Why Children Can't Read

AND WHAT WE CAN DO ABOUT IT

A SCIENTIFIC REVOLUTION IN READING

Diane McGuinness

FOREWORD BY STEVEN PINKER

PENGUIN BOOKS

PENGUIN BOOKS

Published by the Penguin Group
Penguin Books Ltd, 80 Strand, London WC2R 0RL, England
Penguin Putnam Inc., 375 Hudson Street, New York, New York 10014, USA
Penguin Books Australia Ltd, 250 Camberwell Road, Camberwell, Victoria 3124, Australia
Penguin Books Canada Ltd, 10 Alcorn Avenue, Toronto, Ontario, Canada M4V 3B2
Penguin Books India (P) Ltd, 11 Community Centre, Panchsheel Park, New Delhi – 110 017, India
Penguin Books (NZ) Ltd, Cnr Rosedale and Airborne Roads, Albany, Auckland, New Zealand
Penguin Books (South Africa) (Pty) Ltd, 24 Sturdee Avenue, Rosebank 2196, South Africa

Penguin Books Ltd, Registered Offices: 80 Strand, London WC2R 0RL, England

www.penguin.com

First published as *Why Our Children Can't Read* in the USA by the Free Press 1997
First published in Great Britain in this revised edition in Penguin Books 1998
7

Copyright © Diane McGuinness, 1997, 1998
All rights reserved

The moral right of the author has been asserted

Set in 10/12pt Monotype Baskerville
Typeset by Rowland Phototypesetting Ltd, Bury St Edmunds, Suffolk
Printed in England by Clays Ltd, St Ives plc

CONTENTS

PENGUIN BOOKS

WHY CHILDREN CAN'T READ

Diane McGuinness, Ph.D., is a cognitive developmental psychologist and professor at the University of South Florida. She received a first-class honours degree in psychology from Birkbeck College, University of London, in 1972 and her Ph.D. from University College London in 1974. She was Senior Lecturer at Hatfield Polytechnic (now Hatfield University) from 1973 until her return to America in 1976. For the period 1978–81 Professor McGuinness was a lecturer at the University of California, and from 1977 to 1985 was a research associate in the brain research laboratory at Stanford University. She joined the University of South Florida in 1985 and has been a full professor there since 1991. Her son and daughter were educated in England and are graduates of Bristol and Oxford universities respectively. Professor McGuinness is also the author of *When Children Don't Learn*. She lives in Sanibel, Florida.

Every writing system is an abstraction and every transcript is an artefact. Speech can be represented by graphical means only very imperfectly.

Florian Coulmas, *The Writing Systems of the World*
(Blackwell, Oxford, 1989)

'Man has an instinctive tendency to speak, as we see in the babble of our young children; while no child has an instinctive tendency to bake, brew, or write.' More than a century ago, Charles Darwin got it right: language is a human instinct, but written language is not. Language is found in all societies, present and past. All languages are intricately complicated. Although languages change, they do not improve: English is no more complex than the languages of stone age tribes; Modern English is not an advance over Old English. All healthy children master their language without lessons or corrections. When children are thrown together without a usable language, they invent one of their own.

Compare all this with writing. Writing systems have been invented a small number of times in history. They originated only in a few complex civilizations, and they started off crude and slowly improved over the millennia. Until recently, most children never learned to read or write; even with today's universal education, many children struggle and fail. A group of children is no more likely to invent an alphabet than it is to invent the internal combustion engine.

Children are wired for sound, but print is an optional accessory that must be painstakingly bolted on. This basic fact about human nature should be the starting point for any discussion of how to teach our children to read and write. We need to understand how the contraption called writing works, how the mind of the child works, how to get the two to mesh.

It is a national tragedy that this commonsense understanding has been so uncommon. We are turning into a nation of illiterates, the victims of misguided ideas about the nature of reading and how to teach it. All the familiar techniques were devised before we had a scientific understanding of reading, and they are based on theories that we know are wrong. Parents and policymakers are bewildered by contradictory advice from a slew of well-meaning but uninformed romantics, oversimplifiers, entrepreneurs, and quacks.

The book you are now holding is a profound and wonderfully readable essay on reading and writing and how they should be taught. Diane McGuinness is an applied scientist in the best sense of the word – not a self-appointed 'expert' spouting mumbo-jumbo, but someone who works by the guidelines: know what you're talking about, think clearly and logically, and try to let the world tell you whether what you are saying is true. She combines these virtues with style, vigour, insight, and compassion. Anyone who has tried to teach children will recognize the vignettes in this book.

Modern illiteracy is a story of needless misery and waste. *Why Children Can't Read* is part of the solution and one of the most important books of the decade. Read it for your own pleasure and enlightenment, and buy copies for the people in control of your children's education.

Steven Pinker
Professor and Director of the Center
for Cognitive Neuroscience, MIT
Author of *The Language Instinct*
and *How the Mind Works*

When you think back on your schooldays, funny things stick in your mind. These memories stick because of experiences that jolt you into vivid consciousness. My earliest memories were of first grade, probably because I spent a lot of time in the cloakroom that year. I have forgotten the crimes. My main misfortune was to finish my work too quickly and get into trouble. It seemed nothing could be done about this. The whole class worked on the same assignment at the same time. My mother was called in for a conference with Miss Chenette, my teacher at James Madison Elementary in Pasadena, California. They had a discussion about moving me up a year, but Miss Chenette said I was too immature.

I learned to read in Miss Chenette's class, although I don't remember how. I would never have remembered even this fact except for an experience with a neighbourhood boy of twelve who couldn't read. Early most Sunday mornings, I used to read him the comics section from the Sunday paper. 'But everyone can read,' I remember saying. I decided that there must be something wrong with him. If I'd had a larger vocabulary I would have thought he was 'retarded'.

How was it that I could read and he couldn't? These are the twin mysteries of reading research. Fortunately, we have solved the most important one – why children fail. So far, scientists have not studied the reasons why children *don't* fail.

This early experience plus the contrast between my education in the California school system and my children's superb education in Hertfordshire, England, fostered my interest in education. I was witness to what *could be* versus what *is*. However, I didn't realize at that time that 90 per cent of British children were shut out of this experience.

A specific interest in reading and literacy came about through serendipity in the form of being in particular places at the same time as particular people. Phyllis Lindamood was one of my students at the University of California at Santa Cruz. She did her senior thesis project on blind readers learning Braille and introduced me to her parents' work with poor readers. Based on their work, Phyllis predicted that blind people would fail to learn to read Braille to the extent that they are unable to *hear* individual sounds in words. This hypothesis was overwhelmingly supported. The Lindamoods' work on the importance of auditory analysis to reading was virtually unknown by the scientific community at that time. Today, this work has been recognized as one of the major breakthroughs in reading research of this century.

Soon after this, I got an invitation from the Orton Dyslexia Society to present a paper at a conference on sex differences in reading. This prompted me to make connections between the research on poor readers and my own research on the development of perceptual and cognitive skills of boys and girls. This meeting was a major turning point. I met Isabelle Liberman, one of the great pioneers in reading research, who strongly influenced my thinking. I also benefited enormously from future conferences and a close association with the Orton Dyslexia Society, which has consistently supported good scientific research on reading.

Later, I joined the faculty at the University of South Florida. One day, in a class on cognitive psychology, I outlined in detail what the next major step in reading research should be. The following week, some students met me in the hallway, and said: 'We want to do it' – meaning the 'next step'.

Two of these students were Carmen Adams (later to become Carmen McGuinness when she married my son Geoff) and John Donohue. Carmen, Geoff, and John are still intensely involved in research, and Carmen, in particular, in programme and curriculum development. No one realized at the time where this initial project would take us, nor how many hours (years) of testing, data entry, data analysis, and the endless revisions of research reports that would follow. The outcome of this collaboration has been beyond our wildest dreams. This book is the culmination of that work, which has continued for nearly a decade, as well as being a synthesis of modern research on reading. It describes a revolution in teaching methods that so far has escaped the notice of most educators. This revolution is the result of four major discoveries or principles:

1. From palaeography (the study of ancient writing systems) and structural linguistics, we have learned that all writing systems are based upon the syllable structure of the language for which they were written. The way a writing system is designed determines how it should be taught.

2. From cognitive and educational psychology we have learned that children must be trained to hear the individual sounds (phonemes) of their language. They must be able to disconnect or 'unglue' sounds in words in order to use an alphabetic writing system.

3. From an analysis of the structure of the English alphabet code, we have discovered that it encompasses four systems of sound-to-letter mapping logic: simple reversibility (one-to-one mapping), and various forms of propositional logic (one-to-one(two), one-to-many, and many-to-one mapping).

4. From research in the classroom and the clinic, we have discovered that when the sequence of reading and spelling instruction is compatible with the logic of the alphabet code *and* with the child's linguistic and logical development, learning to read and spell proceeds rapidly and smoothly *for all children*, and is equally effective for poor readers of all ages.

Only a handful of reading programmes is based on one or more of these principles. These programmes are unlike anything seen in the classroom or taught in teacher training colleges. This revolution is outside the current debate between 'real books' (also known as 'whole language') and phonics. Neither of these methods, *no matter what form they take*, is based on even one of these principles.

True scientific research on literacy only began about twenty-five years ago. What this means is that every theory or model or method of teaching reading up to now, past or present, has been based either upon human reason alone, or on empty theorizing or fads, rather than on solid scientific research. Because of this, success in learning to read is largely accidental, due to parental input or to the intelligence, talent, and integrity of the classroom teacher, plus the chance connection between the parent or teacher's ability and the aptitudes of particular children. Learning to read in every English-speaking country is like a lottery. It doesn't have to be. The new programmes allow us to teach anyone to read at any age.

This book examines new data on the analysis of writing systems which reveal how they are constructed and, therefore, how they must be taught. It reviews the scientific evidence on the subskills important to mastering an alphabetic writing system, along with exciting new research on reading programmes that work for everyone, including children and adults who can't read a word.

New discoveries lead to new terminology and different ways of describing old events. To help you with technical terms, there is a Glossary at the end of the book. A standard format for pronouncing the sounds of the English language follows this Preface. Please note that all names of persons in the examples are pseudonyms.

This book would not have been possible without the support of some very special people. In addition to those mentioned earlier, I also want to express my appreciation to my agents Felicity Bryan, who believed in this book, and Peter Ginsberg who, with great kindness and tact, guided me through revisions to make the book more saleable. Susan Arellano, my editor for the American edition, was superb, asking just the right questions to force me to have a better perspective on the non-specialist reader. Her ability to remain focused over hours of discussion is amazing and incredibly gratifying to an author. Without her input and guidance this book would have been much more dull and academic than it is. Special thanks too to Eleo Gordon and Martin Toseland at Penguin Books for their enthusiasm and support.

I owe a special debt of gratitude to Carol Tavris and Steven Pinker who liked and understood earlier drafts when nobody else did. Thanks a million. Writers write in a vacuum, and without this encouragement I would probably have given up.

I am especially grateful to Peter Bryant and the Department of Psychology at Oxford University who gave me a home for five months while I did research for this book. Thanks also to the staff of the Bodleian Library and St John's College Library who responded so graciously to my many questions and requests. Thanks to my daughter Julie, who gave me home and hearth at Oxford and listened so patiently while I struggled to put new insights and discoveries into words.

Last, but not least, special thanks to the teachers, the parents and the children with whom I have had the privilege to work over the years. It's their voices that make this book and its message come alive.

Pronunciation Key for English Phonemes

Consonants		Vowels	
sound	key word	sound	key word
/b/	boy	/a/	hat
/d/	dog	/e/	bet
/f/	fan	/i/	sit
/g/	get	/o/	hot
/h/	hot	/u/	cut
/j/	jog	/ae/	cake
/k/	key	/ee/	seem
/l/	log	/ie/	time
/m/	man	/oe/	home
/n/	not	/ue/	cute
/p/	pan	/aw/	law
/qu/ (kw)	quit	/ah/	father
/r/	red	/ou/	out
/s/	sit	/oi/	oil
/t/	top	/oo/	book
/v/	vet	/$\overline{oo}$	soon
/w/	win	/er/	her
/x/ (ks)	fox	/or/	for
/z/	zip		
/ch/	chin		
/ng/	ring		
/sh/	ship		
/th/	thin		
/th/	them		
/zh/	vision		

English phonemes are represented by the most probable spelling rather than the International Phonetic Alphabet, which is unfamiliar to most readers. Sounds are enclosed in slash marks. Letters are underlined. The sound /b/ is spelled b.

Vowel + r

The phoneme /r/ is both a consonant and a vowel. The vowel *r* is spelled <u>er</u>, <u>ir</u>, or <u>ur</u> and pronounced /er/. Other vowels can combine with <u>r</u>. One needs to be taught specifically because the <u>r</u> alters the pronunciation of the preceding vowel: fog/for.

The other vowel + r combinations tend to keep the same sound and spelling pattern with or without the <u>r</u>:

/ah/ (fast/far)
/ee/–/er/ (see/seer)
/ie/–/er/ (time/tire)
/ue/–/er/ (cute/cure)
/ou/–/er/ (out/our)

Why It's Hard to Learn to Read

CHAPTER I

Reading Report Card

The Jamesons were devoted parents to their three children. They valued learning and read their children bedtime stories every night. They often consulted dictionaries and encyclopaedias whenever one of the children introduced an unfamiliar topic. Dinner conversations were lively and filled with accounts of the children's daily activities.

Their youngest son, Tommy, started primary school after a year at a well-run nursery school. Tommy could recite the alphabet, write most of his letters and his first and last names, and could count to 1,000 if anyone would let him. In the Reception class, Tommy got more practice reciting the alphabet, copying out letters, and memorizing some 'sight words'. In Year 1 he taught himself to read simple books and enjoyed writing stories about aeroplanes, guns and robots. The teacher told the Jamesons that Tommy was 'the best reader in the class'. The Jamesons were pleased, his teacher was pleased, and Tommy was pleased. As he told his granny, 'I can read faster than anyone in my class.'

In Year 2 the words got longer. Tommy had trouble remembering all of them. He began to ask his friend, 'What does this word say?' He would try to memorize it for the next time he saw it in a story. As the year went by, he had to ask his friend more and more often. Meanwhile, his stories got more interesting, and his handwriting a little neater. This year he wrote a lot about submarines. He could spell 'submarine' correctly. The word was on the cover of five books he had at home, and he practised copying it over and over again. Here is one of his stories:

THE SUBMARINE RTET

Kpn Jn tol hz cru fl sdm a ked. Tak hr dun. The submarine sek to the osn flor. It was qit. Tha cud ker the daph crujz flng ner by. But tha wr saf.

(The Submarine Retreat. Captain John told his crew full steam ahead. Take her down. The submarine sank to the ocean floor. It was quiet. They could hear the depth charges falling near by. But they were safe.)

This particular story, replete with spelling mistakes, was up on the wall on parents' evening. The Jamesons were alarmed. In fact, they had already discussed asking the teacher about Tommy's written work. The teacher told them not to worry. She pointed out that Tommy was a model student. He worked very hard. She asked them to notice the excellent vocabulary in the story (she was adept at reading her students' spelling). She pointed out that Tommy was the only child who put a capital letter at the beginning of every sentence. She said that this was 'transitional spelling', and the children were now being taught to spell with conventional spelling.

As time went by, the words got longer still. The books had more pages. Tommy couldn't remember lots of these words, even when he asked several times. He had to guess so many of the words as he was reading that he couldn't make sense of the story. It helped if there were pictures. Mrs Jameson spent more time listening to Tommy read and correcting his mistakes as they went along. Despite this extra tutoring, Tommy's reading did not improve. He was now in the bottom reading group (the Kingfishers). When he wrote stories, they looked pretty much the same as 'The Submarine Retreat'. Despite this, Tommy was the best speller in the class. His teacher told the Jamesons that his spelling was perfect. He got 100 per cent week after week on the class spelling words. She said not to worry, because the conventional spelling he was learning would eventually transfer to his creative writing. 'It just takes time.' The teacher saw nothing odd about the fact that despite Tommy's spelling being 'perfect', he was in the bottom reading group and could scarcely spell a word in his creative writing.

When Tommy was in junior school, Mrs Jameson went to see the headmaster about Tommy's poor skills. By now, she had discovered that Tommy could memorize the week's spelling words long enough to pass the test, but forgot them completely only days later. The headmaster said that Tommy's problem was not severe enough for him to be tested, and that he was already receiving special help with his reading from a classroom assistant. They had no further resources to help him. Instead, the Jamesons got Tommy tested by an educational psychologist in private practice. It cost them £400. Tommy was a year and a half behind in reading, two years behind in spelling and had an IQ of 124. The psychologist said he needed private tutoring, and that it could take up to 200 hours, but that she didn't do private tutoring herself and couldn't recommend anyone.

They found a tutor through another parent. The cost was £15 per hour, and Mrs Jameson got a part-time job to meet the extra expense. Meanwhile, they didn't tell anyone about Tommy's problem except the immediate family. They were embarrassed and upset. How had they failed their child? Why was it that Tommy had these problems when the other two children were fine? Did he have some kind of brain damage? What would happen if the reading tutor couldn't teach Tommy to read and spell? Mealtimes were tense instead of joyful, happy occasions, as Tommy was asked to tell everyone *exactly* what he had done in school, *exactly* how many pages he had read, and *exactly* what his spelling words were for that week. The Jamesons argued about who should spend time reading with Tommy, so Mr Jameson listened to Tommy read every night. He wasn't always patient ('I've told you that word a hundred times!') and the session often ended in tears. The Jamesons bought lots of books on 'dyslexia' and 'learning difficulties'. Nothing they read held out much hope. While all this was going on, the other children were pushed into the background and became silently angry and resentful.

What is the ending to this story? It depends upon whether the Jamesons found the right reading specialist. If they did, they would be given an accurate diagnosis of Tommy's problem. The clues are all contained in the story. Tommy's problem was quite simple. He didn't understand the alphabet code. He was using letter-names instead of the sounds the letters stand for, to create his own code ('captain' = 'kay-pee-en' – *kpn*), and trying to memorize whole words by sight. This made it impossible for him to decode text (read) and encode text (write and spell). There was nothing wrong with him. He had the auditory skills to hear individual sounds in words, as indicated by his phonetic use of letter-names to spell words. He had a superb visual memory. Not many children can memorize a list of spelling words entirely by *sight*. He had a terrific vocabulary. These are the ingredients that should have produced an expert reader. A good reading specialist could teach Tommy to read in about twenty hours or less, and family life would quickly return to normal. Tommy would shoot ahead to near the top of the class which is where he should be with an IQ of 124.

Unfortunately, an unhappy ending is more likely. Instead of a knowledgeable reading specialist, the Jamesons found a reading tutor who was kind and patient, but knew as much about how to remedy reading problems as the Jamesons did, especially after all the books they had read on the subject. The tutor merely listened to Tommy read, correcting his mistakes, just as the Jamesons had done. The unhappy ending can continue for a lifetime unless proper help is found. The unhappy ending includes being held back a year, expensive schools for 'dyslexics', more private tutoring, and more family worry and discord. Tommy would eventually finish his special school and end up in a job where he didn't have to read very often. If parents aren't as lucky as the Jamesons and can't afford to pay for outside help or private schools, the situation is even more hopeless. Ultimately, a child with an unremedied reading problem can never function at his full potential and suffers incredible emotional damage and loss of self esteem.

The Jamesons are fictional, but Tommy is not. He is typical of many real children seen by reading specialists and tutors throughout the English-speaking world. In Britain, Tommy is the product of either a 'real books' classroom, or an eclectic approach which includes look-and-say, 'real books', and phonics. In teacher interviews and reports published by the National Foundation for Educational Research in England and Wales (NFER) in 1992, eclecticism reigns supreme under the misguided assumption that no one method works for all children.

As none of these methods work for everyone, either individually or in combination, this raises the question: How many children are like Tommy? In most English-speaking countries there is no answer to this question. There is no literacy testing using accurate demographic sampling and well-controlled objective procedures. A pot-pourri of testing approaches leads to unstable and uninterpretable findings. The Department of Education and Science (DES) reported in 1991 on the performance of 2,000 children, aged four to eleven, who read aloud to school inspectors. Overall, approximately 25 per cent of children were judged to be 'poor readers'. But this figure is suspect in view of these serious methodological problems:

1. The teacher knew that both she and the children were being judged.

2. The teacher was asked to identify children for testing.

3. The child was allowed to choose a book which he or she had already memorized.

4. Each child was rated according to purely subjective judgements of 'accuracy', 'fluency', and 'expression'.

5. The data were reported in a hotch-potch of percentages: 'At the start of Year 3, 70 per cent could read accurately and with understanding; 50 per cent were fluent; 33 per cent were making satisfactory progress; 20 per cent were unable to read with any fluency.' (More than 100 per cent, whichever way you add them up!)

Literacy testing carried out by the NFER is not much better. In a study conducted in 1988, eleven- to seventeen-year-olds read material chosen to be suitable for each age group. There were six fictional and non-fictional texts for each age; children had to locate specific information in the text; every test item was answered by at least 1,000 children. Unfortunately the results are unreliable because the classroom teacher carried out the testing and scored the tests. In any case, the results are uninterpretable. There were no norms or absolute criteria by which children were *supposed* to perform. Performance varied wildly depending on which of six texts the children were asked to read. Sixty-eight per cent of eleven-year-olds scored above 50 per cent correct on one text, but on two other texts for this age group, only 22 per cent scored above 50 per cent, and 40 per cent scored below 30 per cent correct. Does this mean that 40 per cent of eleven-year-olds in Britain are 'functionally illiterate' or that the texts were too difficult? There's no way to tell.

In 1993, the DES published results on Key Stage 1 testing at Level 2 (age seven) under the National Curriculum guidelines. They reported that approximately 75 per cent were reading at the age-appropriate Level 2, 21 per cent at Level 1 (age six), and 4 per cent below Level 1. Testing consisted of subjective ratings by teachers of their own children who read a book 'most likely to allow an individual child to show his or her best performance'.

Julia Davies and her colleagues at Manchester University reported in 1995 on a comparison of teacher ratings to objective test results on the Primary Reading Test (PRT) which is normed on 20,000 children. At the end of Year 2, 342 children were tested using both methods. On the PRT, 25 per cent (1991) and 26 per cent (1992) scored *below* age six. Davies was unable to report how *far* below, because the PRT norms cut off at 6 years 0 months. This means that 25 per cent of seven-year-olds were reading approximately one year or more below age norms. As might be anticipated, there was a discrepancy between the subjective teacher ratings and performance on the PRT, with teacher ratings overestimating true reading skill. Based on the PRT data, reading scores declined between the 1991 and 1992 assessments, while according to teacher ratings, reading scores improved!

None of these methods is satisfactory. To assess literacy properly, you need an objective definition of literacy for each age tested, up to and including adults. This means setting an absolute standard of literacy which is *independent* of the population's reading level, unlike standardized tests which simply reflect a population's ability. This means that if you live in a region where reading scores are poor, then an 'average' performance means you are a poor reader. To date, only the United States and Canada have developed and carried out appropriate testing on large demographic samples, and only the US has tested children.[1] This puts the US in the unenviable position of being the first nation in the English-speaking world to discover the shocking truth about actual literacy rates, truth which has revealed a 'literacy crisis'.

In America, the National Assessment Governing Board, Education Testing Service (ETS) in conjunction with the National Center for Education Statistics (NCES) carried out two studies in 1992. One study involved 140,000 American children in Grades 4, 8 and 12 (approximate ages 9, 13 and 17). The second study tested 26,000 adults in the age range 16 to 65 years. They used careful demographic sampling with accurate proportions of males and females, and all ethnic and racial groups, who were balanced for geographic location in terms of urban, inner city, rural, and so forth. Forty-two states took part in the student sample. The adult sample involved eleven representative states and included 1,000 people from prison populations.

A key innovation was the development of an objective way to measure reading by setting absolute standards or 'achievement levels'. A panel of experts determined in advance what literate adults or children at various ages should be able to do. They emphasized 'functional literacy', the ability to read text, find information, and perform operations ('functions') on that information. Items for the tests were drawn from previously published material and included stories, poems, non-fiction, newspaper articles, and common documents such as bus timetables and simple graphs.

Most important was the rigour with which the testing and scoring was carried out. Testing was done individually or in groups directly supervised by specially trained personnel. Strict guidelines were set up for scoring responses, and this was done by ETS personnel (not the classroom teacher), with the statistical analysis done 'blind' by computer at a central location. All test items were secured, and no school had access to any of them, or even examples of them.

Using a complex scoring procedure and statistical model, NCES established levels of competence based upon the predetermined achievement criteria. For the student population, there were four levels: advanced, proficient, basic, and below basic. Students who were below basic could not understand the overall meaning of what they read and were considered to be functionally illiterate according to expectations for that age. I want to spend some time addressing these findings because they provide a number of clues as to what is going wrong with reading instruction in America, and elsewhere, as we shall see shortly.

The report on the student population provides a detailed breakdown of the fourth-grade data (average age nine years). Buried at the back of the report is an astonishing table. This reveals that, on average, schools claimed that 12 per cent of the students were 'untestable'. ETS personnel disallowed 4 per cent of these exclusions. This left 3 per cent who were excused because of limited English proficiency and 5 per cent who were in special programmes and had an 'individual educational plan', or IEP. This is equivalent to a 'statement of special educational needs' in Britain, which tends to be used in severe cases, averaging around 2 per cent of the student population. The majority of IEP students in America are diagnosed with a 'learning disability', a euphemism for 'can't read'. Thus, otherwise normal children were excluded from a survey on reading because they couldn't read![2]

The states were ranked according to state-wide proficiency scores. The top five states had an average of 29 per cent of all students below basic level reading skills. The bottom five states had over double this rate, at 60 per cent. Overall, the national average for nine-year-olds was 43 per cent 'below basic' in reading skills.

These dismal results continue to dominate the adult survey. In this survey, all materials were drawn from printed text that a normal adult would be likely to encounter in everyday life. For adults there were five levels of competence. Level 1 required only the most minimal level of competence. For example, from an eight-sentence newspaper article, the reader must find this information about a cross-channel swimmer: 'What did Mrs Chanin eat during her swim?'

Altogether, 21 per cent of the population were only able to perform at a Level 1 proficiency or *lower*, indicating that they were functionally illiterate. This translates to approximately 42 million functionally illiterate American adults. Forty-seven per cent of adults scored at Levels 1 and 2, barely literate. Hardly anyone (3 per cent of all adults) scored at Level 5, the 'advanced' level. One Level 5 task was a fact sheet sent to potential jurors outlining the 'voir dire' process during jury selection. It is sobering that only 3 per cent of potential jurors can read and fully comprehend how the jury selection process works.

The Organization for Economic Co-operation and Development (OECD) and Statistics Canada carried out the same kind of testing on adults aged 16–65 in the US, Canada, and five non-English-speaking countries, and replicated the US literacy rates almost exactly. In 1997, the OECD published data on adult literacy rates in the UK (England, Wales, lowland Scotland and Northern Ireland), Ireland, Australia and New Zealand, using the same criterion-based tests. The results are surprising in view of the belief that education in the US is much worse than anywhere else. The UK and Ireland have the highest functional illiteracy rates in the English-speaking world (22 per cent of adults). Canada and Australia have the lowest (17 per cent). The contrast is best illustrated by the proportion of the population who fall into Levels 1 + 2 (illiterate + poor readers) and into Levels 4 + 5 (highly competent readers). Canada has the fewest Level 1 + 2 readers and the most at Levels 4 + 5. The scores are as follows: Levels 1 + 2 – Canada 42.2 per cent, Australia 44.1 per cent, New Zealand 45.7

per cent, US 46.6 per cent, UK 52.1 per cent, Ireland, 52.4 per cent. Levels 4 + 5 – Canada 22.7 per cent, US 21.1 per cent, New Zealand 19.2 per cent, Australia 18.9 per cent, UK 16.6 per cent, Ireland 13.5 per cent. The UK reading scores have been steadily declining. Although Canada came out ahead in these comparisons, 42.2 per cent scoring at minimum literacy levels is nothing to brag about. Sweden has set the benchmark for what school systems can achieve, with only 7.5 per cent at Level 1 (functionally illiterate), 27.8 per cent at Levels 1 + 2, and 32.4 per cent at Levels 4 + 5.

The authors of these reports do not speculate on causes for these extraordinary illiteracy rates, but causes can be inferred from the statistics. There was an extreme range of literacy levels between the states in the US. With a sample of 140,000 children, carefully balanced for sex, race, and geographic region, this cannot be attributed to chance or random variation. We can conclude with confidence that some states train their teachers better and use more effective methods in the classroom.

The student survey included data on Catholic and other private schools. Students from these schools were considerably better readers than those in state schools, even though Catholic schools draw from a similar population to state schools, including a high percentage of Spanish-speaking children. But Catholic schools had 17 per cent *more* students at or above Basic Level skills at all ages tested. This shows that some *schools* have better programmes for teaching reading, and/or are run more effectively, perhaps due to greater academic rigour, higher student expectations, more homework, and better discipline.

Does money matter? Whenever information about falling educational standards is brought to the attention of politicians, the answer is usually: 'more money'. Comparisons of state-wide expenditure on education showed, yet again, that throwing money at the problem doesn't make a difference.

In California, the 'real books' method was mandated state-wide in 1987, and California teachers were overwhelmingly more likely to report heavy use of 'real books'/literature-based reading methods (87 per cent of teachers) than teachers in any other state. California ranked near the bottom in the nation in the 1992 tests, and results from the 1994 survey, published in 1996, showed California in a tie for dead last with Louisiana. In 1996, California passed legislation to reintroduce phonics back into the classroom, along with over one billion dollars of funding for teacher retraining.

When nearly all the teachers in a state report 'heavy use' of a particular method, and the state in which they teach has a 60 per cent functional illiteracy rate, this means the method isn't working. There is simply no other argument for these kinds of numbers. Nor, I might add, is 27 per cent 'below basic' acceptable either, which was the best performance by any single state. A level of 25–30 per cent is also *at least* the likely functional illiteracy rate for British children aged seven to eleven, based on the studies cited earlier, especially as Britain scored consistently below the US in the adult study.

The truth provided by these statistics is that a child's reading problem, and ultimately an adult's reading problem, *is caused by the education system*, and not because there is something wrong with poor readers. It is impossible that 30–60 per cent of schoolchildren have an inherent or 'brain-based' deficit leading to reading failure, and in any case, reading and spelling are not biological properties of the human brain. People are illiterate because none of the current methods of reading instruction work for everyone. Later, I will review evidence which shows that *any child or adult* who isn't mentally retarded or deaf can be taught to read if given proper instruction.

Over the last quarter century, there has been a revolution in our understanding of how to teach reading, the outcome of an explosion of scientific research. So far, the revolution has escaped the notice of most educators. These studies show conclusively that to learn an alphabetic writing system, a child must be taught the sounds of his language and be trained to hear the order of these sounds in words, because it is these sounds that the letters represent. Furthermore, while this ability is easy to train, it doesn't appear spontaneously in all children simply because they are exposed to print ('real books') or taught the sounds of letters (phonics). The next step is to teach children how each of these sounds is spelled in a carefully sequenced way. We now have the knowledge to teach these skills correctly, leaving nothing out. When programmes based on this knowledge are tested in the classroom and the clinic, all children learn to read.

The Plan of the Book

The book is divided into three sections. The first (Chapters 1–6) looks in depth at writing systems and reveals first-hand why children can easily become confused about our writing system and fail to learn to read and spell. It covers incorrect strategies that children routinely adopt; how *all* current teaching methods will fail about 30 per cent of children because they are based on ignorance about how writing systems work; how the English spelling code has evolved over 700 years, and what the structure of this code looks like. The complex syllable patterns in our language, plus the complexities of our spelling system, make the English alphabet code one of the most difficult writing systems in the world to learn. Unless we understand how it works, we cannot teach it.

Section 2 (Chapters 7–9) focuses on the scientific evidence. This has shown that certain subskills must be in place in order for a child or adult to master an alphabetic writing system. Additional research has shown that children's linguistic and logical development are of critical importance in setting up the proper sequence of instruction. The last chapter in this section reviews training studies based upon this research, studies which prove that auditory-linguistic skills are a major missing link to reading success. These skills are so highly trainable at any age, that the terms 'dyslexia' or 'learning difficulties' cease to have any meaning.

The final section of the book (Chapters 10–14) is devoted to method and details the proper way to teach children to read. Chapters 10 and 11 set out the details of such a reading programme for the classroom or for home instruction.

Millions of youngsters and adults have serious reading problems through no fault of their own. Reading and spelling problems are completely remediable with proper training. People who cannot read a word can be taught to read, write and spell, fluently and efficiently, if they are taught by the right methods in the right sequence. Chapter 12 covers remedial instruction, with diagnostic tests for parents and teachers to pinpoint individual learning deficiencies, and guidance on how to deal with the emotional problems of children or adults with severe reading delays.

Chapter 13 offers suggestions about what parents can do to help rather than hinder their children before they go to school, along with some practical ways to help develop skills that are important in learning to read. For parents with a child who has reading or spelling problems, there is advice about how to work with the school system, and how to evaluate a remedial reading programme before enrolling your child or family member. The final chapter deals with the political realities of trying to overhaul the education system and the education bureaucracy, and how the class sytems and teacher expectations profoundly influence students' achievement.

We have the answers to the problem of illiteracy. We have had many of these answers for twenty-five years. So far, members of the educational community either do not know about these research findings, misinterpret them, or are threatened by them, because it would mean an overthrow and a restructuring of everything that is familiar. These new ideas belong in the classroom, because we are harming children and their families by letting even one child slip by.

This book is for the millions of concerned parents, the millions of intelligent people with poor reading skills, the thousands of teachers who are falsely blamed when a child fails to learn to read, for the dedicated scientists and reading specialists who persist and persist, and for the enlightened members of the educational community who care enough to make a difference.

CHAPTER 2

How Do Readers Read?

Everyone who bought or borrowed this book is a reader. Readers don't understand why someone can't learn to read. Many are dumbfounded and troubled by the high illiteracy rates in Britain. They are justifiably upset that no coherent solutions have been forthcoming for more than a hundred years. Some people will have more specific concerns, because they have a child or family member who can't read. Teachers of young children worry that many of their charges will fail to learn to read, and they don't know why. Teachers higher up the school are angry with infant school teachers because children are coming into their classes unable to read, write or spell. This means that they can't move ahead with their lessons as they should. These teachers are not experienced in how to teach reading, nor do their curriculum guidelines include reading instruction, so the problem never gets solved. Instead, children are either held back or passed up the system. Some receive remedial help with few results. At the end of the line, these young people will seek employment where reading isn't necessary.

As a junior school teacher told a friend: 'Your child can't read because no one taught him to read. Get him a good reading tutor now, or he will never learn to read.'

What is reading, and why is there such a problem in understanding how to teach it? To illustrate the problem directly, let's begin with a simple exercise. Read this passage and think about how you did it.

BAD FRUIT

The fructificative goosefoot was foveolariously assembled. The frugivorous and frowsy fricatrice, whose epidermis was of a variegated fuchsinophillic consistency, masticated her chenopodiaceous repast morosely.

[The fruit-bearing goosefoot was full of pit-like indentations. The fruit-loving and frowsy chewer, whose skin was of a mottled and purplish-red consistency, chewed her goosefoot (species) meal morosely.]

(reprinted by courtesy of Read America)

Good readers can read this with relative ease, even though they don't understand many of the words. People who can read this passage know how the English alphabet code works. They know that individual letters, letter-pairs and sometimes three or four letters in a row ('*igh*', '*ough*') stand for only one sound in the English language. These people decoded this passage from left to right, one sound unit at a time. They know this implicitly, and only noticed what they were doing because the words were so unfamiliar, forcing them to slow down and analyse each word sound by sound.

Some people who are reading this book will not be able to read this passage. Most of them are using a 'part-word' decoding strategy in which parts of words are assembled into a longer word. Part-word assemblers search for familiar little words or word fragments inside a longer word. These letter fragments stand for *more than one sound*. Often they reuse letters in different combinations. When familiar patterns can't be located, or aren't helpful in constructing a word, as in the words 'fructificative' (/fru/ /tif/ /cat/ /tive/) or 'chenopodiaceous', (/chin/ /no/ /pod/ /dice/ /ace/ /ous/) the word cannot be read. Instead, they have to ask someone else to read it for them. When I play this game with my university students, it turns out that a surprisingly large number of them are part-word assemblers. They never knew there was any other way to read. These are the students with poor spelling, who misread words, and who have to reread passages with new vocabulary over and over again to understand what they are reading.

The example is here for another reason. Many educators claim that efficient readers read so quickly that they ignore individual letters, regrouping them into patterns of letter strings or 'chunks' and whole words. Therefore, they argue that children should be taught whole words ('sight words') from the beginning. It's true that good readers read quickly, skimming along, unconscious of how they are reading, but they didn't start out like this. Furthermore, careful research has shown that adult good readers look at nearly every letter and can see only about three letters beyond the focal point as they read. When reading complex text, fixation duration is increased, as is the number of repeat fixations, and the number of words read per minute decreases.

Reading is a skilled behaviour and, like all skills, it has to be taught from the bottom up, from the simple parts to the complex whole. No one would dream of asking a novice diver to attempt a difficult dive like a reverse jackknife. Nor would one teach a beginning piano student to use all ten fingers at once at the first piano lesson. All skilled learning builds piece by piece, through practice, until the skills are integrated.

Writing systems are codes for spoken language. Someone has to teach the code, because most people can't figure it out alone. We have learned this lesson from the reports of scholars trying to decipher ancient writing systems. Later, I will be discussing the exact nature of the code for written English in more depth, because the complexity of our alphabet code is a major cause of reading failure. In fact, *nobody* can unravel a written code without knowing something about how the code works, even when they are told that symbols on a page stand for sounds in their native language. Look at this recoded version of the first line of a famous nursery rhyme:

ytoxto hruxsz ub ldyyuos xtmo

The letter–sound relationships are based upon English spelling patterns and recoded by simple substitution. There are even helpful clues here. When more than one letter stands for a single sound (as it does in the original spelling), those letters are underlined. (The answer is at the end of the chapter.)

This example provides the adult reader with some idea of the child's first experience with print. But in many classrooms, the beginning reader doesn't have the advantage of knowing which letters work together to stand for one sound. Nor do they know that letters stand for sounds, or even that there *are* sounds in words. The point is this: if you stared at this passage for *years*, you wouldn't have the slightest idea how to decode it. Why then should we expect a child to teach himself to decipher the English alphabet code, one of the most complex ever designed, without any direct instruction? Yet this is precisely what is going on in classrooms throughout the English-speaking world. Children learn that if they memorize some sight words, look at the pictures, hear the story read while they look at the words on the page, they can teach themselves to read. They are encouraged to do this through getting the maximum information from picture and context cues in a psycholinguistic guessing game.

Let's see how they do this.

First of all, children are taught something. They learn the names of the letters of the alphabet from Mum, Dad, children's television and the classroom teacher. As the names for letters of the alphabet have little relationship to the sounds in speech those letters represent, this sets up the first roadblock for the young reader. To get past this roadblock, the child has to work out that letters have names *and* sounds, or try to memorize words by sight, using clues like shape and word length. This leaves open several possibilities for decoding text.

To illustrate this, I am going to transcribe some lines of 'How the Grinch Stole Christmas' by Dr Seuss. We will look in on several children reading this passage. If your child has a reading problem, you might recognize him or her in these examples.

First is Sally, who is seven and a half. Miss Jones has told Sally, who has just finished reading – or I should say, memorizing – 'The Three Little Pigs' (with considerable help from her Mum and her best friend Jane), to find another book. The teacher is busy and Sally gets no help from her about this book. This means that Sally doesn't know the title and therefore has no 'context clues' to help her read the story. There are pictures. Branches of a Christmas tree are in the first illustration, and a wreath is on the second page, but these pages got stuck together with chewing gum. Sally opens the book at the page where this text appears. On the facing page, the Grinch stands in the opening to his cave, looking mean and disagreeable. The landscape is bleak. There are snow and icicles clinging to the rocky entrance to his cave.

> The Grinch hated Christmas!
> The whole Christmas season.
> Now please don't ask why.
> No one quite knows the reason.

Here's how this passage would have been read by Sally about a year ago when she was using letter-names to decode, just like Tommy used letter-names to spell:

The   jeerienseetch   aitchaiteedee   seeaitchericeteemace
The   grinch   hated   Christmas

It's too painful to continue this transcription. It was also too painful for Sally, who gave up completely until her mother intervened. Sally had been drilled on the letters of the alphabet from the age of four. She could recite them at lightning speed: 'aybeeceedee-ee-ef-gee/ aitchiejaykayelemenopee/kewaresteeyouvee/doubleyouekswhyzed'. When Sally didn't learn to read, her Mum decided to teach her the sounds of the letters as well. Sally's Mum taught these sounds incorrectly, attaching vowels to each consonant (buh, duh, kuh) – extra sounds that shouldn't be there. Now Sally has a mixed strategy. She starts with the letter-name out of habit, knows this is wrong, cancels this in her mind, translates or substitutes a possible sound the letter might stand for, and proceeds along like this (bear in mind, much of this will be subvocal and inaudible): 'The gee/guh, are/ rrruh, ie/i, en/nuh, see/kuh, aitch/huh' (pause: 'umm, umm, umm') 'guhrink'. Not a bad guess. She did this *very* slowly and it has taken about thirty seconds to decode 'Grinch' incorrectly. And so it goes on, and about ten minutes later, Sally may have decoded four lines, most of which will be meaningless because she is so inaccurate and so slow. Personality comes into play here. Sally has always wanted to please her parents and her teacher. She is determined to succeed and just keeps trying. She never gets any better. Most children are not like Sally and would have given up long before this. Sally will give up in Year 3. Sally will think she's dumb.

Let's talk about Nigel. He's in Sally's class. Nigel is reading the same story. Nigel has been taught, via look-and-say, that random letter sequences stand for whole words (sjboidntl = 'football'), and has been encouraged to use context cues. 'What is the story about, Nigel? Look at the picture. Say the whole word. Don't sound it out. Say it fast,' says Miss Jones over and over again. Nigel has memorized some words, so he can read some of the story about the Grinch. Words he's never seen cannot be read, and his memory is faulty because some letter strings look so much alike.

The ——— hat ———
     (hated)
The while ——— ——— .
    (whole)
Now play don't ——— ——— .
    (please)
No one quick ——— the ——— .
      (quite)

Nigel has no way to read words that don't look like words he has already memorized. Nothing he reads ever makes much sense. Nigel has just decided to give up reading 'The Grinch'. He is frustrated. He makes a paper glider and fires it at a classmate's head. He loses the star he got yesterday for good behaviour, and has to move his chair to face the wall.

On the other hand, there is Albert. He has figured out something pretty clever. He has discovered that letters stand for sounds at the beginning of words and sometimes at the end as well. If he can work out the beginning sounds, he can guess the rest of the word because words have different shapes. He looks at the word's overall shape and how long it is. He knows that each string of letters stands for a word, a real word. He knows that stories 'make sense'. So here is Albert's rendition of 'The Grinch'. The individual letters he actually looks at are underlined. The rest of the word is a blur.

The Granny had chocolate.
The while – white chocolate seized.
No plenty don't and won't.
No one quick now the really.

Albert is trying to rely on picture cues to help him guess words. He thinks this story is about Granny and how she has plenty of white chocolate which she 'seized' from someone. The snow and icicles around the Grinch's cave he thinks is white chocolate. Judging by her sour expression in the drawing, she is guarding this chocolate so no one else will get it, even if they're quick. 'Really!' the author says, 'This is too bad!'

Oh dear. If only Miss Jones had given him some context clues, like the title of the story, he would have been in better shape. If he takes the book home, his Mum will tell him the title, read the words he can't read, and Albert will store away some more beginning letter–sound combinations and more word shapes in his brain than he has stored at the moment. After a while his brain will overload and he will give up reading. This will happen during the next year if Albert is very smart and has a good visual memory. If not, he will have stopped by now, and he will just be looking at the pictures.

So far, we have been talking about what children do when they have been misinformed about how our alphabet code works by being encouraged to memorize letter-names or words, and guess whole words from context cues. This means that teaching the alphabet code becomes the parents' problem. These children may have parents who are both working and can't spend time with them, or parents who have tried and failed to teach them to read. Maybe the parents also have a reading problem themselves, or they're doing what the Jamesons did in the story about Tommy – supplying the correct word as the child goes along, but not teaching a system their child can use without their help.

The next examples come from different schools. These children have been taught something about the alphabet code using various types of phonics. I am going to stick to the more generic forms to illustrate the typical patterns of errors children make with phonics instruction. The first type comes mainly from education publishing houses and teaches what are called 'word-families' or 'analogies'. Word-families are parts of a word, usually a group of ending sounds combining a vowel and final consonants. These are often taught in rhyme: 'the cat sat on the mat', and are known technically as 'rimes'. Dr Seuss is a favourite author. The letter strings: ing, ent, unch are examples of word-families. In these examples, the letter strings stand for the following number of sounds in English: two (/i/, /ng/), three (/e/, /n/, /t/), three (/u/, /n/, /ch/). However, children are taught, or led to believe, that these letter sequences *are only one sound*. This means that if they are taught unch as in 'bunch', 'hunch', 'lunch', and 'punch', they will not be able to transfer this knowledge to other similar sounding endings ('bench', 'ranch', 'launch') because they learned 'unch' as one unit or one 'sound'. They don't know that n stands for the sound /n/ wherever it appears in a word, or that ch stands for the sound /ch/ most of the time (except when it sounds /k/ in words like Christmas, character, chaos, choir, anchor, mechanic, etc.). This means each word-family has to be taught one at a time, but there are 1,260 possible rhyming endings in English. Even if teaching word-families was an efficient way to teach spelling patterns (which it isn't), phonics programmes never teach more than a fraction of them.

Here is Sam in Mrs Finch's Year 2 class. The whole school is working in an off-the-shelf reading scheme with a strong phonics emphasis. Sam reads:

> The Ger-inch hat-ate-ted Cris-tams.
> The who-ell Crit-muss see-son.
> Now pless-as do-ont as whee.
> No one quit kuh-na-now the re-are-son.

Notice that Sam is continually reusing letters in different combinations. He knows he has to break the word apart, but he doesn't know how to do this. When he reads 'hated', he sees 'hat', 'ate', and 'ted', and so he reads 'hat-ate-ted'. He also knows he isn't reading real words. He is hoping that what he reads will sound similar to a real word so that he can guess the word. He tries different options. That is why he reads 'Christmas' differently the second time, but it still doesn't make sense. Sam is scanning the words from left to right and from right to left to locate these letter strings standing for word parts. He has done a pretty good job of putting these word parts in the right sequence, from left to right. Some part-word assemblers don't do this. They get the sequence scrambled.

At the beginning of this chapter, I pointed out that many university students use this strategy. If Sam keeps on like this, which he probably will, he will improve to some extent as his vocabulary grows. But this strategy is very prone to error and Sam is seriously at risk of giving up. Even if he persists and becomes more accurate, he will always misread a large number of words on every page and have to reread many sentences.

On the other side of town, there is an experienced teacher called Mrs Earnest. Mrs Earnest is about five years from retirement. She thinks that what is going on in many schools today is nonsense. She particularly hates the 'real books' approach and thinks it's ridiculous that children are supposed to guess words instead of sounding them out. Mrs Earnest strongly believes that phonics is important. She was taught some phonics in her training, and her students do well on reading tests. However, Mrs Earnest never learned the entire alphabet code. She knows the sounds for the twenty-six letters of the alphabet, but she is uncertain about how many other sounds are in the English language. She knows that there are consonant clusters or 'blends' – two consonants side-by-side, as in the letters bl in the word 'black'. She knows that each of these letters stands for a different sound (/b/ and /l/), but she thinks it's easier for the children to learn clusters as one sound, /bl/. She is supported in this incorrect viewpoint by some well-known reading schemes. But neither Mrs Earnest nor the authors of these programmes knows how many clusters there are in the English language (there are seventy-six), and so most clusters are never taught.

She also knows that certain letter pairs can stand for *only one sound* ('each' has two sounds: /ea/, /ch/). She even knows the technical name for this: 'digraph'. It never occurs to her that these two pieces of information are contradictory: two letters stand for 'one sound' which is *really two sounds* (bl), but two letters also stand for 'one sound' which is *really one sound* (ch). Apart from these problems, as Mrs Earnest was never taught the entire spelling code she can only teach as much as she knows. The children have to figure out the rest. Here is Andrew, a seven-year-old, reading 'The Grinch':

> The Grin hatted Chuh-ristmas.
> The wall Christmas seesson.
> Now pleece don't ask wee.
> No one quit k-noass the reesson.

Andrew has a strategy that is partially working. Notice how he corrects 'Christmas' the second time he sees it. First he tries the sound /ch/ and then the sound /k/, which is right and makes sense. He does this because Mrs Earnest has told the children to try out both ways to read ch. But Andrew wasn't taught the final consonant cluster nch. He wasn't taught about 'e-controlled' vowel spellings either. This is where the letter e 'controls' the pronunciation of the vowel letter coming in front of it. It controls this pronunciation backwards across one consonant but not two: hat, hate, hated, hatted. So he misreads 'hated', 'whole', and 'quite' as 'hatted', 'wall', and 'quit'. Mrs Earnest has never taught the children that the sound /z/ is often spelled s or se ('please', 'season', 'reason'). Mrs Earnest has taught the children that final y stands for the sound /ee/ at the end of a lot of words ('baby', 'lady', 'crazy'), but *not* that the letter y can *also* stand for the sound /ie/ at the end of one-syllable words ('why', 'by', 'cry'). Andrew will learn to read eventually, because he has a strategy that is partially working, and this will allow him to figure out more of the code. Right now he is not independent of adult help, but he probably will be in a year or two.

Now let's look in on Mrs Able. She is teaching in yet another primary school. The headmistress is a strong proponent of a 'linguistic' approach to early reading instruction. No child is taught sight words first and phonics last, so that he is misled about how the code works. Within this general framework, the headmistress encourages her teachers to be innovative. Mrs Able had an excellent training about twenty years ago, when she learned the sounds of the English language and the logic of the alphabet code: that letters are arbitrary symbols for sounds in speech. She then went on to make a thorough study of the issue. She tried out various approaches in her classroom and actually noted down the results she got year after year. Her children did better as a result of her efforts. By the time we look in on Mrs Able, she has worked out how to teach the entire alphabet code in a carefully sequenced way, so that no child is ever confused or lost. Mrs Able has had to write most of her own curriculum materials because she couldn't find anything that was complete, accurate, *and* interesting to the children. Here is Tasneem, a little Pakistani girl who is bilingual, reading 'The Grinch':

> The Grinch hated Cheristmas – Christmas.
> The whole Christmas season.
> Now pleass – please don't ask why.
> No one quite knows the reason.

And by the way, I forgot to mention that Mrs Able teaches Year 1, and Tasneem is only six years old.

I hope this exercise has been enlightening for many parents and teachers. Many of you will recognize your child, family member, or one of your students here. It was intended to show that people can decode text in many different ways. When the beginning reader has to decipher the alphabet code without appropriate instruction, he will come up with at least one of the strategies I have outlined here. Most children will use more than one. If a child sticks with any of the first four strategies: letter-name decoding; name-to-sound translating; sight-word memorizing; or real-word guessing, this will *inevitably* lead to reading failure (no exceptions). Failure could come as early as age six or as late as age eight, when the real-word guesser with the fabulous visual memory and terrific vocabulary finally breaks down. A child's poor reading strategy will not self-correct without appropriate remedial help.

Most of the time, a child's decoding strategy is invisible to the teacher and the parent. In order to discover a child's strategy you need to listen to him read individual words and record each misread word phonetically. You need a good ear and knowledge of the spelling code to make these transcriptions. I can share these examples with you only because I have spent hundreds of hours testing children and transcribing and analysing errors, as have other scientists. I can confirm this in a different way, because we see these strategies every day in our reading clinic and some even more bizarre than these. One adult client decoded each unfamiliar word after she chanted letter-names out loud: 'Let's see – double-you, aitch, ay, el, ee – that's "while" isn't it?' (No. It's 'whale'.)

It probably wouldn't surprise anyone that the strategy the child or adult is using is highly correlated to reading test scores on standardized tests. The strategies were introduced in the stories in order from the worst to the best. In our research, children's reading test scores could be predicted from the proportions of each type of strategy error they made at around 65 per cent accuracy. More important, this prediction holds up over time. The types of strategy errors a child makes at the end of Grade 1 (6–7 years) predict his reading ability in Grade 3 (8–9 years) with about 38 per cent accuracy. Examples of the children's errors from our research are shown in Table 2.1.

These illustrate some of the 1,780 errors made by 137 children. The words the child was asked to read are on the left. The errors each child made were phonetically transcribed. Examples are from an easy and a more difficult part of the test. Notice that the margin of error is huge when the child guesses a whole real word or tries to assemble word fragments into something like a word. The test ends when the child makes six errors in a row, which explains why there are so few whole-word errors in the harder part of the test. Most real-word guessers drop out before they get this far.

TABLE 2.1   Children's Errors on Standardized Reading Test

| | Whole Word | Part Word | Phonetic | |
			Illegal	Legal
money	mommy	mo-ness		moany
	mom			
	many			
	morning			
lemon	lawn	lee-mo	leemon	
	woman	lemola		
	none	lev-on		
	loan	el-mon		
without	shouted	witch-shot	withut	
	what	what-out		
	whole	went-about		
	washout	wi-hut		
		withit		
		went-hunt		
		with-ert		
exit	next	ex-is		
	eat	ox-it		
	axe	ex-ch		
	except	ext		
	picket	ex-out		
chew	cherry	ch-wah	shoo	
	cheer	chelm	chow	
	cow	chale		
	show			
	chill			
question	position	quest-unt	questun	
	present	quock		
	construction	quiss		
		plush-on		
		quest		
		quist-on		
		clitton		
		bus-tom		
piece	press	pie-eck	peek	pice
	people	pie	pike	
	picture		pies	

TABLE 2.1 *Cont'd*

	Whole Word	Part Word	Phonetic	
			Illegal	Legal
	price			
	picket			
	place			
	pipe			
	person			
	pick			
strange	starting	star-nag	strang	
	stand	stamp-gate		
	string			
	strong			
	straight			
	starch			
	strain			
	scared			
prudent	parent	pun-dent	proddent	
	pretend	per-dent	pruddent	
	predict	per-dint		
	rodent	por-dunt		
	president	pron-dent		
		prun-tent		
		pre-dent		
		proud-ent		
		per-du-tent		
circumstance	circus	kirkum-ston	kirkumstance	
	Christmas	kircum	kirkumstens	
	cricket	criss-ums		
	customers	circus-tant		
	Christmas/	circus-stance		
	dance	kirkus-men-stem		
		cirma-tense		
		cree-cum-stance		
		cir-quum-stan		
		circum-stess		
		circum-steak		
		cru-cumst		
		curse-come		

TABLE 2.1 *Cont'd*

| | **Whole Word** | **Part Word** | **Phonetic** | |
			Illegal	Legal
occasionally	association	occasion	occa-sinally	occashunally
	o-consequently	os-conally	ockushenally	
	socially	oki-den	occasonally	
		oko-lus		
		ock-us-shun-ality		
		ock-sit-on-ally		
		ocka-sallony		
		ock-ish-inly		
		ock-sin-sin-ly		
		ock-us-on-allay		
		on-son-ally		
		on-cass-on-ally		
		us-colly		
		o-can-selly		
		o-can-sarly		
		ass-ocean		
		o-cash-in-alley		
		ack-sit-olly		
flamboyant		fam-boyantly		
		flam-bio-ant		
		flam-bonnet		
		flam-bout		
		flab-bay-ent		
		fail-boy-ant		
		fan-boy-ant		
		flame-boy		
		flame-bone-yant		
		fame-boy-ant		
		flame-boy-ant		

The errors in the two columns on the right are made by children who decode phonetically from left to right, getting the correct number of sounds in the word. 'Illegal' errors occur when the wrong letter-to-sound decoding is used due to an incomplete knowledge of the spelling code. For example, one child read 'red' as 'reed', using the letter-name for e. 'Legal' errors are accurate phonetic decodings of irregularly spelled words. For example, the word 'money' was often read as 'moany' because o–e is the most common spelling for the sound /oe/ (bone, rode, slope, smoke). Note, however, that errors for phonetic decoders are low, despite the fact that this particular test contains a high proportion of irregularly spelled words.

Are the teachers in the stories unusual? Not really, except perhaps for Mrs Able. Mrs Able is fictional. I have never actually met anyone like this, though I have met teachers who come close. But Mrs Able is very, very lucky. She had excellent training, an enlightened head-mistress, and she took advantage of her freedom to be innovative and carry out her own research. This combination of factors is rare.

Are the children in the stories unusual? This is a harder question to answer. Although we see children use these strategies daily in our clinic and in our research on normal children, there is not sufficient evidence on what percentage of children fit these profiles. You may have noticed that I never mentioned anything about their abilities, other than the fact that some children with superb visual memories can end up reading poorly because they rely so exclusively on this skill. Of course not all children read like the children I have just described. The majority learn to read and score normally on stand-ardized tests. Fifty-seven per cent of American nine-year-olds are reading at 'basic level' or higher according to the national literacy survey. But is this due to something going on in the classroom or something going on outside it?

Reading researchers in Britain often include parents' educational level as one of their measures. Peter Bryant and his colleagues at Oxford University studied factors that predict children's reading ability across the age range four to seven years. The strongest predictor at age seven, on three different reading tests, was *mother's education*, which predicted overall reading skill with 40 per cent accuracy. Mother's edu-cation contributed above and beyond the child's IQ, although this added another 15 per cent to the accuracy of the prediction. The Depart-ment for Education reported in their 1992–3 survey of 2,000 children that 33 per cent of Reception class children could already read.

Mothers with a higher education level are more likely to value education (see Chapter 14), to spend time teaching their children to read, more likely to enrol them in independent schools (especially when they aren't doing well in state schools), and more likely to seek appropriate remedial help. It is also reasonable to assume they are more affluent and have more time and money to devote to their children's education.

What can British mothers be doing that British classroom teachers aren't doing? We can only guess, as this hasn't been studied. There is evidence that the amount of one-to-one instruction you receive is directly related to how fast you learn to read, and how fast you learn to read determines your placement in the classroom. The relative rankings between children have been found to stay fairly constant over several years. The NFER found that despite an almost universal report by classroom teachers that they listen to each child read 'every day', or 'every week', *no child* was seen reading to the teacher during their extensive classroom observations. This could be one factor. From our clinical experience, most parents we meet believe that training children to sound out words is the best way to teach reading. Parents are much less likely to teach whole words by sight or be influenced by fads spawned in departments of education, such as guessing words based on context cues.

Another issue is what is meant by 'being able to read'. Young children can score at 'age level' on standardized tests using quite inefficient reading strategies. Does this mean that norms on standardized tests are essentially meaningless? Certainly, this was the rationale behind the development of 'achievement levels' by the US National Assessment Governing Board, which was borne out by their results.

In our research in the classroom, we found some real-word guessers who were among the best readers in the class at age six, when there are fewer words to memorize, but who fell apart completely later on, just like Tommy in the opening story. So it matters when children are tested. We found that the most common type of reading strategy for eight-year-olds was part-word assembling. And these part-word assemblers all read at or above age norms, showing that this strategy must be common. The next most common is the phonetic decoder who makes 'illegal' decoding errors because of an incomplete grasp of English spelling patterns. Only two children in our sample of 137 children had accurate phonetic decoding skills. One was a six-year-old, whose parents were both teachers, and one was eight. Needless to say, they scored the highest of anyone on the reading test. The six-year-old whizzed through the test and scored at a comparable level to a thirty-three-year-old adult. He was known affectionately as 'the little professor'. He would need a good vocabulary to do this, but he didn't understand all the words he could read; he just knew how the code worked. *Shouldn't every child know how the code works?*

The children in this study attended an excellent private school for children aged five to eighteen which boasted a 90 per cent success rate for university places. Yet after three and a half years of schooling, totalling over 3,600 hours in the classroom, in this best of all possible schools, with dedicated teachers, small classes, and highly involved parents, only 2 per cent of the children really knew the alphabet code. That things are much worse in the average state school is illustrated by the results from the US national literacy survey comparing state and private schools.

How Do Good Readers Learn to Read?

About now, you may be wondering how anybody ever learns to read. How did Tommy's brother and sister learn to read? How did you learn to read? I remember being able to read anything in print in my first year at school, aged six. But I only remember this because of an unusual event: having to read comics to a boy twice my age who couldn't read a word. Beyond this, I remember nothing at all. Many people are familiar with this experience, and parents often report that their child suddenly 'took off' and could read.

How does this happen with the same teaching that fails so many other children? This is a fascinating question that, so far, nobody has attempted to answer. One can only suppose, on the basis of extensive research on poor readers, that good readers have a talent for hearing the individual sounds in words which are the basis for our alphabet code, *and* that they somehow understand that these sounds, and no other combinations of sounds, are represented by a specific letter or letters. These children will also have a talent for remembering visual detail and need less time to memorize letter–sound correspondences. In addition, they will have been given instruction which was sufficiently accurate so as not to be misleading.

How common are people like this?

In the US, good readers are relatively rare. Only 13 per cent of fourth-graders in the bottom-ranked states scored at the combined levels of 'proficient' and 'advanced' in the national reading study. This value was 31 per cent for the top-ranked states and 24 per cent nationwide, about the same proportion of the population who succeed in getting a university degree. No comparable figures are available for Britain. Teacher ratings in Level 2 testing (age seven) in 1991–2 placed 21–24 per cent of children at Level 3, about two years above age norms.

In every skilled behaviour, there are degrees of competence. Reading is no exception. For example, everyone should have swimming lessons sometime in childhood. Whether a child becomes an expert swimmer depends upon the teaching method, the teacher's skill in teaching it, parental support, the child's motivation and talent, and the number of lessons and hours of practice. Few of us are expert swimmers, but most of us could be with appropriate training. We certainly *should* be if we had spent more than 3,600 hours in swimming classes, which is the number of hours our eight-year-olds had spent in the classroom trying to learn to read.

It's nice to be able to swim, but swimming only matters because you might fall into a river or pond. If this should happen, you only need sufficient skill to stay afloat until you are rescued. You don't need Olympic quality style or speed. Learning to read is like learning to swim in one sense (both are skills that must be taught), but completely different in another. To be effective in a modern world, it matters whether or not you are an expert reader. Keeping afloat isn't good enough. Keeping afloat is tantamount to drowning.

So what is reading all about? Is there a better way to teach reading so everyone can become an 'expert'? In the next chapter, we look at exciting new discoveries about how writing systems work. It turns out that every writing system is determined by the sound-based structure of the language for which it was written. This startling new information has important implications for how a particular writing system can and *cannot* be taught. These findings are compared to current teaching methods and to the philosophies behind them.

Answer to nursery rhyme on p. 17: 'London bridge is falling down'. (y=l, t=o, o=n, x=d, etc.)

CHAPTER 3

Transcribing Talk

In the last chapter we saw that when children are given poor or misleading instruction, they develop different strategies or hypotheses about which unit of talk the letters stand for. Some psychologists and educators believe that these strategies reflect stages of reading development. Some go further and argue that these stages mirror the progression of the development of writing itself, an idea which begins to resemble biological determinism. In this view, children are not really making errors, they are behaving 'naturally' as they progress along a developmental path.

There are various forms of quasi-biological models in reading instruction, 'real books' being a prime example. 'Stage' theorists advocate teaching reading in as many as four separate steps. The child is first taught whole words, then whole syllables, then initial consonant plus rhyming endings ('onset-rime'), and finally individual sounds (phonemes). One extreme view advocates using different kinds of symbols for each of these steps. These ideas have had an impact on teacher training and curriculum design in countries around the world. The stages approach typifies some English reading schemes. The phonemic structure of the word is only gradually penetrated, until the child is finally taught the unit for which the alphabet code was actually written, a process which can waste one or two years and derail many children.

The idea that writing systems, or children learning them, go through developmental stages, is incorrect. It is based upon ignorance about how writing systems actually work and also upon a type of reverse logic. Children's confusion and misunderstanding about our alphabetic writing system, instead of being seen as correctable, *becomes the platform* for designing a programme of instruction.

In the next two chapters we will be looking at writing systems in the light of modern teaching methods, to see if there is any fit between the way writing systems are designed and the methods which should be used to teach them.

Scholars have grappled with the mystery of deciphering ancient writing systems for more than 200 years. Eleven writing systems still defy a solution. This extended effort has revealed that writing systems aren't arbitrary; that is, you couldn't use the Chinese writing system for English, and it wouldn't make sense to use the English writing system for Chinese. The evidence shows conclusively that the design of every writing system is constrained by two main factors: firstly, the limits of human memory for abstract visual symbols; and secondly, the syllable structure of the language. This information is critically important in knowing how a writing system should be taught, and in knowing how it *cannot* be taught.

I'm going to start by comparing the development of writing to the 'real books' and 'progressive stages' approaches to reading. Both make specific predictions about how all writing systems should be taught, predictions which can easily be checked against the evidence.

Despite its popularity, there is considerable confusion about what 'real books' actually means. The central idea is that reading is natural in the same way that learning to speak is natural. According to Kenneth Goodman, the leading expert on 'real books', children come to the classroom with a wealth of knowledge about the meaning of words and the grammatical structure of their language. They have acquired this knowledge without any direct instruction. He also assumes that as children speak fluently, they have an awareness of the sounds in their own speech. From this knowledge, which Goodman describes as three 'cueing systems', children can easily acquire an understanding of the written code for their language by maximal use of all three cues: context cues to determine meaning; grammatical structure to anticipate which word is most likely in a sequence; and knowledge of patterns of sounds in speech. Goodman predicts that this approach would work for all written languages, commenting that 'theoretically, any type of writing system would work for any language' *(Phonics Phacts)*.

As reading is supposed to be just like learning to speak, the child needs to be exposed to good children's literature, using books and stories which use 'natural' or 'normal' language, and not unnatural language like the old Janet and John readers, where words were repeated over and over again. ('See Janet, see. Look, look, look.')

The idea is that if children hear natural language from children's books while they are looking at the print as it is being read, and at the same time 'invent' their own spelling system as they're learning to write, children will naturally teach themselves to read and write by trial and error. Goodman states that the reader should 'use the least amount of information possible to make the best guess possible'. By 'information', he means pictures, context, and print. In other words, readers should guess whole words in context and work out what makes sense, rather than sounding out words letter by letter, and should participate in what Goodman has called 'a psycholinguistic guessing game'.

It was this approach that Miss Jones was using in her classroom. This is why she said to Nigel, 'Don't try to sound out the word, just look at the pictures.' What she meant was, that if Nigel could understand the *context* of the story, he could work out which words made sense in that context. As he worked this out, he was supposed to automatically learn the relationship between the sounds in words and the patterns of letters on the page by a process of osmosis.

This certainly makes life a lot simpler for Miss Jones and for the children, and a lot more fun. But is reading and writing 'natural' or not? Can children learn to read by context clues, guessing whole words as they work through text? To find out, we're going to look at how writing was invented in the first place.

Before we begin, here is the problem in a nutshell. Writing is a coded transcription of talk. Talk isn't like words on a page, neat little bundles of sounds separated by spaces. Words are glued together in phrases. Talk sounds like this hypothetical conversation between two people we'll call Mabel and Howard. Howard has just arrived home from the office.

Howard: Hi. Wojjadootuday?
Mabel: Wentootheshops. Haddasale.
Howard: Bynything?

Mabel: Bawtchuapairrasocksannatie.
Howard: Howmuchaycos?
Mabel: Nohmuch. Wanmeetagettumanshowya?
Howard: Inawhile. Wotzferdinner?

Conversations sound like this in every language. Howard and Mabel speak pretty much the same as other people, connecting badly enunciated speech sounds across an entire phrase. Certainly, no one would ever want to create a written record of conversations like this one. Something very important has to be going on to make the invention of writing absolutely necessary.

We are fortunate to have a treasure trove of documents providing a blow-by-blow description of what it was like to design a writing system from scratch. This detailed history comes from ancient Sumer in the Tigris-Euphrates delta. Our alphabet is a distant descendant of the writing systems of Sumer and Egypt. Beginning around 3500 BC, the Sumerians had a problem with storing grain, dates, oil and wine in a communal warehouse. It was the warehouseman's job to remember which farmer was storing which commodity, what kind of grain (emmer, wheat, barley, millet), how much of each type, and what was owed to whom in either exchange or money. He had to keep all this in his head, and no doubt he and the farmers had arguments almost daily. To solve these problems, the farmers and city administrators got together and worked out a code using pictures for the types of grain, for oil, wine and dates, along with little slashes and dots for numbers. These were carved on to clay tablets or tokens. Now they had a method for keeping ledgers and inventory control, a method that got more sophisticated over the next thousand years. An accounting tablet is shown in Figure 3.1.

This solution worked fine until the crime rate started to go up as the harvests increased, artisans flourished and became famous for their wares, and the towns generally grew more prosperous. There were disputes over ownership of land, positions of boundary markers, irrigation rights, and disposable property. This is the awful consequence of owning land and goods. Somebody always gets more than somebody else, and the 'somebody else' hits back.

The Sumerians needed laws, courthouses and judges, and some way to remember the laws and record the judges' case decisions,

FIGURE 3.1   Sumerian Accounting Tablet for Barley

Photo reproduced with permission of Christie's Images

quantity of the product:	type of the product:	accounting period:

c. 135,000 litres	barley	37 months

because the judges couldn't remember them all. But how? Laws aren't commodities, things or numbers. You can't draw pictures of laws. Laws are just talk, and talk sounds like Mabel and Howard's conversation about the socks. It's not easy to represent talk in symbols. What part of the talk do you choose? The most obvious units are words. You could symbolize words with the pictures you already have from the warehouse inventory control system, but this doesn't get you very far with statements like this from a hypothetical plaintiff: 'Hewuzpickinmygrapesoutamyfield. Iknowitwuzim. Isawim.'

It needs a sharp ear and a keen understanding of the language just to find out where the words start and stop. And anyone smart enough to do this and to begin to develop a writing system will know in a hurry that pictures won't work:

He   was   picking   my   grapes   out of my   field.

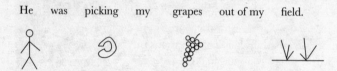

The pictures could mean: 'He was picking grapes in his field', or 'We're hiring men to pick grapes in the field', or 'The man planted seeds in Fred's grape field'.

The Sumerians hit upon the idea of using abstract symbols for words that couldn't be drawn as a picture. These symbols could look like anything at all:

Here's where the trouble began and the story gets interesting, except no one thought so at the time.

These difficulties were not unique to Sumer. They caused problems everywhere during the agricultural revolution, in all the places where it was easy to grow wheat and rice. The same ideas and the same types of solutions cropped up whenever people had to keep inventories, write out wills, contracts, bills of sale, rules, laws and case decisions. This happened in the Nile Delta in Egypt around 3000 BC, in the

Indus Valley around 2500 BC, along the Yangtze river in China sometime around 2000 BC, and in places as remote as the Yucatan jungle, where exactly the same kind of writing was invented by the Mayans, probably in the sixth to seventh century AD.

All early writing systems begin by focusing on meaning. First, words are isolated from phrases. Words that can be drawn (ship, ox) are represented by pictures (pictograms), and words that can't are represented by abstract symbols, called logographs, which is Greek for 'word-writing' or 'word-carving'. After a while the Sumerians had hundreds of these logographs.

Unfortunately, this doesn't work. People may have a natural talent for learning language and rapidly acquire huge vocabularies without much effort, but they have no talent for remembering either thousands of abstract visual patterns or the connection between each abstract visual pattern and a particular word. This meant that the Sumerians couldn't represent most of the words in their language. The average number of words in daily conversations on the streets of any town in the world today is about 50,000. *The Oxford Companion to the English Language* estimates that the total number of all possible English words, including abbreviations and specialist vocabularies, exceeds one million! But when people are asked to memorize what word goes with which abstract visual symbol scribbled on clay, or papyrus, or paper, the upper limit is around 1,500–2,000, not enough for any language. Not even close.

Instead, the Sumerians were faced with a totally different problem: how to limit the number of symbols so that people could remember them, and at the same time transcribe all possible words they needed. They tried to use the symbols more efficiently. For instance, the same symbol was adopted for two words related in meaning. The symbol for 'mouth' was used for the verb 'to speak', and the symbols for 'mouth' and 'food' were combined to stand for 'eating'.

All languages have words that sound alike with different meanings. In English, we bury our dead and pick a berry off a bush. We see a bear in the woods, bare our chest and bear our burdens. We trip on a stair and people stare at us. We pare a pair of pears and reel in a real fish. These kinds of words are called 'homophones' (Greek for 'same sounds'). The Sumerians used one symbol for homophones, instead of inventing different symbols for words like 'berry' and 'bury'.

FIGURE 3.2

 sag (head)

 ka (mouth)

 ninda (food)

 ku (eat)

The reader was supposed to determine which meaning was correct by using context clues.

There were lots of homophones in Sumerian and this made the writing ambiguous. This could have important implications at the courthouse. Arguments might break out in court over whether a man had been blinded by his son, or was blinded by the sun, and this would never do. The Sumerians had another idea. They divided the words in their language into categories, and then invented symbols for each of the categories. In the hypothetical example, if you wrote the symbol for the word 'sun', you could add the category symbol for 'heavenly body', and 'son' could be written beside the category symbol for 'man'. These category signs are called 'determinatives' because they *determine* the meaning of a word. How many of these determinatives you need in the writing system depends upon how many symbols have multiple meanings. Sumerians used determinatives only for nouns.

It's difficult to duplicate these effects in English, because the symbols in our writing system stand for sounds and not words. English homophones usually have different spellings. But it might look something like this:

'Aunt Eloise picked four ripe pears (ⳕ) and took them into the house to pear (ざ) and served them in pears (ᐲ) to the guests.'

Determinatives to help interpret 'pear':

ⳕ = fruit

ざ = utensil

ᐲ = quantity

Alas, this solution was only marginally useful. Most Sumerian words were not homophones. There were still thousands of words without symbols and new words coming into the language almost daily. There was no way to write people's names, and no way to mark grammatical tenses, like past, present and future. To add to the confusion, the pictographs began to disappear after the stylus was invented. It made wedge-shaped marks, known as 'cuneiform' writing. It's difficult to draw with a wedge-shaped tool, so the pictograms were turned on their side and ultimately became as abstract as the logographs. The compound logograph for 'eat' went through these tranformations:

FIGURE 3.3

3000 BC ————————————————————————— 600 BC

So far, the Sumerians had focused exclusively on meaning, developing the writing system entirely at the level of the word. They had pictographs standing for words, logographs standing for words, logographs that stood for several words with the same sound, logographs that stood for words related in meaning, and symbols called determinatives that stood for categories of meaning. From a 'real books' perspective, a writing system that focuses entirely on meaning should have been nearly perfect. The only problem was, *it didn't work.*

No matter how efficiently the symbols were used, they still kept creeping above the limits of human memory.

Eventually, scholars had a better idea. Suppose you invented symbols to stand for fragments of a word, the meaningless *sounds* in the word, instead of the whole word? This would give you two kinds of clues, category clues (determinatives) for words that sounded alike (son/sun), and sound-based codes for words that were ambiguous or had no symbols, like parts of speech. Once they made this decision, they discovered something amazing. There were only three main types of syllables in Sumerian: consonant + vowel (CV), vowel + consonant (VC), and consonant + vowel + consonant (CVC). Furthermore, the total number of possible syllables was incredibly smaller than the total number of words in the language. A syllable is a pattern of sounds with only one vowel. In English, 'I', 'it', 'crunch', and 'sling' are one-syllable words and 'table', 'jumping', and 'forest' are two-syllable words.

From this point on, the Sumerians began to invent symbols for every sound combination in the three types of syllables in their language: CV, VC, and CVC. All new words could be written with syllable symbols alone. So the Sumerian writing system began to accrete symbols that stood for many levels of talk, rather like whales accrete barnacles. Now you might think, with hindsight, that they should have just thrown out the logographs and the category determinatives, and used only the syllable symbols. They couldn't do this right away, just as we have never been able to standardize our spelling system. The reason was that things had gone too far. All the tinkering with the writing system took about a thousand years. The palace archives, temple documents, prayers and sacred myths, laws, case decisions, forms for writs, marriage licences, etc. were written with the old logographs and couldn't be changed just like that.

This meant that by around 2500 BC there were symbols that looked a bit like the old pictures that were used for inventory control, symbols that stood for words you couldn't draw, symbols for words related in meaning, symbols for three types of syllables, and symbols for categories such as 'water', 'mineral', 'plant', 'animal', 'field', and 'farming equipment'. The reader had to shift gears from thinking about words, to thinking about meaningless sounds in words, to thinking about categories as clues to meaning. Samuel Kramer, the famous translator and popularizer of Sumerian literature, writes that not only was this a major stumbling block in deciphering the Sumerian writing system, but often words were written more than one way in the same document. This made it even harder to crack the code because no one believed a writing system could be so wasteful as to have more than one way to write a word. In the same text, you might find the logograph for 'canal' alongside a category determinative for 'water', and later, the syllable symbols (CV-CVC) standing for 'ca'-'nal', depending upon the whim of the author.

The Sumerian writing system wasn't the only one with this many levels of complexity. The Egyptian writing system evolved in the same way and was, if anything, even worse. The hieroglyphic script used by priests to carve or paint on temples and tombs (hieroglyphic means 'sacred carving'), used the same solutions: pictograms, logographs, category determinatives, and sound-based symbols for single consonants (C) and consonant sequences (CC, CCC) (they didn't write vowels). The Egyptians, however, were partial to their pictograms. These pictograms were not only very beautiful, but were considered sacred. When the priests designed the symbols for abstract words and sounds in words, they used their favourite pictograms over and over again. The picture of an owl, 𓅓 meaning 'owl' (the bird), was borrowed to stand for various prepositions (in, to, for, with), *and* for the consonant sound /m/, *and* for words, like 'obedient', where the owl stood for 'good bird', a determinative. The consonant symbols weren't consistent either. The symbol for /m/ was an owl, but the symbol for /ms/ (the word for 'fan') was written like this: 𓏴

The Egyptian priests had a saying which, roughly translated, went: 'Put writing in your heart so you may protect yourself from hard labour of any kind.'[1] They seem to have had a vested interest in keeping the writing system as complicated as possible so only a select few could learn it.

This brief history shows that what is natural for a spoken language isn't natural for a writing system. In natural speech we are only conscious of phrases and words, but to learn a writing system we have to be conscious of sounds in words.

Teaching Sumerian Writing

Even though these writing systems are complex, they are full of duplications and redundancies. There are clues to meaning alongside clues to sounds. From a 'real books' perspective, once these writing systems have been designed they should be easy to learn because there are so many context clues. Were they easy to learn? Could a Sumerian child teach himself to read using context clues?

We can answer this question as well from the thousands of exercise tablets found on the sites of schools all over ancient Sumer. We can reconstruct exactly what happened in these schools with remarkable detail. Let's look in on a typical Sumerian schoolboy in the town of Shurrupak, around 2000 BC. We are at the *edduba*, or tablet-house, which is Sumerian for 'school'. The room is filled with schoolmasters and boys of various ages. One boy, Enkimansi, is the son of a wealthy farmer, and he's sitting beside his best friend on a bench made of clay bricks. He has been there since dawn and will stay till the light fades at sunset. He does this seven days a week and will keep at it until his late teens, about the same number of years that boys and girls go to school today. When Enkimansi first started school, he learned how to prepare his own clay tablets and to make his own writing implement, a wedge-shaped stylus made out of a reed. Next, he had to copy lists of symbols that stood for syllables, starting with the simplest ones for consonant + vowel (CV): *tu, ta, ti, te* [/too/, /tah/, /tee/, /teh/], *ku, ka, ki, ke, nu, na, ni, ne, bu, ba, bi, be, zu, za, zi, ze.*

He did this until his writing was accurate and he had memorized them. Then he learned the symbols for the rest of the syllables (VC and CVC). Next he wrote out and memorized about 900 logographs. Each one had the syllable signs written beside it to help him remember them and pronounce them correctly. Then he learned compound logographs, where two logographs are written side-by-side to stand for a different word (mouth + food = eat). After he had memorized these, he began copying thousands of words in long word lists organized by categories (plants, trees, animals, fish), in order to memorize which category markers (determinatives) went with which words. When he was done with this and could remember everything, he started copying out and reading short phrases, proverbs and fables. And *finally*, when he was about twelve years old, he got to read something interesting.

Here is an example of a popular schoolboy story that Enkimansi was copying (the actual text is illustrated in Figure 3.4). It was written by a schoolmaster in Nippur. Both the masters and the students must have thought it was pretty hilarious because fragments of this story have been found in cities all over Sumer. Like many of the schoolboy stories, it shows the Sumerians' flare for satire. The stories create images of rowdy schoolrooms, full of boisterous, disobedient pupils who were frequently caned for misbehaviour. ('Cane' was written as a compound logograph, combining the symbols for 'stick' and 'flesh'.) Here are some excerpts from the story:

THE BOREDOM

I recited my tablet, ate my lunch, prepared my new tablet, wrote it, finished it; then my model tablets were brought to me, and in the afternoon my exercise tablets were brought to me. When school was dismissed, I went home, entered the house, and found my father sitting there. I explained my exercise tablets to my father. I recited my tablet to him, and he was delighted.

THE DANGER

My teacher, reading my tablet, said: 'There is something missing,' and caned me. The man in charge of neatness said: 'You loitered in the street and did not keep your clothes straight,' and caned me. The man in charge of silence said: 'Why did you talk without permission?' and caned me.

[The caning sequence continues for about twelve more lines and the section concludes:] And so I began to hate the scribal art and to neglect the scribal art. My teacher took no delight in me.

THE BRIBE

[At this point in the story, the student asks his father whether they might be nice to the teacher, invite him to their home, give him presents, and perhaps some extra salary (students paid fees to their head teacher). The father agrees, and the schoolmaster arrives, is seated in the best chair, fed good things to eat, given a new tunic, a handsome ring, and some money. This works wonders. Later in the story the master speaks:]

'Because you gave me everything without holding back, paid me a salary larger than my efforts deserve, and have honoured me, may your pointed stylus write well for you, may your exercises contain no faults, may you walk among the highest of the school graduates.'[2]

FIGURE 3.4   Sumerian schoolboy story

I think you can see that Enkimansi's experience and his typical school day is anything but 'natural', easy or fun. Something natural comes without effort. Instead, the Sumerian and Egyptian pupils had to work awfully hard, for awfully long hours, and for an awfully long time just to learn to read and write. If you look closely at the photograph of the schoolboy story, there is no way anyone could figure it out by guesswork from 'context clues'. It looks like a small wading bird had criss-crossed the clay tablet about a thousand times. You probably can't even tell one symbol from another.

By now it should be clear that writing systems are *inventions* and completely unlike natural language. Even though the Sumerian and Egyptian scholars were eventually able to transcribe talk, it turned out to be monstrously difficult to do. Over the centuries gifted people have invented many types of codes. They have transcribed music into a written notation, and numerical quantities and relationships into a code of number and letter symbols called 'mathematics'. Computer software designers coded the English alphabet into octal, then to binary and back again, so that computers can store this in memory and, at the same time, represent it on a screen. But there is nothing 'natural' about these codes, something that a young child would just pick up by staring at them for a few months. Codes have to be taught.

We learned something else equally important. A whole word (logographic) writing system can't work. There is a *natural* limit on human memory for memorizing codes with too many confusing symbols. This upper limit, from the evidence so far, is around 2,000 symbols. About now, some astute readers may be saying: 'Wait a minute. What about the Chinese? The Chinese have a logographic writing system, don't they?'

Can the Chinese Memorize Logographs?

According to the received wisdom of educators in the early part of this century, English-speaking children can memorize random letter sequences for whole words because Chinese children are supposed to be able to do this. Misconceptions about Chinese writing have fostered the myth that the Chinese people have a 'logographic' or 'ideographic' (idea symbol) writing system, and that Chinese children are taught to read symbols for whole words and ideas.

The earliest examples of Chinese writing are found on oracle bones dated to the Shang Dynasty, at around 1500 BC. Writing was already highly developed with about 4,000 different symbols or 'characters', showing it had originated much earlier. At the close of the Shang dynasty, wars and conquests had divided China into city-states or provinces. Each city-state began to develop the writing system in different ways.

In 221 BC, Emperor Qin unified China and initiated a writing reform. He appointed the scholar Li Su to develop what is called the 'small seal script', which he finished in 200 BC. Li Su's basic job was to standardize the symbols into one uniform system. He assigned one character each to several hundred words (logographs), to CV and CVC syllables (syllabary), and to 'classifier' signs which stood for categories (the same as determinatives in Sumerian and Ancient Egyptian). In other words, the Chinese writing system was almost identical in structure to the Sumerian writing system. During the same century, the Chinese invented the brush, and in AD 106 they invented paper, allowing Xu Shen to compile the first dictionary in AD 120. The dictionary was divided into sections by 540 classifiers organized in a fixed order. The classifiers and their order had to be memorized before you could look up a word. Xu Shen's dictionary included around 10,000 entries.

Over the next 1,700 years, many more characters were created, culminating in the great K'ang Hsi dictionary with nearly 50,000 entries. The classifier symbols were reduced to 214, about the same number there is today. To look up a word in a Chinese dictionary, you decide which classifier sign the word might belong to, you remember the order of the classifiers in the dictionary, and then look up the word based upon the number of brush strokes in each character, which occur in a fixed sequence. As you can imagine this isn't very efficient. Only a few eminent scholars were able to take full advantage of the K'ang Hsi dictionary. In further reforms, the number of entries shrank dramatically. The modern Chinese dictionary contains about 12,000 entries.

The Chinese writing system is largely based on the syllable. Misconceptions about Chinese writing are due to the syllable structure of the Chinese language. Just under half of all Chinese words are only one syllable long ('li', 'chu', 'kao', 'chang') – a word *and* a syllable at the same time. Most Chinese syllables consist of only two basic sound sequences: CV and CVC, and most CVC sequences end in one of only two sounds: /n/ (tan) or /ng/ (tang). The Chinese language has very few consonant clusters and a grand total of 1,277 tonal syllables. In tonal languages, meaning can change by altering the tone or pitch of the vowel. This open, simple syllable structure means that the Chinese language is riddled with homophones, those words that sound alike with different meanings. This makes it necessary to use at least 200 classifiers. Ninety per cent of all Chinese words are written as compound signs, with the syllable sign and classifier sign fused together.

Due to its long evolution, the Chinese writing system is far from perfect. Sometimes the same syllable is written with two or more different characters. Sometimes two or more different syllables are written with the same character. Sometimes a classifier symbol can also be a syllable symbol. Sometimes syllable signs are joined to represent the beginning of one word combined with the ending of another.

There is modern research to show whether or not Chinese writing is easy to learn. In the early 1980s, Harold Stevenson and a group of American, Japanese and Chinese psychologists tested more than 2,000 ten-year-olds in Taiwan, Sendai, and Minneapolis. The children read text of comparable difficulty, with similar vocabularies, averaging around 7,000 words. What they discovered first is surprising. Taiwanese children do not begin by memorizing the 1,260 syllable signs as 'real books' and look-and-say advocates might imagine. Instead, they are taught the individual sounds of their language using a Roman alphabet. For example, they learn that the CVC syllable/word 'tang' has three sounds: /t/ /a/ /ng/. Once the sounds of the language are mastered, they begin to memorize the syllable characters and 214 classifier symbols. For a while, each syllable character (唐) is written alongside its alphabet equivalent (tang), so it can be pronounced correctly. Finally, the alphabet symbols are discarded. Apart from historical tradition, there is a good reason why the Chinese don't use an alphabet. Chinese characters are equally fast, or faster, to read because each character stands for more than one sound.

The researchers set a 75 per cent pass rate for their tests. They found that more of the Taiwan children passed this criterion (69 per cent) than either the Japanese (44 per cent) or American children (54 per cent), but this is just as likely to be a function of their excellent, systematic training as a function of the writing system. Shin-ying Lee found that Beijing children who are taught Chinese characters from the outset (whole syllables or words), did much worse than children in Taiwan, Japan or the US.

Stevenson's research team discovered something else. The majority of the Chinese children who failed the 'pass' criterion, failed entirely because they couldn't understand what they read. There was a discrepancy between the Chinese children's ability to read isolated words

FIGURE 3.5

Classifier			Meaning
	唐	*tang*	
cereal	米	糖	sugar
earth	土	塘	embankment
hand	手 扌	搪	to block
water	水 氵	溏	pond

FIGURE 3.5b Position of the Classifier Can Vary

辟 *pì*

Classifier

亻 僻
言 譬
門 闢
女 嬖

(decoding) and their understanding of the meaning of the text (comprehension), a discrepancy not found for either Japanese or American children. It seems that it is easier to memorize the sound/symbol correspondences for syllable signs than to remember what they mean when they are combined in characters with classifier signs.

I've written a little story in pseudo-Chinese to illustrate this problem. The story is full of homophones, like the Chinese language. The

FIGURE 3.5C   The Syllable Not Consistent with the Symbol

堯 *yáo*

Classifier				Meaning
person	イ	僥	jiǎo	lucky
hand	扌	撓	nǎo	scratch
wood	木	橈	náo	oar
water	氵	澆	jiāo	sprinkle

The diacritics indicate 'tone' or voicing

homophones are written (spelled) the same way, like the Chinese writing system. Each homophone is followed by a classifier in brackets. Try to imagine that each word and each classifier is only one symbol.

THE HUNTER
Frank(name) saw(eye) the bare(animal) in the would(plant). He saw(eye) the marks of paws(animal part) at his feat(body part) and decided to paws(time) and think. He sat on a bare(abstract) rock and looked at the weather(sky) to see(eye) weather(thought) he new(thought) when knight (time) was coming. The sun(heavenly body) was low(position). His sun(family) had already left(movement) to weight(time) by the rode(travel). He decided to leave(travel) too. He rose(position), left(movement) the seen(nature) to meat(greeting) his sun(family) and go home(dwelling).

This doesn't look too 'natural' does it? It certainly isn't the way that Chinese people talk.

All writing systems are imperfect transcriptions of speech. They are very difficult to design, and this can take hundreds and even thousands of years. Writing systems are imperfect even after centuries of tinkering, and most cultures have attempted some type of writing reform. Writing systems do go through stages, not because this is a natural progression, but because writing is so *un*natural. Authors of writing systems always

51

begin with the wrong solution and work backwards to a simpler one.

No culture ever used the *word* as the sole basis for a writing system. Not even the Chinese. A word-based system will always fail. This means there is no such thing as a 'logographic' writing *system*, and there never was. What turns out to be 'natural' is that ordinary people (including children) can only remember about 1,500–2,000 abstract visual symbols. What is also 'natural' is that people don't know the sounds of their language, or whether there are more words or more sounds, or how many kinds of sounds. We are not conscious observers of how we speak.

There are two main choices for converting talk into scribbles on a page, and scribbles on a page back into talk. The first choice for the novice inventor of writing is always based upon what has the greatest psychological relevance, and that is *meaning*. When this fails, scholars scramble to create symbols that are props for decoding meaning. When this also fails, they finally discover they must use the *meaningless* sounds in words, simply because there are far fewer sounds than words in all languages, and therefore the writing system can be made manageable.

There are many choices about which meaningless sounds to use, and the evidence shows that this is critically dependent upon the type of syllable structure or sound-based structure of the language. The Sumerian language had three main syllable types: CV, VC, CVC; the Chinese two: CV, CVC. The Mayans used vowels and CV units. The Egyptians used consonant sequences: C, CC, CCC. There are other units of sound you can use, and I'll talk more about this in the next chapter.

We have a 200-year historical record to show that writing systems are fiendishly difficult to decipher. This is true even when you have good clues and good information, such as knowing ancient place names, or words remaining in the language of the local people, or even knowing the language itself. The reason for the difficulty in deciphering writing systems is that there are several elements of speech the written code can stand for – whole words, syllables, syllable fragments, and consonant sequences – and some writing systems use them all.

These facts explain why the children described in the previous chapter were having such a hard time. They were misled about which unit of speech the letters stand for. Each child came to a different decision, either believing that random letter strings between the gaps on the page stood for a whole word, or by cueing off the first consonant and guessing a real word by its shape, or by combining various fragments of these letter strings: CV, VC, CVC, into nonsense words.

There's one more question a 'real books' advocate might want to ask. As the early writing systems were so hard to invent and hard to learn, maybe these *particular* writing sytems aren't 'natural'. Maybe the people who promote 'real books' are talking about alphabets (so far we haven't seen any alphabets). Maybe an alphabet is the only natural representation of talk, and these other writing systems are unnatural. But if alphabets are natural, why didn't everyone invent an alphabet to begin with, or at least come up with an alphabet in over 2,000 years? And why did people in all these different parts of the world do the *same* thing, in the *same* order? If only alphabets are natural, why are these other ideas so alike?

What Teachers Really Think About 'Real Books'

Let's take a closer look at the 'real books' system, because there's more to it than just 'natural' language and 'natural' reading. If you believe something is natural, this has a number of consequences. The first one is that you don't have to teach something natural in any direct way. The child just needs exposure. Conversely, you would never ask the child to do something *unnatural*, like breaking words up into fragments of sound, and putting the fragments back together again (segmenting and blending sounds). Instead, the child should look at the whole word on the page, notice its shape and overall length and *say* the whole word, or *hear* the whole word pronounced by the teacher or parent. Using this approach, children are supposed to be able to learn to read independently. Context, or meaning, is very important, because it helps the reader anticipate which word might come next in a sentence. Using context means knowing what the story is about ahead of time or using picture clues. This is why there are so many illustrations in the books in 'real books' classrooms.

On the other hand, 'real books' advocates believe that learning to spell is different. Reading is simple decoding based on context and picture clues, but writing is a direct creative act. The most important thing is not to block creativity. If children do lots of writing, according to the theory, they will gradually discover how words should be spelled by inventing their own spelling system. Children can figure out the relationship between sounds in words and the print code *on their own*. They can do this, because they are supposed to have a natural sensitivity to sounds in their own speech. To quote the leading expert on invented spelling, Carol Chomsky, 'Using their knowledge of letter-names and in some cases letter-sounds, children are able to represent the sounds of words quite accurately and consistently.'[3] (This sounds convincing, except it isn't true.)

What happens in 'real books' writing activities in practice, is that many children don't learn to spell anything at all, because they can't *hear* the sounds in their speech. Others learn to spell like Tommy did in the 'Submarine Rtet', using letter-names almost exclusively, because that's all they've ever been taught. As invented spelling is supposed to be 'invented', it is never corrected (no direct instruction is permitted). Children practise errors over and over again, until these errors are fixed in their brains and become very hard to unfix. It would be just like saying to a student just beginning to learn the piano: 'Never mind about all those mistakes. Just remember the tune, get the feeling of the music and you will learn to read the notes correctly.' Anyone who has ever learned a skill knows that practising errors over and over again is always a bad idea.

By now, you should be feeling a little uncomfortable with the notion that a six-year-old should discover how a writing system works without any help, when it took great scholars thousands of years to design them so imperfectly. Let's find out what teachers in 'real books' classrooms really think. Patrick Groff is a professor at San Diego State University, a city where 'real books' was mandated by the State of California in 1987. Groff read the major books on the subject and pulled together the central ideas expressed in those books. He then sent surveys to first- and second-grade teachers to ask for their opinions of a list of statements. He got responses from 275 teachers. Here are ten of the most important statements on his list:

1. Children learn to read best the same way they learned to speak.
2. Children can teach themselves to read. Formal instruction is unnecessary.

3. Children should not learn reading subskills in any type of instructional sequence or 'hierarchical' order.

4. Children should guess at written words, using sentence context cues.

5. Children should be taught to recognize words by sight as wholes.

6. The length and complexity of words is of little consequence in beginning reading instruction.

7. The intensive and systematic teaching of phonics hinders reading comprehension.

8. Intensive phonics makes it more difficult for children to learn to recognize words.

9. No workbooks or worksheets should ever be used.

10. English is spelled too unpredictably for phonics to work well.

This list is remarkably similar to the 'language experience' approach to reading instruction for British teachers set out in *The Primary Language Record* (Centre for Language in Primary Education, London, 1992). The authors date the origin of this new trend in reading to 1970; they also incorrectly infer that Kenneth Goodman, the inventor of the 'real books' method, is a 'psycholinguist'.

The statements compiled by Groff were based upon quotations from books written by 'real books' advocates. These are peppered with hyperbole and unsupported by any scientific research. Absolute certainty in the face of no data is always a dangerous sign. I have italicized such assertions in the quotes below to illustrate this:

'Children *must* develop reading strategies by and for themselves.'[4]

'It is easier for a reader to remember the *unique* appearance and pronunciation of a whole word like 'photograph' than to remember the unique pronunciations of meaningless syllables and spelling units.'[5] [Whoever said English was written as a syllabary?]

'One word in five can be *completely* eliminated from most English texts with scarcely any effect on its overall comprehensibility.'[6] [Let's try it: 'One in five can be completely from most English with scarcely any effect on its overall.']

'English is spelled *so unpredictably*, that there is *no way* of predicting when a particular spelling correspondence applies.'[7]

And the totally contradictory statement: 'Children can develop and use an *intuitive knowledge* of letter-sound correspondences' without '*any* phonics instruction' or 'without deliberate instruction from adults.'[8]

'Sounding out a word is a cumbersome, time-consuming and *unnecessary* activity.'[9]

'Matching letters with sounds is a *flat-earth view of the world*, one that rejects modern science about reading.'[10] [What 'modern science' means here is unknown.]

And finally, an extraordinary statement, considering 5,500 years of historical evidence: 'There is *nothing unique* about reading, either visually or as far as language is concerned.'[11]

What did the San Diego teachers believe about the statements that Groff presented to them? Altogether they disagreed overwhelmingly with all but three. They particularly disagreed with those which claimed that any type of direct instruction or phonics instruction was 'bad'. On the other hand, most teachers thought the child should 'learn to recognize words by sight', and 'guess words using context cues'. (We'll see they should do neither later on.) The teachers were split evenly (true, false, undecided) on their responses to the first statement ('Children learn to read best the same way they learned to speak'), yet were overwhelmingly against the second ('Children can teach themselves to read. Formal instruction is unnecessary.') Only 4 per cent said 'true', and 80 per cent said 'false'. Either these teachers hold contradictory beliefs, or they think that children also need direct instruction to learn how to *talk* (which they don't).

Apart from this, teachers were in opposition to the remaining principles of 'real books'. This is very surprising. They are running 'real books' classrooms, yet they are more likely to *believe* in phonics. American teachers are no longer trained in phonics. My colleagues and I have not seen much phonics in evidence in 'real books' classrooms we have observed in our research in Florida, yet we have also heard teachers *saying* that phonics is important. Phonics instruction took up, on average, only 2 per cent of the language arts period in seven classrooms during more than 100 hours of observation, and teachers clearly did not know what they were doing: 'Today we're going to learn about long ee. It's different to short ee, like in the word "bed", because it sounds like ee in "be".'

Something is clearly amiss when teachers are doing one thing and believing something else, or thinking that the two approaches are compatible when they are contradictory. When they try to do what they believe, they have no understanding of how or where to begin.

Just in case you think that these irrational ideas are something only Americans might believe, here are some quotes from *The Primary*

Language Record, used to guide teachers in Britain through the ongoing evaluative process for the National Curriculum:

'. . . being read to by teachers, and other experienced readers in and out of school, discussing texts, being invited to read familiar phrases – a child develops an understanding that it is the print that carries the message: s/he becomes more aware of the significant features of print itself. Over time and with experience – the experience of reading familiar texts – the child's confidence and competence grow.' (p. 25)

The child is soon 'taking risks with print by making informed guesses based on semantic, syntactic and grapho-phonic information and using a number of strategies . . .' (p. 25) [Translation: children can teach themselves to read.]

Next, the authors move on to the topic of evaluating writing and spelling: '. . . it will be normal for children to "write" texts which look like strings of letters, or in which words are represented by their initial letters, or (later) where words are written as clusters of consonants with the vowels omitted. Early invented spellings are often logical and self-consistent, and it is valuable if children can learn to have a go at spelling words themselves instead of continually asking teachers for words. Early spellings will develop over time given the right experiences, information and support.' (pp. 30–31)

'[Children's] invented spellings will often be logical and self-consistent, good guesses even if they are not absolutely correct. Their invented spellings are likely to approximate more and more closely to standard spellings over time.' (p. 34)

'English . . . is not a phonetically regular language – the sounds of the words do not offer a reliable guide to their spelling. This means that writers must rely on visual memory rather than on the sounds of words to help with spelling.' (p. 33) [It is unclear what is meant by a 'phonetically regular language', given that all languages are as 'phonetically regular' as anatomy will allow.]

The teacher is told to urge the child to 'use visual strategies more consistently, and to focus on the shapes and structures of words and on letter sequences'. And further, that 'It will be a matter of concern if children continue to rely mainly on the sound of words as a guide to their spelling much beyond the middle infants, and they should *not be allowed to sound words out as this is likely to mislead them.*' (p. 34, italics mine) [Translation: children can teach themselves to spell. Sounding out words (phonics) is a hindrance to learning to spell.]

57

In this new revolution, teachers are nothing more than enlightened facilitators. They don't need any skill, and no tips about skills or techniques (not even the words 'segmenting', 'blending', or 'phonics') appear anywhere in this sixty-three-page document. Nobody has to know how to teach reading and spelling because the children already know how! They can work it out 'naturally' and only need a little moral support. One wonders what we need teachers for.

In the final analysis, none of the 'real books' principles are supported by any evidence, not by the historical record, not by structural linguistics – which made it possible to decipher writing systems and understand how they work – and not by any scientific research on how children actually learn to read which will be presented later in this book. Furthermore, the attack on phonics is misguided. There are problems with phonics as we saw in Chapter 2, but phonics programmes are not 'wrong' for the reasons 'real books' advocates claim, that direct instruction about letters and sounds is *bad for you*. Nor is there any evidence that children should be taught each 'stage' in the evolution of writing as if this was a natural developmental progression. This would mean teaching children to mimic every mistake that was ever made, mistakes which took hundreds or even thousands of years to undo.

In the next chapter, we will look at the alphabetic writing system, and how an alphabetic writing system determines the way it should be taught.

CHAPTER 4

Alphabets: Splitting Sounds

The idea that stages of reading development in children are 'natural' and mirror the evolution of writing is based, in part, on the theories of Ignace Gelb, who wrote influential books on early writing systems. Gelb created a myth which still lingers in academic books and encyclopaedias. It goes like this: 'All writing systems develop in a fixed order: pictograms, logographs, syllabaries, alphabets. The alphabet is the highest and final stage of this evolution.' One implication of this myth is that Chinese and Japanese writing are archaic (logographic) forms, historical dinosaurs, kept alive by people who stubbornly cling to tradition.

Almost nothing in this myth is true. People used pictograms for accounting and not for a writing system. Pictograms and logographs could not and *never did* suffice for a writing system. Only two major cultures ever used a syllabary: the Sumerians and the Chinese, and this was entirely because the syllable structure of these languages is so uncomplicated.

All other cultures used different sound-based units. The choice of this unit is not governed by an evolutionary progression but by a simple principle: *use the largest possible phonological unit* (easiest to hear) *which is most economic* (fewest symbols).

In other words, it is the phonological or syllable structure of the language which determines how all writing systems are designed. And in every case, when an alphabet could be avoided, it was. This means that *nobody used an alphabet unless they absolutely had to*.

The purpose of this chapter is to show you why we have an alphabet, and to prove the point that the structure of the language directly determines how it can and cannot be written, and therefore how it must be taught.

If you ask most people what an alphabet is, they will probably tell you that it is a series of letters that stand for sounds in speech, and that the English language is written in an alphabet script with twenty-six letters. Apart from this most people don't know exactly *which* sounds the letters stand for, nor how many sounds are in our language. There are other things that people vaguely know which are mostly incorrect, like 'an alphabet is the simplest writing system to learn', or 'everyone today has an alphabet, except the Chinese and Japanese'.

Our alphabet is a direct descendant of the Phoenician 'alphabet'. Until recently, there was another myth that the Phoenician 'alphabet' was the 'Great Mother Alphabet'. New discoveries have revealed that it was simply one of a long line of 'alphabet' experiments in the Middle East. The earliest found so far was in a turquoise mine in the Sinai Desert. It was inscribed on a stone sphinx in about 1700 BC. Many other 'alphabets' followed this one. The Phoenician 'alphabet' originated much later, around 1050 BC, at Byblos. It became popular not because there was anything revolutionary about it, but because the Phoenicians were great traders and Byblos was an important port. Plus everybody liked the symbols. They were easy to write and easy to read. The Jewish people borrowed the Phoenician letters for the Old Hebrew writing system and so did the Greeks. The name 'alphabet' comes from the Greek, as you can see from the letter-names that begin the old Greek alphabet: *alpha, beta, gamma, delta, epsilon*. Actually, they are nonsense names. They don't make any sense in Greek either. The Greeks borrowed the letters *and* the names from the Phoenicians. Each letter was named with a Phoenician word that started with the same sound. Here are the first six letters in the Phoenician writing system along with their Phoenician names and the sounds they represented:

Letter	Name	Sound
⊀	'alpu (ox)	– /'/ a glottal stop made by the soft palate and tongue
⊰	beth (house)	– /b/ as in 'boat'
⊤	gimel (camel)	– /g/ as in 'get'

◁	daleth (door)	– /d/ as in 'door'
ⅎ	he (not a word)	– /h/ as in 'hot'
⊏	zain (weapon)	– /z/ as in 'zip'

If we went through all twenty-two of the Phoenician letters, you would see that there are only consonants and no vowels in this 'alphabet'. That doesn't mean there were no vowels in the Phoenician language. What kind of alphabet is this? Is this an alphabet at all?

To answer these questions, we need to go back to Egypt briefly. By 2700 BC, the Egyptians had developed several sets of symbols for sounds in their language. One set was for each consonant and one vowel sound. The other symbols were for double and triple consonant sequences: CC, CCC. Remember, the picture of an owl stood for the consonant sound /m/, and the funny-looking symbol 𓅓 stood for *two* consonants, /m/ combined with /s/ (/ms/). The Egyptians used pictograms, logographs, determinatives *and* these consonant symbols

FIGURE 4.1   Theban Title for 'Book of the Dead'

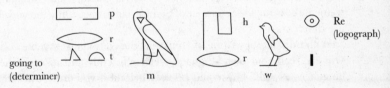

prt   m   hrw   Re
literal translation: going to the light of Re (Sun God)

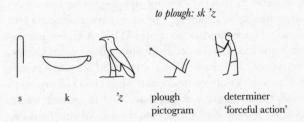

all at once, so there was absolutely no confusion about meaning.

The Akkadians to the north of Sumer borrowed the Sumerian writing system. They discovered that the Sumerian syllable symbols didn't fit their language. They adapted what they could and created many more symbols. At first they used three syllable types, like the Sumerians, but later they found that two types of syllables (CV, VC) fit most Akkadian words. This meant they could throw away the Sumerian logographs and determinatives, and they did precisely this around 2000 BC. At this time, about 90 per cent of the Akkadian writing system consisted of syllable symbols.

The next step was to combine these two solutions. It turned out that there was a simpler way to do it. Old Egyptian and Akkadian were languages of the Hamito-Semitic group, and Semitic languages have a unique property. The most important sounds in Semitic words are the consonants. They are so important that *you don't need to mark the vowels at all*. It seems the ancient Egyptians had already figured this out. Most words in Semitic languages have a fixed consonant frame, called a 'root'. This consonant frame, or skeleton, is C-C-C, or C-C. Vowels can change in and out, but the consonant sequence stays put. Table 4.1 shows an example using the Semitic verb 'to carry'. It is written *qbr*, but it isn't *read* 'qbr'. You can see that this consonant frame is the same for a number of Semitic languages. Only the vowels are different.

With this kind of writing, if you know the consonant–symbol code you can read your own language pretty efficiently and several other languages as well. This could be very helpful if you are a travelling salesman doing business around the Middle East, or a diplomat or emissary trying to negotiate peace settlements or trade agreements.

In the Phoenician writing system the reader has to *fill in the vowel sounds* as he is reading. These types of writing systems are known as 'consonantal alphabets', but they are not alphabets as we know them. They are something quite different. The twenty-two consonant symbols actually stand for a consonant + vowel (CV or VC) even though the vowel isn't marked. Consonantal alphabets are a kind of abbreviated syllable system. The reader's task is to figure out *which* missing vowel sounds to supply from context clues. This doesn't always work, and sometimes the meaning is ambiguous. Modern Semitic writing systems, such as Hebrew and Arabic, use special diacritic marks for

TABLE 4.1   **qbr** 'to carry' (imperative)

	Hebrew	**Syrian**	**Arabic**	**Ethiopian**
Singular				
Masc.	qebur	qebor	uqbur	qeber
Fem.	qibri	qebor	uqburi	qeberi
Plural				
Masc.	qibru	qebor	uqburu	qeberu
Fem.	qeborna	qebor	uqburna	qebera

missing vowel sounds. These are sloping lines and dashes written above or below the text. These marks are usually omitted in newspapers and books and only appear consistently in sacred texts and in children's primers and books.

Introducing Diphones

When babies begin to talk, they babble in CV units: ba-ba, ma-ma, ga-ga-ga. There are hundreds of languages that build on this basic speech pattern, and there are hundreds of writing systems in the world that use CV symbols exclusively. These systems are mistakenly called syllabaries or alphabets. There are so many CV writing systems in the world, I'm going to give them a special name, since nobody else has. I will call them '*diphone*' systems (diphone means 'two sounds' in Greek). By 'diphone' I am referring only to CV diphones and to no other combinations. In a diphone system, *one symbol* stands for two sounds: C + V. In English, the word 'baby' would be written with two symbols instead of four: ✢ ℰ (bay-bee). The word 'trap' would be written with three symbols instead of four: ⵊ ∧ ◁ (ta-ra-pa).

Here's how a diphone systems is set up. First, you discover all the consonant and vowel sounds in your language and assign a symbol to each of these sounds. We'll take an imaginary language as an example. Our imaginary language has the vowel sounds /a/, /e/, /i/, /o/, /u/ and five consonant sounds – /b/, /t/, /g/, /s/, /f/. (The slash marks indicate these are *sounds* and not letter-names.) To create a CV diphone writing system, you set up a matrix:

	a	**e**	**i**	**o**	**u**
b	ba↓	be	bi	bo	bu
t	ta⟩	te	ti	to	tu
g	ga₀⊢○	ge	gi	go	gu
s	sa⟨	se	si	so	su
f	fa⟩	fe	fi	fo	fu

We started out with 10 symbols (an alphabet) and we will have to create 25 new symbols, one for each of the diphone combinations. This doesn't seem very efficient, especially as most languages have about 40 consonant and vowel sounds altogether. If you multiplied the 25 consonants and 18 vowels in English to create an English diphone writing system, you would need 450 symbols instead of 43. So why would anybody do this? Is this just another historical milestone, a step along the thorny path to alphabets?

There are three very good reasons. The first reason is that 400 to 500 symbols are well within the human memory limit for abstract visual symbols. The second reason is that diphone systems are just as fast, or faster, to read as an alphabet. The more sounds a symbol represents, the fewer symbols you have to look at to get out the same information.

The third reason is the most important. CV diphones are much easier to *hear* than consonants or vowels alone. We have proof of this from modern scientific research. Computer scientists struggled for decades to generate speech by computer – the robot-like 'voice' you hear on some telephone answering systems. They found they had to use the acoustic signals across two adjacent sounds as the *smallest* speech fragment that could be recombined into words. They called this overlapping acoustic pattern a 'diphone'. Consonants split off from a vowel don't sound like speech at all, but more like chirps and wheezes.

We have proof of a different kind from the historical evidence showing how scholars developed CV diphone writing systems. We can show that an alphabet is not the final stage of the evolution of writing, or a 'perfect' solution for all languages, by an example of such evolution going *backwards*, from alphabets to something else. There are many such examples. In India, writing was invented at the same time as in Sumer and Egypt, but no one has ever been able to decipher this script. A completely new type of writing appeared around the fifth century BC. One script, the 'Brahmi script', became the prototype for over 200 writing systems used today throughout India and for most writing systems across Southeast Asia, in countries such as Thailand, Burma, Tibet, Mongolia, and Kashmir.

The Brahmin scholars set up a matrix of consonants and vowels, like the one I invented. Next, they created a separate diphone symbol for each C V pair. The main or primary diphone symbol always stood for a consonant plus the vowel sound /ah/, which was the most common vowel sound in the language. Next, the diphone symbol was modified systematically to mark each different vowel sound.

FIGURE 4.2   Brahmi Script, Fifth Century BC

Examples of diphone symbols for two consonants and nine vowels:

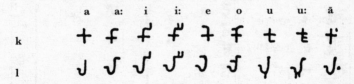

We have a more precise record of how one of these diphone systems is set up from the Buddhist priests who developed the famous Devanagari script for the Sanskrit language. They designed this script in the eleventh century AD. They had already invented symbols to stand for each of the thirteen vowels and thirty-five consonant sounds in the Sanskrit language. These were written in a fixed (alphabetical) order to teach novices to chant mantras and recite the sacred texts with the correct pronunciation. The priests had a complete understanding of the phonetic structure of the Sanskrit language, classifying each sound according to which parts of the mouth move to make it. You can see how clever this is in Figure 4.3.

Next, they set up a matrix and created new symbols for all the C V diphone combinations in the Sanskrit language. It's clear that this

FIGURE 4.3   The Devanagari Alphabet for Sanskrit

Vowels		Consonants			

*	+							
अ	− a	क	k	gutturals	प	p	labials
आ	ा ā	ख	k-h		फ	p-h	
		ग	g		ब	b	
इ	ि i	घ	g-h		भ	b-h	
ई	ी ī	ङ	ṅ		म	m	
उ	ु u	च	c	palatals	य	y	semivowels
ऊ	ू ū	छ	c-h		र	r	
ऋ	ृ ṛ (or ṛi)	ज	j		ल	l	
ॠ	ॄ ṝ (or ṛī)	झ or झ	j-h		व	v	
ऌ	ॢ ḷ (or ḷi)	ञ	ñ				
ए	े e	ट	ṭ	cerebrals	श	ś (or ç)	spirants
ऐ	ै ai	ठ	ṭ-h		ष	ṣ	
ओ	ो o	ड	ḍ		स	s	
औ	ौ au	ढ	ḍ-h		ह	h	
		ण	ṇ				
		त	t	dentals	: ḥ (visarga)		
		थ	t-h				
		द	d		·ṃ or ·ṁ (anusvāra)		
		ध	d-h				
		न	n				

* initial form of letters   + medial form of letters

system was not designed by accident, or because the priests weren't clever enough to figure out that an alphabet was the most perfect writing system. It was done this way on purpose, with the utmost skill. The Brahmi writing system of the fifth century BC and the 200 writing systems related to it today, go *backwards* down the so-called 'evolutionary path'.

Why didn't the Brahmin and Buddhist priests stick with the straight-forward alphabet they had designed? There can be only one possible reason. They knew it was *hard for people to hear consonant sounds separated from vowels*. This is clear from their understanding of the structure of their language, and from the way they linked the symbols to mimic the natural flow of human speech, where words are connected in phrases. A long bar was drawn across the top of several words to show that they were strung together, like Howard and Mabel's conversation ('Wojjadootuday?'); the bar broke where people would naturally pause or breathe (Figure 4.4). The priests knew how difficult it was to pick out isolated consonants and vowels from a stream of speech sounds. They knew that if something was hard for them, it would be hard for everyone else. And if something is too hard, many people can't use it.

This evolutionary reversal wasn't unique to India. It happened in Korea as well. In 1446, King Sejong issued a writing reform 'out of pity for the people'. Up to that time, the Koreans had been using Chinese syllable and classifier symbols as logographs for Korean words. They had the same problem memorizing logographs that everyone else did. In the writing reform, Korean scholars analysed the individual sounds in the Korean language, wrote out a set of symbols for them into an alphabet, set this up in a matrix, and turned the alphabet into a CV diphone system of 140 symbols, called Han'gul. Figure 4.5 shows what this looks like today. It is beautifully systematic. The vowel symbols and consonant symbols are fused to form unique pairs.

Once you know they are there, diphone systems pop up all over the place. They were the ancient writing systems for mainland Greece, Crete, and Cyprus. They are the modern writing systems in Ethiopia and for the Cherokee Nation. The diphone is the basis of the katakana and hiragana scripts used in Japan, introduced from India through Buddhist writings. Each of the two diphone scripts is written with a different set of about 75 symbols. The diphone turns out to be a

FIGURE 4.4 Sanskrit Text in Devanagari Script

व्यवहारान्नृपः पश्येदिद्धद्विद्विर्ब्राह्मणैः सह ।

धर्मशास्त्रानुसारेण क्रोधलोभविवर्जितः ॥ १ ॥

FIGURE 4.5 The basic combinations of vowels and consonants in the Korean diphone system

Consonants		Vowels ㅏ	ㅑ	ㅓ	ㅕ	ㅗ	ㅛ	ㅜ	ㅠ	ㅡ	ㅣ
		a	ya	ŏ	yeo	o	yo	u	yu	eu	i
ㄱ	g(k)	가	갸	거	겨	고	교	구	규	그	기
ㄴ	n	나	냐	너	녀	노	뇨	누	뉴	느	니
ㄷ	d	다	댜	더	뎌	도	됴	두	듀	드	디
ㄹ	r(l)	라	랴	러	려	로	료	루	류	르	리
ㅁ	m	마	먀	머	며	모	묘	무	뮤	므	미
ㅂ	b	바	뱌	버	벼	보	뵤	부	뷰	브	비
ㅅ	s	사	샤	서	셔	소	쇼	수	슈	스	시
ㅇ	※	아	야	어	여	오	요	우	유	으	이
ㅈ	j	자	쟈	저	져	조	죠	주	쥬	즈	지
ㅊ	ch	차	챠	처	쳐	초	쵸	추	츄	츠	치
ㅋ	k	카	캬	커	켜	코	쿄	쿠	큐	크	키
ㅌ	t	타	탸	터	텨	토	툐	투	튜	트	티
ㅍ	p	파	퍄	퍼	펴	포	표	푸	퓨	프	피
ㅎ	h	하	햐	허	혀	호	효	후	휴	흐	히

perfect fit for the Japanese language, as most words are built out of CV-CV-CV sequences, like 'ka-ta-ka-na'.

In addition to the katakana and hiragana scripts, the Japanese still use the ancient Chinese symbols as logographs for Chinese loan-words and Japanese words (kanji), though many also contain phonological cues. The Ministry of Education has set a minimum target of 1,850 kanji for 'an educated person'. This puts the upper boundary of abstract visual symbols (including hiragana, katakana and Roman letters) over 2,000, the highest number for any written language today. Japanese children learn hiragana first, followed by kanji logographs, then katakana and alphabet symbols for foreign words, making Japanese writing the hardest system in the world to learn. It isn't surprising that many children fail. As we saw earlier, Harold Stevenson's research shows that 56 per cent of Japanese schoolchildren failed to meet the 75 per cent pass criterion for ten-year-olds' reading, compared to 46 per cent of American children and 31 per cent of Taiwanese children. Shin-ying Lee's research on six-year-olds showed that Sendai children were considerably less likely to have advanced reading skills than children in Taipei and the US. Takeshi Hatta and Takehiko Hirase tested 871 eleven-year-olds in Japan on a standardized reading test. They found that 30 per cent were one or more years below age norms. The Japanese could solve this problem by standardizing on *one* of their two diphone systems and by eliminating kanji. This would give them one of the easiest writing systems to learn. So far, there has been no attempt to do this.

Diphone writing systems, or abbreviated diphone systems like consonantal alphabets, dominate in India and across Southeast Asia and Korea. They form the core of the writing system in Japan. They are found everywhere in the Middle East. If so many people can get along without an alphabet, *and* their scripts are equally fast to read and write, *and* use a unit of speech that is much easier to hear, then why do we have an alphabet?

True Alphabets Split Sounds

The answer is actually quite simple. It started with the Greeks in the eighth century BC, when they borrowed those Phoenician symbols. The Greeks already had a writing system. Modern scholars deciphered it about forty years ago and we know it as 'Linear B'. Linear B is a diphone system, which also includes five vowel letters used only at the beginnings of words. Archaeology has revealed no evidence that Linear B was ever used for anything more sophisticated than invoices, ledgers and inventory control. The Greek language cannot be written accurately in a diphone writing system because Greek has too many consonant clusters. Unlike Semitic languages, the vowel sounds in Greek carry as much of the meaning load as consonants do, so it is impossible to represent it with a consonantal alphabet either.

Let me show you why neither a consonantal alphabet or a diphone system could work for the Greek language or for any other European language. The first example is a letter written in a consonantal alphabet, not too different from the Phoenician script the Greeks decided to borrow:

Dr Sm,
    Wl — gs ths s gdb. Ftr r ft lst nt — n t wnt wrk. — m mvng w t tr t frgt. — dnt nd t b rmndd f ths pls nd l th sd mmrs.
Pls s gdb t Ls fr m. — wl ms hr.
Sdl,
    Ls
[The letter reads: 'Dear Sam, Well, I guess this is goodbye. After our fight last night, I know it won't work. I am moving away to try to forget. I don't need to be reminded of this place and all the sad memories. Please say goodbye to Alice for me. I will miss her. Sadly, Eloise.' The blanks are at the places where one whole word is a single vowel sound.]

I think you can see the important work that vowels do in the English language, as they did in the old Greek language.

Here's another letter written with a slightly more complex vocabulary. This is transcribed as it would sound if it was read out loud, from a CV diphone system like Linear B. Linear B had five vowel symbols used in the initial position in a word, plus a symbol for every possible CV combination. When it is read out loud it sounds CV-CV-CV-CV-CV, whether this speech pattern fits the word or not. In this example all the unnecessary vowel sounds are written with the letter a̠.

Deara Fareda,

    I canata parovida u witha caleera paroofa ova the sapeeseesa ova theeza sataraynja palanatas. Ifa I ama correcata ina my asasumapashunasa, they ara a raira bareeda ova dawarafa karysanathimuma – wuna thata Iva never comma acarossa befor.

    Satumapata,

    Joraja

    [Dear Fred, I can't provide you with clear proof of the species of these strange plants. If I am correct in my assumptions, they are a rare breed of dwarf chrysanthemum – one that I've never come across before. Stumped, George.]

Neither of these writing systems work for European languages, although from the last example, diphones might do a fair job with Italian!

The Greeks used the Phoenician letters to create the first 'true' alphabet. A true alphabet is a writing system in which *each* consonant and *each* vowel is represented by a symbol. These individual sounds (consonants and vowels) are the smallest or finest sounds in speech that people can hear. They are known collectively as 'phonemes', which simply means 'units of sound'. Hence, a *true* alphabet is a 'phonetic' alphabet.

To set up their alphabet, the Greeks began by using the Phoenician letters that stood for the same consonants in the Greek language. They used left-over letters for vowels and invented some new vowel letters. The Greek alphabet was tailor-made for the Greek language, a perfect fit, one symbol for each phoneme or sound. The alphabet was revised as the Greek language changed over time. It was borrowed by the Etruscans, and then by the Romans, who brought it to Britain at the time of the Roman invasion. The Anglo-Saxons borrowed it for an English alphabet (see Chapter 5). The alphabet changed over time as it was modified to fit one language and then another.

This history explodes the myth that an alphabet is the ultimate writing system, and shows instead that *the alphabet is the most unnatural writing system ever designed*. Alphabetic writing is unnatural because it splits sounds in speech in a way they don't normally split. Consonant clusters hang together. Consonants are very hard to unglue from vowels. Many consonants in English are hard to *say* separately from a vowel sound, even when they are isolated from words. Try saying

FIGURE 4.6

1050 BC Phoenician		8th cent. BC Old Greek		8th cent. BC Etruscan		5th–4th cent. BC Classical Greek		Old Latin	
�461	,	A	a	A	a	A	a	A	a
9	b	�.B9	b	B	b	B	b	B	b
⁊	g	⁊	c	⟩	c	Γ	g	⟨	c
◁	d	△	d	△	d	△	d	D	d
∃	h	∃	e	∃	e	E	e	E	e
—	—	∃⁊	f	⁊	f	—	—	F	f
I	z	I	g	—	—	—	—	⁊	g
⊞	h	⊞	h	⊞	h	⊞	ẽ	H	h
⊗	th	⊕	th	—	—	Θ	th	—	—
⊌	y	⟨	i	I	i	⊖	i	I	i
↗	k	⤨	k	⤨	k	K	k	K	k
㇄	l	⥮	l	⥮	l	∧	l	L	l
⅏	m	⅏	m	⅏	m	M	m	M	m
⅄	n	⋎	n	⋎	n	N	n	N	n
⧧	s	⧧	ks	—	—	⹀	ks	—	—
O	,	O	o	O	o	O	o	O	o
⊃	p	⟅	p	⟅	p	Π	p	⌐	p
℣	ṣ	—	—	—	—	—	—	—	—
Φ	q	Φ	q	Q	q	—	—	Q	q
⁊	r	⁊	r	⁊	r	P	r	R	r
W	š	⟩⟨	s	⟨	s	Σ	s	⟨	s
⊤	t	T	t	T	t	T	t	T	t
Ψ	w	Ψ	y	V	u	Y	u,ü	V	u
—	—	X	x	—	—	X	chi	X	x
—	—	—	—	—	—	Φ	phi	—	—
—	—	—	—	—	—	Ψ	psi	—	—
—	—	—	—	—	—	Ω	omega	—	—

/b/ all by itself without saying 'buh'. This is exactly what you must be able to do to use an alphabet efficiently. This is why Sally's mother wasn't helping her all that much when she taught her 'the sounds of letters' incorrectly (buh, duh, guh). It is even more difficult to split sounds apart when they are embedded in a word, or when words are strung together in speech. This is what the Brahmin and Buddhist priests understood so well. See if you can hear every sound in these one-syllable words: 'strong', 'scratch', 'shrink', 'dwells', 'crunch'. Each word has five sounds. (The number of sounds doesn't match the number of letters.)

In case you don't believe that many people find it hard to hear phonemes in words, here's an example of what we see regularly in the clinic. This is an early session with eight-year-old Jake:

'Jake, can you say the first sound in "frog"?'
Jake: 'Frog.'
'You said the whole word. Try to say just a little bit of the word "frog".'
Jake: 'Frog.'
'Now try this. Start to say the word "frog" and stop before you finish.'
Jake: 'Frog.'
'Say /g/.'
Jake: '/G/.'
'OK, now say "frog" again but *don't* say /g/.'
Jake: 'Fro.'
'Very good. Now try to make it even shorter.'
Jake: 'Fro.'
'Say "fro" for me.'
Jake: 'Fro.'
'Good, now say it again without the /ah/ sound at the end.'
Jake: 'Fr.'
'Terrific. Now listen to me carefully. What is the very first sound in "ffrr"?'
Jake: 'Fr.'
'You said two sounds: /f/ and /r/. Try saying the first sound in "ffffrr".'
Jake: 'Fr.'
'That's still two sounds.'

Jake is having a very tough time, but he is by no means unique.

One of the main points of this chapter is to show *why* the English language had to be written in an alphabet and in no other way. Think about what this means. Any teaching method which tampers with the alphabet principle, trying to turn our writing system into something else, like a logographic system (look-and-say, 'real books'), a diphone, syllable or part-word system (phonics 'word-families'/onset-rime analogies), will inevitably cause many children to fail to learn to read. It is difficult to hear sequences of isolated phonemes, and this problem is compounded when children are taught to make the wrong choices about how words are broken into sounds. This is even more critical with the English alphabet, because in our spelling system, two or more letters can stand for one sound. Here's what the eyes have to look at to be able to read 'strawberry ice cream':

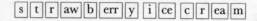

Despite the fact that alphabets make extreme demands on auditory analysis (ungluing sounds in words), they turn out to have an unexpected bonus. All languages have a small, finite number of phonemes, usually around forty. If alphabets are taught properly, they are very efficient, especially when they are well designed so that only one symbol stands for only one sound. Unfortunately, only Spanish and Finnish come close to this ideal.

Alphabets are 'transparent' writing systems in the sense that they directly represent speech, and are only as ambiguous as spoken language itself. Ambiguity has been a consistent problem throughout the history of writing. Consonantal alphabets need diacritic marks to indicate vowels. Indian languages also have consonant clusters. The Brahmin priests added little loops to the symbols ('ligatures' or 'connectors') to show where vowels should be dropped between two consonants. This makes the writing visually confusing. Everybody who still uses a CV diphone system, like that of the ancient Mayans, Cretans, and Cypriots, has to remember to drop vowel sounds between consonant clusters or when a word ends in a consonant. The Japanese say 'kanji' when they see the written symbols for: ka-na-ji. The Mayans said 'balam' (jaguar) when they read the diphones for ba-la-ma.

The English alphabet shares all the good features of other alphabets, but has one enormous drawback. *It lacks a one-to-one correspondence between each sound in the language and the symbol that represents it.* This means that learning to read the English alphabet system can be a trap if taught badly or not at all. If there was a simple answer to teaching children to read an English alphabet, we would have found it before now, especially since schools have been common since the sixteenth century.

Let's pause for a minute and take stock. There are many important lessons from this historical account. Writing systems based on the whole word don't work: languages have too many words. Because people are limited in their ability to memorize abstract symbols, speech sounds are the basic unit for all writing systems. This means that *no child should ever be taught to memorize or guess whole words by sight*. This will never work, and we now have 5,500 years of evidence to prove it.

All writing systems are designed to fit the syllable structure, or sound-based structure, of the language for which they are written. When the language has an open, simple syllable structure, like Sumerian or Chinese, you can use syllable symbols (a syllabary). When it has mainly a repetitive C-C-C or CVCVCV sound structure like Semitic languages, Indic languages, or Japanese and Korean, then a consonantal alphabet or diphone writing system will work. When the language has a complex syllable structure, riddled with consonant clusters, it must be written with an alphabet. There is no other way.

Individual phonemes embedded in words are hard to hear and disconnect, which is why so many cultures abandoned the alphabet solution. It's hard to detach consonants from vowels and consonants from each other. Many children can't *hear* the units of sound the letters of the code stand for, and if nobody teaches them these sounds, they won't have a clue what the code is about. This means that many children can't learn the code. It's just that simple. The 'real books' claim that all children will automatically be sensitive to phonological units of speech simply because they can talk, is an erroneous and dangerous assumption. We now have an avalanche of data to show this isn't true.

A final lesson relates to the logic of writing systems. Writing systems are designed to transcribe *talk*. Speech sounds are the basis for the code. It is the sounds in speech that are 'real', consistent, and stable. The letters *are the code*: unreal, arbitrary, and, in English spelling, unstable. Of course, *all codes are reversible*; you can put something into a code (encoding) and translate it back out again (decoding), otherwise it wouldn't be a code. The alphabet code is no exception. But teachers must understand what the code was designed to do. They must know the *direction* in which the code was written.

If you teach a child that abstract squiggles on the page (letters) are 'real', and that these squiggles 'have' arbitrary noises (sounds), she won't understand what you're talking about. By contrast, if you tell her that letters on the page stand for specific sounds in *her own speech*, the process of matching letters to sounds will make sense.

Does Phonics Teach the Alphabet Principle?

This brings us to phonics. In Chapter 1, we saw how children can develop reading difficulties in classrooms where teachers are supposedly trying to teach the alphabet code using phonics. The word 'phonics' simply means 'sounds' in Greek, and is used by educators as a generic term for any reading method which teaches sounds rather than whole words. (The overuse of the word 'phonics' and the confusion this creates will be discussed in the following chapter.)

Authors and publishers have churned out scores of phonics programmes over the past 100 years, with different charts, different worksheets, different readers, different vocabularies, and a different number of phonics rules. Some have attempted to classify these programmes. Jeanne Chall made a valiant effort in her book, *Learning to Read: The Great Debate*. They have been given names like 'analytic', 'synthetic', 'intensive', 'structured', or 'linguistic'. This makes them seem as if they are different, and though some are much more comprehensive than others, in principle they are pretty much alike.

To begin with, all phonics programmes teach 'the names and sounds of letters'. This is even in the dictionary definition of phonics, and this definition fits every phonics programme I have seen. This means that *all phonics programmes teach the alphabet principle backwards* as I described above. Phonics teaches that 'letters have sounds', rather than that 'speech has sounds' and these speech sounds 'have letters'. Even when they know better, and confess that really, strictly speaking, 'letters don't *have* sounds' (if you put your ear to the page, you hear nothing), teachers like Mrs Earnest believe it's easier to teach children that they do. It's easier to do it this way because letters seem 'real'. After all, they are there on the page, visible, concrete and permanent. Sounds are invisible, fleeting and ephemeral. We'll see how much havoc this can create when we analyse how the sounds in the English language map on to the English spelling system.

Most phonics programmes *don't teach the sounds in English for which the code was written*. They teach the 'sounds of letters'. But there are twenty-six letters and forty-three sounds. How is this supposed to work? No child is ever told what the alphabet code really is. This is because the teachers don't know what it really is. No one ever taught them. You can prove this yourself by asking any primary school teacher how many sounds there are in the English language. Most will tell you 'twenty-six', or that they have no idea.

Here's another thing most phonics programmes have in common. They set up a schizophrenic writing system in which they mix up the number of sounds in speech that letters stand for. This makes it impossible for the child to figure out the unit of speech for which our alphabetic code was written. And it is doubly impossible to learn the code for those children who can't *hear* the sound units to start with, like Jake in the example.

We saw in Chapter 2 that children in phonics classrooms were struggling with this problem. They were taught letters that stand for units of one phoneme: <u>b</u>, <u>t</u>, <u>ch</u>, letters that stand for two phonemes, like the clusters: <u>bl</u>, <u>dw</u>, <u>shr</u>, letters that stand for three phonemes (word-families): <u>enth</u>, <u>ond</u>, <u>unch</u>, as if all of these letter-patterns stood for *only one sound*. This is why Andrew decoded 'hated' as 'hat-ate-ted', which he thought was three sounds, instead of /h/, /ae/, /t/, /e/, /d/ (five sounds). If you don't understand what you're teaching, you will mislead your students and risk causing them to fail.

We will be examining these and other problems with phonics programmes in the following chapter when we look in depth at the sounds in the English language and how these sounds are transcribed or 'mapped' to letter symbols.

CHAPTER 5

The English Alphabet Code

As a child, I remember waiting with bated breath for the closing moments of my favourite serial, when the announcer read a series of numbers that you had to 'decode'. Only then could you find out whether the hero or heroine burned to a crisp or was rescued in the nick of time. (I always knew they would be rescued but I wanted proof now.) These messages could be decoded with a special device that had to be purchased with wrappers from Ovaltine jars. This kind of code is a *translation* from one symbol system into another. My decoding device translated numbers into letters that spelled words, a 'code of a code': 1=p, 2=a, 3=f, 4=s, 5=i, etc.

Writing systems are also codes of codes. Language itself is a code. Languages are based on an agreement between language users that things, persons, places, actions, intentions, and feelings can be represented by combinations of vocal noises. The noises are utterly arbitrary and have no meaning in and of themselves. Because of the way the vocal apparatus works, there is considerable freedom of choice about the available noises, though not absolute freedom. Our mouth parts and vocal cords can move in just so many ways, and most languages share a number of speech noises in common.

All languages are composed of two main kinds of sound: vowels and consonants. Vowels are 'voiced', causing the vocal folds or cords to vibrate, and vowels pass freely, unconstrained by touching mouth parts. Vowels add volume to speech. When Stephen's Mum calls him for dinner, the vowel carries her voice: 'Steeeeeeeephen.' A language can't be constructed of vowels alone: eeeeeeaaaaaaaouououououououoooooooo. Consonants add features to a barren landscape of vowels, separating one group of noises from another into little packets of syllables, words and phrases. Consonants are made by touching various mouth parts together. Some consonants are 'voiced' and the vocal cords vibrate. Some are not. Put your fingers on your neck, near your vocal cords, and feel the vibration at the beginning of the word 'dot', but not at the beginning of the word 'tot'. The sounds /d/ and /t/ are produced by the same mouth movements, tongue tapping behind the front teeth, but only the /d/ is voiced, so they sound quite different.

Until this moment, you probably never knew this. We speak fluently and effortlessly without any conscious awareness of how we do it. This happens because we learn the sounds of our native language when we are too young to be conscious observers of what we do or think. When we learn a second language later in life, it takes months to pronounce the sounds only tolerably well, and even with years of intense conscious effort, most of us will never sound like native speakers.

Perhaps you can imagine how difficult it was for people to design an alphabetic writing system. No one is aware of these speech sounds in the first place, and once you become aware of them, it's still hard to calculate how many different sounds are in your language, especially before you have a way to write them down. Imagine too, how difficult it is for children, who are just as unconscious of how they speak as you are, to analyse the sounds of their own speech and decide which sound goes with which letter or letter combinations.

Most major languages of the world have a similar number of individual sounds, or phonemes. (The range for all languages is eight to eighty.) English is pretty much on target with other languages, having approximately forty-three. I say 'approximately' because there are endless disputes over this number. There are twenty-five consonants and eighteen vowel sounds in English, similar to Chinese, or Semitic, or Indian languages. Yet we saw in the last two chapters that these languages don't need to be written in an alphabet because of the way that consonants and vowels are combined into syllables and words. English must be written with an alphabet because our language is awash with consonant clusters due to its Germanic roots. There are twenty-eight adjacent consonants or clusters that come at the beginning of syllables (*bl*, *dw*, *str*), and forty-eight clusters that come at the end (*nd*, *lk*, *nch*, *mpt*), and only *three* of these clusters occur in both positions.

They are /sk/ /sp/ and /st/ as in the words: skunk, spoon, stamp, and ask, wasp, and past.

We have already seen why English can't be written with a consonantal alphabet (the vowels are too important) or a diphone system (too many consonant clusters). Nor can it be written as a syllabary, like Sumerian or Chinese, and here's why. In English, consonants and vowels can combine in fifteen different syllable patterns: CV, CCV, CCCV, CVC, CCVC, CCCVC, CVCC, CVCCC, CCVCC, CCVCCC, CCCVCCC, VCCC, VCC, VC, V.

The way that the twenty-five consonants and eighteen vowels can combine in these syllables means that there are more than 55,000 'phonetically legitimate' English syllables – more syllables than words in common use. And this is the tip of the iceberg. Most English words are two or more syllables long. 'Phonetically legitimate' simply means that a word or syllable has consonant-vowel patterns that are recognizable as English. A writing system must be able to represent every legitimate syllable pattern in the language, though not all of them are used at the time. You could read the word 'Grinch' in Chapter 2 and recognize it as 'English', because it obeys the syllable structure of English. If we couldn't use the writing system this way, we wouldn't be able to write new words or people's names. One beauty of an alphabet system is that it is as flexibly expandable as language itself. Without this flexibility, we wouldn't have words like 'bonk', 'thwack', 'nerd', 'twit', 'doodle', or 'scrumptious'. Dr Seuss and Lewis Carroll couldn't have written their books. There would be no Grinch, no Yertle, no Loraxes, grickle grass or truffula trees, and no 'gyre and gimble in the wabe'.

Other new English words can be created by compounding existing words (household, desktop, firefighter, doughnut, football) and by compounding with prefixes and suffixes, a trick which exploded when we borrowed thousands of Latin words. We can draft and ratify a statute, create an institute, or institutionalize Aunt Dorothy, or complain about the institutionalizing of the Arts, or deinstitutionalize a bureaucracy, a process known as deinstitutionalization. (Note that 'instatute' ought to be the correct spelling.)

It is hard to pick individual sounds out of these complex words. Simple arithmetic will show why children can have trouble learning an alphabet right from the start. We have seen that consonants are hard to unglue from vowels. There are 22 consonants that begin words, and each can be followed by 18 vowels. This makes 396 CV sound combinations that are hard to unglue. Consonant clusters are even harder to unglue, both from each other and from the following vowel sound. Each of the 28 consonant clusters that come at the beginning of words can be followed by 18 vowels. This adds another 28 + 486 ungluable combinations, a total of 910 so far, and we're only talking about the beginning of words.

It is because of these problems that children must be taught the individual phonemes in English, and how to unglue these phonemes from each other, as we saw in the example with Jake. Next, they need to learn how each phoneme is transcribed or 'mapped' to letter symbols. We can't teach reading and writing using a minimalist fraction of the code, taught backwards (phonics), because many children will never understand how the code works. Nor can we harbour the delusion that the length and complexity of words is irrelevant (look-and-say, 'real books') and expect children to become able, fluent readers and spellers, and sophisticated users of the language. Later on we will be looking in great detail about how to teach children to hear and be able to manipulate sounds in words. Here, I will be addressing the final problem of the English writing system, our formidable spelling code.

What Went Wrong With English Spelling?

In a perfect alphabetic writing system, each of the forty-three English sounds would have *one*, and only one, symbol. But the English alphabet has only twenty-six letters, four of which are wasted. Spelling reformers want them eradicated or put to better use. The letter c doubles for the sounds /k/ and /s/. The letters qu stand for the two sounds /k/ /w/ pronounced simultaneously. The letter x is used for the consonant cluster /ks/ when the word *isn't* plural: tax, box, fax (versus tacks, blocks, flicks), and for /ks/ or /gz/ in words like 'exit' and 'exact'. Y doubles for several different vowel sounds which already have letters: fly (flie), baby (babee), yes (ee-es). Some argue that as the sound /w/ is really a very short /oo/ sound, the letter w could be thrown out as well: 'winter' would be spelled 'oointer'. These ideas have not met with any success.

Too many sounds chasing too few letters creates a major roadblock for the young reader. Instead of designing new letters for these leftover sounds, like the Greeks did, the old letters were *reused* in different combinations. The Romans started this habit by using letter-pairs to stand for one sound. These are called *digraphs*. The missing consonants in English were spelled: <u>ch</u> (church), <u>qu</u> (quit), <u>sh</u> (shoot), <u>ng</u> (ring), and <u>th</u>. The voiced and unvoiced sounds /th/ and /th/ as in 'this' and 'think' share the same spelling. (Put your hand on your throat again to check this out.) One consonant sound never got its own spelling. This is the sound /zh/ we inherited from Norman French, which usually appears in the middle of words (Asia, azure, pleasure, measure, vision), and is spelled <u>si</u>, <u>z</u>, <u>s</u>, or <u>ge</u> (camouflage).

When something can be classified in two or more overlapping ways, this is known in logic as a 'class inclusion problem'. Later, I will talk about the difficulty children have with class inclusion logic. Digraphs create a class inclusion problem. For example, the letter <u>h</u> can stand for the sound /h/ when it's beside some letters (house, hear, ahead), but entirely *different* sounds when it's beside other letters: <u>ch</u>est /ch/, <u>th</u>em /th/, <u>sh</u>ine /sh/, <u>gh</u>ost /g/, <u>ph</u>one /f/, tou<u>gh</u> /f/. The spellings for ghost, phone, and tough show that the basic idea of using one consonant digraph to stand for one sound didn't hold up, and <u>h</u> was combined with other letters to stand for sounds that *already had letters*, like /g/ and /f/. This gives you the flavour of the problem, but by no means the substance. The situation is far, far worse with vowels. We will look at the entire structure of our spelling code at the end of this chapter. First, we need to find out what went wrong.

The English spelling system evolved over a period of 1,150 years until it ran up against the mighty pen and intellect of Samuel Johnson. Since that time, in the mid eighteenth century, there have only been minor skirmishes of the spelling reformers, which have never had any impact. Johnson was not a reformer. He knew he could do nothing to turn back the clock and start again. One of his main objectives was to stop the rot and keep our spelling system from running amok.

It wasn't always thus. The Venerable Bede, who wrote the first history of England, describes how King Oswald of Northumbria worked together with Bishop Aidan from Ireland to translate Irish into English. Bishop Aidan had come from the monastery at Iona to establish the Christian Church in Northumbria. He couldn't speak English, but Oswald could speak Gaelic – he had grown up at Iona. Together, in about AD 635, they developed a written code for English, borrowing the script that was used in Ireland to write Latin. They taught the boys and novices at the monasteries to read in English and then Latin by translating from Latin to English. Almost no examples of this writing have survived. The Danes attacked Northumbria in 793 and burned everything in sight.

The Danes marched relentlessly on through most of the next century, attacking by land, river and sea, finally ending up in the Kingdom of Wessex in the south-west. Here they were defeated by King Alfred in 878, after several years and many fierce battles in which Alfred lost his father and three brothers. Alfred was thirty years old when he secured peace. He not only saved England, but he saved the English language and the English writing system. If it hadn't been for Alfred, we might all be speaking Danish.

Alfred began a campaign to unify England, building fortresses (burghs), and restoring the spirit and pride of the people. As part of this enterprise, he had major Christian texts translated from Latin into English, a novel idea at the time. He recreated English writing by tracking down any monks or clerics he could find who knew it. Alfred was an intellectual and a Latin scholar and he personally translated many of these works.

Alfred was eager to educate his people to read and write in Saxon English, and he maintained two large scriptoria at Canterbury and Winchester. It isn't known what documents Alfred and his priests used to reconstruct English writing, but their translations survive today. They show that the English spelling system was nearly perfect, and it got a little more perfect over the next 100 years at the hands of Ælfric, the great Saxon scholar.

A perfect spelling system has no alternative spellings for the same sound like we have today: be, been, bean, believe, deceive, baby, donkey; and no overlap in the code where one spelling pattern (ou) stands for different sounds (out, soup, soul, tough). In Table 5.1, I have illustrated the spelling alternatives and code overlaps in the Old English spelling system. If the spelling system was perfect, this table would be a blank page. At the end of this chapter you can compare Table 5.1 to the tables I have prepared for modern English spelling.

TABLE 5.1   Deviations from a One-to-one Correspondence in the Old English Spelling Code

Sound	Spelling Alternatives Spellings		
/i/	ı	y	
/gh/ guttural	h	c	
/k/	c	k	
/s/	s	ʀ	ſ
/th/	ð	þ	

Letter	Code Overlap Sounds
ı	/i/ or /ee/
u	/u/ or /oo/
y	/i/ or /ü/
c	/k/ or /gh/
F	/f/ or /v/
ð	/g/ or /j/
p	/p/ or /w/

The detour back to Saxon England is of interest because many spellings today resemble spellings from 1,100 years ago. There isn't space to discuss them all, but you can see in Table 5.2 where some of our strangest spellings come from. In the Old English spelling system, all letters in the word were pronounced. There were no 'silent' letters. The Old English spellings are on the left, followed by their phonetic equivalent. Saxon was a Germanic language with two guttural sounds, spelled with an <u>h</u> and a <u>c</u>. In Middle English spelling, the <u>h</u> was changed to <u>gh</u>. Then the guttural sounds dropped out of the language, leaving their gutteral ghosts behind. The /l/ and /e/ sounds in 'sholde' and 'wolde' were pronounced, as was the /k/ sound in 'cnawan'.

Not long before Bishop Ælfric died in 1020, England was invaded by Canute of Denmark (later to become King of Denmark and Norway). Skirmishes between Denmark and England continued until

TABLE 5.2   Old English Spellings of Some Familiar Words

Written	Pronounced	Modern Spelling
ſcolde	sholde	should
polde	wolde	would
ælmihtiʒ	almighty*	almighty
brohte	broghte	brought
ſohte	soghte	sought
noht	noght	nought
meahte	meaghte	might
ðohte	thoghte	thought
ðurh	thurgh	through
hpile	hwile	while
hpær	hwar	where
hpelce	hwelch	which
hpæðer	hwather	whether
cnapan	cnawan	to know
cniht	cnight	knight
feapa	fe-ah-wa	few
andpyrde	andwyrde	answered

gh is pronounced as a guttural sound.

the Battle of Hastings in 1066, which brought William the Conqueror to the throne. From this point forward, England and the English language was never to be the same, and the English spelling system went haywire.

William, his barons, relatives, and acquaintances – whom he installed in every church and on every estate and farm – spoke Norman French, a patois of Danish, Romanz (Old French), and Latin. Everybody who was important spoke French, and the 'unimportant' peasants, artisans and merchants spoke English in the dialect of their region. The English aristocracy fled to Wales and the continent. All education and affairs of the Church, the Chancery, and the courts were conducted in Latin, the official language of state. English writing all but disappeared, kept alive by a few obscure monks who did their best to avoid any direct encounter with William or his cronies.

After about 200 years, English writing began to reappear, mainly in sermons and secular poetry. In this brief time, the English language had changed almost out of recognition. The case grammar of Old English, with special endings that marked gender, the subject of the sentence and the object of the action, had disappeared. The words for 'learn' (verb), 'learning' (noun) and 'learned' (adjective) originally had these forms: lar, lare, lareda, laera, laeren, leorn, leornian, lerne, lernan, lareo, lareowas, liornunga, geleara, geliornod, geliornodon, geliornode. By the end of the thirteenth century, all that remained of this grammar was a vestigial e left behind on the ends of words, the spellings familiar to us in 'Ye Olde English Tea Shoppe'. Thousands of French words had entered the language and strange French spellings (au, ai, ay, ou, oi, eu) were adopted for the new English vowel sounds.

Meanwhile, extraordinary events in the fourteenth century helped save the English language from oblivion. The Black Death struck in 1348, and again in 1361 and 1368–9. Modern estimates put the death rate at between 35 and 50 per cent of the population. Farmers and merchants were thrust to the forefront as the only people left in England who could run successful farms and businesses. The severe labour shortage led to skyrocketing wages. As these families began to acquire wealth, they started to buy up land around the villages deserted after the plague, and by the fifteenth century, farmers were the largest landowners in England. Farmers and merchants became the new aristocracy and they wanted their children educated in English.

Edward III, who was on the throne from 1327 to 1377, initiated the Hundred Years' War with France. It was an unpopular war, and it was hard to rally support, especially when the aristocracy spoke French. In the meantime, Parisian French had become the language of diplomacy, and Norman French was becoming something of an embarrassment. Pressure was felt at all levels of society to speak English. Parliament was opened in English in 1362. Chancery documents started appearing in English in 1380, and when Henry IV took the throne in 1399, he was the first king in more than 300 years to speak English. He spoke in the dialect of London, the state and commercial capital of England.

Here is how he might have sounded. These are the opening lines of *The Vision of Piers Plowman*, a fourteenth-century book-length poem in alliterative verse, written by William Langland in the London dialect:

In a somer sesonn, whan softe was the sonne
I shop me in to a shrowde as y a shep were,
In abite of an heremyte unholy of werkes,
Wente forth in the worlde wondris to here.
And saw many sellis and selcouth thynges
Ac on a May mornynge in Malverne Hullys
Me bifel for to slepe for weryness of walked
And in a lannde as y lay pened y and slepte
And meruailous lichte me metter as y may gow telle
At the welthe of the world and the woo bothe.[1]

[In a summer season, when soft was the sun, I changed me into a
shroud, as I a sheep were, in 'abit of a hermit, unholy of works, went
forth in the world, wonders to hear. And saw many good and various
things. Ah, on a May morning in Malvern Hills, me befell for to sleep for
wearyness of walking, and in a land as I lay, I was in pain, and slept.
And marvellous light met me, as I am going to tell you, at the wealth of
the world and the woe both.]

The words are nearly modern, but the spellings are strange. If you
look closely, you will see that the same sounds have more than one
spelling, the sound /ee/ is spelled be, bifel, slepe, shep, here, wery; the
sound /oe/ is spelled gow, woo, bothe, holy. The variety of spellings
for the *same* sound actually increased over time, despite all the efforts
to stop it.

The English Renaissance is dated from 1476, the year William
Caxton brought the first printing press to England. He opened a
bookshop in Westminster called the Red Pale. Cheap books, increasing
prosperity, and a renewed interest in the classics of Greece and Rome
changed the language once more and spelling along with it. Scholars
became fascinated by the origins of words, and began altering spellings
to reflect their Latin, French, or German origins, creating a discipline
called 'etymology'. Words about science, philosophy and medicine
were borrowed into the language from Greek and got special 'Greek'
spellings (etymology, metaphysics, philosophy, phonology). Authors of
books tended to favour the spellings which reflected their idiosyncratic
knowledge of word origins, or their special point of view, or simply
their personal preference.

Three main groups were struggling to standardize the spelling
system. These were the Chancery, who drafted documents of state;

printers, who needed a 'house style' for their publications; and school-masters who had to teach pupils how to write and spell. This isn't easy to do if there are three or four or five ways to spell the same word – 'Well, John, you can spell the word "great": gret, grete, great, greate, greet, grate. Just use whatever looks best on the page.'

Here's a letter written by Sir Walter Raleigh's wife, Elizabeth, to Sir Robert Cecil, announcing news of Raleigh's return from South America. Elizabeth was an educated woman, and had been a lady-in-waiting at Queen Elizabeth's court.

> Sur hit tes trew i thonke the leving God sur Walter is safly londed at Plumworthe [Plymouth] with as gret honnor as ever man can, but littel riches. i have not yet hard from him selfe. Kepe thies I besech you to your selfe yet; only to me lord ammerall [Admiral]. In haste this Sunday.
>   Your pour frind
>   E. Raleg[2]

Disagreements about spelling created two major factions. There were the spelling reformers, who wanted to scrap everything and design a perfect system, like King Alfred used to have. There were the pragmatic tinkerers, mainly schoolmasters, who said this was impossible, and wanted to tidy it up and agree on one spelling for each word. These groups fought each other in books, pamphlets, lectures, and in the trenches (the classroom). The printers sometimes paid attention, sometimes not, and went doggedly about trying to standardize their own in-house spelling systems, with marginal agreement between them.

In the meantime, dictionaries were called for as a possible solution. There were no dictionaries of the English language until late in the sixteenth century, and most were written for schoolboys. In a dictionary, each word can have only one entry. Dictionaries standardize spelling by default – that is, if everyone buys the same dictionary. The first dictionary of any merit was published anonymously in 1702 by someone who signed himself J.K. (probably John Kersey), but nobody paid much attention to it. After a succession of mediocre dictionaries appeared on the scene, friends of Samuel Johnson, along with a consortium of booksellers (the publishers of their day), urged him to write a dictionary. Johnson was highly regarded for his brilliant books and essays, and if anyone could make an impact, it would be him. He got an advance of approximately £31,500 in today's currency for a project lasting nine years.

Meanwhile, sounds in the language had started changing again, even faster than the spellings. Until Henry IV came to the throne in 1399, the aristocracy could demarcate themselves from the hoi polloi by speaking an entirely different language. Now they sounded just like everybody else, and this would never do. This is just speculation, but it answers a very puzzling question: Why did vowel sounds change so dramatically during the fifteenth and sixteenth centuries, a phenomenon called the 'Great Vowel Shift'? One plausible reason was a conscious effort on the part of the aristocracy to modify their pronunciation of English. They wanted to put as much distance as possible between the way they spoke and the 'cockney' English of London and other regional dialects. Later, the accent of the aristocracy became known as 'received pronunciation' (RP) or 'the King's English'.

This was Johnson's legacy in 1746: the 700 years' accumulation of changing sounds in the language, the conscious efforts to alter vowel sounds even more by the aristocracy, intellectuals, and social climbers, the practice of spelling any way you felt like it, the thousands of French, Latin and Greek words entering the language, the scholars who zealously created more and more special spellings to mark the etymological roots of these words, and the failure of any one person or group to influence *everyone* to agree on a standard spelling system. That Johnson succeeded is nothing short of a miracle.

Standardized Spelling

Johnson's *Dictionary of the English Language* was published in 1755 and was soon on the bookshelf or library table of everyone who considered themselves literate. It did just what everyone hoped it would do.

Johnson's major goal in writing his dictionary was actually more ambitious than standardizing spelling. He wanted to provide comprehensive and accurate definitions for words and establish a standard *pronunciation* for the English language. He complained about the 'non-standard' and 'incorrect' pronunciation of words and thought that fixed spellings would help, although he recognized that it would be impossible to fix pronunciation over time.

Linguists know that languages 'drift' over time and nothing can stop them doing this. Yet, since Johnson's dictionary appeared, English hasn't drifted very far. It was as if he tied the English language to a stout oak tree to which all dialects of English are connected by shorter or longer pieces of rope. Today, over 240 years later, most people of America, England, Scotland, Wales, Ireland, Australia, New Zealand, Canada, South Africa, and India have little difficulty understanding each other's English. Contrast this with the extraordinary changes in the language from 1066 to 1300.

Johnson compiled the words for his dictionary from the vocabularies of Hooker's Bible, Shakespeare, Spenser, and Francis Bacon, plus his own prodigious knowledge of the language. In addition to standardizing pronunciation through phonetic spellings, he also emphasized word derivation as a major source for spelling, and he provides etymological roots (in five languages) for many of the words. Other than this, and stating that he found it impossible to work from other people's dictionaries, he provides no further insights or guiding principles for why he spelled words in particular ways.

Throughout the dictionary, a few consistencies stand out, and these ideas were not original to Johnson. Words with the sound /j/, previously spelled i, were now standardized to j (iump > jump). The confusion between how to use the letters v and u was resolved (vnless > unless; heauen > heaven). The letter y was banished from the middle of words (wylle, kyng, hym, eyght), unless the word was Greek (myth, symbol). A long-standing plea to systematize those final es at the ends of words was heeded. The letter e was retained when it signalled a change in a vowel sound: 'mate'; but not 'seeme'. Johnson also left a final e on some ending consonants as a cue or diacritic to signal pronunciation: ce (fence not fenc), se (dense not dens), ge (barge not barg), the (bathe not bath), and/or when the spelling was originally French: le (table), ve (pensive). The ve combination creates problems in words like above, dove, give, have, love, live, shove (abov, dov, giv, hav, lov, liv, shov), where the e works with the v and not the vowel.

The use of the letter e as diacritic for five different vowel sounds (/ae/ tame, /ie/ time, /ee/ teem, /oe/ tone, /ue/ cute) became known as the 'e-control principle'. Its effect on spelling is far-reaching, and constitutes one of the few spelling patterns that has any consistency. Basically, the principles are these:

1. E signals the pronunciation of the preceding vowel letters: a, e,

i, o, u only, backwards across one consonant but not two: mut/mute/mutter; mate/mated/matted; mar/mare/marked.

2. To cancel e-control, you must double the consonant: bat/batter; tin/tinned.

3. Other vowel letters can substitute for e when adding a suffix: whine/whining; shine/shiny.

But like all spelling 'rules' for English, this doesn't hold up a hundred per cent of the time: fable, table, maple, paste, waste, haste, are but a few exceptions. If they followed the rule, two consonants in a row would cancel e-control, and the words would be read: fabble, tabble, mapple, past, wast, hast.

Johnson ensured that most homophones (words that sound alike with different meanings) got a different spelling. He managed to locate more than 600 of them. He systematized plural and past tense spellings so they were always consistent, regardless of how they sounded in the word. The plural is always spelled s or es, even when it usually sounds /z/: trees, chairs, tables, peaches. Past tense is mainly spelled ed, though the letter e may not be sounded, or the d sounds like /t/: pact/packed; past/passed; bold/bowled; board/bored; find/fined.

Perhaps Johnson's changes can be observed most clearly in comparison with the spellings of one of the most famous of all publications, the First Folio of Shakespeare's plays, published in 1623 by Jaggard and Blount. I have listed the non-modern spellings from Hamlet's soliloquy and compared them with the spellings in Johnson's dictionary. Only one of Johnson's spellings has since been changed to reflect its French origin: 'unkle' to 'uncle' (from *oncle*), and Johnson made a mistake with 'shooes'. He should have left it alone. Instead, he removed an o and left the e to reflect its old Saxon spelling, ſceo ('sheo'), which had a different pronunciation.

Johnson's knowledge of the individual sounds (phonemes) of the English language was incomplete, and he was inaccurate about some of the complex vowel sounds or diphthongs, which he occasionally confused with digraphs. He comments on 'mute' letters in spellings of words, specifically consonant spellings, but did nothing to get rid of them. His examples were debt, subtle, lamb, gnash, sign, ghost, though, right, sought, damn, condemn, psalm. He says he leaves these mute letters in the spelling because of custom or because of etymology: debt/debit, sign/signature, damn/damnation, condemn/condemnation.

TABLE 5.3   Changes in Spelling from Shakespeare to Johnson

Hamlet's Soliloquy (1623)	Johnson's Dictionary (1755)
fixt	fixed
selfe	self
seemes	seems
growes	grows
growne	grown
possesse	possess
grosse	gross
meerely	merely
louing	loving
heauen	heaven
shooes	shoes
poore	poor
teares	tears
vnkle	unkle
vses	uses
moneth	month
vnweeded	unweeded
vnprofitable	unprofitable
breake	break
euen	even
mourn'd	mourned
vnrighteous	unrighteous
breake	break
encrease	increase
windes	winds
beteene	between

Johnson was very aware of his shortcomings in tackling this formidable problem. I'll let him speak for himself:

I have laboured to settle the orthography, display the analogy, regulate the structures, and ascertain the signification of English words, to perform all the parts of a faithful lexicographer: but I have not always executed my own scheme, or satisfied my own expectations. The work, whatever proofs of diligence and attention it may exhibit, is yet capable of many improvements: the orthography which I recommend is still controvertible, the etymology I adopt is uncertain and perhaps frequently erroneous . . .

if our language is not here fully displayed, I have only failed in an attempt which no human powers have hitherto completed.[3]

These spellings are original. Nothing has changed.

Johnson's success in standardizing spelling had an unforeseen consequence. Now that there was only one 'right' way to spell a word, the task of every schoolboy or girl was to memorize that one right way, otherwise their written work would reflect their ignorance. From this point on, teaching spelling began to diverge from teaching reading and took on a life of its own.

Noah Webster's Great Mistake

Webster was a brilliant linguist who wrote the first American dictionary and is responsible for any differences in American spelling. He borrowed mainly from Johnson, and the changes he made were minor. For example, he decided that words ending in the sounds /ik/ should be spelled *ic* and not *ick*: 'music' not 'musick'. He applied this principle religiously to multi-syllable words: panic, terrific, atomic, frantic, endemic, septic, etc., but left the one-syllable 'ik' words untouched: trick, stick, flick. He abolished the letter *u* from words like labour, colour, and favour.

Webster studied classics at Yale and was admitted to the Bar in 1781 at the age of twenty-three. He was a schoolteacher for a while and realized that children were having problems pronouncing English correctly and learning to read and spell. He saw that their books had no accurate or systematic content about pronunciation, spelling or grammar. At the ripe old age of twenty-five, he set out to change this once and for all, and published Part I of the *Grammatical Institute of the English Language*, in 1783. This became known as the *American Speller* or *Blue-backed Speller*, the most popular speller on both sides of the Atlantic for nearly 100 years.

Although the *Speller* eventually sold over 100,000,000 copies, due to absent or ineffective copyright laws in the various different states, the income from it during Webster's lifetime was never sufficient to support his family. He continued to supplement his income with his legal work, teaching, founding a newspaper, and writing and lecturing about the English language, politics, history and other topics. In 1801, he began work on his first dictionary, published in 1806. He wasn't proud of it and wrote later: 'I found myself embarrassed at every step for want of a knowledge of the origin of words, which Johnson–and others–do not afford the means of obtaining.'[4] Webster took eighteen years to study and compare more than twenty languages. These included all the obvious ones, plus Arabic, Hebrew, Chaldee, Russian, Amharic, Persian, Syriac, Icelandic, and others. Finally, in 1828, he published his magnum opus, a 70,000-word dictionary. He was seventy years old.

It's the *Speller* that created problems in the teaching of reading and spelling in American and British schools, although they might have happened anyway. Some of these problems were due to Webster's emphasis, and others were created by publishers who imitated Webster but omitted most of the spelling code and his systematic exposition of syllable patterns.

Webster's goal was to reform the teaching of spoken and written English. He saw himself, like Johnson, as a champion of 'correct' pronunciation and felt that this could be accomplished by teaching spelling properly, and marking syllable boundaries and pronunciation with various diacritic marks. Proper spelling was mainly what Johnson had established. Webster writes: 'In spelling and accenting, I have generally made Dr Johnson's dictionary my guide.' Webster devised a set of exercises which gradually took the student through word lists of simple to complex spelling and syllable patterns.

In the Preface to the 1783 edition of the *Speller*, Webster began by outlining the sounds of the English language. First he derived sounds from their spellings, and then sounds independently of spellings. Webster writes as if he is thinking out loud, so it's easy to follow his train of thought. He knew that a writing system is an arbitrary code for sounds in the language. As he put it: 'letters are the marks of sounds'. After all, he was a student of languages. He was surprised to discover that he didn't know the sounds in his own language. In the Preface he 'discovers' thirty-eight sounds. Later, he found one more (/ng/).

In the same edition, Webster wrote out the spellings in two directions: first, from each sound in the language to its various spelling alternatives. The sound /ae/ 'can be spelled: hate, fair, day, they, vein, gauge.'

Next, he wrote out the various sounds each letter could represent: the letter a 'can sound: fate, hat, halt.' I described these two patterns earlier as *spelling alternatives* and *code overlaps* (my terms not his). So far, so good. If he had developed both these ideas, he would have revolutionized the teaching of reading and spelling.

Instead he made a mistake. The *Speller* itself consisted of word lists of increasing complexity and syllable length, interleaved with short phrases and little stories. Rather than organizing the lists by *sounds* (phonemes) in the language, he decided to do this by letters, word-families, and syllable length, set out alphabetically. In some ways this is understandable, because it is hard to represent 'sounds' in print. Lessons begin with short word lists: ba, ca, da, fa, ga; ab, ac, ad, af, ag; can, man, pan, ran, van; brag, drag, flag, stag. The child encounters consonant digraphs (two letters = one sound) almost immediately, mixed together with consonant clusters (two letters = two sounds). On page three we find: glut, <u>sh</u>ut, smut, slut(!), and <u>ch</u>ub, club, drub, grub (digraphs are underlined). Next come a series of e-controlled vowel spellings: hide, ride, side, wide; face, lace, pace, race, etc. After a couple of dozen pages of these lists the child is plunged without warning into word lists containing these vowel digraphs: <u>ai</u>, <u>ay</u>, <u>ey</u>, <u>ee</u>, <u>ea</u>, <u>oa</u>, <u>oi</u>, <u>oy</u>, <u>ou</u>, <u>ow</u>, none of which have been seen before.

In succeeding editions, his detailed analysis of the sounds in English along with the various spelling alternatives for different sounds was either abbreviated or put in an Appendix, and sounds were explained and organized in the *Speller* as if they were derived from letters. The following quotes are from the 1870 edition:[5]

> The regular long sound of *a* [meaning the letter] is denoted by a
> horizontal mark over it, as in āncient, profāne.

When the vowel letters run out, he switches logic from letter to sound, but often this is muddled:

> The short sound of oo in pool is that of *u* in pull and *oo* in wool.

Here Webster presents oo as a 'sound', when what he actually means is that the *letters* <u>oo</u> can represent two different sounds, as in 'pool' and 'wool', and that the *sound* /oo/ can also be spelled <u>u</u> as in 'pull'.

Consonants are presented in the Introduction in alphabetical order (visually) rather than by sound, with sounds derived from letters. When a letter has only one sound, and a sound has only one letter (one-to-one mapping), then this works fine. But look what happens here:

F has only one sound: life, fever, except of, in which it has the sound of v.

The letter f̲ may stand for only one sound (no code overlap), but the *sound* /f/ has four spelling alternatives: deaf, cliff, phone, rough. If you never introduce the *sound* /f/ to the student, there is no way to get to this information.

When Webster's approach breaks down (as it must), he tries to solve the problem by switching logic, as illustrated with the example for 'pool', or by inventing spelling 'rules'. Here is one of his rules:

Gh are mute in every English word, both in the middle and at the end, except in words like cough, tough [etc.] when they close with the sound of f.

He should have added: 'unless they appear at the beginning of the word, when they have the sound of g (ghost)'. Yet Webster (accurately) cautions teachers never to teach rules to children, because they 'can't understand them'.

If this is getting confusing already, you can imagine that Webster's imitators were only going to make things worse. What happened as a result of Webster's emphasis was that the sounds of the language, which he had carefully worked out, got lost. Today, in phonics lessons, the alphabet is taught from letter to sound, which destroys the logic of the alphabet code. This will be explained in more detail below.

Webster made other decisions which affected phonics teaching methods. His *Speller* begins with ten vowels, actually five vowel letters, described as being 'long' or 'short' vowels. The short vowels are /a/ bat, /e/ bet, /i/ sit, /o/ hot, /u/ cup, and the 'long' vowels are /ae/ gate, /ee/ seem, /ie/ tie, /oe/ toe, /ue/ cute (in other words, vowel sounds with e-controlled spellings). Webster actually believed that the word 'made' took longer to say than 'mad'. Webster didn't invent this idea. The terms 'long' and 'short' vowels were used by Johnson and by earlier writers. No one knows exactly when this practice began. Some people thought that the old Saxon language had long and short versions of the same vowel sound: 'mad' and 'maaad', but there is no evidence for this.

The 'long' and 'short' distinction here is meaningless. It doesn't hold up in terms of duration or in any other way, and it doesn't even correspond to what phoneticians call 'long' and 'short' vowels. There are simply ten different vowel sounds related only because they share the same letters. Children have no idea what the teacher means when she says vowels are 'long' and 'short'. They think she is talking about physical size, a long A and a short A.

Johnson informed his dictionary readers that he was leaving certain 'mute' letters in words, which he identified only in consonant clusters (sign, doubt). In Webster's hands, 'mute' letters began multiplying like some dreaded virus. They invaded all vowel digraphs, and he marked these 'silent' letters with italics so children would be sure to notice them (lif*e*, gr*ie*f, thou*gh*, b*ui*ld, pe*o*ple, tau*gh*t, he*a*d, go*a*l).

Later, someone invented the saying: 'When two vowels go walking the first one does the talking.' This means that when you see a vowel pair, the second letter is silent and you say the *letter-name* of the first vowel (beach, feet, and soap, follow the rule). This is supposed to be a useful mnemonic device for decoding vowel digraphs. During phonics lessons, children can devote the greater part of their reading time to searching for 'silent' letters and blocking them out with a fingernail. Having to do this is bad enough, even if the rule worked, but it only holds up about 40 per cent of the time. If the rule was true, you would pronounce the words

> dawn, launch, soil, boy, pouch, cow, bread, touch, eight, thief, grew, group, pear

like this:

> dane, lainch, sole, boe, poach, coe, breed, toach, eat, thife, gree, groap, peer

And these are just a few of the *common* spelling patterns that don't follow the rule.

In every edition of Webster's *Speller*, it is clear that Webster was fully aware that sounds in English are the basis for the code. For example, he writes in a footnote: 'Children may be much assisted by being told how to place the tongue and lips to make any sound.'[6] Perhaps because this was so obvious to him, it got de-emphasized over time, and in setting up the lessons entirely *from* letters *to* sounds, the importance of the sounds was obscured and then lost.

At the end of the nineteenth century, there was a brief ray of hope in the work of Nellie Dale, a schoolteacher at Wimbledon High School for Girls. She developed the first true linguistic reading programme. Unfortunately, any such innovative leftovers from the nineteenth century were soon crushed into oblivion by the Universal Education movement and the bureaucracy it spawned. These topics will be addressed in the following chapter.

Meanwhile, I leave you with the English alphabet code.

The True Logic of the English Alphabet Code

There are 43 phonemes in English. These phonemes can be represented by approximately 100 letters or letter combinations. In order to teach this, you must set up a Basic Code where each of the 43 phonemes is represented by only *one* letter or digraph. The remaining structure of the spelling code should be taught as 'spelling alternatives' for those sounds with more than one spelling, and 'code overlaps' for those letters that represent more than one sound. The structure breaks down as follows:

Consonants

Twenty-four consonant sounds can be spelled with a total of 50 spellings. Twelve consonants have only one spelling, or one spelling by position in a word:

/b/, /d/, /h/, /l/, /p/, /t/, /v/, /ng/, /qu/, /sh/, /th/, /<u>th</u>/

A further 12 are assigned one spelling (the most probable or least ambiguous), which completes the Basic Code for consonants:

/f/, /g/, /j/, /k/, /m/, /n/, /r/, /s/, /w/, /x/, /z/, /ch/, /sh/

(The 25th sound /zh/ (vision) isn't taught at this stage.)

This leaves *26 spelling alternatives for 12 consonants* which must be taught. (Example: the sound /f/ can be spelled: <u>f</u>, <u>ff</u>, <u>gh</u>, <u>ph</u>.)

Consonant Clusters

Seventy-six consonant clusters are spelled exactly like single consonants, and 73 have only one spelling. There is no new logic and no new complexity.

Vowels

Eighteen vowels can be spelled with a total of 50 spellings. Two vowels are mainly spelled one way, and one (/oi/) by position in a word:

> /a/ cat, /i/ sit, /oi/ toil/toy

The remaining 15 vowels are assigned one spelling (the most probable), which completes the Basic Code for vowels:

> /e/, /o/, /u/, /ee/, /ae/, /ie/, /oe/, /ue/, /aw/, /o͞o/, /oo/, /ou/, /er/, /or/
> (/ah/, spelled a last or ar far, is an exception)

This leaves 32 spelling alternatives for 14 vowel sounds which must be taught. (Example: the vowel sound /oe/ can be spelled o–e tone, oa goat, o told, ow low, ough dough.)

Code Overlaps

There are 21 vowel letter-patterns that overlap more than one vowel sound (consonant overlaps are much less of a problem). For example, the letters ou stand for five phonemes: /ou/ out, /o͞o/ soup, /oe/ soul, /u/ touch, /o/ cough. These 21 code overlaps must be taught.

Notice that this process whittles away at the complexity so that it becomes smaller and more manageable. Beyond the Basic Code level (42 sounds/42 spellings), this is what remains:

> 26 consonant spelling alternatives
> 32 vowel spelling alternatives
> 21 code overlaps
> Total complexity: 79

Outcome: the complexity of the code shrinks. The child has a logic to read and to spell. *The code is reversible.* This makes it possible to read (decode) and spell (encode) using the same logic. The child sees that the alphabet is a *code* for sounds in speech. *The code makes sense to the child.*

Phonics Logic

Most phonics programmes teach *from* the letters *to* sounds. Most commercial programmes teach only a fraction of the code, forcing the child to work out the rest on his own. This is how the complete code would be if it were taught with phonics logic:

50 consonant letter-patterns representing 62 sounds
76 consonant cluster letter-patterns representing 76 sounds
50 vowel letter-patterns representing 95 sounds
Total complexity: 176 letter(s) representing 233 sounds.

Outcome:

1. You have destroyed the logic of the alphabet code. There are not 233 sounds in the English language.

2. You have greatly increased the complexity rather than reducing it.

3. You have taught 76 clusters as if they were 76 new sounds instead of combinations of old sounds.

4. You have made it impossible to categorize what needs to be taught or to arrange lessons on the basis of spelling probabilities.

5. You have created a trap from which there is no escape. The code can't reverse and only works to decode but not to encode, because *you can't teach spelling alternatives for 233 'sounds'*! To solve this problem, authors of phonics programmes have developed scores of unmemorable rules.

To make matters worse, many phonics programmes teach 'word-families' or rimes (VC, VCC, and VCCC endings – *ing, unch, est*) as if they were one sound. Here's what happens when you do this. There are 1,260 word-families in English (more than 820 in common English words alone), adding another 1,260 sounds to the 233 sounds you already have, a total of 1,493 sounds. Rimes are syllable fragments. The child is taught <u>est</u> as a single sound, so that it can be recognized anywhere in a word, even though it may cross over syllable boundaries and change in pronunciation: blest, west, establish (est-ablish), destiny (dest-iny), destroy (dest-roy). The number of these syllable fragments is likely to come close to infinity, given that English has more than 55,000 syllables to start with.

In the late 1980s, the US Center for the Study of Reading was awarded a grant to investigate the impact of phonics on reading skill and to collate this research. Marilyn Adams was selected to write the review of the research literature, and her well-known book *Beginning to Read* was published in 1990. Adams maintains a cool and scholarly approach in her assessment of the research findings until she begins to review phonics instructional programmes and finds little support for their validity. She writes:

> 'Given the diffuse and complex nature of English spelling–sound translations, there is no obvious path through the phonic correspondences and generalizations; along that path, there are no obvious landmarks to let the teacher or student know which way it will turn next or how much headway has been made towards its end.' (p. 287)

> 'Experts have invested enormous efforts in finding the most coherent and teachable way to do so [teach phonics]. Yet chaos prevails.' (p. 286)

Adams' frustration is heard in these remarks:

> 'On scrutiny, the notion of phonics first turns into a pedagogical morass.' (p. 285)

> 'The teachers are responsible for teaching this mess . . .' (p. 286)

The problems are twofold. The developers of phonics curricula have never analysed the structure of the spelling code, so that phonics programmes are not only seriously impoverished, but chaotic. The second issue is that even if phonics programmes were complete, as illustrated in the analysis of phonics logic above, they still couldn't work, because phonics logic is backwards, and the spelling code cannot be categorized with this logic.

The *word* 'phonics' is problematic as well because it is used in two entirely different ways. In Adams' book, 'phonics' means *anything* to do with teaching sounds rather than whole words. The second meaning refers to types of reading programmes. But there are diametrically opposing ways to teach sounds. Traditional phonics teaches the 'sounds of letters'. The other way, which doesn't yet have a name, teaches the sounds (phonemes) in the English language *and* how each of these phonemes is mapped to letters.

Misunderstanding this fundamental difference has been the major cause of the failure of reading programmes probably well before Webster. In this century, it has been the cause of the endless flip-flops and shifts in emphasis between memorizing whole words (as in look-and-say and 'real books'), and phonics, or has led to the notion that all methods should work at once (eclecticism). As a start on the path to a complete understanding of the new way, let me introduce you to the code.

The Code

This chapter closes with the sounds of the English language and the structure of the English spelling code. All codes are based on what is called 'mapping' or mapping transformations. When a phoneme is coded with only one letter, this is the simplest type of mapping: one-to-one. Because there aren't enough letters for all the phonemes in English, letters have been combined in pairs to stand for the remaining sounds. These letter pairs, or digraphs, introduce a more complex variation: one phoneme to one letter pair, or one-to-one(two) mapping. Many phonemes have multiple spellings or spelling alternatives. Also, a letter or digraph can represent multiple sounds or code overlaps, creating two further mapping logics, known as one-to-many, and many-to-one mapping. The Latin layer of language represents still another mapping relationship which will be discussed in Chapter 10.

These mapping relationships can be seen in the following tables (5.4–5.7). The first group of tables present the spelling alternatives for each phoneme in English, and the second group shows the code overlaps for vowel letter-patterns only. You may want to compare these tables to the spelling alternatives/code overlaps in King Alfred's spelling system in Table 5.1.

There are few consistent patterns or 'rules' in our spelling system, especially for vowels, but there is a way around this problem. The tables are arranged according to spelling *probabilities*, based upon how many words have that particular spelling. Perceptual learning or perceptual memory occurs by a process called 'probability matching'. The brain is specially adapted to learn visual and auditory patterns automatically by seeing or hearing them a few times. *If, and only if, the eye is trained to look at the letter(s) representing one sound*, these patterns will be coded without effort. The brain searches for 'reoccurring regularities'. What is frequently encountered will be remembered. What is very strange or discrepant will be noticed.

When a system, such as our spelling system, cannot be easily classified, the solution is to organize it according to its probability structure, and teach it by systematic exposure to this structure. This probability structure must be based upon how the code was written. Phonemes are the *categories* and letter(s) are the *code*. This means teaching the child the *most likely spelling* for each phoneme first (Basic Code), then the next most likely spellings, and so on. In order to do this, you have to know which spellings *are* most likely or unlikely. Someone has to work this out ahead of time. The tables present this probability structure for common English words, for the first time.[7] We'll be looking at this issue in depth in Chapter 11, the chapter on how to teach spelling so that it's consistent with the logic of the English alphabet code.

How to Read the Tables

Phoneme sounds are on the left, spelled in Basic Code, which is the most probable or least ambiguous spelling for that phoneme, along with a key word as a cue for pronunciation. Spelling alternatives, or multiple ways to spell that sound, are listed separately for beginning and ending consonants in words or syllables, and also for vowels.

Spellings are set out in the tables according to probabilities, from the most likely spelling to the least. The probability order is based upon the number of *common* English words with that spelling, and does not include the Latin layer of the language.

The final set of tables show the code overlaps for vowels only. These illustrate the number of different sounds each vowel spelling pattern can represent.

Rare spellings, like those that some people love to use to prove our spelling system is totally chaotic (sew, people, yacht, debt, who) are not included in this probability structure. There are less than fifty of them in common English words.

TABLE 5.4   Single Consonant Spelling Alternatives

Sound	Key Word	Word Beginning			Word Ending			
b	big	b			b			
d	dog	d			d			
f	fun	f	ph		f	ff	ph	gh
g	got	g	gu	gh	g	gue	gg	
h	hot	h	wh		—			
j	job	j	g		ge	dge		
k	kid	c	k	ch	k	ck	c	
l	log	l			l	ll		
m	man	m			m	mb	mn	
n	not	n	kn	gn	n	gn		
p	pig	p			p			
r	red	r	wr		r			
s	sat	s	c	sc	ce	se	ss	s
t	top	t			t	bt		
v	van	v			ve			
w	win	w	wh		—			
x /ks/	tax	—			x			
z	zip	z			se	ze	zz	s z
ch	chin	ch			ch	tch		
ng	sing	—			ng			
qu/kw/	quit	qu			—			
sh	shop	sh			sh			
th	thin	th			th			
t͟h	then	th			the			

Spelling alternatives are ordered by most to least likely.

TABLE 5.5 Consonant Clusters

| **Beginning** | | **Ending** | |
Clusters	Spelling Alternatives	Clusters	Spelling Alternatives
bl br			
dr dw		dth	
fl fr		ft fth	
gl gr			
kl kr	**cl cr**	(kt)	**ct**
	chl chr		
		ld lf (lj)	**lge**
		lm ln lp lt	
		lch lsh lth	
		mp mpt (mf)	**mph**
		nch nd (nj)	**nge**
		nt nth	
pl pr		pt pth	
		rb rc rd	
		rf rg (rj)	**rge**
		rk rl rm rn	
		rp rt rch	
		rsh rth rve	
sk skr	**sc** sk sch **scr**	sk sm sp st	
sl sm sn			
sp spl spr			
st str			
sw squ			
tr tw			
		xt	
		(ngk) (ngkt)	**nk nct**
		ngth	
shr			
thr			

Clusters in brackets are never spelled this way. Optional spellings in bold are the most likely (or only) spelling.

TABLE 5.6   Vowel Chart

Sound	Key Word	Spelling Alternatives (in order of most to least frequent)						
		1	2	3	4	5	6	7
a	had	a						
e	bed	e	ea	ai				
i	it	i	y	ui				
o	dog	o	a					
aw	law	aw	au	ough	augh			
ah	father	a	ar					
u	but	u	o	o–e	ou			
ae	made	a–e	ai	a	ay	ei	eigh	ey
ee	see	ee	ea	y	ie	e	e–e	ey
ie	time	i–e	i	y	igh			
oe	tone	o–e	o	oa	ow	ou	ough	
ue	cute	u–e	u	ew	eu			
oo	look	oo	u	ou				
o͞o	soon	oo	u–e	ew	u	ou	ui	
ou	out	ou	ow	ough				
oi	soil	oi	oy					

Vowel + r

er	her	er		ur	ir	or	ear	ar
or	for	or	ore	oar	our	ar		
e + er	bare	are	air	err	ear			

TABLE 5.7 Code Overlap: The Code from Letters to Sound
(In order of most to least common)

Letters	Sound/Word		Sound/Word		Sound/Word		Sound/Word	
a	/a/	cat	/ae/	table	/au/	father		
e	/e/	bed	/ee/	be				
i	/i/	sit	/ie/	find				
o	/o/	dog	/oe/	cold				
u	/u/	but	/oo/	pull	/ue/	pupil	/o͞o/	ruin
a–e	/ae/	made						
ai	/ae/	sail	/e/	said				
ee	/ee/	see						
ea	/ee/	meat	/e/	head	/ae/	break		
i–e	/ie/	tie	/ee/	believe	/e/	friend		
o–e	/oe/	tone	/u/	done	/o͞o/	shoe		
oa	/oe/	boat						
u–e	/ue/	cute	/o͞o/	rule				
aw	/aw/	law						
au	/aw/	haul						
oo	/o͞o/	soon	/oo/	look				
ow	/ow/	how	/oe/	low				
ou	/ow/	out	/o͞o/	soup	/u/	touch	/oe/	soul
oy	/oy/	toy						
oi	/oy/	oil						
y	/ee/	baby	/ie/	fly	/ee + V/	yes	/i/	gym
ay	/ae/	day						
ey	/ee/	key	/ae/	they				
uy	/ie/	buy						
ye	/ie/	lye						
ui	/i/	build	/o͞o/	juice				
ew	/ue/	new	/o͞o/	blue				
eu	/ue/	feud						
ei	/ee/	seize	/ae/	vein				
eigh	/ae/	eight	/ie/	height				
igh	/ie/	high						
augh	/aw/	caught	ah	laugh				
ough	/aw/	ought	/ow/	bough	/oe/	dough		

TABLE 5.7   Code Overlap: The Code from Letters to Sound
(In order of most to least common)   *Cont'd*

R-controlled Vowels

ar	/ah/	far	/or/	war	/er/ collar
er	/er/	her			
ir	/er/	sir			
ur	/er/	fur			
or	/or/	for	/er/	work	
air	/e + er/	hair			
are	/e + er/	bare	/ar/	are	
arr	/a + er/	carry			
err	/e + er/	error			
ear	/eer/	ear	/air/	bear	/er/ learn
eer	/eer/	peer			
ere	/eer/	mere	/air/	there	/er/ were
iar	/ire/	liar			
ire	/ire/	hire			
ore	/or/	ore			
oar	/or/	roar			
our	/our/	hour	/or/	four	/er/ colour
oor	/or/	door			
ure	/ue + r/	pure	/er/	measure	

Irregular spellings used to spell only one or two words are omitted: aigh (/ae/ straight), oir (/ie/ choir), yre (/ie/ lyre), ai (/ie/ aisle), awer (/or/ drawer), etc.

A Comment on Dialects

The forty-three phonemes in the English language are the basis for our alphabet code. There is an argument by some educators against teaching the sounds of English to children learning to read and write because people speak in different dialects.

A reading programme was withdrawn from one local education authority under orders from a national authority because it advocated teaching speech sounds in the local dialect rather than in standard English. The national authority disapproved because they believed this would enhance class divisions, and be socially harmful.

This is not a valid argument. People who speak in non-standard dialects understand the standard dialect perfectly (as heard on TV or radio, for example), yet this does not cause them to change their dialect or feel bad about themselves. Britain and America share a nearly identical spelling system, yet have different standard dialects and different pronunciations for these spellings. This does not create special problems in either country.

The key issue is the degree of deviation of a regional dialect from the standard. There is no harm in teaching speech sounds in a dialect that approximates standard English. Using a key-word code makes this possible. However, there would be considerable harm in teaching sounds of a dialect which is too remote from the standard. This will cause major difficulties with the spelling code (not with self-esteem).

CHAPTER 6

Not So Universal Education

Universal education began in earnest in the nineteenth century and ran a remarkably parallel course in the United States and Britain, as it does today. Governments saw the necessity for universal literacy as the only way to foster democracy and provide opportunities for all its citizens. This was partly an economic decision (literate people make better workers in rapidly industrializing nations) and partly idealistic, due to an increasing sensitivity to the fact that illiteracy not only wastes potential talent, but condemns citizens to the lowest and most impoverished levels of society.

The way in which universal education was implemented failed to preserve what had been good about schools in the private sector. Children from wealthy families had been educated by tutors or in exclusive schools with small classes. Teachers could work with each child individually. The curriculum was based upon language and language-related skills. Children learned Latin and French, which made them sensitive to sounds in speech and enriched their understanding of the English language.

Even the sixteenth-century guild schools for children of guild members (Merchant Taylors' and Haberdashers' Aske's still survive), emphasized languages along with mathematics. In the US, the first fledgling attempt to educate children from different social backgrounds was the founding of the Boston Latin school in 1635. This was the first town-supported school and its name illustrates the focus of the curriculum at that time. The de-emphasis on learning languages and on the value of memorization is one of the most unfortunate consequences of universal education.

State funding for education in England and Wales began in 1833 when the government allocated £20,000 to schools for poor people. At this time, there were about 700 grammar schools for the middle classes and more than 2,000 schools sponsored mainly by churches or local patrons. In 1856, an Education Department was established, and legislation for funding was approved in 1858 for £663,000 to be spent on schools. The government also funded a special commission (the Newcastle Commission) who reported in 1859 on the state of the nation's schools. The conclusions were notable for their hyperbole: 'Our middle classes are nearly the worst educated in the world.'

The impact of the Newcastle Report led to the Education Act of 1870, a lengthy document spelling out what needed to be done. The Act reinforced class divisions by outlining the purpose of state expenditure on education, not so much for the poor, but rather 'for the education of children belonging to the class who support themselves by manual labour'. The negative attitude towards 'manual labour' (or in fact 'labour' of any kind) has worked against designing an education system that is effective for everyone. This bias also seriously affects expectations, as we shall see later in this book.

The 1880 Mundella Act made school compulsory, and in 1882 the school leaving age was raised to twelve. This caused enormous difficulties for the churches, who were responsible, by default, for educating all children without financial means. By 1888, this constituted 69 per cent of all schoolchildren, and the problem became even more acute when Parliament abolished school fees entirely in 1891. Finally, as some churches were on the verge of bankruptcy, 'rate aid' was granted to all denominational schools in 1902, which effectively made education in England and Wales a government-funded programme for everyone.

A report in 1895 by one of the many committees convened over the years to investigate the state of literacy in Britain claimed that there was a very high level of functional illiteracy, poor or absent reading comprehension, impoverished vocabulary, and 'the inability to remember anything'. As a consequence, school inspectors were hired to study practices in classrooms across England and Wales. In reports from Her Majesty's Inspectorate (HMI), comments abound about 'the imbecility with which reading is taught in the elementary schools'. These comments do not reflect any kind of Victorian golden age of literacy, and sound very much like criticisms raised today.

The school leaving age was raised to fourteen in 1918, although for most pupils this just meant an extension of their elementary school education. It wasn't until after the Second World War that the 1944 Butler Education Act came into effect and funded compulsory secondary education, although it was only in the 1960s that the school leaving age was raised to fifteen and in the 1970s to sixteen.

A similar chronology occurred in America, but with a different outcome for secondary education, and a different set of attitudes about 'manual labour' and the 'working classes'. In 1918, the US government passed legislation for state-wide compulsory school attendance through high school (up to the age of fourteen). In the same year, the National Education Association (NEA) teachers' union set up curriculum guidelines for high schools, which added instruction in health, family life, vocational studies, citizenship, ethics, and use of leisure time.

During the long build-up to universal education, a number of prominent people were agitating for spelling reform. The peculiarities of English spelling were seen as one of the major stumbling blocks to true literacy – which meant absolutely correct spelling. Correct spelling was stringently enforced throughout the nineteenth and early twentieth centuries. In the US, spelling lessons were taught throughout secondary school. The spelling standard became so rigid in Britain, that in the late nineteenth century an HMI wrote that out of 1,972 failures in the Civil Service examination, '1,866 were plucked for spelling' (quoted by J. L. Dobson – see references).

The fact that the curriculum emphasized spelling such a long time after reading instruction had been completed is informative, because it reflects a schism in classroom practice between teaching decoding (reading) and encoding (spelling) that is still with us. Spelling and reading were seen as two entirely different skills having little to do with each other.

The concern of spelling reformers was that the standardization of the code by Johnson and Webster was not efficient, for all the reasons noted in the previous chapter. In 1876 the National Union of Elementary School Teachers in England voted to support Isaac Pitman's shorthand, called 'Phonotype', with its forty special characters for forty sounds in English. But the characters were too dissimilar to conventional letters to catch on.

The British Philological Society was formed in 1869 to improve spelling, but the founders fell out over how to do this. Ten years later, the British Spelling Reform Association was established and included such prominent figures as Alfred, Lord Tennyson and Charles Darwin. They invented three different schemes and then couldn't agree on which was the best. One scheme consisted of twenty-four different rules for improving spelling, one of which was to drop all unnecessary letters: liv, fether, gess, activ, tripl, abuv, fonetic, flasht, etc.

The American Spelling Reform Association was founded in 1876 by Francis Marsh, S. S. Haldeman and W. D. Whitney. These gentlemen had more success in agreeing on what to do, but nobody paid any attention to their recommendations. Andrew Carnegie got into the act in 1906, by funding the Simplified Spelling Board, and industrialists in Britain followed suit in the same year by funding the British Simplified Spelling Society. These groups invented such systems as 'Anglic', 'Nue Spelling', and 'Regularized Inglish', but their 'nue' spelling ideas made no impact whatsoever.

The only spelling reform ever to reach the classroom was Sir James Pitman's (grandson of Isaac) Initial Teaching Alphabet (i t a), brought into a number of state schools in Britain in a vast experiment in the 1960s. The script had specially designed letters for several English phonemes. There was support for the idea that this script would help in teaching the logic of the alphabet code, and children who used it could read and write with greater accuracy and fluency. The problem was that this wasn't spelling reform at all, because i t a was confined to books and readers in infant school classrooms. After this, the child had to relearn standard writing and spelling conventions to be able to read anything else. (I remember this well, because my son was in the experiment.) Because parents were concerned about their children learning two writing systems, one of which had to be unlearned, i t a was withdrawn. The last gasp of spelling reform was a 1962 publication of Bernard Shaw's *Androcles and the Lion* printed with a spelling system he designed.

Although spelling reform never got off the ground (and unfortunately will never work), throughout the nineteenth and early twentieth centuries other changes took place that had a dramatic impact on the character and quality of schools and the teaching profession. One overriding concern was how to finance this vast social experiment and control runaway costs. New printing methods were developed that made textbooks much less expensive. Salaries were sharply reduced from the typical wages paid to the mainly male teachers in the private sector. In the United States as state schools began to replace private schools and salaries shrank, male teachers left the field in droves, their numbers declining by 47 per cent during the nineteenth century. The number of female teachers, who were paid less than half of the average male wage, increased during that same time by 156 per cent. As women began to replace men, earning much lower wages, the prestige of the teaching profession declined. With loss of prestige came loss of power and the loss of a voice.

Instead, power shifted to people who often knew nothing about education. At the city level, school boards and local education authorities made up of local businessmen and other important citizens were set up as watchdogs for the general public to prevent the misuse of public funds by school officials and teachers. This was accompanied by a shift of power to central agencies. As wage earners in the classroom lost representation to other professional groups, a bureaucracy was launched which grew exponentially in the US. In Boston in 1890 there were seven supervisors of schools. By 1920, there were 159. In New York City the comparable numbers were 235 and 1,310. Supervisors took over teachers' functions of developing curricula, scheduling classes and setting standards. Teachers in remote one-room schools were the only lucky ones to escape. Today, teachers in the US and Britain are at the mercy of local, county, and national regulations and layers of bureaucracy. The teacher has become disenfranchised from local educational policy and decision-making. In Britain, this situation has considerably worsened with the 1988 Education Reform Act.

The attempt to reach the poor and weaken the class system by government decree has continued throughout this century. Butler's 1944 Education Act mandated an examination at the age of eleven (the 11-plus) to determine who would go to grammar schools (and so to college or university), and who to 'secondary modern' schools. The goal was to enable bright children of middle- and working-class parents to go on to higher education, which had been nearly impossible due to the different curriculum structure of independent and state schools. This backfired. The 11-plus exam was criticized for being taken far too young, was uniformly feared and despised by the 'underdog' 80 per cent who failed it annually, and by their parents and the teachers who had to teach them. All believed they were second-class citizens in second-class schools, and few realized they were the vast majority. Indeed, secondary modern schools *were* second class, receiving one-third of the funding of the grammar schools.

After nearly twenty years of the 11-plus exam, the government passed legislation to encourage local authorities to establish comprehensive secondary schools, similar to American high schools. In 1980, Margaret Thatcher introduced 'parental choice' (Parents' Charter), an idea picked up by President Bush. Children were supposed to be able 'to vote with their feet', but instead, parents voted with their cars. Those who can afford cars and have the time to drive children miles to and from the better schools, are the people with 'choice'. Working-class children are still stuck with the local neighbourhood school, good or bad.

The problems inherent in controlling state education from the top down are vividly captured in Margaret Thatcher's autobiography, when she sets out her original intentions for the 1988 Education Reform Act. There were seven major goals:

1. Improve education standards.
2. Use central authority and control to establish uniform standards in three subjects: English, mathematics, and science.
3. Monitor these standards with objective tests.
4. Improve teacher training and allow for different routes to certification.
5. Encourage school choice and competition via the 1980 Parents' Charter.
6. Allow for innovation by bypassing the bureaucracy and LEAs (local education authorities) via 'grant-maintained schools'.
7. 'Ease the state out of education.' (Chapter 20, *passim*.)

Ten years later, nothing like this has happened. Instead, Thatcher's admirable goals, funnelled through the Secretary of State for Education, through the Department of Education and Science (DES), through HMI (now Ofsted), through the teachers' unions, and through a myriad of curriculum specialists, created a monster. The tail has wagged the dog.

It's quite remarkable how unsuccessfully the first four goals were met. Instead of standards and objective testing for three subject areas, Britain got a complete National Curriculum. The three targeted areas were expanded to nine. Outside, objective testing was abandoned in favour of 'diagnostic' testing by the classroom teacher. Thatcher reports on demands made by the education establishment for new ways to bloat the already bloated education bureaucracy. They recommended a 'National Curriculum Council' (NCC), a new 'Schools Examination and Assessment Council' (SEAC), plus 800 new LEA inspectors along with a fleet of senior inspectors to oversee the LEA inspectors. How could this happen to someone as shrewd and adroit as Thatcher? She confesses that she was overwhelmed by jumbo reports containing hundreds of pages of edu-babble (the education establishment's weapon of choice the world over). The timing was always impeccable as these reports typically arrived one or two days before the crucial vote in the House. Melanie Phillips has documented how the DES used the same delaying tactics with the NCC committee. (By the way, it will be interesting to witness President Clinton's ten-step plan for education unfolding. The largest teachers' union, the National Education Association, has already found a nearly foolproof way to foil his 'charter schools', which are similar to grant-maintained schools.)

The New Classroom

As bureaucrats in both Britain and the US took over the education system, they often worked hand-in-glove with the businessmen who stood to profit by the vast new market for educational materials. This is especially true in the US where textbook publishers and powerful people in the educational establishment came to dictate how whole school districts, and even whole states, would educate their children. US educational publishers also have effectively locked out publishers from Britain and elsewhere as far as classroom curriculum is concerned.

During this century, vast quantities of materials, including readers, spellers, worksheets, workbooks, flash cards, story books, 'big books', have streamed forth from the educational publishing houses. If parents complained about the lack of progress of their children, schools could spend rate revenues on new materials. In the US, the pattern was to discard everything and replace it with something completely new in the burgeoning spirit of planned obsolescence. In Britain, teachers did the opposite and never threw out anything. Their affection for eclecticism evolved not so much as a consequence of a well-thought-out theoretical position, but as a result of conservatism, thriftiness, and the mistaken belief that different children learn how to read in different ways. New materials, along with their incompatible methods and philosophies, are simply added to the teacher's bag of tricks.

The influence of business was seen in the parallels with the newly emerging, assembly-line models of industry. Schools were organized along the lines of a factory. In the US, children, like battery chickens, were martialled through 'grades', neatly sorted by age. The teacher (the factory foreman) conducted lessons from the front of the room and had little opportunity to work individually with the children in her class. There was an implicit assumption that all children could learn the same material, at the same rate, in exactly the same way. This assumption was challenged very quickly when it became obvious that reading could not be taught the 'old fashioned way' (where a teacher would divide a varied class into small groups and circulate around the room) using this kind of model.

This trend was unfortunate, because the early stages of universal education began with an explosion of creativity. New reading programmes were introduced that were less spartan than Webster's *Speller*. Some programmes were excellent, and one or two, extraordinary. A remarkable programme was developed by Nellie Dale at Wimbledon High School for Girls. Dale's efforts first appeared as the *Walter Crane Infant Readers* in 1898. These had colour-coded print to indicate vowels (red), voiced and unvoiced consonants (blue and black) and 'silent' letters (brown). In 1902, the books were expanded and published as *The Dale Readers*, selling widely in Britain and the US. Dale's methods were set out in two detailed teacher manuals. Given what we know today, based upon the last twenty-five years of scientific research, Dale was at least sixty years ahead of her time. For this reason, I want to present her approach in some detail.

Dale's method was based on linguistics. Phonemes in the English language were identified and categorized according to articulatory features. The code for each phoneme was worked through to about one or two spellings. Dale designed a wooden frame to stand at the front of the classroom where 'sounds' could hang (as coloured letters) as they were discovered, one by one, by the children. The frame was constructed so that vowels and consonants were separated, as was place of articulation. At the bottom of the frame was a 'word assembly' space to hang letters to make different words.

Dale's use of discovery techniques to engage children and make the lessons memorable predated Montessori, who subsequently became famous for the discovery method of learning. Dale outlined eighty-six lessons in the manuals. Children were asked to listen to their speech. Their attention was initially directed to the beginning sounds in short CVC words, then to final sounds, and last to middle sounds. They listened to how sounds are ordered in words, made comparisons between one sound and another, and noticed how sounds are produced by movements of the jaw, lips and tongue. The next step was to create CVC words by the children moving in space. Individual children 'became' sounds in words and ordered themselves from left to right in front of the class.

Children discovered sounds before they saw any letters, and then letters were introduced in conjunction with simple words. As each sequence of sounds was discovered and the appropriate letters chosen, these were placed in sequence on the frame. The children copied the words on to a blackboard inside the lid of their desks as they said each sound (phoneme) out loud. These exercises make the logic perfectly clear: *Letters are symbols for phonemes in words* and are ordered from left to right. After several sound–letter correspondences in words had been learned, children wrote stories and practised spelling using these words. They could see that reading and spelling are reversible processes.

Dale wrote: 'Writing is delayed until all sounds are learned and *even with classes of seventy children* writing is all the better for being delayed.' (my italics) This shows how children were crowded into classrooms, even at Wimbledon High School, one of the more prestigious girls' schools of the time.

It's not possible to outline more than a fraction of Dale's advice about teaching the alphabet code and about teaching in general. Here are a few of her ideas:

Never teach anything you will have to discard later.
Children need to move to learn and to engage many senses.
Never teach letter-names. This confuses the child about the sounds the letters stand for.

If you teach sounds according to the principles of phonetics, you will automatically promote good spelling. [She also explains why spelling reform will never work.]

The eye should help, not hinder, the ear. [Relates to teaching precisely which letter or letter combination stands for one sound.]

Group together words with a particular spelling to avoid meeting them scattered in text.

Some of her tricks:

Children discovered which sounds are voiced or unvoiced by putting their hand over their windpipe as they spoke. The eight voiced/unvoiced sound-pairs (/b/, /p/) were called 'brothers'.

Consonant sounds with multiple spellings are 'sisters' (/c/, /k/, /qu/).

The vowels /a/, /e/, /i/, /o/, /u/ were taught using a modified vowel circle, called a 'vowel triangle', to illustrate in which vowels the jaw is closed/open and the tongue back/forward.

Mnemonics were created to teach vowel sounds spelled with digraphs: 'trout /ou/', 'boiling /oi/'.

We will never know whether Dale's method was effective, because there was no way to test children in 1900. We do know that she had an amazing insight into how to teach the English writing system, and based on current research, she was probably highly successful. We also see from her ideas what an innovative teacher she was.

It is unlikely that there were many Nellie Dales around in classrooms of that time, and for teachers who were merely human, a true phonetic method is difficult to teach from the front of the room. Children need to be monitored until their mastery of phonology and knowledge of the alphabet code is secure. If this doesn't happen, some children will fail to learn to read. Dale, for example, never describes how she could listen to seventy children read individually.

How the problem of overcrowding was solved has been our legacy for the past hundred years. Most teachers did not have Dale's amazing insight and skill, and needed individual contact with their students to teach even rudimentary phonics. With so many children in the classroom this became difficult to impossible. Instead of changing the structure of the classroom to make it possible for teachers to teach reading properly, educators decided to *change the nature of the alphabet* by voiding the alphabet principle altogether.

Professors from prestigious universities decreed that it didn't matter how reading was taught. A 'whole word' method would work just as well as the old-fashioned phonetic one. Dr Huey advocated this approach as early as 1908 in his influential book, *The Psychology and Pedagogy of Reading*. Huey believed that children should read for meaning, and never mind if they misread words here and there. Context is the important thing and not accuracy.

> It may even be necessary, if the reader is to really tell what the page suggests, to tell it in words that are somewhat variant; for reading is always of the nature of translation and, to be truthful, must be free.
> (E. B. Huey, quoted by R. Flesch)

After the First World War, university professors, in tandem with educational publishing houses, began designing a series of reading programmes that came to be known as 'look-and-say', where children memorize words by sight as if they were logographs and chant in unison as the teacher holds up flash cards at the front of the room. Look-and-say took the English-speaking world by storm. It was only during the Second World War that the dismal literacy levels of the armed forces were revealed. Joyce Morris (formerly Reading Director at the National Foundation for Educational Research) reviewed the history of the 'phonics debate' that followed this revelation. What is surprising about this history is that despite the intense controversy, the innovative programmes that were created, and the overwhelming research support that phonics worked better than look-and-say, educators refused to budge. Phonics was considered non-progressive, dull and boring, and had no connection to meaning. Meaning was the important thing to motivate children to want to read. Instead, look-and-say remained the dominant method, and nothing much has changed. Lip service is paid to phonics as a useful adjunct, or 'good for poor readers', but is rarely taught on teachers' training courses. Over the past two decades, look-and-say has merged with 'real books', where children look and say whole words in meaningful contexts.

It's the Child's Fault

The failure of look-and-say to teach everyone to read flew in the face of the conventional wisdom of the time, which was that all children are supposed to learn at the same rate to the same degree of expertise. Instead of changing the structure of the classroom to accommodate children in difficulty, and finding out how to teach reading properly, educators decided to *classify the children according to whether they suited the curriculum*! In a 'factory' mentality there are perfect widgets and imperfect widgets. Widgets that fail inspection are called *rejects*.

If a child failed to learn to read, this was viewed as unnatural. The child was considered to have a deficiency. In the US, national norms were established for intelligence, for vocabulary, and for achievement in reading, spelling and maths, to determine exactly who was imperfect and should be rejected. All other children were supposed to be normal, or the same. As the ultimate example of woolly thinking along these lines, for decades US federally funded research on education focused on the issue of 'reading readiness', in the belief that all children became magically ready to read at a specific age. As no one knew how to teach reading properly, it was never clear what the children were supposed to be ready *for*. This research ground to a halt in a sea of conflicting data and was abandoned.

Teachers were trained to teach to the norm or the average. If children fell outside these norms they were considered truly (not just statistically) deviant. Over time the list of 'non-normal' categories began to explode, especially in the US, culminating in the Special Education Act: Public Law 94–142. Today, children who have IQs in excess of their reading skill are placed in remedial classrooms from which they rarely escape, indicating that the term 'remedial' is a misnomer. In Britain, the Warnock Commission report led to the 1981 Education Act which supported services for special education. The commission reported that 2 per cent of children had 'special needs', approximately 18 per cent had academic problems (translation: reading problems), and 2 per cent had behaviour problems. However, funding to support special education for the 22 per cent of the school population that needed it has never been forthcoming. On average, only 2 per cent are served, and this figure varies enormously from one local authority to another.

When children failed to learn to read, instead of blaming the system – the structure of the classroom, the inadequate training of teachers, the woefully ineffective methods of instruction, too much uninformed political interference – educators blamed the child. Soon everyone began to believe that reading is a property of the child. If a child can't read then it is his fault. And if the child shows normal persistence and willingness to learn (neither lazy) and normal intelligence (nor stupid), then the child must have a brain disorder called 'dyslexia', a label applied to children who are so confused by their poor reading instruction that they can't overcome it without special help. In the following chapter, we will see that there is no validity to the diagnosis of 'dyslexia', nor do so-called 'dyslexic' children have any more trouble learning to read than other children *if* they are taught with an appropriate method.

For more than one hundred years we have been using misleading and incomplete reading methods, and these methods are getting worse. Look-and-say, phonics, and 'real books', either singly or in combination, don't work for many children. Advocates of phonics and 'real books' assume that children can spontaneously access sounds in words without any instruction. The most important breakthrough in research on reading has been the discovery that phoneme-awareness is critical to mastering an alphabet script. This aptitude is both a talent and a trainable skill, but can remain latent unless it is taught. There is a small minority of children, like Jake, who seem deaf to individual phonemes and need careful instruction. This is not because they have anything wrong with them, but because of the way that language systems of the brain reorganize during development. Most people, even those who read 'phonetically', are not consciously aware of the phonemes in the English language and have difficulty hearing individual sounds in words.

This is where we are today in the classroom. But this is not where we are in our knowledge. For more than twenty years we have had the methods to teach children so that *everyone can read and spell*. In the following chapter we look at the scientific research on which subskills are critical for mastering an alphabetic writing system.

A Reading Revolution

CHAPTER 7

Science to the Rescue

Earlier I introduced you to several children who were having trouble learning to read.

Tommy was using letter-names to spell words ('full steam ahead' = 'fl sdm a ked') like 'real books' experts said he should, and guessing whole words when he read ('the rabbit crossed the road' = 'the ranger climbed the rock'), like 'real books' experts said he should. But he didn't develop into a good reader and speller.

Sally was using letter-names to decode text, until her mother taught her 'letter-sounds' (incorrectly). Sally translated from each letter-name to a letter-sound slowly and painfully: 'rabbit' = 'are/ruh, ae/a, bee/buh, bee/buh, ie/i, tee/tuh: "rabies-it".'

Nigel was told by his teacher *not* to sound out words. Instead, he was told to 'look at the pictures' and memorize a string of letters standing for a whole word: 'bdextntk' = 'football'. Nigel knew this strategy wasn't working, but he couldn't figure out a better way.

Albert was told the same thing, but Albert was more adventurous. Albert, like Tommy, noticed that the first letter or letters in each word stood for a sound, and this sound was a clue to the word. Then he used his excellent visual memory to memorize the *shape* of the rest of the word. He could read short words correctly, but he was extremely inaccurate when words got more visually confusing: 'matter' = 'mother', 'horse' = 'house', 'swimming' = 'sailing'.

Sam was misled by an off-the-shelf reading scheme into thinking that the alphabet code was about groups of letters standing for little words or bits of words. This strategy was hopeless for decoding multi-syllable words: 'hated' = 'hat-ate-ted'.

Tommy, Sally, Nigel, Albert and Sam will not learn to read without help. They are definite candidates for the diagnosis of 'dyslexia' or a 'learning difficulty'.

Now we're ready to answer the question: If other children can learn to read given the *same* instruction, in the *same* classroom, is there something wrong with these children? Here's where science enters the picture. Scientists and educators alike ask: '*What do these children have in common?*'

What do *you* think these children have in common? Here is a checklist of possibilities:

Brain damage/brain anomalies affecting
    language systems of the brain
    low IQ/borderline intelligence
Genetic predisposition
Defect or delay in subskills important to reading
Poor instruction
Inadequate support from parents/family members
Developmental issues: delays in
    logical reasoning
    language development
Attentional difficulties
Child's strategy choice
Chance

In the next three chapters I will be addressing these issues. The central problem in reading research is that there are many variables which influence a child's ability to learn to read. It's the scientist's job to control for all of these variables, but that is easier said than done.

In this chapter I will be reviewing the research on brain damage/ anomalies, genetic predisposition, and subskills related to reading such as auditory processing, visual processing, speech and language, and IQ. Topic headings are provided so that you can read about what is of interest to you, but before you start turning pages, let me explain how science works.

If everybody learned to read effortlessly, we wouldn't need any scientific research on reading. It is because of the 'failures' that parents, other family members, and scientists alike begin to ask questions. Scientists ask the same kind of questions that parents and family members ask, and then design research studies to answer them. Scientists study groups and use a 'statistical' model. If each individual case was unique, science wouldn't work. Instead, scientists are searching for patterns that fit the majority of poor readers. By contrast, parents, family members, and reading specialists look at the individual. The questions, however, are the same. Parents of a poor reader want to know:

1. Does my child have low intelligence?
2. Does my child have a brain disorder?
3. Is there something wrong with my child's eyesight? Does he see letters upside down and backwards?
4. My husband had a reading problem. Is my son's reading problem genetic?
5. Does a reading problem stay with you for life?
6. Is my child's teacher doing an adequate job?

What Science Is and Isn't

To understand how to assess the research designed to answer these questions, I need to talk about the word 'research', one of the most misused and misunderstood words in the English language. Journalists do 'research', by telephoning their sources for information. Many academics do 'research' by going to the library to read up on some topic. They rely on information published by people who went to the library before they did and wrote a book or paper about it. The first section of this book is partly based on this kind of library research. Some educational 'research' consists of observing children in classrooms and forming subjective opinions about this experience.

None of these activities qualify as *scientific* research. Science can only work when things can be measured and recorded in numbers. If you want to find out if a particular teaching method is good or bad, *ask to see the data* from research on the method. The data should be reported in comparisons of test scores on standardized tests. Statements such as 'the children really like it', or 'Research in Liverpool showed that the teachers and parents report that children are reading "better" using this method' don't count.

In the past few decades, some educators have begun misusing the word 'science', calling something 'scientific research' when it is nothing of the sort. When people with influence misuse language, this can have dangerous consequences, leading people to believe that a statement is a scientific fact when it is not. In a recent book, *Phonics Phacts*, 'real books' advocate Kenneth Goodman repeatedly stresses that his ideas are based upon scientific research, especially his. On pages three and four, in explaining the purpose of the book, Goodman uses the words 'research', 'science', and 'scientific' ten times, for example: '. . . show how these misunderstandings [phonics] conflict with scientific realities' and '. . . came to understand the science of how sounds and letters work together in an alphabetic language'. This 'science' demonstrates his conclusion that 'phonics relationships are between the patterns and systems of oral and written language, not between individual letters and sounds.' He says he will avoid technical language and 'still keep my explanations scientific', and that 'This book is . . . my personal statement of scientific belief.'

If you are a scientist, or if you think logically, these statements are strange. There is no 'science' of how sounds and letters work together in an alphabet. This is strictly an issue of categorization and mapping relationships. Science doesn't 'demonstrate a conclusion'. Either the data are there, and replicable, or they are not. In any case, our writing system was designed for individual phonemes and *not* for 'patterns' of sounds. This is simply a *fact*. As all the evidence is in conflict with his claim here, one wonders where his 'conclusion' comes from.

Lastly, how can you have a 'personal scientific belief'? You can have a model or a theory based upon a set of data. But this is not a personal belief.

Goodman proceeds to discuss rudimentary phonetics and linguistics, leading the reader to believe that they are sciences. They are not. They are descriptive disciplines and depend upon other phoneticians and linguists agreeing with you. (Not one of the phoneticians referred to in Chapter 5 had the same list of English phonemes as any of the others!) Classifying things is not science. It is the first step to *begin* to do science.

Goodman's claim that he is doing 'science' has convinced educators in Britain that he is. In *The Primary Language Record*, one of the most highly recommended books for trainee teachers, the authors state that Goodman's 'research findings demonstrated so clearly the way in which beginning readers brought all their linguistic knowledge and experience of life to the task of processing text . . . As a result of these research findings we are now in a position to consider how children learn to read.' (p. 24)

Be that as it may, let's take a look at Goodman's research. In 1965, 1967, and 1969 (the only peer-reviewed research cited in *Phonics Phacts*), he reported on errors children make when reading stories, which he calls 'miscues'. This is similar to the research described in Chapter 2 on children's errors in decoding isolated words. Goodman became intrigued about why children don't rely more on context and grammar to avoid making mistakes. In other words, why do children read 'nonsense words' or real words that don't make any sense in the context of the story? This is a very interesting question and completely amenable to scientific inquiry, but instead Goodman blames this on phonics instruction, and simply talks about these errors in subjective language (my italics):

> Patricia starts out her reading *preoccupied* with getting the words right . . . *perhaps* her teacher has been *admonishing* Patricia and her classmates to say the final <t> and <d> . . . since that's a phrase that *makes sense* to her . . . She *seems to be trying* to do two things: get the words right and *make sense* of the story. But *she can't do both*, so she *swings from one way* of reading to the other.[1]

How does Goodman know that Patricia is 'preoccupied' or that her teacher has been 'admonishing her', or that she is 'trying to do two things', or 'swinging' from one way to another? There are ways to find out if you want to do science. Otherwise you can just speculate.

Here's what Goodman might have done to answer his question:

1. Create some data. So far he has none.

    a. Get inter-judge reliability scores for the 'miscue' categories he uses. This means that at least two people can code the errors independently and classify them into the same categories.

    b. Calculate the proportions of each kind of error per unit of text for each child observed.

    c. Calculate the total number of errors per number of words in the text.

2. Compare the types of errors made by children receiving different kinds of reading instruction. Do context or syntax errors diminish with a 'real books' approach?

3. Measure reading comprehension using a standardized test and correlate this to the proportions of the types of 'miscue' errors the children make. Do certain types of errors make comprehension more difficult?

4. Create text specifically designed to generate more syntax errors or more context-based errors, or more phonetic errors. See if 'real books' training makes a difference to these types of errors or to reading comprehension.

5. Carry out long-term studies to see if any particular types of miscue errors or the overall number of errors predicts reading ability later in time.

This is doing science.

Science is a search for the truth and is open to being falsified. If you never do scientific research, you can never be proven wrong. The truth is reached through the scientific method. This method is procedural. It dictates the way studies to answer a particular question should be designed.

Another major error in educational research has been to rely exclusively on average scores of small groups. If Classroom A scores at an average of 6 years 8 months at the end of first year, and Classroom B, using the new, revolutionary reading programme X, scores at 7 years, is this a difference that matters? To find out, each child's test score must be submitted to statistical analysis. This will tell you whether a pattern of reading scores could occur entirely by chance (random), or whether there is a consistent effect caused by the reading method. Statistics is based on the mathematics of probability. This allows the researcher to predict the likelihood that using reading programme X would produce a consistent effect again and again on different groups of children. You can't make this prediction on the basis of average scores alone.

Statistics is particularly important in behavioural research because it allows scientists to use small populations (samples) and estimate what would happen if they had access to large populations, such as all the children in Oxfordshire. In the US literacy survey reported in Chapter 1, they didn't need to use such statistical methods to show that American children were in trouble. They tested 140,000 children. With numbers like these, percentages or averages alone are sufficient.

All the research findings reported in this and the following chapters are 'statistically significant' unless otherwise stated, meaning that the probability of a particular result is well above the possibility of a chance or random outcome. A scientific 'fact' is established when several research studies produce the same results.

Scientists try to be objective in that they accept their results even when the data show the opposite of what they had predicted. Scientific data are nature's way of knocking at the door and saying: 'Hey, there's a real world out here, and it doesn't conform to what you think.' This doesn't mean that scientists never have biases or hunches about their research. But real scientists are not wedded to their theories, and when the data run counter to these theories, they must change them to accommodate the data.

This does not mean that scientists never make mistakes. Subjective bias can enter into the scientific process, even though scientists do their best to guard against it. It can affect the way you ask a research question. It can affect what you choose to measure and what you leave out. It can affect the way you interpret your data. This doesn't mean that the scientist is dishonest, but it does mean that the real world has to knock louder and louder to be heard. In other words, it takes more research and a lot more time.

Before we move on to the true scientific breakthroughs in reading research, I need to dispel two powerful myths. One is that persistent reading failure is due to brain damage, and the other is that reading is encoded in genes.

If you have read the first six chapters carefully, you will be way ahead of the game. You will have more insight into the complex nature of reading and how children fall through the cracks than some scientists working honestly and rigorously in the field right now. Let me explain why. You have seen the list of possible reasons why children might have difficulties learning to read. There are items on this list that some scientists forget all about, especially if they work from a clinical or 'deficit' model. Stripped to its essence, this model relies on only two variables: (1) humans' ability to decode a writing system is determined by their brain and (2) whether someone was taught to read.

Thus, 'dyslexia' is viewed as a property of the child, and nothing to do with current methods of reading instruction or the child's strategy. The main reason for a persistent decoding problem is because you have something wrong with your brain. To explore the fate of this idea, let's begin with the modern research on dyslexia.

Is Dyslexia a Special Reading Disorder?

'Dyslexia' is Greek for 'poor with words' or 'poor reading'. 'He has dyslexia' sounds medical and scientific. 'He has poor reading' doesn't have quite the same impact. Like many medical terms, 'dyslexia' merely describes a state of affairs and has no diagnostic utility. 'Strabismus' means that your eyes are not properly aligned. But the word 'strabismus' doesn't explain *why* your eyes are misaligned.

The term 'dyslexia' was coined by a nineteenth-century ophthalmologist who observed that some brain-damaged patients could no longer read. It was popularized by Samuel Orton, a neuropathologist, who believed on the basis of his observations that severe reading problems were due either to cerebral dominance, or to abnormalities of the language systems of the brain. Though Orton was right about the connection between language and reading, unfortunately these ideas led to the belief that poor readers have brain damage.

This belief reflects a serious misconception about the human brain, along with a failure to consider normal variation in traits. We call complex human traits 'talents'. An inability to sing in tune is due to lack of musical talent not brain damage, and singing is far more natural (biological) than learning to read. Normal variation is on a continuum, but people working from a medical or clinical model tend to think in dichotomies: perfect/imperfect, healthy/diseased, intact/damaged.

We have just reviewed 5,500 years of evidence to show that writing systems are inventions, and that humans do not spontaneously and effortlessly develop writing systems or find it easy to learn them. We have seen that the alphabet is a particularly non-natural writing system. Reading is definitely not a property of the human brain. If reading problems were due to brain damage, they would be immutable or only partially fixable. Progress would be slow and the client never really cured. Some reading programmes for 'dyslexic' children take *years*; a self-fulfilling prophecy.

Of course humans use their brains to learn to decode a writing system. We need the primary visual system (visual cortex) to see and discriminate letters on the page. We need visual-motor commands (frontal eye fields) to control eye movements to scan text smoothly from left to right. We need language systems to remember the order of words in phrases and to analyse meaning and grammatical structure (posterior left hemisphere). We need auditory analysis of sounds in words in order to use a phonetic alphabet (left-brain auditory cortex). We need speech output and articulatory control to read aloud (left-brain speech-motor systems). We need brain systems that integrate these processes (Wernicke's area, parietal lobes, subcortical white matter, basal ganglia). We need to keep our attention focused on what we are doing from one moment to the next (frontal lobes/basal ganglia), and if we're bad at something, it takes more effort (hippocampus) and more brain cortex to do it. Reading engages the entire brain. There is no 'place' or 'box' for reading in the brain. Only when a child shows a clear and enduring deficit in one of these natural abilities, should parents be concerned about a possible biological basis for their child's reading problem, but a biological basis usually means normal variation, not brain damage.

Do dyslexics have brain damage? Twenty years of data from brain-imaging studies and EEG recordings have shown conclusively that people diagnosed 'dyslexic' have no damage to any part of their brain. Studies using modern imaging techniques, such as computerized tomography (CAT) and magnetic resonance imagery (MRI) search for anatomical differences between poor and normal readers. So far, nothing has been found. The only result that is even marginally consistent is a tendency for more poor readers to have symmetric brains. But 35 per cent of the population have symmetric brains. Symmetry is not pathology.

There is research on the microstructure of brain tissue in eight people who had reading problems as determined by school records. But there are serious methodological problems with this study. It wasn't possible to measure reading properly before the people died to verify the nature of their reading difficulties. Many had other brain-related problems which could affect the results, such as epilepsy, severe language disorders, and extreme old age. They found greater brain symmetry and evidence of abnormal cell migration (ectopic nests) in the left and right hemispheres. Whether these abnormalities correlate with reading, or language, or epilepsy, is unclear.

There is an even more serious problem than trying to find 'dyslexia' in the brain. A number of studies on very large populations of children show conclusively that the diagnosis of dyslexia is invalid. This calls into question all research on dyslexics. The diagnosis for many years was based on these assumptions: if a child has a serious reading problem, but normal or above normal intelligence, the child must have a special type of reading disability – 'dyslexia'. Children with low reading scores and low intelligence are supposed to read badly because they have low intelligence.

In 1975, Michael Rutter and William Yule reported their findings from several studies on large populations of children carried out in London and on the Isle of Wight. They were interested in whether there were two types of poor reader: children whose reading test scores were highly discrepant to their age and IQ ('specific reading retardation') versus children with low IQs *and* low reading scores ('general reading backwardness'). They identified a group of children with extreme deviations between IQ and age and a reading score. For example, at age 10, the formula selected children whose reading test scores were 30 months below age and IQ.

Next, they plotted the reading test scores expecting to see a normal, bell-shaped distribution curve. Instead, children with reading/IQ discrepancies had reading test scores that were abnormally distributed. Too many scores clustered at the bottom end of the curve, forming a 'hump', or discontinuity. In a symmetrical distribution, only 2.28 per cent of children should score in the bottom group. Instead, there were 1 per cent (10 years) and 2 per cent (14 years) more of the Isle of Wight children than expected, and 4 per cent more of the London children (10-year-olds) than expected. Rutter and Yule pointed out that these results were just as likely to be due to methods of teaching as to any biological factors.

To find out more about these two types of poor readers, they compared them to a control group of normal readers on a battery of tests. More of the low IQ children had neurological and motor problems. However, poor readers, regardless of type, differed to the controls on these measures: family history of reading difficulty; family history of speech delay (first word spoken after 18 months, first phrase spoken after 24 months); and current speech/articulation problems. These language problems occurred in both groups of poor readers at three times the rate of normal readers. It is clear that speech delays are a predictor for subsequent reading problems. However, this does not mean that reading problems are always caused by speech delays (or that speech delays are due to brain damage).

Rutter and Yule did not believe they had identified 'dyslexia'. They argued strongly against the vague definitions of 'dyslexia' currently in vogue, and the idea that 'dyslexia' is a unitary disorder with a high genetic component. Instead, they cite additional evidence to show that they also found strong environmental effects on reading, such as large family size, the child's temperament, and teacher turnover-rate at the school. They also point out that if dyslexia was a true genetic syndrome, then the heritability should be identical in different geographic regions. Yet the poor readers scoring in the bottom range were four times greater in London than on the Isle of Wight, evidence for an environmental effect. They conclude as follows:

> In short, there has been a complete failure to show that the signs of dyslexia constitute any meaningful pattern. It may be concluded that the question of whether specific reading retardation is or is not dyslexia can be abandoned as meaningless.[2]

Rutter and Yule's clearly stated arguments were ignored, and instead educators decreed that at last proof for 'dyslexia' had been found. For almost ten years, no one even challenged their results. Everybody used a discrepancy measure (reading age considerably lower than IQ would predict) to select subjects for research on reading disabilities (or, in Britain, 'learning difficulties'), and to identify children for special reading services. The discrepancy model underpins US Federal guidelines for the diagnosis of learning disabilities in Public Law 94–142. This law provides funding to school districts for special education. The discrepancy measure is taken so literally in some school districts that a child with a high IQ, around 130, with an average reading test score of 100 (normal reading), would be diagnosed as learning disabled and qualify for special services, but someone who had a very poor reading score, around 85, with a normal IQ of 95, would not. (Both sets of scores are standardized so that 100 is average. Scores in the range 92.5 to 107.5 are normal.)

The first study to challenge Rutter and Yule's findings was carried out in Australia by David Share and his colleagues in 1987. After testing 1,037 children, they found no evidence for two types of reading disorder. They concluded that Rutter and Yule's 'hump' in the data occurred as a result of the way in which the reading tests they used had been designed and normed. The Australians argued strongly that a diagnosis for a special reading disorder must be based on other tests besides a reading test.

The remaining studies date from 1992. Jack Fletcher is one of the team leaders of the Connecticut Longitudinal Study which began in 1983. He and his colleagues reported on 199 poor readers aged between seven and nine. They were divided into four groups on the basis of different statistical methods of computing a discrepancy between IQ and reading. A fifth group (controls) had no reading problems. All children were given a battery of nine tests, some of which were known from previous research to be related to reading. The discrepancy model did not hold up. Children with reading problems, regardless of IQ, all scored badly on one particular test which measures the *ability to hear individual phonemes in words*, a skill required by an alphabetic writing system, but by no other writing system. Children with low IQs did worse on a memory test, but otherwise all the poor readers scored normally on the remaining tests.

Fletcher and his colleagues concluded that there is no evidence for any special type of reading disorder like 'dyslexia' and that reading scores are on a continuum from good to bad. They comment that if children with lower IQs and reading problems were included in the learning disability diagnosis, 'this would mean that 25 per cent of the population could be defined as reading impaired, a figure that would probably frighten policymakers and state-federal funding sources'.[3] (The national literacy survey data for Connecticut schoolchildren showed that 34 per cent are below basic skills in reading.)

Fletcher was also a collaborator in a Canadian study with researchers at Windsor, Ontario. They tested 1,069 children referred to a clinic for reading problems. Children were aged between nine and fourteen. The children were divided into four groups based on different calculations of IQ/reading discrepancy scores, and were given a battery of ten tests by the Canadian psychologists. All children with poor reading scores, regardless of IQ, regardless of group, did badly on the same two tests. One test measured the ability to blend isolated phonemes into words, and the other, the ability to decode letters into phonemes. Once again the results were the same, and the conclusion was that there is no basis for any special category of reading disorder.

Sally Shaywitz, project director, and other researchers on the Connecticut Longitudinal Study, followed children over time to see if the discrepancy diagnosis of 'dyslexia' was constant from one grade to another. They tested the same children many times from first to sixth grade. Twenty-five children were diagnosed 'dyslexic' in first grade, and 31 in third grade, but only 7 were classified as 'dyslexic' in both grades. The same thing happened at fifth grade. Of the 24 children classified as 'dyslexic' at fifth grade, only 14 were also 'dyslexic' in third grade. The chance of being diagnosed 'dyslexic' in sixth grade as a function of being diagnosed 'dyslexic' at first grade was only 17 per cent.

Similar findings are reported by scientists Keith Stanovich and Linda Siegel of the Ontario Institute in Toronto. They reanalysed data from a database of more than 1,500 children, fitting poor readers into various groups based on discrepancy scores. They could find no differences in the performance of types of poor readers on a wide variety of tests, except for tests requiring the child to read phonetically spelled nonsense words. All poor readers had the same problems with these tests regardless of their IQ. Stanovich and Siegel conclude as follows:

> If there is a special group of children with reading disabilities who are behaviorally, cognitively, genetically, or neurologically different, it is becoming increasingly unlikely that they can be easily identified by using IQ discrepancy as a proxy for the genetic and neurological differences themselves. Thus, the basic assumption that underlies decades of classification in research and educational practice regarding reading disabilities is becoming increasingly untenable.[4]

Finally, a study on twins has been carried out by Bruce Pennington and his co-workers at the University of Denver. They tested 538 pairs of twins, dividing the children into four groups based on age, IQ and reading scores. They had the same results. All poor readers, regardless of group, IQ or age, had problems reading phonetically spelled nonsense words and nothing else. The authors concluded that there is no evidence for any test that can identify groups of poor readers who do or do not have a discrepancy between IQ and reading scores.

These studies sound the death knell of 'dyslexia' and 'learning difficulties' as a category of specific reading retardation. The truth is simply that if a child scores badly on a reading test, he or she has a reading problem and needs to be taught to read. There is no evidence from any of the studies or any of the tests that most poor readers have anything wrong with them, except the inability to read an alphabetic writing system, and this in turn is related to a difficulty in accessing the phonemic level of speech. In other words, children with reading problems have a hard time ungluing sounds in words, exactly what the Brahmin priests must have predicted 2,500 years ago when they opted not to use an alphabet. Humans have no reason to unglue sounds in words unless they have to learn an alphabetic writing system. So whether or not this ability is brain-based or genetic is really moot.

A Gene for Bad Reading?

The demise of the dyslexia diagnosis is a serious blow for heritability studies and genetic models of 'dyslexia'. These studies use a formula to diagnose 'dyslexia' based upon discrepancies between reading scores, age and IQ. In family studies, a discrepancy score is used to identify children, their parents and other family members. If scores are not discrepant, you are not included in the study.

Three scientists, Bruce Pennington, John DeFries, and Richard Olson, are studying the heritability and genetics of 'dyslexia'. They have carried out a number of studies on families and twins. Their findings seem impressive. Between 35 per cent and 40 per cent of first-degree relatives of very poor readers also have a reading problem. Sons of affected fathers have a 40 per cent risk, sons of affected mothers, a 35 per cent risk. Daughters of affected mothers or fathers have a risk of only about 18 per cent.

Studies on twins are a more powerful research tool because monozygotic twins (one egg splitting) have 100 per cent genetic inheritance, and dizygotic twins (two eggs) only 50 per cent inheritance. Comparing the heritability of 'dyslexia' in populations of the two types of twins, it was found that with IQ controlled (subtracted from the equations), 'dyslexia' is 30 per cent heritable.

What does this actually mean? Superficially it means that you can predict a reading problem with 30 per cent accuracy knowing the family history. This means, also, that the miss-rate in this prediction is 70 per cent. However, there are two other factors to consider. Now that the diagnosis of dyslexia has been shown to be invalid, what would happen if *all* poor readers, regardless of IQ, were included in the heritability and twin studies? What exactly is being inherited: the reading problem, the discrepancy effect, or the inability to unglue sounds in words?

The second issue is that 43 per cent of American nine-year-olds are below basic-level skills. You could predict that a child would be reading poorly in *any household in America* with 43 per cent accuracy, knowing nothing about the family members' reading skills. There are 40 per cent of children below basic skills in reading in Colorado, where many of these family and twin studies have been done.

Nevertheless, something very interesting came out of these studies. In a twin study by Richard Olson and others reported in 1989, they found that 'dyslexics' had difficulty *ungluing phonemes in words and manipulating them*. They couldn't use 'Pig Latin'. In Pig Latin, you remove the first consonant in a word, put it at the end and add /ay/. 'Cat' in Pig Latin is 'at-cay'. The Pig Latin score was almost as powerful in estimating heritability as the reading score. Subsequent research on twins showed that phonological decoding had a heritability of around 80 per cent.

Pennington, in his book on learning difficulties, reports on the efforts to discover what kind of gene mechanism or type of genetic transmission can explain how 'dyslexia' is inherited. Here are two of his conclusions:

> 'It was estimated that dyslexia is linked to chromosome 15 in about 20 per cent of families.'
>
> 'Existing data support genetic heterogeneity in the transmission of dyslexia, and the recent analyses provide support for a partially dominant major gene or genes.'[5]

Genes for bad reading?!

If reading is a biological property of the brain, transmitted genetically, then this must have occurred by Lamarckian evolution. (In Larmarckian evolution, what parents learn during their lifetime is transmitted to their offspring, a theory for which there is zero scientific support.) A genetic model for reading cannot work by Darwinian evolution, because universal education is only a hundred years old, much too short a time-span for such a complex behaviour to evolve.

Reading cannot be coded in genes any more than other highly skilled behaviours. For example, skateboarding might be found to have high heritability. Obviously, what is inherited is not 'skateboarding', it is the necessary aptitudes to *be able to skateboard*. It is these skills that are properties of brains, such as *balance* and *visuo-motor* integration. If skateboarding was as highly valued socially as reading, it would be no more nonsensical to look for a skateboarding gene than a reading gene. Here are other possibilities of disorders that might be genetically transmitted:

Dysmechanica: the inability to repair machines.
Dysmusia: the inability to read musical notation.
Dysmobilia: the inability to drive a car.
Dyscarpenteria: the inability to build things out of wood.

Pennington doesn't really mean 'dyslexia' is inherited, because he says, 'the final common pathway in most of developmental dyslexia is a deficit in phonological coding.'[6] In other words, he recognizes that it is phonological processing (the auditory skill to hear and manipulate sounds in words) that might be inherited and not reading. Pennington's use of habitual language trails behind what he actually thinks and knows. The problem here is that the layman, not familiar with twenty-five years of research, is confused by this habit. Parents or family members of poor readers need to know that there is no valid diagnosis for 'dyslexia', no such thing as a 'reading gene', and no such thing as 'inheriting bad reading'. Nor is a weakness in discriminating phonemes due to organic brain damage.

Although it is meaningless to look for a 'reading gene', subskills or aptitudes that are important to learning reading may be heritable, just as balance and visuo-motor skills may be heritable. It is the *natural* abilities of people that are transmitted genetically, not unnatural abilities that depend upon instruction and involve the integration of many subskills. This does not mean that these subskills are untrainable, or that they would spontaneously be brought to bear on a task when instruction was misleading. There is now an enormous literature on subskills related to reading. These studies will be considered next.

Phonological Awareness and Reading

Subskills important in learning to read were first studied using correlational research designs. Correlational research is used at the outset of scientific inquiry. It helps determine what things or events go together or predict each other. Here is an example of a simple correlation: the speed at which you drive to the supermarket is highly correlated to the time it takes to get there. Here is an example of a more complex relationship: weight loss is correlated to the intake of total calories and fat calories, *and* to the amount of exercise you get, *and* to your basal metabolism or 'set point'.

Correlations don't allow you to determine *causes* of the relationships. You can get the flavour of this problem and the complexity created by correlational patterns if you ask these questions: Does metabolic rate cause eating which causes exercise which causes weight? Does weight cause exercise which causes eating which causes metabolic rate? Or, does exercise cause metabolic rate which causes eating which causes weight? I think you get the point. You can't discover causes just by calculating what goes together. The only way to answer these questions is to do an experiment: for example, change fat calorie intake, while you hold everything else (exercise, total calories) constant.

With these reservations in mind, correlations are a powerful tool for any initial inquiry. Experiments are only practical when all possible connections have been mapped out. You wouldn't want to waste time training poor readers' eyesight unless vision was correlated to reading. In the early stages of research on reading, scientists began by looking at simple relationships: does a single test score predict a single reading score? Many different tests were tried: eye-movement control, visual acuity, auditory discrimination, memory, vocabulary, IQ, and so forth. This was followed by more ambitious studies using several of these tests at once. Next came the 'kitchen sink' phase, in which batteries of tests were given to large populations of children to find out what the tests had in common (which tests are redundant), and which test was the most powerful predictor of reading, the next most powerful, and so on. Finally, there is the fine-tuning period, which is where we are right now. Fine tuning can go on until everybody gets tired of it, or another breakthrough takes place.

In the research presented so far, we have seen that one subskill consistently predicted reading scores and that is sensitivity to sounds in speech. 'Phonological awareness' and 'phonological processing' are major buzzwords in reading research today. The term 'phonological' is broad and means any kind of analysis of sounds in words: syllables, syllable fragments, and phonemes.

Several important scientific discoveries took place during the mid 1960s and early 1970s. That these discoveries were, in fact, major breakthroughs has only been recognized for about ten years. This is an example of the real world knocking and only a few people listening. The research came from different parts of the United States and was conducted by people who had never met and who were in entirely different disciplines.

Jerome Rosner was working at the University of Pittsburgh at the Learning Research and Development Center. Rosner and his colleague Dorothy Simon began a quest to develop a test of auditory analysis that would correlate with (predict) reading-test scores. They reasoned that while children needed to learn a phonetic alphabet, they would do this efficiently *only* to the degree that they could hear and manipulate sounds (phonemes) in words. Up to this time, simple auditory tests did not correlate well with reading.

They designed the Auditory Analysis Test (AAT), in which the child has to mentally remove a sound from a word he hears, close up the remaining sounds, and then repeat back the word that's left.[7] The simplest part of the test uses compound words. The tester reads the statement: 'Say cowboy. Now say it again without the cow.' The child must respond with the word that remains: 'boy'. The test has various levels of difficulty including removing the initial consonant ('smile without the /s/' = mile), removing a consonant from a cluster ('steam without the /t/' = seam), or removing an inner syllable ('continent without the /in/' = content).

Rosner and Simon gave this test to 284 children aged five to twelve. The children were also tested on the reading subtests of the Stanford Achievement Test and the Otis Lennon IQ test. Rosner and Simon found that the AAT was too difficult for the five-year-olds, but for the other children, the AAT scores were highly correlated to reading in every year, with correlations ranging from .59 to .84. (A perfect correlation is 1.0.) The AAT was also correlated to IQ. This relationship was statistically subtracted to get a pure measure of the correlation between AAT and reading, independent of the children's intelligence. When this was done, the AAT and reading scores were still strongly correlated, with values ranging from .40 in six-year-olds to a high of .69 in eight-year-olds. You can estimate the accuracy of predicting one score from another by squaring these numbers (.40 x.40, .69 x.69).

These values range from 16 per cent to 48 per cent predictability between scores on the AAT and scores on a reading test.

The order of difficulty of the forty items on the test (grouped under six headings) was calculated:

1. Remove a word from a compound word.
2. Remove the initial phoneme from a CVC word.
3. Remove the final phoneme from a CVC word.
4. Remove the initial phoneme from a cluster: CCVC.
5. Remove an inner phoneme from a cluster: CCV or VCC.
6. Remove an inner syllable from a multi-syllable word.

Performance on this test was highly dependent upon the age of the child. The test was too difficult for most of the five-year-olds, and 60 per cent of the six- and seven-year-olds got only about half the items correct. After this age, the scores fit a normal distribution.

Rosner and Simon demonstrated that there was a powerful connection between the ability to *hear* and manipulate sounds in words (to unglue sounds) and the ability to read and comprehend text. But they were left with the tantalizing question: does some innate ability to hear sounds in words *cause* a child to be able to learn a phonetic alphabet, or does learning a phonetic alphabet *cause* a child to be able to hear sounds in words? 'The logical position is that the two are completely interwoven,' Rosner and Simon concluded in their discussion of the data.

Meanwhile, in a small university town halfway up the California coast, Pat Lindamood had another breakthrough. Armed with two masters degrees, one in reading and one in speech and hearing sciences, Lindamood opened a clinic for children in the sixties. Despite her extensive training, she found that most of what she had been taught was irrelevant, and nothing really worked at all for the serious cases of reading disability or speech disorders. Because she had two kinds of clients and two types of training, she was able to make connections that someone else might not have made. She observed that people with speech disorders had reading problems as well. Her initial insight came from an unanswered question: does the person with a speech disorder suffer from a motor disability (an articulation or output dysfunction) as she had been taught, or do they also suffer from an auditory processing deficit (a perceptual or input dysfunction)? Could it be that the reason people with speech difficulties speak in such a peculiar manner, is because that's the way they *hear other people speak*? And could an auditory processing problem explain their inability to use a phonetic alphabet? Given these questions, how could you ever find the answer? All the tests and materials she had at her disposal required a spoken response from the client. This made it impossible to tease apart a motor dysfunction from an auditory processing dysfunction.

Lindamood pondered on this problem for months. One day she was working with a young girl with a severe speech disorder who was clearly in a state of despair and who could scarcely make eye contact. Lindamood's sense of frustration at her inadequacy was overwhelming. That night she awoke around 3 a.m. with an image of a row of coloured blocks. She roused her husband Charles, a linguist, and together they worked until dawn on the basic elements of a test of auditory discrimination. This eventually became the LAC test (Lindamood Test of Auditory Conceptualization). Lindamood's reasoning was identical to Rosner and Simon's, that a valid test of auditory processing had to involve the manipulation of phonemes in words. Unlike Rosner, she couldn't use a vocal response to answer her particular question. Instead, she had clients represent sequences of phonemes *silently* as rows of coloured blocks, first individually: /b/, /b/, /v/, and next in nonsense words in a sequence or chain. The tester says: 'If that is /i/, show me /ip/. If that says /ip/, show me /bip/. If that is /bip/ show me /bop/,' and so forth. Each sound is represented by a different colour (any colour will do) and blocks are added, exchanged or removed as the chain proceeds.

This basic tool became the foundation of a new method for remedying not only speech disorders but reading disabilities as well. Her initial insight was correct. Children and adults with speech deficits failed this test. They cannot speak clearly because they cannot *hear* speech clearly. Children who speak normally can also have serious reading problems, and many of these children, it turned out, also had weak phonemic processing skill but to a much milder degree.

In a team effort with Robert Calfee at Stanford University, the Lindamoods gave the LAC test to 660 normal children aged five to eighteen. The children were also tested on the reading and spelling subtests of the Wide Range Achievement test. There were high correlations between the LAC scores and reading and spelling, ranging from .66 to .81. The average correlation between LAC scores and reading for the 660 children was .73. These values would be lower if the relationship of IQ to reading had been subtracted, but they are very similar to Rosner and Simon's results. They are also subject to the same criticism: there is no way to confirm the direction of causality based upon simple correlations.

On the opposite seaboard, in New Haven, Connecticut, research was being conducted at the Haskins Laboratory on the perception and production of speech by Alvin Liberman and Donald Shankweiler and their colleagues. Isabelle Liberman, a psychologist, and wife of Alvin, joined the faculty at the University of Connecticut and began an important collaboration on the relationship between the perception of speech and reading. She reasoned that there must be a connection between the ability to hear individual sounds in words and reading an alphabetic writing system, but that this relationship was not obvious. Most poor readers speak normally and can recite the alphabet fluently. To decode an alphabetic writing system, you must be consciously aware of the order of phonemes in words. This aptitude is not essential to understanding speech, which is produced in co-articulated chunks of sound – syllables, words and phrases. Alvin Liberman and Donald Shankweiler proposed in 1967, on the basis of their extensive research on speech perception, that the language systems of the brain reorganize to process speech at the level of the syllable and not the phoneme. This topic will be revisited in the chapter on children's language development.

Isabelle Liberman, Donald Shankweiler, and their students published research in which they attempted to discover which kinds of phonological processing were critical to learning to read. They explored sensitivity to rhyme, the ability to segment by syllables and by phonemes, the ability to remember the order of words in word lists and the order of sounds in words. Their results revealed that children do not spontaneously learn to segment words into their constituent parts just because they are exposed to an alphabetic writing system. Many children are not even aware of a 'word' as a separate unit of speech. Syllables (counting beats) are easier to segment than phonemes, and the ability to segment phonemes is predictive of subsequent reading skill. Liberman found that at the end of first grade (age seven), approximately 30 per cent of children had *no understanding that words can be segmented into phonemes*.

Their research also indicated that poor readers had more trouble repeating back lists of letters or words in the correct sequence (spoon, tree, floor, dog, sheet, etc.), but no problem remembering sequences of environmental sounds (animal calls, bird calls, various noises), or visual patterns. The researchers concluded that children with reading problems have difficulty in one or more aspects of phonological processing. Liberman's extensive research, and the number of graduate students she inspired to carry on this work are responsible for putting phonological processing on the map. These early studies have been supported by hundreds more from countries around the world.

A similar discovery was made by Lynette Bradley and Peter Bryant at Oxford University in the late 1970s. They developed a simpler test of phonological awareness which four- and five-year-olds could do. The child had to say the 'odd one out' from a list of three words. Words varied in first sound (alliteration): 'Which word has a different first sound – hill, pig, pin,' or in whether the rhyme changed ('cot, pot, hat'). Performance on this test correlated with subsequent reading and spelling test scores.

In addition to the phonological processing and verbal memory difficulties in poor readers, there was one other discovery from this period that has stood the test of time. Patients with brain damage to the left hemisphere can have word-finding or 'naming' problems. Martha Denckla, a neurologist at Columbia University's College of Physicians and Surgeons, reasoned that reading difficulties may be due to a language-based dysfunction. Therefore, children diagnosed dyslexic may also have problems in naming similar to those of brain-damaged patients. In particular, she was interested in naming fluency for well-known, over-learned ('automatic') words. In 1972, she published a test called Rapid Automatized Naming along with test scores for children in the age range five to eleven years. The children had to name fifty squares of colours as rapidly as possible. The colours were red, green, blue, yellow, and black, arranged in rows and repeating randomly. The norms were used to compare children referred for reading problems. Ten per cent of these poor readers were found to have abnormally slow naming times.

In 1976, Denckla and Rita Rudel expanded the test to include naming of pictures, letters and digits. They tested 128 children, aged seven to eleven, diagnosed with a learning disability (either reading or maths), and 120 average readers. Charts of pictures, letters, and digits were prepared in the same way, five different items repeated randomly for a total of fifty items. Denckla and Rudel found that the poor readers had the slowest naming speed, the low-maths learning disabled children were faster, and normal controls faster still. There was a strong developmental trend for children's naming speed to increase with age, and the naming fluency measure did not level out by the age of eleven.

More recent studies on naming speed, particularly the work of Maryanne Wolf, have shown that letter and digit naming speeds are more highly correlated to reading skill (correlations ranging from .50 to .57) than naming speeds for objects or colours, which correlate to reading at around .35–.38, about a 10 per cent prediction rate, which is what Denckla originally found. Naming objects and colours is a truer reflection of natural or biologically based ability than naming letters and digits, and though these correlations are low, they are consistent across many studies.

We now have evidence of the following tests correlating to reading scores: auditory analysis of phonemes; verbal short-term memory; sensitivity to alliteration and rhyme; ability to segment syllables and phonemes; naming or word-finding speed.

These initial breakthroughs prompted other researchers to begin investigations of a variety of language-related abilities. There are now hundreds of such studies and it is only possible to summarize the findings. Tests that involve an analysis and manipulation of phonemes (phonemic awareness) correlate with each other. These are tests like Rosner and Simon's AAT, the Lindamoods' LAC test, tests of sounding out words (segmenting), combining individual phonemes into words (blending), Pig Latin, and so forth. All of these tests are measuring some aspect of the same skill, and any one of them is a powerful predictor of reading ability in absolutely everyone's data. This is the real world knocking with a sledgehammer.

The developmental aspects of children's ability to hear and discriminate phonemes in words have been worked out in detail by Margaretha Vandervelden and Linda Siegel, in Toronto. They tested 108 children aged five to seven, and developed simpler tests for the younger children.

They found that the sequence for being able to hear individual phonemes in simple one-syllable words, was initial consonant first (what's the first sound in 'bat?'), then final consonant, then vowel, and last, separating consonant clusters (what's the first sound in 'frog'?), which was the most difficult task of all, confirming Rosner and Simon's original report. The most powerful predictor of reading and spelling for the younger children was a test of segmenting, and the most powerful predictor for the seven-year-olds was Rosner and Simon's AAT. This single test predicted reading scores at .85 and spelling scores at .78.

Sensitivity to rhyme has not been shown to be a strong predictor of reading skill. In the study by Bradley and Bryant mentioned above, the combined alliteration and rhyme scores predicted reading and spelling three years later by only 5–10 per cent, once IQ, vocabulary and memory test scores had been statistically controlled. These authors replicated this result in 1990, but found that alliteration (first phoneme) was a more consistent predictor than rhyme, though neither effect was robust once mother's education and IQ were taken into account.

The importance of early rhyming sensitivity, and especially the ability to decode by analogy to words with rhyming endings ('beak', 'weak') has been stressed by some British researchers. Usha Goswami and Peter Bryant suggest that children first master 'onset-rime' segmenting, begin to decode by analogy to words with rhyming endings, and only later develop phoneme awareness. They also advocate that rhyming and onset-rime ('word-families') training be an integral part of early reading instruction. Some educational publishers have incorporated these ideas into their reading schemes. Usha Goswami, for example, is an author for the 'Oxford Reading Tree'. The notion that 'rhyming' = 'phonological awareness' = 'phoneme awareness' has permeated the National Curriculum guidelines. Teachers are led to believe that teaching rhyming games and segmenting by onset and rime will have a direct impact on learning to read and spell.

Several recent studies in the US, UK and Sweden have shown conclusively that children do not use rhyming endings to decode words; hardly ever decode by analogy to other words; and that ability to dissect words into onsets and rimes has no impact whatsoever on learning to read and spell. Kate Nation and Charles Hulme tested seventy-five lower-middle-class children (Year 1, Year 3 and Year 4) in York, on tests of rhyming, alliteration, and segmenting onset-rimes and phonemes. Only phoneme-segmenting strongly predicted reading and spelling test scores. Onset-rime was not easy for the children and scores were a constant 55 per cent correct across all ages. Phoneme-segmenting improved noticeably with age. The authors concluded: 'Children's ability to perform onset-rime segmentation was not in any way related to literacy.' Also of interest in this study, was that children's reading and spelling scores began in the normal range but steadily declined with age compared to national British norms. They had lost six months by age eight, and one year by age nine.

My own research on strategies, discussed in Chapter 2, revealed much the same result. Altogether 132 reading tests were classified by types of decoding errors. Children made virtually no errors by 'analogy' to other words. Out of 1,780 errors, only seven (0.03 per cent or .003) could have been possible analogies to other words. However, these errors were also highly probable *phonetic* decodings. One example was reading 'money' as 'moany'. This could be a possible analogy to 'phoney', but it is much more likely that children recognize o–e as a common spelling for the sound /oe/ (cone, phone, broke, home, etc.), than it is that children search in visual memory for a word that 'looks like' the one they are looking at, mentally swap out letters and then sounds, and finally say the word. Adults with a vast experience of print may decode unfamiliar words by analogy to other words, but children do not.

The Belgian psychologist José Morais found this was true for adults as well. He tested illiterate poets, none of whom had any difficulty rhyming, but who were unable to read. Other research has shown that neither simple rhyming tests nor syllable segmenting are good predictors of reading test scores.

Tests that combine rhyming and memory are correlated to reading, but the data are conflicting. The first evidence for this effect was a study by Donald Shankweiler and Isabelle Liberman. They found that good readers were more susceptible to 'rhyming confusion' when they were asked to repeat back letters that rhymed – D, C, P, G, B, versus letters that did not – L, H, J, F, X. Later, Virginia Mann and Isabelle Liberman found the same effect with lists of rhyming words. However, David Share, Anthony Jorm and their colleagues in New Zealand, using a much larger population of children, found that good readers were consistently *better* than poor readers in remembering sentences that rhymed. My students and I replicated this effect on ninety-four six- and seven-year-olds, who were asked to repeat back lists of rhyming words. Good memory for rhyming words was strongly correlated to reading skill but *only for girls*. The scores of the boys were uncorrelated.

Most of the studies reported so far measure the connection between subskills and reading in real time. They measure what 'goes together' now and not whether a particular test can predict reading scores *later* in time. In the study by Bradley and Bryant they measured phonological awareness in young children who couldn't read, and then correlated this score to reading test scores when children were older. A prediction over time provides tentative evidence for cause, on the assumption that time does not go backwards. Several studies of this type have been carried out in the US, Britain, Australia, Denmark and Norway. They all report more or less the same result. The major predictor of reading skill from ages five and six (independent of reading scores themselves) is a test of phoneme analysis. These are tests like the AAT, the LAC, and tests of segmenting and blending phonemes. Simple rhyming, sensitivity to rhyme, and syllable segmenting are not good predictors of reading scores over time.

However, while phoneme-awareness skill predicts well for about a year or two in the early school years, it doesn't predict well over longer periods. For example, we found that LAC test scores for six-year-olds as they began first grade could predict reading test scores at the end of the year with about 40 per cent accuracy, but did not predict reading ability when the same children were tested in third grade (aged eight). This is a function of the rapidly changing skill in phoneme-awareness in young children, and also of correlational research designs. As time goes by, *reading predicts reading* more than anything else. When two measures are nearly perfectly correlated, no other test score can contribute further to the relationship.

This does not mean that phoneme-awareness becomes less important for poor readers as they grow older. Phoneme processing deficits in adult non-readers were found in a landmark study by José Morais and his colleagues in 1979. They tested adult illiterates in Portugal who had never been taught to read, and compared them to other former illiterates who had been taught to read. They measured the ability to segment words into phonemes. The people who had been taught to read were superior on the phoneme segmenting tasks. Charles Read and three Chinese colleagues found that Chinese people who had originally learned to read by memorizing whole characters were poor at segmenting by phonemes. Those who had learned with a phonetic alphabet had good segmenting skills.

Ilana Ben-Dror, Ram Frost and Shlomo Bentin tested two groups of adult bilingual speakers of Hebrew and English. One group had learned to read and write English as children, and the other group had learned the Hebrew consonantal alphabet, where letters represent CV or VC units (diphones). They were asked to delete the 'first sound' from spoken words. The group who had learned English writing first, deleted the initial consonant – /b/ in 'bat'. The group who had learned Hebrew first deleted CV diphones instead – /ba/ in 'bat'.

These studies show the strong impact of the type of writing system and type of instruction on the development of phonemic awareness – an environmental effect – and restate the point that you do not acquire this aptitude unless you need it. So far the evidence could support four possible conclusions:

1. The ability to access the phoneme level of speech is heritable. Phoneme-awareness is on a continuum of innate ability (normal variation), and good/bad phoneme-awareness runs in families, just as musical talent does.

2. Phoneme-awareness is acquired through learning an alphabetic writing system.

3. Phoneme-awareness fails to be acquired in learning to read because the instruction is poor.

4. Phoneme-awareness is excellent but never applied by the child as a decoding strategy.

I want to close this section with a cautionary tale to explain the fourth point. Having good phonemic awareness is no *guarantee* that someone will automatically use it. This connection is not a given.

Let me introduce you to Alice.

Alice was a subject in one of our research projects. At the age of six she scored at the top of almost every test we gave. Her vocabulary score placed her in the highly gifted range with a score of 140 (comparable to a 140 Verbal IQ). She was the only child we tested to score 100 per cent on the LAC test of phoneme-awareness. Her verbal and visual memory were excellent. Her reading score placed her a full year ahead for her age. By third grade (aged eight), Alice was the second worst reader out of two third-grade classes and was making no further progress. I also discovered that she got 100 per cent correct on spelling tests for words she could not read (like Tommy in the opening story).

When I retested her at third grade, I looked in detail at both sets of transcriptions of her errors on the reading test. It was almost as though no time had elapsed. Alice succeeded in reading only ten more words on the test. She made exactly the same mistakes on many of the same words that she made nearly two years before, reading 'grade' for 'garage', 'curl' for 'cruel', 'rake' for 'wreck', and 'incure' for 'inquire'. When Alice got to a certain point on the test, she turned to me and said: 'I can't read any more of these words because I have never seen them before.'

Translated this means: 'I can only read words that I have been individually taught. I have no understanding of the principles of a phonetic alphabet and cannot use these principles to decode unfamiliar words.'

Alice was using a combination of two strategies. Most of her errors were whole-word guesses. Occasionally, she decided to slow down and sound out chunks of words (word-part assembling), but this didn't work much better. How could this have happened to someone who was predicted to be the best reader in the class, according to all her scores in first grade? Meanwhile, Alice had become a total nuisance in class, disobedient, disruptive, and sometimes rude.

I asked to work with her to discover more about the nature of her processing strategy. I was curious about what had become of her phenomenal ability. Had her phoneme analysis skill deteriorated over the past two years, withered away with disuse, or was it still intact? I got permission from her parents to work with her during the lunch hour. We used the Lindamood programme, and as I proceeded through the step-by-step exercises, Alice continued to surprise me. Having worked for hours with poor readers, I knew how long it took for some of these exercises to be mastered. Alice mastered them immediately. After about six hours of work, she was reading (decoding) multi-syllable nonsense words (pseudo-words) up to twenty sounds long ('prerauncherchoidingly') with no difficulty whatsoever, that is, as long as we were working with the movable alphabet tiles which had digraphs clearly demarcated from single letters.

Alice could even *create* these complex nonsense words and check me to see if I read them correctly. I couldn't trick her. But the moment we tried to move back to print on a page, she began to experience difficulty and promptly fell into her old routine of guessing whole words and assembling word parts. It was a habit reinforced by many years of practice and was now imbued with a visible sense of panic. This panic forced her on through the text at an ever increasing pace, misreading word after word. To try to solve the problem, I forced her to stop at every misread word and represent it in the movable alphabet. This allowed her to experience a direct relationship between how the word looked with the letter tiles and how it looked on the page. But this activity was frustrating and took much longer to complete than the initial training. It provided me with keen insight into how difficult it is to shift a habit that has become so ingrained, even for a child of remarkable intelligence who could effortlessly decode phonetically, and who now had a complete grasp of the logic of the alphabetic code.

I want to emphasize how important this case is for understanding the reading process. Since working with Alice, we have seen many 'Alices' in our clinical research:

1. Children who are taught by the same teacher in the same classroom with the same method will nevertheless, unless carefully monitored, each adopt their own strategies for learning to read.

2. Children are surrounded by print. Many begin to try to read at very young ages. Letting them drift along using their invented strategies, without intervention, may harm them for life.

3. Children with high verbal intelligence and good visual memory can score in the normal or even superior range on reading tests in the early school years, *despite* using a whole-word guessing strategy. These children will go undetected until the second or third year, when their memory capacity becomes overloaded.

4. When children begin to fail, their behaviour deteriorates. Alice's parents had been asked to 'think about whether she might be better off in a state school'. (This private school prided itself on excellent SAT [Scholastic Aptitude Test] scores and college admissions.) Her misbehaviour was an added impetus to get her out of the classroom. In a state school, Alice would have been reading at grade level (according to test norms) whereas the children in this school were

reading well above grade level. For Alice, grade-level (score of 100) would be 40 points below her verbal IQ of 140.

5. Possessing *all* the talents to be an expert reader is no guarantee that you will use them if the teaching is inappropriate or inadequate. Alice's outstanding ability in phoneme analysis had never been engaged at any point in her reading instruction.

This story answers one more question raised at the beginning of this chapter. Yes, a child can fail to learn to read entirely by chance, unless the teacher is careful to monitor what each child is doing, *and* knows how to prevent bad habits from continuing. This makes it all the more important to teach reading correctly in the beginning, the focus of the final section of this book. (A strategies test is included in Chapter 12.)

The remaining topics in this chapter cover three areas of research that may be of concern to many parents and teachers. These are speech and language delays and their link to phonemic awareness and reading; the relationship between IQ and reading; and the relationship between vision and reading. The findings from these studies will be summarized briefly at the end of the chapter. If these topics are of little interest, you may want to skip ahead to the conclusions.

Speech and Language and Reading

We have already seen, from Michael Rutter and William Yule's research, that speech problems predict reading problems and, from Pat Lindamood's discovery, that speech problems can be caused by the inability to hear speech accurately. It is not surprising that children with speech and language delays have trouble with an alphabetic writing system. Severe and persistent inability to hear and reproduce speech sounds is a candidate for a possible biological marker for potential reading problems in some children. This does not mean that biology is destiny, because speech problems are remediable. It does mean, however, that if a child has speech difficulties, these could affect their ability to read if uncorrected.

So far, science has not resolved all the important issues on this topic. Research on language and speech development has been ongoing for decades, and the different types of disabilities have been well documented. Unfortunately, tests used to measure these types of disabilities are poorly designed and unreliable, and this makes it hard to determine which kinds of language and speech problems affect reading and which do not.

Speech perception and production in early childhood is highly variable from one child to another. My students and I tested nearly 200 children aged three to seven. The children were asked to repeat back 40 nonsense words (in 'Martian') which conformed to the syllable structure of English, gradually increasing in length and syllable complexity. They had to hear the sounds accurately and reproduce them. Three-year-olds performed erratically, scoring as low as one or two correct to over 75 per cent correct. By the age of four the average was around 50 per cent correct. At five, the average was 75 per cent correct. At age six, 80 per cent of the children scored 75 per cent correct or higher, and nearly half of the seven-year-olds scored at or above 90 per cent. Table 7.1 illustrates the range of scores for each age group, as well as the fact that high individual variation in speech analysis and production is common throughout the period that children are beginning to read. (The nonsense-word repetition test is in Chapter 12.)

Accuracy in speech production continues to improve until adulthood and perhaps beyond. In 1971, F. M. Hull and others in the US published the National Speech and Hearing Survey on 38,800 children, each individually tested on various measures of speech production by trained specialists. These data are illustrated in Figure 7.1. The children's speech was rated as 'acceptable', 'moderate deviation', and 'severe'. The graph illustrates a trade-off. The number of children

TABLE 7.1   Percentage of Children Scoring at Five Levels on the Nonsense-word Repetition Test

Age	Below 25%	25–49%	50–74%	75–89%	90–100%
3	27%	27%	36%	9%	0
4	0	29%	51%	15%	5%
5	0	0	38%	50%	12%
6	0	3%	17%	45%	35%
7	0	0	16%	37%	47%

with 'acceptable' speech increases with age, while the number in the other two categories declines. Severe speech problems dip sharply between the ages of six and eight. Girls have a consistent developmental edge in speech production and clarity, which may explain why reading difficulties have not been found to be 'heritable' for girls.

Taken together, the findings show that the developmental path for speech and language is rapid in early childhood, that speech clarity continues to improve over very long periods of time, that speech perception and production varies *within* age groups until around age eight, and this is partly determined by sex. These complex factors make it difficult to predict language development from an early age. Dorothy Bishop and her colleagues in Britain have found that just under half of the children referred at ages three and four for speech and language problems (those with normal IQs) spoke normally when they were retested at the age of five and a half. When the children were tested again at the age of eight, the children who had had speech difficulties at five also had reading problems.

Research has been carried out on children with reading problems to see if they also have speech or language difficulties. The major finding has been that some poor readers have speech abnormalities. There is not a strong connection between learning to read and vocabulary skills. The relationship of reading and grammatical accuracy is much less clear. William Tunmer and his group found that if reading skill was matched in older poor readers to that of younger good readers, the poor readers performed significantly worse on tests of syntax (grammar), even though, being older, they had more experience with spoken language. They were less able to correct errors in word-order ('The boy home goes'), or supply the correct missing suffix ('Sally went swim—'), or supply the correct missing word ('Peter was born a long time —'). On the other hand, Donald Shankweiler and his colleagues found that what appeared to be a problem with syntax might actually be due to something else. They gave 353 children a number of tests of syntax, such as saying whether a picture matched a spoken sentence. The poor readers had trouble on only one test, which involved adding suffixes to words (four/fourth, five/fifth, courage/courageous), especially when the root word has to change: (five/fifth). They found that scores on the suffix test were almost entirely predicted by phoneme-awareness skill, whereas none of the other tests of syntax related either

FIGURE 7.1 Articulation Development

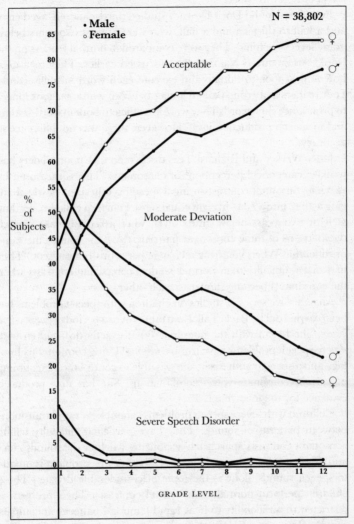

Adapted from: Hull et al., 'National Speech and Hearing Survey (1971), ASHA, 3, 501–9.

to reading or to phoneme-awareness test scores. Obviously, the jury is still out on this issue.

Lynn Snyder and Doris Downey studied thirty children, aged eight and a half to thirteen and a half, who were at least two years below grade level in reading. They were compared to normal readers on the Rapid Automatized Naming test, discussed earlier. They measured how long it took to initiate and execute each word in milliseconds. Poor readers as a group paused longer between words *and* took longer to pronounce each word. They were less efficient both in word-finding and in speech production itself. However, there was no difference in accuracy.

Janet Werker and Richard Tees discovered that poor readers had weaker 'categorical perception' of consonants. This is measured by varying consonant contrasts using a speech synthesizer, slowly changing a /ba/ into a /da/ in eight equal steps. Fourteen children, reading at least two years below grade level, were asked to make various comparisons of these consonant patterns. ('Are the sounds the same or different? When you hear a change press this button,' etc.) They had more difficulty than normal readers comparing contrasts when the consonants became similar to each other.

An extensive series of studies on children with speech problems has been carried out by Paula Tallal and others over a period of twenty-five years. She began with the question: What exactly do children with severe speech problems have trouble *hearing*? Using computer technology and a speech synthesizer, she was able to control the exact timing of various consonant-vowel combinations. She has now produced evidence for the following:

Children with severe speech problems cannot hear rapid transitions between patterns of sounds. They have particular difficulty telling consonant contrasts apart, such as noticing whether the sounds /ba/ and /da/ are the same or different. (Whether this problem is unique to speech sounds alone is the topic of considerable debate.) These children perform normally with vowel contrasts. Their problem is restricted to an inability to hear rapid temporal patterns in complex sounds. The critical information in consonant contrasts like /ba/ and /da/ lasts only about forty milliseconds. When Tallal artificially slowed down these components tenfold by computer, the children could hear the difference easily, just like normal children.

Tallal also studied 20 children, 8–12 years old, who were 1–5 years below grade level in reading, and attended a school for children with learning disabilities. Forty-five per cent of these children were found to be worse than normal readers in discriminating rapid contrasts of complex speech-like sounds. The score on the auditory test correlated at .81 to a nonsense-word reading test, and .64 to word recognition.

This problem does not appear to be due to a developmental delay. Even infants have little trouble discriminating between consonant contrasts. In fact most children can tell consonants apart far better than similar vowel sounds, such as in the words /bet/ and /bit/. Tallal concluded that children with severe speech difficulties may have abnormal development of parts of the brain responsible for processing sounds with rapid transitions, areas in and around the auditory cortex of the left hemisphere.

The ability to detect finer and finer contrasts ('discrimination') is something our brains learn easily, and at all ages. Discrimination is highly trainable. People can learn to tell wines apart by developing their sense of smell. Artists and decorators can discriminate very fine shades of the same colour. The discrimination of musical pitch improves dramatically with learning to play a musical instrument, especially those you have to tune (guitar, violin). Recently Tallal, in collaboration with Michael Merzenich, developed a computerized training game for children with severe receptive speech problems. The game artificially slows down acoustic components of consonants in connected speech until the child can hear them clearly. The speech sounds as if it was recorded underwater. During practice, the contrasts are gradually speeded up in a series of trials. With about sixty hours of training, the seven children in the study made two years of developmental gains in speech perception, and these gains held up at retesting three months later. Standard methods of speech therapy had failed. However, there is *no evidence* that there is any connection between this type of training and reading, despite a media blitz making this claim. Severe speech disorders affect a very small number of children – 3 per cent or less in the US according to the National Speech and Hearing Survey.

The final story is not yet in. So far, there is no definitive breakdown on exactly which children with which kinds of speech and language difficulties will have reading and spelling problems. In clinical observations perhaps the most common auditory problem of poor readers is an inability to hear similar vowel contrasts: bit, bet, bat. Yolanda Post reported in 1996 that very poor readers had striking difficulties with hearing similar vowel contrasts and *no* greater problem with consonant contrasts than good readers. We have also observed in our clinic that children who appear delayed in speech development often learn to read just as quickly as children with no speech delays. These are children who are still saying 'wabbit' at the age of six.

The main issue for parents is that if their child's speech problem persists past the age of four, they should have the child tested and have speech therapy if necessary. Speech difficulties predict problems learning an alphabetic writing system. Equally predictive are the teaching methods currently used in most classrooms. If your child has a speech problem, he or she is in double jeopardy. The earlier the child is taken to a good reading specialist and taught to read *correctly*, the better. Information on how to find one is presented in Chapters 12 and 13.

Intelligence and Reading

A major concern of parents and of researchers has been whether or not low intelligence leads to reading difficulties. The short answer is 'no', unless a child is mentally retarded. Children with low or marginal IQs may be slow in word finding because of poor vocabulary or poor verbal memory, but although they may be slow in matching print to a word, they can still learn to read, if they are taught the code.

Intelligence is moderately and positively correlated to reading. Keith Stanovich and his colleagues compiled results from studies carried out in the US between 1955 and 1982 comparing total IQ scores to reading ability. Here are the median values for these correlations for each grade level: Grade 1 (ages 5–6) = .45; Grade 2 (ages 6–7) = .47; Grade 3 (ages 7–8) = .45; Grades 4–8 (ages 9–14) = .60; and Grades 9 and above (ages 14–18) = .66. This tells us that IQ becomes more closely connected to reading with age. This would be expected as IQ scores are affected by what you learn at school, and what you learn is related to how well you can read. A major problem with these studies is that reading tests at the higher grades include measures of comprehension, verbal reasoning, and spelling. This makes it difficult to know which intelligence subtest is correlated to which kind of reading test.

The IQ subtest with the highest correlation to verbal IQ is a vocabulary test. For this reason, vocabulary tests are often substituted for verbal IQ in research on reading. The most reliable vocabulary test is the Peabody Picture Vocabulary (PPVT). In this test, the child hears a spoken word and must point to one of four pictures that matches the word. Tests that require the child to *read* are, of course, invalid as a measure of vocabulary for a poor reader or a non-reader.

Stanovich and his group presented data on 49 first-graders (aged 5–6), who were tested individually on a variety of tests, including the PPVT. Vocabulary was correlated to reading comprehension (Metropolitan Reading Readiness Test) at a very modest .34, showing only about a 12 per cent connection between the two skills. Further, they found that vocabulary scores were unrelated to performance on any other reading tests or phonological processing tests.

Recent long-term studies show little support for the impact of verbal or performance IQ on reading scores. In 1989, Hans-Jörgen Gjessing and Bjorn Karlsen published their results on 3,090 children in Bergen, Norway who had been tested since 1977. The children did hundreds of tests over that period. Gjessing and Karlsen, along with various collaborators, focused most of their efforts on a group of severe 'dyslexics', who constituted 6.6 per cent of the sample. This group was compared independently to another group classified as 'mentally retarded' (1.6 per cent of the population), and to normal readers. Correlations for the dyslexic group were computed between intelligence tests (total score, verbal and performance subtests) and reading and spelling. The correlations ranged around .30 (9 per cent of the variance).

The Norwegian children identified as dyslexic at the ages of six and seven were given remedial instruction and followed on until they were eight and nine. The authors looked closely at every measure in order to determine the best predictors for successful response to remedial help. The IQ score showed no prediction whatsoever. Furthermore, they also found no support for a special 'dyslexic' type based on a discrepancy measure, confirming the research cited earlier. The highest predictors for successful response to remedial teaching were tests classified as 'complex phonological functions', in other words, tests of phoneme-awareness.

Richard Wagner, Joseph Torgesen and Carol Rashotte studied 244 schoolchildren in Tallahassee, Florida from kindergarten to second grade (ages five to seven). One of their measures was the vocabulary subtest from the Stanford–Binet IQ test. Vocabulary correlated to reading in kindergarten at .26; in first grade at .36; and in second grade at .48. However, they found that vocabulary scores did not predict reading later in time either from kindergarten to first grade, or from first to second grade. The strongest single predictor was a test of phoneme-awareness similar to the AAT.

My students and I tested ninety-four first-grade children on a battery of reading predictors including the Peabody Vocabulary test. The Peabody test scores were uncorrelated to reading scores, nor did vocabulary predict reading ability in a group of forty-two children who were followed over the year.

In contrast, Lynette Bradley and Peter Bryant in Oxford tested children between four and five years of age and followed them for three years. They found that vocabulary was *the* strongest predictor of reading skill, and IQ added even further to this prediction. These robust effects have not been found in most other countries, and may be due to differences in the British educational system, or the British tests. In another study by the same group, children were followed from the age of four to the age of seven. As mentioned earlier, the mother's education predicted 40 per cent of the score on a reading test, and the child's IQ added another 15 per cent to this prediction.

Apart from the findings in Britain, most studies show that intelligence only marginally affects reading skill. Vocabulary does not predict early reading skill, but is more highly correlated to reading in older children and adults, probably because reading a lot improves vocabulary. Nevertheless, as we have seen, a child or adult can have high intelligence and an excellent vocabulary and still have a serious reading problem.

Vision and Reading

Research on vision and reading has been extensive because reading begins with the visual perception of letter forms. One impetus to the study of vision and its connection to reading was the technical advances in eye-movement recording devices in the 1960s. It was soon discovered that poor readers had erratic eye-tracking patterns when they read. They did not scan the text smoothly; they repeated fixations; their eyes frequently jumped backwards, and so forth. Today, everyone agrees that eye movements do not cause reading problems, but that reading problems cause erratic eye movements. In 1985, Keith Rayner in the US did a simple but elegant experiment to prove this point. He had poor readers read very simple text, well within their ability level. Their eye-tracking patterns were completely normal. Next, he had good readers read very difficult material. Their eye-tracking patterns became erratic and looked just like those of the poor readers.

Let's be clear about what is and is not important in this research. To see objects in the normal world, eyes scan multiple directions. Scanning in straight rows from left to right, down one line, and so on, is unnatural and must be trained in a child learning to read. Smooth and efficient scanning develops slowly over childhood.

Reading specialists report that a small minority of poor readers have serious trouble scanning print from left to right. These children are unable to maintain binocular fusion (both eyes consistently in focus) while the eyes are scanning rows of print. This sends the print in and out of focus. Research support for this clinical observation has been provided by J. Stein and M. Fowler at Oxford University. Older children with severe reading problems were compared to younger good readers, matched for reading ability. The older poor readers had poorer binocular control, and visual training *alone* improved reading test scores for these children.

Children with serious problems in binocular control tend to telegraph this in noticeable behaviours. They frequently rub their eyes, squint at the page, cover one eye or turn sideways to read, or move their head from left to right instead of their eyes. Any one of these behaviours, if persistent, is an indication that parents should have their child tested by an optometrist specializing in diagnosing and treating visuo-motor problems. Binocular fusion and controlled scanning are highly trainable.

Most of the time, when children show erratic, unplanned or unsystematic eye-movements as they read, they do not necessarily have something wrong with their eyes. It's not the eye-movement control that's the problem, reading is the problem. Poor readers, like Albert in Chapter 2, who look at the first letter of the word (in focus), and then globally scan to estimate word shape and length (out of focus), also have strange eye-movement patterns. These are caused by a *strategy* problem and not an eye-movement control problem.

Scores of studies on the relationship of vision and reading were based on the popular belief that 'dyslexics' see letters upside down or backwards. Young children sometimes write letters backwards or in mirror-image transformations, because they look at visual patterns globally and not in a sequence. But they do not confuse letters when they are asked to compare them. They can tell you that b and d are different. Robert Calfee and his group at Stanford discovered that young children outgrow any tendency to confuse the orientation of visual symbols. Nevertheless, this belief spawned surveys on children's eyesight and its connection to reading.

In the Norwegian study mentioned above, H. Aasved reports on the visual screening of 2,590 children. They were divided into five groups according to reading ability. There was no difference between the groups on any of the visual tests, which included stereopsis, measures of strabismus, convergence, and central suppression. A group of 259 children, classified as dyslexic, were compared to a group of normal readers. There was no difference between the two groups in the incidence of abnormal eye conditions. Included were measures of acuity, refraction error, strabismus, squint, convergence, accommodation, fusion, stereopsis, eye dominance and reference eyedness. This was true even when the dyslexics were separated into subtypes. Visual problems were no more evident in the visual subtype than in any other subtype. When Aasved measured the progress of dyslexic children receiving remedial teaching compared to their visual sensory function, no prediction was found between a prior eye condition and reading progress. He concluded: 'Dyslexic children did not differ from other children with regard to eye characteristics. Most children with eye problems do not have dyslexia. In general, there appears to be no particular causal relationship between eye characteristics and reading and spelling difficulties . . .'[8]

In the same study, Hans-Jörgen Gjessing divided poor readers into categories or subtypes based upon a battery of tests. He found a small group of children with particular problems in visual memory and visual processing. They had trouble on various spelling tasks, difficulty in copying and identifying letters, and appeared to have visual confusions when they read text. They were normal on auditory/phonological tasks. This group consisted of only 10 per cent of the 'dyslexic' population who, in turn, constituted only 6 per cent of the entire sample. Ten per cent of 6 per cent is less than 1 per cent of all schoolchildren. If only a fraction of the population has visual problems, they aren't going to be observed very often.

These findings cast strong doubts on claims that poor readers as a group have problems fixating, controlling vergence movements of the eyes, and abnormal oculomotor dominance. I would be just as cautious of any statements that reading upside down and wearing coloured lenses 'cures dyslexia'. There is little research support for these claims.

Visual memory has also been an area of interest. Teachers and reading therapists report that there are some children who cannot remember their letters, no matter how often they are told their names or their sounds. Most of the time this is not because they can't remember the difference between the shapes of the letters, but because they can't *hear* sounds in words. It is impossible to connect something that you cannot perceive to anything else, such as a visual symbol. There is a large literature on attempts to discover whether poor readers have problems in visual memory in general. Unfortunately, it is almost impossible to test visual memory independently of language (verbal memory). When children or adults are asked to look at something and then remember it, they automatically recode it into language, *even* when they are shown abstract patterns that would seem hard to label verbally. For this reason, studies on visual memory and reading are contradictory and inconclusive.

Conclusions

Here is a summary of the findings so far:

Children with reading problems do not have brain damage.

There is no diagnosis and no evidence for any special type of reading disorder like 'dyslexia'.

There is no logic to the notion of a gene for 'bad reading'. Genes do not code complex skilled behaviours that have to be taught. Genes code natural subskills which are combined to produce that behaviour.

Of all the subskills measured by the hundreds of tests that have been given over the past twenty-five years, tests of phonemic analysis or phonemic awareness are consistently the most predictive of reading skill. No other type of test comes close in predictive power. Yet, phonemic awareness is also enhanced by learning to read an alphabetic writing system (an environmental and not a biological effect). We will see in Chapter 9 that phoneme-awareness is also highly trainable.

Children with severe speech problems have trouble hearing rapid transitions between individual speech sounds (and other sounds). In some cases this is not caused by a developmental delay, because even infants can hear these transitions. This problem is remediable with proper training. Children with more minor speech problems generally grow out of them. In the Hull study illustrated in Figure 7.1, 13 per cent of boys and 7 per cent of girls were classified as having 'severe' problems in speech production at the age of six. Yet only 3 per cent of both sexes were found to be 'severe' at the age of eight.

Most children with reading problems do not have speech or language problems.

In general, IQ does not predict reading skill unless the IQ is so low that memory and vocabulary are severely impaired. If a child with a low IQ has reasonably intact language skills, the child can be taught to read. It may take a little longer, or the child may read a little slower, but fluency will improve with time.

Visual problems are not a factor in the vast majority of children with poor reading skills. However, maintaining binocular fusion while scanning from left to right is unstable in early childhood, and a small minority of children will have problems focusing as they read. This is easy to spot because it is accompanied by noticeable behaviours. Visual scanning and binocular control are trainable by optometrists specializing in this problem.

In the following chapter we look at developmental research which provides important clues for curriculum development and setting up a sequence of instruction.

CHAPTER 8

The Child's Mind and Reading

A friend related this experience at a scientific meeting. Jim was attending a three-hour symposium on child development. On the stage were several leading experts in the field of child psychology, seated at a long table. The room was packed with eager listeners. After hearing the first speaker, Jim began to feel slightly uncomfortable, because he couldn't quite see the connection between the speaker's point of view and his own extensive experience with his four children. His feeling of discomfort didn't go away. Instead, it mounted with each speaker, until at the end of the symposium, Jim was in a state of bewilderment and confusion. The experts seemed to be doing research on robots, making all sorts of assumptions about children that were simply untrue, such as believing that five-year-olds can be tested for one to two hours at a stretch and produce reliable data. He wondered if any of these speakers had ever actually met a child in their life.

At question time, Jim put up his hand. He had one question for all of the speakers on the platform: 'Do any of you have children?' To his amazement, not one of them did!

In the last chapter, I mentioned that in research on reading, the child is often left out of the picture. Sure, children are given batteries of tests, on auditory perception, eyesight, IQ, memory, reading skill, and so forth. But there is rarely any mention of what might be going on in a child's mind, or how children *think* when they are learning to read.

In Chapter 2, we saw that children were using different strategies in response to the *same* instruction. Sally did what her mother told her to do, basically ignoring what the teacher was saying. In the same class, Nigel faithfully adhered to the teacher's advice: guess words in context as if random letter sequences were logographs. When an unfamiliar letter sequence standing for a new word appeared on the page (one that wasn't stored in Nigel's brain), he couldn't read the word. He had no way to begin and he didn't even try. He just got mad.

Albert liked to figure things out for himself. He discovered, completely on his own, that beginning letters stood for the beginning sounds in words. Albert was actively problem-solving. Nigel was not.

Sam interpreted his basal-reader phonics lessons absolutely literally. He thought that various short letter sequences like 'ing' (two sounds) and 'unch' (three sounds) stood for only one 'sound' in words, and that the number of these letter-patterns and sounds was likely to be infinite. He could never have put it this way, because children are very bad at explaining how they think. At the rate he was going, Sam probably thought that learning to read could take a lifetime.

Our research on children's strategies showed that whether the child was using an effective or ineffective strategy was not caused by an inability to analyse sounds in words, or weak vocabulary skills. In fact, children with the *worst* strategies had the highest vocabulary scores. These children seemed to be relying on their excellent vocabulary to guess words in context. When reading instruction is inadequate, incomplete, or misleading, children can adopt a particular strategy by relying on their most efficient skill *or* more or less by chance. Children can follow blindly, but most of them actively try to figure out what to do.

Children are not empty vessels waiting to be filled. Children have expectations. My son, aged five, announced at breakfast one morning that he was quitting school. As he put it: 'I have been in school a *whole* week. It seems like a hundred years, and I haven't even learned to read.' In Year 1, when he did learn to read, he informed us again that he was quitting school. Now that he had learned to read he could teach himself what he wanted to know. Nothing would convince him that his teachers might teach him something interesting he hadn't thought of yet.

Children are not robots. They are active and inquisitive learners. They do not all do exactly what the teacher is telling them to do, especially when what she is telling them doesn't work. Children go home to families at the end of the day. Mums and Dads, as well as reading tutors, say many things about learning to read that can directly contradict what the teacher is trying to teach. From these various pieces of information, plus their own analysis of the problem, children try to make sense of their experience and what they are being taught. After all, it's what they have been doing almost since the day they were born.

In this chapter we will be examining those developmental issues which have a direct impact on learning to read. The way skills develop throughout childhood determines the appropriate sequence of reading instruction.

Making Sense of the World: Initial Steps in a System of Logic

There is a consensus in developmental psychology that children have different patterns of thought and process information differently at different ages. Children learn some things much better at younger ages than they do when they are older, something that Maria Montessori observed and called 'sensitive periods', and scientists now call 'critical periods'.

According to Jean Piaget (who did have children), a child's first task is to develop an inventory of his body, his motor capabilities, and then learn how to integrate movement with sensory impressions in order to create a perceptual schema. Schemata are concepts, or frameworks, for building knowledge about the world. Piaget has called this first phase the sensorimotor period. By 'motor' he did not necessarily mean physical action. You can learn about an object by *moving* your eyes around it. In fact, if you don't move your eyes you can't 'see' it. Experiments have shown that when eye movements are temporarily stabilized, the world disappears. Blind children 'see' objects by *moving* them around in their hands.

Piaget carried out extensive research on the performance of children in tasks of logical-mathematical reasoning, such as understanding the properties of objects and object relations in the physical environment. The importance of his work to teaching a writing system is that every code also has a logical structure. This is called a 'mapping relationship', as described in Chapter 5. For this reason, Piaget's discoveries are important in understanding the child's emerging skill in discriminating sensory elements and written symbols, and her ability to fathom the logical structure of the spelling code.

Piaget has been under attack from experimental psychologists for about forty years. There is no space here to enter into this debate, except to say that there are problems with Piaget's estimates of the average ages at which his tasks could be solved. In cross-cultural studies, ages vary by as much as four years, and this is strongly determined by the type of education the child receives. Piaget developed a 'stage' model, arguing that the stages remain invariable regardless of age or culture. That is, Stage 1 comes first, Stage 2 next, and so forth. In a paper by myself, Karl Pribram and Miriam Pirnazar, we reviewed evidence to suggest that Piagetian stages (meaning levels of skill and understanding) are reinvoked every time you learn something completely new, even if you're an adult. The difference is, you run through the stages much faster.

A related difficulty for Piaget's model is shown in studies where children (and adults) can use higher levels of logical reasoning when tasks are based upon something *familiar*, but use lower levels on unfamiliar tasks. No doubt this debate will continue for decades to come, unfortunately without Piaget's brilliant participation. Despite the debate and the problems with aspects of Piaget's model, no one has been able to come up with a better one, and no one has done more to provide an analysis of the different types of children's logic, such as understanding reversibility, transitivity and class inclusion.

What does any of this have to do with a writing system? Earlier, you met the Sumerian boy, Enkimansi. In the Sumerian school, the children copied symbols from clay tablets and then recited the words or sounds that they had written. Each day was spent in exercising this *reversible* process: Copy–recite; recite–copy. This provides a concrete understanding of the basic logic of a writing system: reversibility. It works in two directions: decoding–encoding.

But Enkimansi's story teaches something more. While I was doing research for this book at the Bodleian Library in Oxford, I had my first encounter with authentic Old English writing. Figure 8.1 gives an example of it, from Ælfric's *Grammar* circa AD 990.

The opening lines read:

FIGURE 8.1

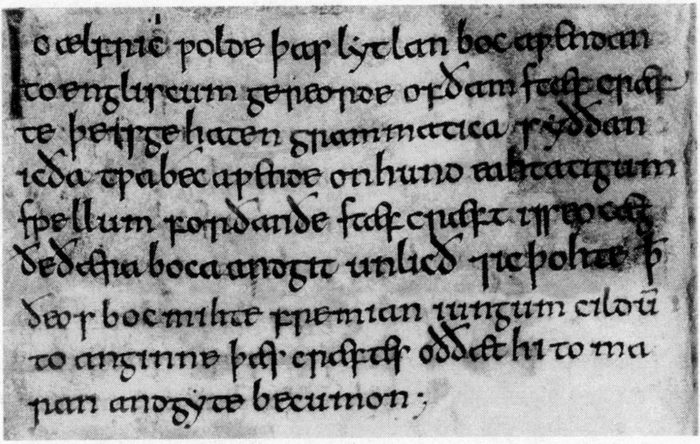

Photo reproduced with permission of the President and Scholars of St John's College, Oxford

Ic ælfric wolde thas lytlan boc awendan to englishum geweorde of tham staef craefte the is gehaten grammatica sythan ic tha twa bec awende onhund eahtatigum spellum forthan the staef craeft is seo caeg the thaera boca andgit unlicth and ic thohte that theos boc mihte fremian iungum childum to anginne thaes craeftes othaet hi to maram andgyte becumon'[1]

[I, Ælfric, would this little book to translate to English words of the letters craft that is called grammar since I (into) two books translated eighty sermons, because the letters craft is the key which these books understanding unlocks, and I thought that this book might help young children to begin this craft until they to great understanding come.]

I had a little paperback book which allowed me to translate each Old English letter to its modern equivalent, along with a pronunciation key. I memorized this without much trouble, because many of the letters are the same. However, I found that I was completely unable to read Old English phonetically from the text. I literally couldn't *see* where one letter stopped and the other began when they were combined into words, especially as words wrap around lines and are often joined together. I found this very frustrating.

Fortunately for me, the Bodleian Library doesn't permit readers to make photocopies of ancient documents. If you want to study the documents, you order photographs (which are expensive) or *you copy them by hand*. To my surprise, once I began copying text, I was able to 'see' each letter clearly. It didn't take long before I could read Old English fluently, though not with the correct accent, or much understanding of the words.

This is a perfect example of sensorimotor integration. It was the *movement* I made with my hand combined with the visual comparison of my writing with the print on the page (eye movements scanning the letters), that forced me to *really* look, and allowed me to see the letters. I became aware of *how* the letters were formed by the writer, and that there was an efficient and an inefficient way to write them, such as a vertical stroke first, horizontal next, or vice versa. In a fairly short space of time, the individual letters seemed to pop off the page, rather than being blurrily wedged in words. This is what Piaget would call a 'transformation', the creation of a new schema. And it doesn't go away. Even though I don't look at Old English script for months at a time, the moment I look at it, I 'see' it just as vividly.

What this experience shows is that sensorimotor learning can occur at any age, and that it is a necessary first step to learn any task with which you are completely unfamiliar. Remember when you first learned to drive, and every movement and every perception was completely (overwhelmingly) conscious? Once the individual movements are mastered, and the timing of those movements with the perception of landmarks, stop signs, and other moving vehicles is integrated, a 'transformation' takes place. When this happens, everything appears to run off automatically, without the need for conscious reflection. It's only when the road conditions become dangerous that you suddenly become acutely conscious, and you realize that something in your brain had been monitoring everything all along, otherwise you never would have noticed the danger.

This transformation of an acquired skill into a semi-automatic process has been measured in the brain. A skill that has become automatic uses fewer neurons in highly specialized locations, and the brain needs far less glucose (brain food). When scientists first began to use positron emission tomography (PET), which measures glucose uptake in various regions of the brain, they were amazed to find that if you are good at something, reading for example, fewer brain regions are active, and neurons need less glucose to do it. If you are bad at something, more and different areas of the brain gobble glucose. The brain lights up like a Christmas tree. Previously, people thought that the better you are at something, the more neurons in your brain were involved and specialized for that task. Instead, it turns out that the better you are at something, the *less of your brain is actively involved*.

It makes sense when you think about it. The neurons of the brain reorganize through facilitating new connections into efficient neural networks. This is just as Piaget suggested in his concept of higher-order schemas. Computer programmers call these schemas 'subroutines'. You can drive a car along a highway, listen to music on the radio, carry on a conversation with your passenger, and drink coffee at the same time. Some people shave and talk on a mobile phone while they negotiate heavy traffic! This is because all of these activities have been turned into semi-automatic subroutines through practice. When this happens the brain can handle multiple subroutines at the same time, and switch attention from one task to another almost instantaneously.

Here is the main message of this section. If you want a child to be a good reader, a good speller, and a creative writer, then your first goal is to create efficient and automatic subroutines in the necessary sensorimotor skills that should not require overt attention, such as encoding and decoding. An efficient reader looks at text and does not see letters, nor does he see words; he experiences *meaning* directly. An efficient writer puts *meaning* on a piece of blank paper, not letters and words. He has to stop and think only when he is unsure of a particular spelling or is seeking for a particular word to convey a special meaning. You can't get to meaning unless everything else is efficient and automatic. This is why look-and-say and 'real books' don't work. The important subskills are never put in place, and the emphasis on whole-word recognition undermines the child's ability to internalize the code.

Let's look at the subskills a young child needs to master the simplest type of writing system:

Sensorimotor processing

1. Visual discrimination of letter shapes. Occurs by eyes moving around the shapes and by hands copying them.

2. Putting letter shapes in a left to right sequence across the page. Occurs by copying or writing letters in a left to right sequence, training eyes to move from letter to letter.

3. Auditory discrimination of the exact sounds in speech which the letters represent. Occurs by listening and through kinaesthetic or motor feedback from articulation of speech sounds. ('Say /m/. Watch my mouth. Feel your lips close to make this sound.')

4. Cross-modal association. The integration of these new skills, one auditory, and one visual, into a cross-modal schema. Sounds are matched to letters; letters are matched to sounds.

Logic

1. Symbolization. Knowing that an abstract symbol can stand for a sound in speech.

2. Transitivity. Knowing that this symbol can stand for that speech sound *anywhere* in the word: beginning, middle, end. B̲ stands for /b/ in 'big', 'boy', 'cab', 'about'.

3. Reversibility. Knowing that the code is reversible. You can read (decode) letter sequences into sounds in words, and write (encode) the sounds in words into letter sequences.

The more that these new sensory units are anchored in something *already known*, the better and more efficient the learning. An alphabet script uses abstract visual patterns to represent phonemes in speech. The primary sensory components of the task are the *sounds the child already makes when he talks*. For the adult with a severe reading problem, these sensorimotor schemata are missing and must be put in place. It is never too late to do this.

So far we have only discussed the simplest level of logic. We have introduced a writing system that involves one-to-one mapping only, which is *concretely* reversible. The letter b̲ *always* stands for the sound /b/, and the sound /b/ is *always* spelled by the letter b̲. The English alphabet code, however, is not this simple, and the reversibility of the code can get lost unless great care is taken.

Logics for the Advanced Code Level

Young children have difficulty handling more than one sensory dimension at a time. A child may be able to sort objects easily by colour alone, or by shape, or by size, but cannot solve the task: 'Put the largest red squares in the box'. 'Red squares' as a portion of 'all squares' represents what is known as a class-inclusion problem, a type of problem that Piaget studied extensively. One of Piaget's class-inclusion problems goes like this: 'Imagine I have a lot of flowers. Some of my flowers are yellow. Do I have more *flowers* or more *yellow* flowers?'

This problem can be diagrammed like this:

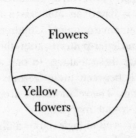

Piaget found that Parisian schoolchildren couldn't solve this problem until around the age of nine. Others have found that by changing the wording ('larger number' instead of 'more'), this problem can be solved at slightly younger ages.

Categorical language is also slow to develop. Eleanor Rosch showed that during language acquisition children first learn 'basic level' category words. Children notice and remember words like 'dog' but not 'collie'; 'tree' but not 'oak'. Steven Pinker points out that basic-level category words also contain the maximum amount of information. They are not too general ('plant') or too specific ('dwarf rhododendron'). Children also learn names for category members. 'This is my dog. His name is Rover.' They don't learn words that represent complex categorical relationships, and cannot fathom these relationships, such as 'Rover is a cocker spaniel, a breed of dog, and member of the animal kingdom.'

As children start to master simple category relationships, a system of logic begins to develop. Logic in the Piagetian sense means an understanding of the way entities are put together. Francis Richards and Michael Commons have continued the analysis of logic based upon Piaget's model. They emphasize Piaget's important point that subsequent abilities are always based upon preceding abilities. As Piaget wrote in 1964, 'Learning is possible if you base the more complex structure on simpler structures, that is when there is a natural relationship and development of structures.'[2]

This means that to handle the complex logic of our alphabet code, the child must have mastered each level of complexity in carefully sequenced steps. It does *not* mean that the child needs to know the logic in any formal sense. However, as Richards and Commons note, 'each of these logics is based on abilities to detect, measure, and relate the features of an environment.' Children must be able to *hear* phonemes, *see* letters and letter-patterns, know their extent (how many/ how much), and relate these features to one another. When there is a one-to-one match between these features this is known as an equivalence relationship. The relationships are perfect and mutually imply each other (one-to-one mapping).

The more advanced levels of logic in our alphabet code are known as the logics of 'classes' and 'relations'. 'Classes' simply means categories where objects or events that share similar properties are grouped together ('all the red ones'). Relations refer to relationships within and between categories. In relational logic, objects share certain features but not all features: most birds have beaks, feathers, wings, and fly. A penguin has a beak, furry feathers, wing-like flippers, and doesn't fly. Is a penguin a bird? Is a penguin a 'kind of' bird? Is a penguin something else?

An analysis of the complex relations between sounds and letters in the English spelling code is illustrated in Table 8.1. The chart shows one example: using the *sounds* /i/ (sit), /e/ (bed), and /ie/ (tie), the *letters* i and e, and how these units are related across several transformations.

These complex patterns of relations occur with most vowel spellings and some consonant spellings. Nearly half of the sounds in English are mapped to digraphs. Digraphs *reuse* two letters to stand for a different sound. This means that a letter can be in two categories at

TABLE 8.1   Mapping Complexity For Sounds and Letters

Sound	Spelling Alternatives				
/i/	i (bit)	y (gym)	ui (build)		
/e/	e (bet)	ea (head)			
/ie/	ie (bite)	i (find)	igh (sigh)	y (cry)	ai aisle

Letter	Code Overlap				
i	/i/	sit	/ie/	find	
e	/e/	bet	/ee/	be	
ie	/ie/	tie	/ee/	believe	/e/ friend

the same time. In one category the letter exists by itself: t, and in the other category it can only function as a member of a pair: th.

The digraph problem fits a higher level of logic called 'propositional logic'. Propositional logic involves *integrating* the logics of classes and relations, the ability to simultaneously think of the same entity in two or more combinations. In formal statements of propositional logic, these combinations are connected by relational terms such as '*and*', '*not*', '*or*', '*if – then*', and '*if and only if*'. The digraph problem is stated accurately as: '*If* the letter t is followed by an h, *then* say /th/ (thank); but *if* the letter t is followed by any other letter or no letter *then* say /t/ (tank, bent).'

Here is a more familiar problem in propositional logic:

1   This is one
2   This is two
12   This is ??
21   This is ??

Richards and Commons point out that an understanding of relations which are governed by propositional logic typically emerges around the age of eleven or twelve. And while propositional logic may present no problem whatsoever to adults, it is simply unavailable to a child learning to read. This means that children can't sort out the systems of complex relationships between patterns of letters and sounds because they haven't the logical capacity to do this on their own. Nor should we be surprised since curriculum designers can't either! But we'll see shortly that someone else can do it for them.

We're not done yet, because there are still two more types of relational logic structures in our spelling system, as shown in Table 8.1. There are multiple spelling alternatives for the same sound. This is true of almost all vowels. The sound /ie/ (tie) can be spelled ie or i (find), or igh (high), or y (cry), a relationship expressed by the logical term '*or*'. There is also *code overlap*, where the letter(s) can stand for more than one sound. The *letter* i can stand for the sounds /i/ (sit), or /ie/ (find); the letter e can stand for the sounds /e/ (bet), or /ee/ (be), and the letters ie can stand for the sounds /ie/ (tie), or /ee/ (believe), or /e/ (friend). This is also expressed by the logical term '*or*'.

Think how difficult arithmetic would be if a child had to learn that the number 1 could stand for 'one' in 81, but stood for 'three' in 91! This is not too far off from the way our alphabet code is set up.

The level of complexity produced by digraphs, plus the unstable and shifting relationships between sounds and letters, and letters and sounds, means that accurate and automatic sensorimotor processing becomes even more critical. A child absolutely must notice which letters work together and which do not as he scans across rows of text. These complex relations in our spelling system must be sorted out *by an adult* (curriculum designer, teacher) before they are taught to a child. Although some children may be able to grasp our spelling system intuitively and ultimately become good readers and spellers, most children cannot do this on their own. Remember that children actively seek to make sense of everything they do. When adults fail to make sense of what they are trying to teach, children will struggle to impose some kind of logic on how a writing system works. More often than not, this will be the wrong logic.

Formal descriptions of logical operations are complex and formidable, and neither the child nor the teacher needs to understand them as formal descriptions. Nevertheless, these complex logics are embedded or implicit in the code, and *someone must understand them* because they dictate how the code should be taught.

According to Richards and Commons, the types of logical reasoning essential to mastering the English alphabet code are not available to children learning to read. If we followed their timetable to the letter, children should not be taught to read our alphabetic writing system until they are between nine and eleven. Recent research has shown that this timetable doesn't always apply in real-world contexts. The key lies in the difference between real problems and abstract problems. If reading is taught as a real problem: 'How do letters represent sounds in *your* speech?' then we have an opportunity for success. If we are aware of the logical pitfalls that are created by our complex spelling code, we can avoid confusing the child by careful sequencing of the learning process. This means starting with a real problem, stabilizing the first step (one-to-one mapping/simple logic) so that it in turn becomes real (in Piaget's terms: creates a 'structure') before moving on to the second step (digraphs/one-to-one(two) mapping/propositional logic), and so on.

Research on some dramatic examples of the importance of context in making problems 'real', has been described by Stephen Ceci and Antonio Roazzi. If problems in class-inclusion logic were presented in a familiar real-world context they could be solved expertly, whereas when they were presented in a different context, or in their abstract form, they couldn't be solved at all. Experienced racetrack gamblers couldn't solve a familiar problem presented in a stock-market context, until they were told that a 'price-earnings ratio' was similar to predicting 'post-time odds'.

Illiterate street urchins selling fruit and vegetables in Brazil could solve class-inclusion problems related to the sale of fruit and vegetables that they couldn't solve in other formats. They could add up the costs of fruit and vegetables with ease ('A small coconut is 50 cruceiros, a large coconut is 76 cruceiros; if you buy both, you pay 126 cruceiros'), but couldn't add up the identical numbers given to them verbally ('How much is 76 plus 50?'). In their own setting, they were actually better at certain types of mathematics than children the same age with several years of schooling, scoring 60 per cent correct on a context-specific class-inclusion problem (involving different flavours and quantities of chewing gum) that only 27 per cent of the educated children got right.

If you mislead the child into thinking that the alphabetic code is completely abstract and arbitrary, and ignore the complex logic in the way our spelling code is structured, you will inevitably fail to teach most children to read and spell efficiently. Seen this way, you can understand why look-and-say and 'real books' are actually 'anti-reading' methods, because they actively discourage teachers from presenting consistent information about the exact units of speech and letter-patterns that constitute our alphabet code. This effectively blocks the child from using his emerging skill in categorizing because there is nothing to categorize. There is only chaos.

You can see also why most phonics instruction will fail for a large number of children. First, phonics never establishes a 'real' problem; *sounds in the child's speech* are not usually taught as the basis, or key, to unlocking the code. Second, phonics confounds the logic of digraphs (one-to-one(two) mapping) with the logic of consonant clusters (one-to-one mapping). Third, phonics never addresses the most complex level of logic at all: one-to-many and many-to-one mapping (spelling alternatives and code overlaps). In many phonics lessons, children are given spelling lists containing words that have no relationship to what they are reading or are able to read. No chance for learning reversibility here. Children are taught to read and spell with 'word-families' ('unch' = one sound), introducing a relational logic that *doesn't even exist* in our spelling system or in anyone else's: i.e., 'Everything in the word except the first letter is one sound'.

The Development of Language and Learning to Read

In the last chapter, we learned that phonemic awareness is one of the most critical skills in learning to read and spell. Is there a developmental timetable which has an impact on this ability?

Young infants babble in most sounds of every known language. Even deaf children babble just like hearing children. If this wasn't the case then Chinese babies couldn't learn Chinese, or French babies learn French. Over time, sounds in the native language increase in frequency and foreign sounds drop out, because only the native sounds are heard again and again in 'conversations' with adults. At one stage in language development, an infant has complete ability to hear (discriminate) any consonant or vowel in any language with great accuracy.

Janet Werker has carried out research on what happens to this early skill as language develops. Infants' ability to discriminate (tell apart) speech sounds which are absent in their native language starts to disappear during the first year of life. At around ten to twelve months children act as if they are deaf to non-native speech sounds, and hear them instead as the most similar sound in their own language. The skill doesn't disappear entirely, but declines slowly over childhood. Young children are much less likely to speak with a foreign accent if they learn a different language. Older children and adults can only learn to pronounce foreign speech sounds after years of consistent drill and conscious training, and rarely ever sound like native speakers.

Once the infant has learned which sounds of her language to notice, her next task is to hear them clearly enough to be able to produce them. Toddlers only gradually develop a more acute sensitivity to complex combinations of sounds. The most difficult of all are consonant clusters. A toddler will say 'poon' for 'spoon', and 'wing' for 'ring' because the beginning /r/ sound is actually *two* sounds produced simultaneously: /wr/. The most difficult of all, both to hear and to reproduce, are triple clusters. Pre-school children say 'teet' for 'street', and 'plash' for 'splash'.

What happens when children change languages at an early age? Do sensitivities to the phonemes in their first language disappear? Richard Tees and Janet Werker did a fascinating study on American college students learning Hindi, a language with several phonemes that are completely absent in English. They compared students with five years of training to two types of beginner: those who had heard spoken Hindi until the age of one or two years, but not since, and those who had never heard the language before. From time to time, the students were given a test of their ability to discriminate (tell apart) various Hindi sounds that don't exist in English. At the end of the first year of training, the group never having heard Hindi before were still performing badly. But after only two weeks, the students with early childhood exposure were as good as the students with five years of training. This shows that the awareness of the phonemes in one's native language is permanently stored in the brain. Even if these sounds have never been heard since early childhood, they can be recovered with relative ease *provided they are taught*. This means that everyone can be trained to become aware of the individual phonemes in his or her language.

This raises the question of why these phonemes are not immediately accessible when the child needs them, when he or she begins to learn to read an alphabetic writing system. There is another developmental milestone that has an impact on phonemic awareness. As speech accuracy and clarity improve throughout childhood, the brain begins to reorganize the basic unit of speech production. Speech output increases in speed with age, so that a continuous flow of sounds becomes effortlessly and fluently connected in a phrase or sentence. Children repeat words and phrases over and over again to exercise this skill and increase fluency. We saw earlier that naming fluency increases with age. To accomplish this, the simple speech segments produced in infancy – ba-ba, da-da, bi-bi – are incorporated into larger units of speech: syllables and words.

Research at the Haskins Laboratory in Connecticut, under the direction of Alvin Liberman and Donald Shankweiler, showed that from about the age of four or five, we speak so rapidly that the final phoneme in a word alters the way phonemes coming earlier in the word are physically produced. The acoustic patterns of the phoneme /d/ in the word 'dog', as shown on a speech spectogram, are noticeably different from the patterns in the phoneme /d/ in the word 'day'. This is because the movement of the tongue to make the /d/ is controlled by where the jaw and tongue move *next* and next, and next. Phonemes in words *overlap* each other in speech, a process Liberman and Shankweiler called 'co-articulation'. This, incidentally, is why it is so difficult to program computers to process and analyse natural speech. When this reorganization takes place in the child's brain, the primary speech units are syllables or words, and phonemes are lost to conscious awareness.

Fortunately, human speakers, unlike computers, do not hear these variations as different sounds or misperceive them. Through another process called 'categorical perception', anything approximating a /d/ will be perceived as a /d/. Nevertheless, as speech becomes fluent, consonants and vowels become perceptually glued together, and it becomes difficult for the auditory system to unglue them. Individual phonemes become embedded in the flow of co-articulated speech. The auditory system hears them as shifting sets of overlapping sounds in syllable chunks, and not like individual beads strung on a necklace.

These major developmental milestones in speech production are

FIGURE 8.2   Co-articulation

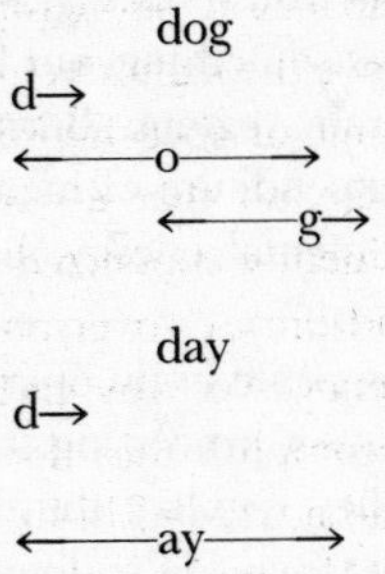

dog

d→

←——o——→

←——g→

day

d→

←———ay———→

always preceded by similar changes in speech perception. This means that for the child learning a phonetic alphabet, just at the point when he begins to master his native tongue effortlessly and fluently, his ability to hear individual phonemes within words or syllables declines, sometimes to zero. The phonemic level of speech becomes unavailable to conscious awareness because it is inefficient to be aware of it. The only reason you would ever need to hear phonemes is if you have to learn an alphabetic writing system.

For these reasons, a child must be taught to hear individual phonemes in speech, because he doesn't know they're there. To create a real problem, something that is tangible and concrete for the child, and a familiar context for learning the rest of the code, children must be made aware of what the letter symbols stand for.

Control of Attention

Attentional control has become an important issue, especially in American schools, due to the belief that 'deficits in attention' are causing learning failure, which usually means reading failure. This overly simplistic notion seems immune to twenty years of scientific research showing conclusively that children diagnosed with 'attention deficit disorder' (ADD) have no attentional problems, at least none that can be demonstrated in controlled laboratory conditions. Instead, research has shown the opposite: Learning failure causes an inability to attend.

183

The worse you are at something, the more brain cells you need to do it, the harder it is to keep doing it, and the harder it is to keep your attention focused on what you're doing. As we saw earlier in this chapter, when we're bad at something, our brain burns more glucose in more and different brain regions. Burning glucose uses energy and a high, continuous expenditure of mental energy is exhausting. Frustration also reduces mental energy, because it interferes with concentration.

The attentional systems of the brain operate in two major ways to facilitate efficient information processing. One set of brain systems controls distractibility. They regulate the degree to which you are interruptible or distractible when you're doing something. If you aren't doing very much (going for a nature walk, washing the dishes) then being distractible is fine, and the attentional control systems go into standby mode. If you're doing something difficult (studying for exams) then distraction is bad, and the control systems go to work to partially shut out the world. Activating these systems takes effort: energy. Studying for exams is exhausting not so much because what you are learning is difficult, but because of the mental effort to shut out distracting noises and thoughts and stay focused.

The second type of attention involves the amount of information that can be held in the mind at any one time, variously called 'attention span', 'span of awareness', or 'conscious awareness'. Both types of attention have a strong developmental timetable. Young children are highly distractible. When everything is new, newness or novelty is compelling. Distractibility has a purpose. It alerts the young mind to what is novel and possibly important. The young brain has to code everything important into memory, and until this coding has continued for some time, there is no yardstick to measure what is and is not 'important'. One reason that adults seem less distractible than children is because to them, everything is 'old' and predictable. If adults were suddenly transported to an alien planet, they would become as distractible as children.

Children vary in their level of distractibility. Some children can focus attention on a task and stay focused until they finish what they're doing. Other children, at the same age, cannot. Noises interrupt them. Sudden movement across a room attracts their attention. Curiosity (the pull of the novel or the unexplained) engages them and they leave what they are doing to watch others. There are maturational differences as well as individual differences underpinning these behaviours. In general, the older the child, the more he is able to sustain attention to a task, and girls seem to have a developmental edge. This is not to say that distractibility is 'bad' or even 'childish'. We all know highly curious people who stay excited about life in a way that we might envy. Furthermore, distractibility can be useful. Teachers who find novel ways to engage children keep their interest.

The ability to hold information 'in mind' (attention span) varies from one individual to another depending upon a number of factors. Some children can keep several requests in mind at once: '[1] Take your shoes upstairs, [2] put them in the closet, [3] wash your hands and [4] come down to dinner.' Girls are more likely to rely on the verbal channel than boys, and so do a better job of remembering requests. Boys are more attentive to visual information and more likely to remember only one request at a time: 'Take your shoes upstairs.' Children can have difficulty storing all these requests in memory in the first place, or they can lose information because something distracts them. Jimmy, heading upstairs to put his shoes away, might notice his Nintendo game on the way, drop his shoes on the bed, neglect to wash his hands, and forget all about dinner.

Attention span *and* the ability to focus and keep from being distracted are obviously connected. Both are affected by temperament, interest, motivation, and *competence* in a particular skill. When a child is good at something, she can perform with less effort, be aware of more elements in the task, and stay focused for longer periods of time. That is, she can hold more information in mind (greater attention span) and find it easier to avoid being distracted. The brain is working efficiently, and this is a function of ability as much as a function of maturation. When a child is bad at something, she can only perform with great effort, find difficulty staying focused and is more likely to become distracted.

Many children with reading problems exhibit behaviour problems due to their inability and unwillingness to stay focused and 'on task'. Being asked to do something you can't do for six hours a day, for hundreds of days a year, year after year, knowing that your peers are fully aware of your shortcomings, must be the most distressing experience imaginable. It is scarcely surprising that children fail to stay on task and cause trouble for the teacher, their classmates, and their parents.

There are scores of studies which show that the majority of children diagnosed with 'attentional' problems have serious reading or other learning problems, and most of the remainder have serious emotional problems, or both. This means that the inability to pay attention in classrooms is a *symptom* and not a cause.

Another reason for acting out is to get attention paid to you. Peter Williamson writes that for some children any attention is 'good' attention, and whether it takes good or bad behaviour to get it doesn't matter. Any attention is purely rewarding. While this may be true for some, most children are more subtle than this. There are limits to the kinds of rewards that children will accept. Praise or 'tokens' for good behaviour are not always as effective as people once thought. It turns out that children are more likely to maintain interest in a task and to accept praise when they have done something that merits it, just like most adults. They respond best to praise when it provides some feedback in the form of what Lilian Katz has called a 'tribute'. A tribute is a statement that tells a child what is competent about his performance. Reinforcement works to create or maintain interest when it is deserved and informative. Reinforcement for the sole purpose of manipulating a child so he stays on task, Katz calls an 'inducement', and it is ineffective once it is withdrawn.

Stephen Ceci and Richard Ryan did a fascinating study which proves this point in another way. They observed children and discovered what it was that each one liked to do. Then they gave the children 'rewards' (smiley faces) for doing something they had already chosen and were enjoying. The reward caused them to stop preferring this activity. The children interpreted this experience as follows: 'Smiley faces are only given to get you to do something you don't want to do. Therefore, I shouldn't like doing this.'

A reading programme should be good enough to make every child competent. Because teachers are never provided with the training and skills to teach reading correctly, their classrooms are filling up with children who are 'dyslexic', or 'can't pay attention', or who 'aren't motivated', or 'have emotional problems'. We are blaming the victims because teachers aren't properly trained to do their job. We need to stop and think what would happen to attention, to behaviour, to emotional stability, if every child was *competent* in the skills he is supposed to be learning in the classroom, where he spends over 1,200 hours per year, year after year.

Conclusions

Understanding the mind of the child is critical to our attempt to teach anything in a classroom, much less a complex skill like reading. To summarize the key points, here is what must be considered in setting up a curriculum that works for the young child about to begin to learn to read.

Children and adults alike re-enter a sensorimotor phase every time they learn a new skill. In learning to drive, every movement of each part of the body has to be made completely conscious until the movements become integrated. Each important sensory and motor component of the task must be identified and the integration of the sensorimotor elements must be trained. In a sensorimotor phase of learning, competency is the primary goal. Competency stems from practice (repetition). Children willingly practise or repeat actions to obtain mastery. Just because repetition may look boring to an adult doesn't mean it's boring to a child.

Children in primary school have trouble processing more than one or two perceptual dimensions simultaneously. When children begin to be able to classify objects and events, they can only handle one or two categorical levels. Children can't learn new skills that involve complex logics unless the categorical relations in these logics are worked out ahead of time and taught in a carefully sequenced way. Understanding complex relations like those in our spelling code is made simpler and more accessible when a child is working on a 'real' problem. Real problems are tangible and concrete, and anchored in a familiar context. Learning gets easier (automatic) when a problem has become familiar.

Children are unaware of phonemes in speech, and it is easier for them to become aware of syllables or whole words. If a child can only hear words or syllables, she won't understand how to use our writing system. For this reason, *no reading method should teach children to read whole words, syllables or syllable parts (word-families)*. These are the wrong sensory units for our writing system. These incorrect sensory units will be stored in memory, programming the brain, becoming more and more automatic with time, and making it harder to learn to read correctly. Children must be trained from the start to become aware of the individual phonemes in speech. The earlier this is done, the easier it will be for a child to learn to read.

When children are highly distractible, overly disruptive and unable to stay 'on task', this usually means they can't do the task.

Children appreciate praise or rewards when they are deserved (a 'tribute') and inform them about their level of competence. Don't bribe children to keep them on task. Tell them something good about what they are doing, and be sure that you're accurate.

This chapter has answered most of the remaining questions raised about the potential causes of reading problems listed in the last chapter. These were questions about causes of reading failure due to developmental issues such as logic, language, and attentional control in the normal child. Children's language development precludes them from being able to use a phonetic alphabet unless the phonemes are specifically taught. Phonemic awareness can be recovered at any age, but for children learning to read, the earlier the better. At the time when children learn to read, their logical development makes it difficult for them to grasp the complex structure of our spelling code. Some children may work out basic one-to-one mapping logic by themselves, but the remaining levels of the code must be explicitly taught. Furthermore, each step must be grounded in something that has already become 'real' (familiar context). Only then can learning proceed evenly and effectively.

Children, like adults, have problems paying attention to something they can't do or don't understand. They have a limited capacity to hold information in mind, and this capacity shrinks to zero when that information makes no sense.

Just about everything I have talked about in this chapter is directly or indirectly connected to instruction. It is only in the *absence* of clear, appropriately sequenced, unambiguous instruction, that these developmental issues can cause problems in learning to read. This is a *normal* consequence of the child's developmental level and not due to something wrong with the child.

In the next chapter we will be looking into the future at new methods to teach reading that are based on the research discussed so far. These studies provide the ultimate answer to the most important question: Can every child be taught to read?

....

CHAPTER 9

The Proof of the Pudding:
Reading Programmes That Work

Up until now, we have looked at the world as it is. In this chapter we're going to look at the world as it could be. Most of the research presented so far has been descriptive or correlational. Descriptive research counts things and calculates averages, percentiles, or standard deviations. Correlational research tells you precisely what things go together, and whether a particular skill will predict another skill, either now or later in time. Tests of phoneme-awareness correlate with reading skill. So far, we have no proof that phoneme-awareness plays any *causal* role in reading skill. It is just as likely that learning to read an alphabetic writing system causes phoneme-awareness.

No matter how clever and how thorough correlational studies are, they will never tell you whether reading skill can be caused by something you do or do not do. Only an experiment can tell you that. In an experiment, a researcher introduces a new teaching method to one group of children, while another group of children (the control group) are taught in the usual way. Children are tested both at the beginning and the end of training. A significant difference in gains between the two groups is a positive indication that the new method had an effect. In other words, the researcher *caused* something to change.

Experiments on real people doing real things in the real world aren't easy to carry out. All sorts of unforeseen things can interfere with your results. One of the most powerful effects discovered in reading research this century is known as the 'teacher effect'. If the teacher doesn't understand or believe in what you are asking her to do, she will sabotage your most carefully planned experiment day after day. This can happen even when teachers sincerely think they are doing what they were trained to do. The 'teacher effect' tells us that teachers need to be given a clear rationale for being asked to change their teaching methods. The new method has to make sense and be designed so that it works in the classroom, with curriculum materials and lesson plans. The teacher must be thoroughly trained, so that she feels confident and comfortable with the new approach.

As young readers lack the ability to unglue and manipulate phonemes in words, an obvious component in an effective reading programme is training in phonemic awareness. This is assuming it can be trained, or that the training will affect reading ability. An improvement in reading-test scores after phoneme training would be direct evidence for a *cause* of reading success. Another important experimental question is whether children must be taught the alphabet principle directly (that phonemes in words are represented by letter symbols), or whether they can discover this principle without instruction. Another issue concerns the best way to teach our formidable spelling code so that a young child can learn it.

Training studies fall into two main types. In the first type, the research team is directly involved in teaching the children. This type of study has high internal validity, which means that it has the highest level of control, because at all times the researcher proceeds according to a strict plan.

The second type of study has high external validity. In this type, the classroom teacher is trained and monitored. This shows that the training can be transferred to the real world: the classroom, where it matters most. If teachers can train skills that help children learn to read effectively, we could dramatically reduce the number of children lagging behind, or referred for special education. There would be no more children diagnosed 'dyslexic' or with a 'learning difficulty'. This would put an end to the enormous suffering of these children and their families.

Hundreds of studies on reading methods have been carried out over the past century. For the most part, these studies suffer from serious methodological problems, such as missing control groups, or the absence of baseline testing. I have already discussed the fact that most reading programmes in today's classroom are deficient and misleading. For these reasons, this chapter focuses on studies where teaching methods are in line with the research findings detailed in the last chapter. These studies meet most of the following criteria:

1. They teach phonemes in words as the basis for the code.

2. They include a phoneme-awareness training component.

3. They include instruction in both phoneme-to-letter and letter-to-phoneme correspondences.

4. They use appropriate methodology.

5. They present clearly described procedures.

6. They include control groups when possible.

7. They measure outcomes with objective or standard tests.

Surprisingly few studies pass muster by these criteria. Because of this, it is difficult to organize them into a coherent sequence. Each study has a slightly different focus. The children are of varying ages, sometimes trained individually, sometimes in groups, sometimes in the normal classroom, or in a pull-out programme, or in a private clinic. Each study has its own story to tell because of these differences, yet the overall picture is one of remarkable agreement. A list of commercially available programmes and where they can be obtained is included in the Appendix to Chapter 10.

Training Studies on Pre-school Children

We're going to start in Australia with an important series of studies by Brian Byrne and Ruth Fielding-Barnsley. They began with a basic question: what is the minimum amount of information you need to teach for young children to understand that phonemes in words are represented by letter symbols? Pre-school children, three to five years old, participated in a series of five studies. None of the children knew any letter-names or sounds. Different groups of children were taught various tasks ranging in difficulty and complexity. The simplest was word–symbol association. The children were taught words like 'dog' and 'house' and that each could be represented by a 'word token' (coloured shape). These word tokens could be combined into compound words: 'doghouse'. Another task was to listen for the first sound in a word and match a picture of this word to another picture that started with the same sound: 'bag', 'bat'. Next, children had to match these words to word tokens that stood for words starting with the same sound. Another group of children were trained in the same way, only using *letters* instead of tokens. At each stage of the training, the children were tested for their ability to *transfer* what they had been taught to similar tasks in order to discover if the child could generalize her knowledge about the relationship between sounds in words and symbols for those sounds.

The researchers found that many children had great difficulty with these tasks. For those who could be trained, the results were clear. Letter-sound knowledge alone and phoneme-awareness alone were not enough for the child to comprehend the alphabet principle. For a complete understanding of how an alphabet writing system works, the child must have a thorough grasp of this information:

1. The ability to analyse words into phonemes.
2. The knowledge that these phonemes occur in all words.
3. The knowledge of which letter symbol represents which phoneme.
4. The understanding that there is a consistent relationship between each phoneme and a letter across all positions in a word and across all words. The letter b stands for the phoneme /b/ in the word 'big', and *also* for /b/ in the word 'bat', and *also* for /b/ in the word 'tub'.

What seems so obvious to an adult is not obvious to a child. Each of these four elements must be taught because children this age cannot figure this out on their own.

Byrne and Fielding-Barnsley also carried out a study in which they trained pre-school children in small groups to listen and identify beginning and final phonemes in words. The children had only twenty minutes a week of this training for twelve weeks. Another group of children spent the same amount of time learning to categorize on the basis of shape, colour, animate/inanimate, etc. One year later, at the age of about six, towards the end of their first year in elementary school, the children were given various reading and spelling tests. The children with the phoneme training were superior on a test of decoding regularly spelled nonsense words. These children could use the alphabet principle to decode unfamiliar words significantly more accurately than the children without any training.

Children in these studies were trained for short periods of time. What happens when there is a more consistent and extensive training programme for this age group? Eileen Ball and Benita Blachman devised a training programme for kindergarten children (five-year-olds) just beginning to learn to read, in Syracuse, New York. For Group 1, they designed various games, such as having the child manipulate blank squares to stand for the number and order of phonemes in a word, which was cued by a picture, an exercise first developed by Elkonin in 1963. Most of the training was devoted to segmenting each phoneme in words: /b/–/a/–/t/, blending them back into words, and training in listening for beginning, middle and final phonemes in words. The children were also taught letter-names and letter-phoneme correspondences. They restricted the training to nine phonemes and letters: a̲, m̲, t̲, i̲, s̲, r̲, f̲, u̲, b̲. The children worked in groups of five, twenty minutes daily for seven weeks (nearly twelve hours altogether).

There were two other groups of children in this study. Group 2 spent twenty minutes a day learning letter-name/letter-sound correspondences (phonics) on the same letters, plus general language activities, such as vocabulary development, listening to stories and categorizing things. Group 3 continued with their normal classroom activities.

At the end of training, the children were given phoneme-awareness and reading tests. Group 1, who had both phoneme-awareness *and* letter–sound training, was superior on the phoneme tests to the other two groups. Groups 1 and 2, who had the letter–sound training, were superior on the phoneme tests to Group 3 with no training. All three groups were equally accurate in knowing letter-names.

The most important results were on the reading test which the authors developed. The test consisted of twenty-one two- and three-sound regularly spelled words using the same nine letters (mat, sub, at, fit). Group 1 could read five times more words correctly than Group 3 (ordinary classroom), and three times more words correctly than Group 2 (the phonics group). Group 3 could read, on average, only two of the twenty-one words.

These results confirm what Byrne and Fielding-Barnsley report, that teaching phoneme-awareness *and* the phoneme–letter connections are equally important. Further, these results show unambiguously that knowing *letter-names* is not much help in being able to read, and that a phonics approach is inferior.

Since this study, Blachman and Darlene Tangel have developed an eleven-week programme for this age group. They reported on the first test of this programme in 1992. Seventy-seven kindergarten children received phoneme-awareness training using various activities and games, plus training on letter-names and letter–sound relationships.

They were taught only nine letters in two- and three-sound words. They were taught by their regular teacher or a classroom assistant, who had fourteen hours of training. Another group of seventy-two children simply participated in the usual classroom activities. The children were all from low-income, inner-city families in Syracuse, New York.

At the end of the year, the children with phoneme-awareness training and letter–sound training were superior on tests of phoneme segmenting, letter–sound knowledge, and reading two- and three-sound real and nonsense words. They were also well ahead in spelling skills, using more developmentally advanced spelling strategies on measures of 'invented spelling'.

The entire study was replicated in 1994 with identical results. Children were followed into the first grade (aged six), where they continued to receive a more advanced programme designed by Blachman. The training was expanded to include reading and writing exercises along with a continuation of lessons in phoneme-awareness. The control group worked with the Scott–Foresman reading and spelling programmes, which were phonics-based.

The phoneme training group was superior at the end of first grade on phoneme-awareness and on every measure of reading and spelling accuracy on both specially designed tests and standardized tests of reading and spelling. These children maintained their superior performance on all measures when tested again, one year later, at the end of their second year at school.

Jolly Phonics is a linguistic programme developed by Sue Lloyd and Sara Wernham at Woods Loke Primary School in Lowestoft. It is designed for whole-class teaching. Forty-two sounds are taught using the most common single letter or digraph spelling. Letter names are taught later. Sounds are introduced in groups, the first being /s/ /a/ /t/ /i/ /p/ /n/. Next, children learn words spelled with these sounds. Children learn to say the sounds separately then blend them into the word, and also to identify individual sounds in words. Writing is stressed, including tracing, copying and writing from memory. Several types of materials and a video were developed to teach these skills. Children read books with a graded vocabulary as soon as possible. A new sound is taught every day in lessons lasting about an hour or longer. Each lesson includes all the skills components. The sounds and their most common spellings are taught in ten weeks, and children move on to regular books. Later, they learn alternative spellings as part of reading practice.

Research on this programme has been carried out by Rhona Johnston at St Andrews University, and also by Dale Willows at the University of Toronto. In 1997, Johnston and Watson compared a 'synthetic' phonics programme (Jolly Phonics) to an 'analytic phonics programme where children begin with whole words, then word parts (rhymes), then individual sounds, with blends and digraphs coming in a Years 2 and 3. Two classes of children with an average age of 4.8 years were matched in ability. By December, the synthetic phonics group was eleven months ahead on a standardized test of reading, and by March they were sixteen months ahead. In a comparison of children in Year 3, matched on vocabulary and age, the synthetic phonics class was nine months ahead in reading. In the analytic phonics class, 31.5 percent exceeded one year below age norms, compared to the synthetic phonics class with 9 per cent below.

In a second study in county Clackmannon, Scotland, this programme was used in the Reception classes in three schools with the poorest families. Eight classes in largely middle-class schools were taught using analytic phonics. In March of the following year, children in the synthetic phonics classes were one year ahead in reading and fourteen months ahead in spellling. (Data are unpublished.)

Similar results were found in a study on 281 kindergarten children in Toronto. Compared to children receiving the 'normal' curriculum, Jolly-Phonics-trained children were 6.2 standard score points ahead in reading and 6.7 points ahead in spelling. They were also significantly ahead on all other measures, letter-sound skills, word-attack skills, and non-word spelling. (Data are unpublished.)

The message is that young children can be taught to read if they are taught quickly and in depth, *and when* the lessons are based on the logic of the alphabet code. Not only this, but gains hold up well over time, and far fewer children are left behind.

A Swedish team led by Ingvar Lundberg studied two groups of children in different geographic regions of Denmark, matched for socio-economic class. Children begin kindergarten in Denmark at the age of six, and parents are encouraged to refrain from helping their children learn to read until the age of seven. One group of 235 six-year-olds received training on a number of phonological tasks, and the control group of 155 children did not.

The training consisted of 15–20 minutes daily for 14 weeks of rhyming games ('What rhymes with or sounds like "fish"?'), segmenting words in sentences ('wunssaponnatime' = 'once-upon-a-time'), and segmenting syllables in words (ta-ble, flow-er). This was followed at Week 15 by training in listening to initial phonemes in words (*b*ig, *b*at, *b*ug), and at Weeks 17 and 18 (Month 5) by phoneme segmenting and blending tasks of increasing complexity. At the end of the school year, the children were given various tests of their phonological ability. The only real difference between the groups was in segmenting and blending phonemes, and *not* in the ability to rhyme or segment sentences and syllables.

The children were retested eight months after the start of first grade, when they were about seven-and-a-half years old. Children were asked to read individual words and match each one to a picture. They were also tested on spelling dictation. The trained group was only marginally ahead on reading, but did much better on the spelling dictation test, scoring an average of 10.7 correct to the control group's 6.7 correct. Here is an example of phoneme-awareness training working *independently* of direct instruction in letter–sound relationships.

This study showed that training in parsing sentences into words and words into syllables, and playing rhyming games had no real effect. The groups did not differ in these skills after training. None of these skills were found to correlate to reading and spelling scores later in time. These activities took up 50 per cent of the training, time that was essentially wasted. This finding was replicated by Barbara Foorman and her colleagues in Houston, Texas. When they compared children trained in the same programme to a control group, the only significant difference was on the phoneme-awareness tasks.

Preventive Programmes for At-risk Children

One of the most famous training studies in the literature was carried out in Oxford by Lynette Bradley and Peter Bryant. The children in this study were at risk for reading failure due to extremely poor scores on a phoneme-awareness test. Altogether there were sixty-five children, average age six years, who were divided into four separate groups matched for reading and IQ. The children were trained individually in pull-out sessions across a two-year period, for a total of forty ten-minute sessions for each child (approximately seven hours). The rest of the time they were in the main classroom. Group 1 was given phoneme-awareness training using three-sound words. They were taught to listen and compare words that did or did not match in initial, middle, and final phonemes, and rhyming units. Words were cued by pictures or generated by the child. It is unclear whether segmenting, blending or digraphs were taught. Group 1 was also given training in letter-to-phoneme correspondences.

Children in Group 2 were given phoneme-awareness training only (no letters). Group 3 spent the same amount of time doing language-related tasks, such as sorting the pictures into linguistic categories: pets, people. Children assigned to Group 4, the control group, remained in their regular classroom.

At the end of this training, children in Group 1 were the only ones to score at age-level in reading and spelling. They were over one year ahead of the control Group 4 on the Schonell and Neale reading tests, and two years ahead on the Schonell spelling test. They were also significantly ahead of Group 3, the categorizing group. Group 1 was also over one year ahead of Group 2 (phoneme-awareness and no letters) in spelling. The authors concluded in much the same vein as the research reviewed above. An understanding of the alphabet principle has to be based on two separate skills: the ability to hear individual phonemes in words, and knowledge of which phonemes are connected to which letters of the alphabet. The evidence shows that phoneme-awareness training *by itself* does not automatically transfer to an understanding of letter–sound correspondences. Nor do children spontaneously pick up this extra knowledge in the classroom.

Lynette Bradley carried out follow-on testing when the same children were thirteen years old. Group 1 was about one year ahead of the control group (no treatment) on the Schonell and Neale reading tests, and one-and-a-half years ahead on Schonell spelling. Group 2 (phoneme training only) fell in between. However, *all groups were well below age norms*. Group 1 was now two years *behind* their normal peers in both reading and spelling, despite the early training in phoneme-awareness and letter–sound knowledge. Although the results show a strong positive effect from only seven hours of early training, the programme was not sufficiently comprehensive to allow the children to maintain their age-level standing over the long term.

Other studies have been designed to teach reading to at-risk children in the classroom. These studies were carried out either by the classroom teachers, or by specially trained tutors working in the classroom.

One of the first studies of this type was carried out in Chicago in the early 1970s, in two inner-city schools, using a programme designed by Michael and Lisa Wallach. The children were six-year-olds just starting school, who had scored below the 40th percentile on the Metropolitan Reading Readiness Test. There were thirty-six children who received special tutoring, and fifty-two children who were taught in the usual way in the main classroom. The tutors were adult volunteers from the community who were trained to use special materials and lesson plans designed by the Wallachs. The tutors saw each child for about half an hour each day.

Children were initially taught about phonemes in words by matching a sound they heard to the beginning sound in a word. A wide range of materials and games were used to teach this. Children learned to trace letters and to match letters to phonemes. Phonemes were taught in alphabetical order, and only those that matched the twenty-six letters were taught.

At the next step, children learned to blend and segment three-sound words, first just by hearing them, and then by using a movable alphabet. When the children had completed these lessons, they began to read simple books. Through reading, they discovered the remaining phonemes in English and the more complex phoneme–letter relationships such as consonant clusters, digraphs, and alternative spellings for the same sound.

At the end of the first year, children in the two groups were given a variety of tests of reading, comprehension, and letter–sound knowledge. The tutored children were superior on all of them. This is not to say that all children in the tutored group were equally successful. About one-third still scored at beginning first year level or worse. The main difference between the groups was that nearly two-thirds of the control group had made no gains. A problem with this study was the lack of a balanced research design. To prove the effectiveness of the programme, a control group should also have had the advantage of thirty minutes of daily individual instruction. These results also show that teaching only 26 letters/26 sounds and letting the child figure out the rest of the code on his own is not enough, and doesn't help about a third of the children.

Another study on at-risk inner-city children was carried out by Benita Blachman in New Haven, Connecticut. She developed a programme for small group instruction for first-grade children (six-year-olds) that could be delivered by the classroom teacher. She created a variety of materials for teaching phoneme-awareness, including picture cue cards for segmenting and blending sounds in words. The children were given daily practice (a thirty-minute lesson) in segmenting and blending syllables and phonemes. Children were also taught letter–sound correspondences. The teaching extended to consonant clusters, vowel digraphs, and e-controlled vowel spellings. Children also read stories largely drawn from basic phonics book series, and were given spelling dictation lessons on the same kinds of words they were learning to read. Later, another school joined in and the project was extended.

Much later, in fourth grade, aged about nine, the children participated in schoolwide testing for the Iowa Test of Basic Skills. The children with the special training scored well above national norms, whereas previously the children from these two schools had scored either seven months or one year below national norms. Both schools with the special training programme were now close to the top in city-wide ranks, whereas before they had been close to the bottom. This shows the persistence of appropriately sequenced training in phoneme-awareness and letter–sound decoding, and the advantage of a more in-depth programme which held up over a three-year period.

There are important findings from the studies reviewed so far. Children can be taught to unglue sounds in words and learn the alphabet principle at the age of five or younger. These skills orient the child to the correct strategy for decoding and spelling, and this persists over time. However, teaching *only* the basic 26 letters/26 sounds formula without teaching the remaining 21 phonemes, extensive work on clusters, digraphs, e-controlled vowel spellings, or any elements of the advanced spelling code, is not sufficient to keep at-risk children at age-level over the long haul. It is important that there is consistency in methods and careful sequencing of skills-training throughout the early school years.

Undoubtedly the most ambitious programme for at-risk children has been developed by Robert Slavin and his group at Johns Hopkins University. Slavin was approached in 1986 to design a reading programme for local inner-city children in Baltimore, Maryland. These are mainly black children, and most qualify for federal aid to disadvantaged children. The initial work has expanded, and a curriculum, including a tutorial component, has been designed for pre-school children (four-year-olds) up to sixth grade (eleven- to twelve-year-olds). The programme is called Success for All (SFA). The overriding philosophy is that everyone can learn to read. The goal is to teach every child to read, write and spell, and ultimately to do away with special education altogether.

In 1996, Slavin and his group published a detailed report on the structure of the curriculum, its programmatic aspects, teacher training, and so forth. It is only possible here to touch briefly on the components of reading instruction and the results of their research over a six-year period.

There are many innovative components to this programme, and perhaps the most notable is how lessons for reading instruction are set up. They use the Joplin Plan, in which reading groups cut across three age groups. The entire school reassembles in different classrooms based upon each child's reading skill, which is assessed every eight weeks. The reading/literacy period lasts for ninety minutes each day and is directed by a trained reading specialist. The specialist spends half her time in the classroom and half in one-to-one tutorial sessions with the poorest readers. In addition, there is a parent-involvement component to the programme, in which parents participate in school-related functions and are encouraged to listen to their child read for at least twenty minutes each night.

The pre-school and Reception class reading exercises (for four- to six-year-olds) involve rhyming activities, training in awareness of the first sound in words, and syllable segmenting. Children are also taught letters of the alphabet. (Remember, research has shown rhyming, syllable segmenting, and learning letter-names have no direct impact on reading skill.) Next, children begin a reading programme which includes phoneme-awareness training plus components of phonics and 'real books'. There is a strong emphasis on story analysis and story comprehension, as children lack experience with print and have limited vocabularies. This is a very strong test of an eclectic reading programme, which in Britain (minus the phoneme-awareness training) is the major teaching approach.

The phoneme-awareness training is comprehensive. It begins with listening for initial consonant sounds in short words and expands to include extensive work in sounding out and blending three or more phonemes in phonetically regular words. Children are also taught to be aware of how they produce phonemes in speech by listening, feeling, and watching the teacher's mouth. Children match sounds they hear to pictures of objects containing those sounds. They do tracking exercises, which involve changing one sound to make another word: fat, fast, fist, fit, fin, fun, sun. At the same time, they begin to apply this new skill when reading specially written stories with phonetically regular words mixed with short and long 'sight words'. As well, children learn to write letters in the air, trace letters, write letters on paper, and spell words from dictation by sounding out phonemes in words and writing each sound one by one on the page.

Complete information about the reading curriculum is not provided in the report. It appears from the examples that twenty-six letters are taught and, presumably, twenty-six sounds. It is unclear how clusters are taught initially. There is no mention or example of how digraphs are taught, except when reading text, nor of any elements of the advanced spelling code.

From this point forward Success for All switches to an eclectic approach in which phonetic decoding is combined with training à la 'real books' and phonics. Children work at thinking about meaning based on story context and grammatical structure ('Does what you just read make sense?'). When a child encounters a difficult word in a story, the teacher reads the word instead, *or* the child is told to look at the pictures and guess using context cues. Children read and reread and reread the same story until it is memorized. 'Word-family' (part-word) drill is borrowed from phonics. A story about 'Fang' is used to teach 's-ang', 'b-ang', etc.

Examples of tutoring lessons provide a vivid illustration of how eclectic reading programmes combining incompatible logics fail many young readers. Tim is a beginning reader in first grade. He is up to Story No. 11, which is about a fancy dress party. Tim has obviously seen this story many times before. The story contains many phonetically regular words, plus several 'sight' words that are well beyond a beginning reader's skills. As Tim begins to read, he first has trouble decoding the word 'Nick', which he sounds out connecting all the sounds: 'Nnnniiiiiicccckkk', instead of segmenting them: /n/–/i/–/k/. As he never hears the individual phonemes *or* learns which letters represent them (n, i, ck), he has the same trouble each time this word appears. He consistently confuses 'cat' and 'cot', and 'sad' and 'says', and corrects himself by context cues. On the other hand he has no trouble whatsoever reading: 'baseball', 'player', 'dragon', 'pirate', 'policeman', 'jacket', and 'badge' (the 'sight words' in the story). After Tim has read the story, he is shown isolated words from the story on cards. He still has to laboriously sound out 'Nick' once more. He reads the word 'in' as 'on'. He is told to spell it with letter-names: 'oe'–'en'. He reads 'be' as 'did'. A note tells the reader that 'be' and 'did' are 'sight words' (?) which Tim consistently confuses (why?). Tim sounds out the word 'Fang' as if it had *four* sounds (/f/, /a/, /n/, /g/) instead of *three* (/f/, /a/, /ng/) and the teacher says this is 'very good'.

In another example, Terrell is shown the story of 'Fang'. The teacher asks if he remembers the story and asks for the title, which Terrell supplies without hesitation. He has seen this book before. Later, when he encounters 'Fang' in the text, he can't read it and has to laboriously sound it out, again incorrectly, with four sounds instead of three. This causes him to read it as 'fan' several times, because 'fan'-'g' isn't a word. Terrell reads 'in' as 'on', and 'fast' as 'fat' and then 'far'. The teacher tells him that the word 'off' is a word 'that you can't sound out' and must be memorized by sight. ('Off' is perfectly phonetic.) When he reads, 'The ball is off the fence,' the teacher responds, 'Does that make sense?' (It does to me!) Then she asks him to look at the *picture* to see if there *is* a fence. The correct word is 'field'. The child has not been taught the spelling option ie for the sound /ee/, so he learns that this is another 'sight word'. The story of 'Fang' is peppered with final triple clusters like 'nts', 'mps', 'sts' which the child is supposed to 'sound out' as 'nnnntttttsss' rather than segmenting individual phonemes: /n/, /t/, /s/. Triple clusters are the most difficult sound combinations of all to hear and unglue and come last in speech development. They should not be taught to a child having this much trouble with simple decoding.

These examples show that Success for All actually encourages children to become 'whole-word guessers' and abort the phonetic strategy the teachers had worked so hard to establish. They also show why a whole-word strategy would be preferred by the child. It has a much higher initial success rate and takes far less effort. This is especially true for children like Tim and Terrell who haven't a clue how the alphabet code works, and don't know how to segment phonemes in words to apply that code. It is never made clear to the child why he is asked to sound out some words and not others. He learns that 'little words' and 'long or funny words' must be memorized by sight, but that 'medium-sized words' are sounded out. *This is the only logic he has to work with.* The examples show that whole-word guessing is less effective for little words (too visually confusing) than for longer words which are visually distinctive and highly contextual. Remember that a whole-word guessing strategy will break down completely later on.

Another source of confusion is that most of the 'little' sight words the child is told to memorize are phonetically regular in spelling: in, on, did, be, she, me, off, up, etc. Telling the child these are 'sight words' sends the message: 'You might think you can sound out these words but, trust me, you can't.' This hidden message undermines his fragile knowledge of the code.

Success for All is a powerful example of what is wrong with eclectic reading programmes, and how the best intentions can go awry. This is a terrible pity, because the authors have worked hard to develop an excellent programme structure for all the right reasons. The research findings reflect the good and bad elements of the programme. It is consistently more effective than anything going on in the control classrooms. It has more impact than the internationally popular Reading Recovery programme (see 'Remedial Programmes', below) *and* has been subjected to more rigorous experimental research. Unfortunately, it still fails too many children.

By 1996, Success for All was in classrooms in more than 300 schools in 70 school districts in 23 states. Thousands of children have been tested (8,000 for Grade 1 alone) and so data are extremely robust. The Woodcock Reading Mastery subtest scores for word identification (real words) and word attack (phonetic nonsense words) for Grades 1 to 5 (ages six to ten) were compiled and are shown in Table 9.1.

The table presents average grade-equivalent scores for children taught with Success for All and for the control groups. Controls were matched for Chapter 1 eligibility (children from low-income families

TABLE 9.1 Success for All: Average grade-level equivalent scores for Grades 1–5

Woodcock Reading Mastery: Word attack subtest

	All Groups		Lowest 25%	
Grade	SFA	Controls	SFA	Controls
1	1.82	1.50	1.53	1.16
2	2.42	1.86	1.74	1.34
3	2.91	2.32	1.87	1.57
4	3.35	2.35	1.68	1.27
5	4.50	2.61	2.15	1.51

Woodcock Reading Mastery: Word identification subtest

Grade	SFA	Controls	SFA	Controls
1	1.79	1.60	1.45	1.28
2	2.52	2.15	1.93	1.63
3	3.24	2.64	2.30	1.88
4	4.13	3.21	2.62	1.87
5	4.79	3.74	3.12	2.24

Note: This programme is cumulative. Children in higher grades had more years in the programme.
Data were compiled from tables presented in *Every Child, Every School: Success for All* by R. E. Slavin, N. A. Madden, L. J. Dolan and B. A. Wasik.

who qualify for federal aid), ethnic group, and/or socio-economic status. Data from the lowest scoring 25 per cent are shown on the right side of the table. Two things stand out in this table. The SFA-trained children, as a whole, are more on track than the controls, and are close to age-level over the years. They are one year ahead of the control groups in reading from Grade 3 (age 8) on. On the other hand, the lowest 25 per cent of SFA children are in serious trouble. On the word attack test (nonsense-word decoding), both SFA and control children are stuck at first-grade level for four years. The SFA children break through to second-grade level (age 7) only by fifth grade (age 10). It should be noted that SFA is a cumulative programme and fifth-grade children have been in the programme for several years.

Although the bottom 25 per cent of SFA children are consistently ahead of the controls, this is not very heartening when children score three years below age-level in decoding. The suggestion that this programme is promoting a whole-word strategy is confirmed by a comparison of the word ID and word attack test scores. In competent readers, these two scores are similar, and for the SFA groups combined, they are reasonably close. However, in the lowest 25 per cent, the scores begin to deviate noticeably at third grade. By fourth grade, SFA children score one year higher when reading real words than when reading nonsense words. A discrepancy this large is a tell-tale sign that these children can't decode and are relying on visual memory and guessing as their main strategy. It also shows that the effort spent in 'sounding out' (rather than segmenting properly) has largely been a waste of time. (Note too that the controls show this same discrepancy.)

The issue remains as to whether a programme with such an innovative structure and so many good aspects could be dramatically improved by incorporating a logically consistent reading component, one which would never mislead any child.

School-based Studies Using Average Children

Earlier, I introduced you to Pat Lindamood, who was one of the pioneers in recognizing the importance of phonemic awareness to reading skill. She developed a reading method for one-to-one training for poor readers. In the late 1970s, Marilyn Howard began a project in Arco, Idaho to teach first-grade (six-year-old) children to read by adapting the Lindamood programme Auditory Discrimination in Depth (ADD) for the classroom. The first-grade classroom teacher was trained in the method, and a special assistant was also in the classroom for an hour or so each day to work with individual children.

ADD is a true linguistic programme which follows the correct logic throughout. Briefly, the children are taught forty-four phonemes in English by a process of discovery – feeling movements of the mouth, and watching these movements in a mirror. They are trained to manipulate sounds in words using coloured blocks, pictures of mouth postures representing the way sounds are produced, and subsequently using movable alphabet tiles. The movable alphabet represents the forty-four sounds, and digraphs are printed together on the same tile so the logic is clear.

Phonemes are taught in categories based upon their similarity in place and manner of articulation. Sixteen consonants are grouped into voiced and unvoiced pairs, or 'brothers' (/b/, /p/; /d/, /t/), etc. Nasals are taught as one group (/m/, /n/, /ng/), aspirants as another (/h/, /w/, /wh/). Phoneme sequences are taught both in isolation and in tracking exercises, or chains. The child is asked to make changes to rows of coloured blocks, or mouth pictures, or letters, when told: 'If that says /ip/ show me /pip/; if that says /pip/ show me /sip/,' and so forth. The programme includes extensive work on consonant clusters, taught correctly as sequences of single consonants. There is also training at the multi-syllable level, and some spelling alternatives are taught. Thus, the ADD programme goes well beyond most of the training methods described so far.

Howard's work in Arco has produced dramatic increases in first-graders' reading performance on the Woodcock Reading Mastery test. The trained children were one year ahead of the control group after only seven months of training. This has persisted over time. Children in Arco used to score close to national norms (50th percentile). With the new reading instruction, they now scored at the 92nd, 91st, and 86th percentiles at Grades 2 (aged 7), 3 (aged 8), and 6 (aged 11) respectively.

Reading specialists from the Lindamood reading clinic carried out a similar project in Santa Maria, California. A first-grade classroom teacher was trained in the method, and a clinician/aide was in the classroom for about an hour each day. The goal was to teach forty-four phonemes and their letter correspondences, as well as how to manipulate, segment and blend phonemes in words, prior to reading any text. The ADD-trained children received *no books* until January of the school year. A control class was selected by school administrators that was taught by a teacher who consistently had the best test results in the district. So the cards were stacked against success. These children were taught in the usual way. Many of the children in this school district were sons and daughters of migrant farm workers with poor English-language skills.

The ADD programme was enormously successful. On the Wood-cock Reading Mastery test, children could read real words at an average of two years above age norms at the end of first grade. On nonsense-word decoding, they were six years above age norms. They were one year ahead in spelling. On nonsense-word decoding, even the lowest scoring child was one year above age norms, reading at a third-grade level when beginning second grade.

These children have been followed for a number of years and are still well ahead of their age group on national norms and for the school district as a whole. At the age of ten, the scores for reading comprehension, nonsense-word decoding, and spelling for the rest of the school range from 39.4 to 56.5 percentile points. The ADD-trained children scored in the range 63.6 to 81.7. There is no overlap in these scores. This shows that the powerful effect of appropriate training using a consistent logic persists long after the training has been discontinued.

Despite the fact that there were control classes in both of these studies, the children in the control groups did not receive any individual training. This design flaw was remedied in a study my students and I carried out using the Lindamood method. Instead of one-to-one training, the programme was adapted for the classroom teacher, who used the programme during her normal language arts period. There were two first-grade classes using the method in two different schools. There was also a control classroom where the teacher taught children for the same amount of time, using a combination of phonics, 'real books' and invented spelling. Children were matched for ability, and all three teachers had produced consistently good reading test scores over the years. Teachers had small classes and worked with small groups of between five and eight children for about thirty or forty minutes a day on reading and language arts. After eight months, children were retested on the Woodcock Reading Mastery Test for real-word reading and for nonsense-word decoding. The two ADD-trained groups gained 11 and 14 months in reading real words, and 19 and 36 months in decoding nonsense words. The control group made exactly the gains in reading they were supposed to, based upon time elapsed (8 months' gain) but actually fell behind expected gains (+4 months only) in decoding nonsense words, again suggesting that many children were drifting into a whole-word strategy.

These results show that this highly structured clinical programme can be successfully adapted to work in a normal classroom situation, and that teachers can be trained to use this method effectively. Obviously, the gains are not as spectacular as when children receive one-to-one tuition, but they are remarkable and consistent none the less.

Remedial Programmes

Clinical studies on children who are falling behind at school, or diagnosed with a 'learning difficulty' or 'dyslexia', provide the final test to answer the one remaining unanswered question: 'Are poor readers, poor readers for life?' We certainly have evidence that this is true when children are left to the mercy of the school system.

In the late 1970s, Jack Fletcher and Paul Satz tested 426 boys in five counties in Florida at the end of second grade (aged seven) and again at the end of fifth grade (aged ten). On the basis of standardized reading-test scores, they classified each child as: superior, average, poor, or severe. What they found was alarming. Not only do poor readers never catch up, but a large percentage of children actually get *worse* over time. Of the poor readers, 38.5 per cent became severe readers; 30 per cent of the average readers became poor or severe; and 51 per cent of the superior readers became average or poor. The number of children in the ranks severe and poor *increased* from second to fifth grade by 14 per cent, while the proportion of superior readers increased by only 6 per cent. This shows that there is a tendency for good and poor readers to get worse over time, and also to become more discrepant in reading ability.

Since this study, the general finding has been that relative differences between good and poor readers stay fairly constant over time. For example, in Texas Connie Juel found that first-grade reading scores correlated to fourth-grade reading scores at .88. We found the same effect when we followed the six-year-olds in our ADD experiment up to the age of eight. In the Connecticut Longitudinal Study discussed in Chapter 7, Bennett Shaywitz and others followed 445 children from the age of six to the age of eleven. Children who were well behind their peers at six tended to improve at the same rate as good readers, but they never caught up or even came close.

Any reading programme that can have a positive impact on a poor reader's skill, bringing him up to the level of his peers, is obviously of great importance. Steven Truch in Canada, and Robert Slavin and his colleagues in the US, report that the vast majority of children in special education classrooms make no progress whatsoever.

In the remedial reading literature, there is a general finding that it is easier to help poor readers when they are young, at the age of six or seven, than when they are older. This could happen for several reasons. First, the intervention process is easier when children are younger. The training studies on very young children showed that they could grasp the alphabet principle quite well by being taught sounds in three-sound words and how these sounds are mapped to letters. This early training tends to persist over time *if* classroom reading instruction continues in a way compatible with this logic.

Teaching at this basic level may not work for older poor readers, because they try to memorize words by sight or by word fragments. The more that these bad habits become ingrained, the harder they are to shift. The brain sets up the wrong perceptual units for decoding print. Maybe it becomes impossible to shift them.

A second possibility is that if children can't learn to read by the age of eight or nine, they have something wrong with them. This is the crux of the dyslexia model which proposes that children will never be truly expert readers because they have a brain disorder.

Finally, older children may not be able to learn to read as well as younger children simply because the remedial programme isn't effective for this age group. In other words, this is an instructional issue. Fortunately, we now have the answers to these questions.

We will be looking at three programmes of remedial instruction, all of which contain a phoneme-awareness training component. Before I begin, I need to point out that there are many well-known remedial programmes which *do not* train phonemic awareness, or if they do, do not integrate this appropriately into the main programme. In case you encounter these programmes, I will describe them briefly.

The first is the tutorial method where the child reads and the tutor corrects the mistakes by supplying the correct word. Sometimes the tutor may also help the student sound out the word, but does not provide any information that allows the student to be independent and to self-correct his errors. This method is largely ineffective. Most parents can do this, and it is a waste of time and money to get somebody else to do it. (It's also a waste of time for the parents to do it.)

Reading Recovery is a popular remedial programme which targets 20 per cent of the poorest readers in Year 1. It combines reading practice (à la 'real books') using a graded book series, along with training in sound-to-letter correspondences in creative writing and spelling. It was developed by Marie Clay in New Zealand, is used in many schools around the world, including Britain and forty states in the US. It's a pull-out programme of one-to-one training for thirty minutes daily, delivered by highly trained, expert teachers. Children in the US need to receive about sixty hours of training to produce any gains.

Reading Recovery has had an enormous amount of research devoted to it, though most of this is unpublished. Recently, Timothy Shanahan and Rebecca Barr published a detailed critique of this research. Because this is an expensive programme and is so common worldwide, I want to review some of the methodological problems with the research and report on two studies that are methodologically sound.

1. A major methodological weakness is that only the Reading Recovery children get daily one-to-one help. What would happen if the control group (the children left back in the classroom) also had one-to-one help with their reading?

2. Shanahan and Barr could find only two studies where there were pre-test scores for the control children. This makes it impossible to know whether the children left in the classroom were *really* better readers, or what kind of gains *they* had made over the school year.

3. Few studies measure gains using standardized tests. Instead, the children are tested on the same book series and exercises *on which they have been trained and on which they had practised during the remedial sessions*. The book levels have been found to be uneven in difficulty, with greater 'gains' occurring in the lower levels than in the upper levels.

4. The failure to use standardized tests leads to another problem known as regression to the mean. Without proper test construction, people who score badly on a test usually get better at the second testing, and people who score very well, usually do worse. This would make the Reading Recovery group look better at second testing *without any intervention at all*.

5. Reading Recovery teachers are better teachers. They are specifically selected for training on the basis of their teaching skill. Plus, they receive a year's training in how to teach reading that most classroom teachers never receive.

6. There is a high drop-out rate in Reading Recovery groups.

Estimates in both New Zealand and the US are comparable. On average, 7 per cent are referred on to special education programmes and an additional 25–30 per cent fail to complete the programme. They are either returned to the classroom due to lack of progress, or they don't finish the sixty hours' training. The US National Diffusion network, which tracks children going through Reading Recovery programmes, reports that of 22,193 children, only 62 per cent successfully completed it – a drop-out/fail rate of 38 per cent.

7. The children who fail to complete the programme for whatever reason *are never included in the statistics to measure student gains!*

In view of these serious methodological problems, it is not surprising that in properly controlled studies using standardized tests, the gains for Reading Recovery children are not impressive. In one large-scale study by Gay Sue Pinnell and others, involving forty schools in ten school districts in Ohio, the standard Reading Recovery method was compared with three different programmes. One was a Reading Recovery programme in which the teacher training was compressed into two weeks. Another was a small-group version. The third was a teacher-initiated one-to-one tutoring approach. The only children to make gains were the Reading Recovery children with the highly trained teacher (possible evidence for a teacher training effect). They gained seven standard score points (about six months) during one semester (four months). The other groups made no gains. However, when the children were retested in May, these gains had disappeared.

Yola Center and her colleagues tested 296 children in ten schools in Australia. They compared the standard Reading Recovery programme to two groups: poor readers in the classroom who had not been selected by their teacher for the programme; and children who were scheduled to receive Reading Recovery but who had not yet been tutored. At the first test after initial training was completed and at a retest fifteen weeks later, the Reading Recovery children were superior on a standardized reading test. However, eight months later there was no difference between any of the groups. One-third of the Reading Recovery children failed to learn to read, while one-third of both control groups *did* learn to read.

Reading Recovery is expensive and has been estimated to cost local US taxpayers more than $4,600 per child in addition to the $5,938 per child the taxpayer already pays. This estimate was based upon average teacher salaries, teacher training costs for one year, travel to training centres, teacher benefits, etc. The average Reading Recovery teacher is estimated to tutor only about ten children a year.

There is another large group of remedial programmes, most of which lack a phoneme-awareness training component, and have either no research support or research with similar methodological problems. (Diana Clark wrote an excellent book reviewing these programmes, updated by Joanna Uhry in 1995.) They are best described as sophisticated phonics, and many are derived from the Orton–Gillingham or Slingerland model. This model is based on the premise that there is a brain condition causing dyslexia, a premise that tends to seriously limit expectations and slow down progress. These programmes are often highly structured with extensive curriculum materials. They are found in the school system for groups of poor readers, in special education classrooms, in the clinic, and in private schools for dyslexics. Like all phonics programmes, they emphasize learning letter-names and letter-sounds, and letter-names are taught as a primary decoding strategy at all levels of the curriculum. (Letter-names are particularly problematic for poor readers and consistently get in the way of learning automatic connections between print and sound, and sound and print.)

I call these programmes 'sophisticated phonics' because they make a genuine attempt to teach most letter-patterns of the spelling code. Unfortunately, they teach the advanced spelling code backwards, as all phonics programmes do, from letters and letter-patterns *to* 'sounds'. This can lead to the problem described in Chapter 5, where the child is taught as many as 200 'sounds of letters'. Once this reverse logic is set up, there is no coherent way to teach spelling. In an attempt to solve this problem, some sophisticated phonics programmes have developed scores of elaborate spelling rules that must be mastered and memorized. These programmes take an inordinate amount of time, often two to three years or more to see minimal gains. They tend to work better with younger children, perhaps because they are too young to get bogged down in memorizing rules. The published research on these programmes shows it is difficult to get gains after the age of eight or nine.

There are three remedial programmes which include a phoneme-awareness component, use the correct logic to teach the code, and also have research support. Bear in mind that these programmes teach the children that other programmes like Reading Recovery, Success for All, and 'sophisticated phonics' *can't teach*. So, in one sense, the control groups for these studies consist of millions of poor readers making no progress in special education classrooms or other remedial reading settings.

The first programme, The ABDs of Reading, was developed by Joanna Williams of Columbia Teachers' College for small group instruction in special education classrooms. The other two programmes are used in one-to-one sessions in private clinics.

The ABDs of Reading

This programme was developed for children aged seven to twelve who had been referred due to extremely poor reading skills. The children were in schools qualifying for federal aid because they served low-income families in Harlem, New York. In the first year of the project, children in twenty-one special education classrooms were tested and divided into experimental and control groups, comprising a total of 127 children. The ABD-trained children were taught in groups of about four. The control children stayed in special education classrooms. Lesson plans were written for the teachers, who were trained in workshops. Teachers were supervised by staff on the project.

A phonological training component began with syllable segmenting and blending exercises up to and including three-syllable words. Following this, phoneme segmenting and blending exercises began. Children were also taught letter-to-sound and sound-to-letter correspondences and how to decode simple words and nonsense words. They were trained on a restricted segment of twelve consonants and three vowels. Children spent about thirty minutes daily on these exercises.

At the end of twenty-six weeks, the children were retested. The ABD groups were significantly better on the phoneme tests, but no differences were found at the syllable level. Unfortunately, these results tended not to hold up well over time when subjects were retested in January of the following year. Williams reasoned that the syllable work had taken up too much time. In a second study, much of the syllable work was dropped, and the main emphasis was on phonetic analysis, focusing more time on single-phoneme segmenting and blending. Six new sounds were added and training was expanded to include teaching clusters up to the CCVCC level, along with decoding two-syllable words. Teacher feedback led to a revision of the manual and some of the materials.

In the second project, new children were tested, assigned to the ABD or control groups, and taught in groups of four children (102 children in total). After nineteen weeks (a total of fifty-eight half-hour sessions) they were retested. There was now an overwhelming superiority in the trained children compared to the controls on all measures of phoneme analysis. When children were tested on reading simple words and nonsense words composed of the letters they had been taught, the trained children could read four or five times as many words. They could read real words and nonsense words equally well, whereas the control children read real words twice as well as nonsense words, evidence that they were using a sight-word strategy.

This study provides important information on what does and does not work for teaching poor readers. First, just as for beginning readers, extensive training in syllable segmenting is a waste of time. The control groups could segment by syllables just as well without any special training. Readers' problems are at the level of phoneme analysis. Second, the more time that is spent teaching children the phoneme segments in words, their order, and their connection to letters, the faster their progress in learning to read.

Williams' study used a subset (twenty-one) of the sounds in English, and we still don't know whether this new knowledge would transfer to the rest of the alphabet code. Even after nineteen weeks of training, the children in the ABD groups could read less than half the words in a reading test composed of the letters and sounds they had been specifically taught.

Lindamood ADD

I have already discussed the Lindamood method (Auditory Discrimination in Depth). This programme is notable for the consistency with which the *phoneme* is used as the organizing principle throughout all lessons, and unlike Williams' programme, forty-four phonemes in the language are taught (including /w/, /wh/). The results for the thousands of children who have attended the Lindamood–Bell clinics have never been published, but there are two research studies in the literature that used this programme.

One was carried out by Steven Truch and included all the children and adults (281 people) who were helped over a two-year period at the Reading Foundation clinic in Calgary, Alberta. Clients were taught in intensive sessions of four hours daily, five days a week, for four weeks, a total of about eighty hours of instruction. Truch states that he expanded the multi-syllable component of training beyond the teacher's manual. Clients were taught some alternative spelling patterns for various phonemes and read text as part of the training sessions.

Measures were taken both prior to and following training on the Woodcock Word Attack (nonsense-word decoding), the Wide Range (WRAT) reading and spelling tests, and the Gray Oral Reading Test. Everybody gained on all measures, with the possible exception of some of the youngest children on spelling. The greatest gains were for nonsense-word decoding, ranging from several months to four years or higher. Seventy-two per cent of the older children (ages thirteen to seventeen) and 84 per cent of the adults made gains of four or more years for nonsense-word decoding, much greater gains than those of the younger group (ages six to twelve). Across all age groups, the majority of clients had gains in the range of 16–30 standard score points on the WRAT reading test and 8–15 points on spelling. The overall gain for all clients, regardless of age, was 17 standard score points for WRAT reading (approximately 1 to 1.5 years, depending on age). Truch comments that these results are the reverse of what is commonly reported, where older children and adults either cannot learn to read or make much poorer gains than younger children.

Another remedial study using the same programme in the same format was conducted by Ann Alexander and her colleagues in Gainesville, Florida. They report on ten children, ranging in age from seven to twelve. All had a diagnosis of dyslexia based on extreme discrepancies between reading scores and IQ. The children averaged 65 hours overall of training (ranging from 38 to 124 hours). They gained about 1 year on average in reading real words, and over 1.5 years in decoding nonsense words. The actual gains per hour of clinical time in reading-test scores were identical to those in Truch's study.

Read America: Phono-Graphix™

The last remedial study is research carried out in Orlando, Florida at the Read America clinic. The reading programme is called Phono-Graphix™, as mentioned earlier, and is designed from the bottom up to take advantage of all the research to date. It includes phoneme-awareness training, plus a complete curriculum based on the structure of our spelling code, sequenced to match the child's developmental level. The programme and the curriculum were developed by Carmen and Geoffrey McGuinness.

Two primary goals propelled the development of Phono-Graphix™. First they asked the same question that Brian Byrne and Ruth Fielding-Barnsley asked: What is the *minimum* amount of information a child needs to be taught in order to be a fluent and accurate reader and speller? Second, Carmen, in particular, was interested in how fast a child could be taught to read. She began with pilot studies in a Montessori school, testing each component of the programme against the response of the child, so that the exercises at each level were aligned with the child's developmental capacity.

A more detailed analysis of this approach will be provided in Chapter 12. The basic framework is set out below. The platform for the programme was built upon a thorough analysis of the English spelling code. This foundation made it possible to organize a sequence of instruction which would work for everyone from five years old to the adult level. The programme proceeds in this order:

1. Teach phonemes (sounds in words) as the basis for the code. Introduce by phoneme alone, and then immediately connect this to a letter-symbol.

2. Teach that phonemes in words are written from left to right across the page.

3. Teach three types of phoneme-awareness: auditory analysis (manipulating sounds in words); segmenting (separating phonemes from each other); and blending (joining isolated phonemes into words) using real and nonsense words.

4. Start with phonemes that obey simple one-to-one mapping: one sound = one letter-symbol. For younger children, start with a subset of sounds.

5. Teach segmenting and blending of all possible phoneme combinations within a syllable, including consonant clusters at the one-to-one mapping level only. Most clusters obey one-to-one mapping.

6. Introduce the five remaining consonants, each written with a digraph (one-to-one(two) mapping).

7. Teach the remaining vowel sounds, using the most probable spelling (Basic Code), and move on immediately to spelling alternatives for each vowel sound (one-to-many mapping).

8. Teach overlaps in the code when they appear.

9. Teach multi-syllable words, the remaining spelling alternatives/ code overlaps, and Latin suffixes.

There are common elements at each step of the programme. First, a complete curriculum was designed for each of these steps using different story vocabularies for three age groups (young child, older child, adult). The curriculum includes manipulatives (hands-on movable materials), worksheets, games, and stories in specially coded text which helps the child see which letters work together to represent one phoneme. Digraphs and phonograms are printed in bold type, and children learn that these are 'sound pictures' for individual phonemes. For example, **ough** is a sound-picture for the phoneme /aw/ in 'thought', the phoneme /ou/ in 'bough', and the phoneme /oe/ in 'dough'. Stories were written to emphasize a single phoneme and its various spelling alternatives. The curriculum is designed to be fool-proof, so that it is difficult to use it incorrectly.

There are three important principles that inform the teaching method. First, *teach reversibility*. The code works in two directions. The child should copy words he reads, write words he hears (spelling), and read what he writes.

Teach fast. Let the child do the work and the thinking. Keep verbal instructions or questions absolutely clear and to the minimum. Never use misleading or meaningless language such as 'long' or 'short' vowels or 'silent letters'. Avoid adult logic, such as training in complex categorizing exercises. Leave out *everything* that would have to be discarded later on, like learning special mnemonic devices or labels for sounds ('tappers'), or reading funny script that has to be unlearned, or relying on colour-coded text. Eliminate everything that gets in the way of automatic decoding and encoding, *especially letter-names*.

Teach the whole code, including useful examples of consistent spelling patterns, *by exposure*. Never teach 'rules', as children cannot remember them, and most will be broken anyway.

A diagnostic test battery was developed to ensure that the client starts at the appropriate level in the curriculum, and doesn't have to waste time being taught something he can already do. (This battery is presented at the end of Chapter 12.) Finally, a parent or adult mentor is brought into the process. The mentor receives a book containing more than 250 worksheets and stories for all levels of the programme. These materials are used in weekly homework. Worksheets are assigned to reinforce what was taught at each session. They are designed so that the mentor and child must use the correct strategy.

Test scores of every child who enrolled in the programme were analysed over a two-year period. There were 87 children ranging in age from 6 to 16. The programme was set up in one-hour sessions, one a week for 12 weeks. Some children did not need 12 hours; some needed more. The average time in the programme was 9.33 hours. The minimum was 3 hours and the maximum 18 hours. All children were tested at intake and again at 12 hours, or earlier if it was their last session. Forty per cent had been diagnosed with a learning disability and were in special education programmes at school. Four children had IQs in the 70s. Nineteen had large discrepancies between IQ and reading scores ('dyslexic'). Some children were having speech therapy. Four children were referred for vision therapy. Several children couldn't read a single word.

Averaging gains to a constant 12 hours, the children gained 1.5 years on the Woodcock Reading Mastery test for reading real words, and over 2 years in decoding regularly spelled nonsense words. Nearly all of the children were at ceiling (100 per cent correct) on tests of phoneme analysis, segmenting, blending and knowledge of 50 letter–sound correspondences.

Children who met the criteria for dyslexia made nearly twice the gains of children who did not, averaging an increase of 2.5 years in reading real and nonsense words in 12 hours. The four children with IQs in the 70s made the same gains in phoneme-awareness as everyone else, along with a 2-year gain in nonsense-word decoding, within 12 hours. An updated study on more than 300 clients shows that average gains are 1.7 years for real words and 4.3 years for nonsense words within an average of 9.65 hours.

These gains are similar to those of Steven Truch and Ann Alexander in almost every respect. The difference is that they happened *seven times faster* per hour of clinical training. We interpret this as due to a number of factors: no loss of time in memorizing categories and category names, or teaching the client what he already can do; the extensive curriculum which provides appropriate sequencing and novelty; the analysis of the entire spelling code and the incorporation of all elements of the code into the curriculum; the high involvement of parents.

An anonymous survey was sent to parents at the end of the second year. Fifty per cent responded. It's impossible to know why the remaining 50 per cent did not respond, except to note that surveys sent by mail have an average response rate of around 10–15 per cent. Children previously diagnosed learning-disabled were no longer so. The lowest grade in language arts was now a C instead of an F. Grades prior to doing the programme had been Cs, Ds, or Fs. Now nearly everyone was getting As and Bs. One-third of the children were now on the honour roll (getting top marks) whereas none had been before. Parents reported that 100 per cent had increased self-esteem, and any behavioural problems had disappeared (87 per cent reported improved behaviour). All the parents reported that they were still using the worksheets and stories with their children each week.

Taken together, these studies provide overwhelming evidence that there is no such thing as 'dyslexia' or a 'learning difficulty'. If there was something wrong with these children's brains, the remedial instruction wouldn't have worked, and certainly not in twelve hours. Children fail to learn to read in school because *they aren't being taught correctly*. They fail to learn to read in remedial programmes because *they aren't being taught correctly*. Everyone, it turns out, can be taught to read unless they have such deficient mental and/or linguistic skills they can't carry on a normal conversation. Note that the Lindamood ADD programme and Phono-Graphix™ *teach everyone to read*, including adults, *and* the 90 per cent who never escape special education classrooms, *and* the children that other remedial programmes fail.

The most important message from the research reviewed in this chapter is that *a good reading programme looks similar whether it is in the classroom or the clinic. There is only one right way to teach an alphabetic writing system.* The evidence from other research, particularly the Success for All programme, suggests that not only is there one right way, but that this right way can be subverted if it is mixed up with wrong ways, such as trying to teach a linguistic-phonetic approach combined with phonics and 'real books'. The Santa Maria study also shows that *no books* is preferable to the *wrong* books until children are secure in phoneme-awareness, segmenting, blending, and in phoneme–letter correspondences.

Overall, the evidence in this chapter points to some inescapable conclusions. The earlier children are taught to decode our alphabetic writing system correctly, the less likely they will be to have reading problems, and the sooner they will be able to read stories and books accurately and fluently. Progress in learning to read, either in the classroom or in the clinic, is determined by the quality, consistency, and comprehensiveness of the programme, and also by the *amount* of one-to-one time each child receives. Children learn much faster in one-to-one sessions than they do in small groups. This finding was reported by Slavin and his colleagues, and is also evident in the comparison of the greater effectiveness of the ADD programme with individual help (Arco and Santa Maria) versus our ADD classroom study using small group instruction.

Finally, the clinical data for Phono-Graphix™ show that if the entire spelling code is worked out (*all* spelling alternatives and *all* code overlaps) so that this structure controls the sequence of instruction, you will get much greater gains in much less time. One of the major discoveries in our clinical research is that poor readers of all ages do not understand the alphabet code. *They do not know it IS a code.* Children and adults often say: '*Oh*, it's a code! I never knew that!'

We can now answer our last question. No, poor readers don't have to stay poor readers for life. They don't even have to stay poor readers for more than twelve weeks. If your child or a family member has been held back in school, is languishing in a remedial reading programme, or in a school for dyslexics and making no progress, then he is in the wrong programme or the wrong school.

In the next section of the book, I outline the correct way to teach reading and spelling from the beginning for the parent and for the teacher. An in-depth analysis of the remedial reading process is provided in Chapter 12. Information on where to find materials, curricula, and good reading specialists will be found at the end of each chapter.

Practical Solutions

CHAPTER 10

Beginning Reading Right

What does a reading programme look like that is based on all of the information presented so far? This is the topic of this final section. We will be looking at a detailed analysis of a good reading programme in the classroom and in one-to-one teaching with a reading specialist. The first two chapters are about the beginning reader. They are for the classroom teacher, reading curriculum specialist, elementary school principal, and for parents who are home-schooling a child, or who just want to ensure that their child will learn to read. (Giving remedial help is covered in Chapter 12.)

Let's recap the important points from the analysis of writing systems, the English alphabet code, and the scientific research on reading. This knowledge dictates the overall structure of a good reading programme.

1. Phonemes are the basis for our writing system. Don't teach larger phonological units, such as whole words, word-families, or analogies. This can create reading and spelling problems.

2. The alphabet is a letter code for phonemes in speech, not a 'sound code' for letters on the page.

3. When you teach the code the way it was designed, it is *reversible* as shown in Chapter 5. Spelling, writing and reading can be integrated at all levels of the curriculum.

4. Reading, spelling and writing are skilled behaviours, and like all skills, must be taught from the bottom up, from the simple to the complex.

5. The English alphabet code contains four mapping logics that are beyond the understanding of most young children (see Chapter 8).

Solve this problem by making the simple logic familiar first, and then the next most simple, and so on.

6. The ability to analyse and manipulate, segment and blend isolated phonemes in words is the basis for unlocking an alphabetic writing system.

I will guide you through the basic mechanics and sequence of instruction, but you need to do something too. Most importantly, you need to hold the firm belief that all children can be taught to read. Clear your mind of notions like 'dyslexia', and 'learning difficulties'. The research data are overwhelming that these terms are invalid. If you base your thinking on a deficit model, this will mean you won't expect rapid progress. If a child has a reading problem you must do something about it fast. Don't hope the problem will self-correct. It won't.

Most teachers lack proper training in reading instruction. Teachers have told me over the years that they discovered they had no idea how to teach reading when they faced their first class in their own classroom. Often teachers are taught nothing more than how to manage a sequence of language activities over blocks of time. Seventy per cent of trainee teachers in Britain reported to the National Foundation for Educational Research that they had no confidence in how to teach reading.

In order to teach reading effectively, you must have adequate phoneme-awareness yourself and be fully informed about the sounds in the English language. Teachers and parents alike have little awareness of phonemes in speech, even though they may read and spell adequately. Almost no one knows the structure of our spelling code. I can teach you about the code, but I cannot help you develop phonemic awareness if you do not have it. If you mispronounce words or are unable to decode unfamiliar words in print, you need to receive special help or remedial sessions yourself before you try to teach anyone to read. On the other hand, if you feel confident about your reading ability, have a good ear for speech patterns, such as being able to tell dialects apart, then all you will need is the phoneme charts in this chapter and a good audiotape of English phonemes (see Appendix).

Never forget that the teacher of the young reader is the custodian of that child's destiny. Be alert. Many things can go wrong. Don't assume that a primary school child is using the correct strategy even if he seems to be a fluent reader. The evidence shows that children are much more likely to adopt an inefficient strategy than an efficient one. Many children do not change their strategy no matter how inefficient it becomes. Highly intelligent children, like Alice and Tommy in Chapter 2, can go for years before anyone is aware they have a serious reading problem. Teachers must monitor each child's strategy and know how to keep the child on the correct path. This can't happen unless the teacher has time for one-to-one interactions with each child. (A test to uncover a child's reading strategy and other diagnostic tests are given in Chapter 12.)

Teachers and parents must also be aware of other problems that will have an impact on reading. Children with serious speech delays will have difficulties with an alphabetic writing system. By the time these children begin to read, most will be in speech therapy, but some may not. Teachers should (and most do) request testing for children who they suspect need help with their speech.

Visually scanning across rows of text from left to right, down one line, and so on, is an unnatural act, and this aptitude is slow to develop. For a small minority of children, it is nearly impossible without special help. These children will fall into the habit of guessing whole words because they can't see each letter in a word. If a teacher suspects that a child has a visual problem, she should reread the section on vision in Chapter 7, and notify the child's parents. They will have to get outside help from an optometrist specializing in vision therapy.

Due to the fact that there are many ways a child can fall through the cracks, this makes the first three years of school *the* most important in the child's life. It also means that primary school teachers are the most important teachers in the entire system.

This chapter is about teaching the Basic Code of forty-two English phonemes and their most probable spellings. (The final one, /zh/ as in 'vision', isn't taught at this level.) The Basic Code includes two types of logic. The first is where a phoneme maps to a single letter symbol (one-to-one mapping): /b/ = b in 'big' and 'cab'. The second type of logic is a by-product of having too few letters for forty-two sounds. This is when a phoneme maps to a letter-pair or digraph (one-to-one(two) mapping): /ch/ = ch in 'church'. (The advanced levels of the code involving spelling alternatives and code overlaps [one-to-many mapping/many-to-one mapping] are dealt with in the following chapter.)

I will be presenting the overall structure and sequence of a good reading programme, rather than a detailed curriculum and lesson plans. There is simply no space for this here. At the end of this chapter there are word lists to help you get started and information about how to obtain good curriculum materials.

Here is an overview of the major components of a good beginning reading programme:

1. Phoneme-awareness: training in awareness of phonemes in speech and the ability to segment (separate) and blend isolated phonemes back into words.

2. Alphabet principle: teach the alphabet code the way it was written – from sound to print.

3. Sound-to-symbol association: teach how to connect phonemes in words to individual letters or letter combinations.

4. Logic: instruction is sequenced from simple to complex and conforms to the child's developmental level. It should include the entire spelling code, not just a fraction of it.

5. Curriculum: materials should cover all possible skill areas – phoneme analysis, segmenting, blending, reading, writing, spelling. Materials must be related in content so that children learn that reading and spelling are reversible.

6. Pedagogic style: teach by exposure and example, using brief, clear explanations. Make sure the child is actively problem-solving and not passive.

7. Fail-safe: monitor the child's model of the reading process and his performance at frequent intervals.

Parents have the advantage of working one-to-one with their child. Teachers have to manage a class of twenty or thirty youngsters. Some exercises can be carried out with the whole class, but the bulk of teaching must be done in small groups and with individual children who are slower to learn. Four children per group is about the maximum. This will allow the teacher to monitor each child at some time during the week. Small group instruction should take from ten to twenty minutes daily, depending on the age of the child. Many teachers have a support assistant or a parent volunteer, making life much easier. If a teacher isn't so lucky, she will have to accommodate the rest of the class while working with groups. Here are some suggestions:

1. Assign the rest of the class some activity.

2. Arrange with other teachers to trade off time by sharing some teaching activities that involve larger groups.

3. Ask for parent volunteers to help in your classroom.

4. Ask the head for a support assistant who can be shared among teachers.

The lessons in this chapter are designed for the beginning reader starting at the age of five. This chapter is oriented to children who have not had much exposure to formal training in reading and presents an overview of lessons that would continue to the middle or end of Year 1. Working in small groups helps to keep track of who is having problems. These children should be given one-to-one sessions of five or ten minutes, preferably daily. It is important to ensure mastery at each level before children move ahead. Over time, it can be seen who is moving quickly and who needs more help.

Reception Class

As a first principle, skills training in mastering English phonemes and the alphabet code does not preclude other language-related activities going on at home or in the classroom. These activities are just as important as learning to read and write. They include story time, building new vocabulary through stories or lessons, and discussions of topics of interest. 'Real books' did not invent good children's literature. There is no reason why good skills training cannot coexist with quality literature, nor, as you will see later, why good skills training can't employ materials of good literary content.

It's important to be aware of what is or is not helpful in teaching reading and spelling. The studies reviewed in the preceding chapter show conclusively that extended training in rhyming and clapping out beats for syllables in words does not have any impact on learning to decode an alphabetic writing system. As part of early skills training, these activities are a waste of time. That does not mean that rhyming should not be included in other activities. Children love rhymes and rhyming games, and a sense of rhyme and metre (patterns of strong and weak syllables) is important for an appreciation of poetry and song.

The issue about teaching letter-names is more problematic. In the systematic studies reviewed in the last chapter, knowledge of letter-names did not promote reading skills, whereas the knowledge of phoneme-to-letter correspondences did. Reading specialists working with poor readers report that letter-names get in the way of training automatic decoding skill, and recommend that they not be taught until the child has a clear understanding of the fact that phonemes are the basis for our writing system. I would recommend that letter-name teaching form no part of the skills training I am about to describe. I would suggest that it form no part of any training until Year 2. Memorizing the alphabet sequence of letter-names has one major purpose, and that is to assist the child in looking up words in a dictionary. But you don't need letter-names to do this. The child can memorize the sounds the letters represent.

Another issue concerns capital letters. If capital letters were just larger versions of lower-case letters this would present fewer problems, but most capital letters look entirely different from lower-case letters: A a, B b. Lower case is used far more often and should be taught first. Learning two sets of symbols with different visual appearances adds an unnecessary memory load. Capital letters can be introduced later during lessons in creative writing.

Finally, *no cursive (joined-up writing) allowed*. Cursive should never be taught until the child is familiar with the Basic Code. Children need to see how individual phonemes map to individual letters and digraphs. If they join the letters together they can't *see* how this works. Further, books are not printed in cursive, so it makes no sense to have a child write in one way and read books printed in a different way.

The four main skill areas for five-year-olds are: awareness of phonemes and sequences of phonemes in words – that is, how to match phonemes to letters; the logic of the alphabet code; fine-motor control; and visual scanning and analysis of visual detail. All are equally important and reinforce each other.

Sounds and Symbols

Isabelle Liberman discovered that children had to be able to hear and understand the concepts of sequence and number in order to be able to segment and blend sounds in words. She used a simple task where children listened to someone knock under the table and told how many sounds they heard. The knocks could vary from one to three. ('Close your eyes and tell me how many sounds you hear.') This can be turned into a game played by the children. It provides a good first step in learning about sequences. The teacher or children can make different kinds of sounds, using a bell, a triangle, or a woodblock. Once a child can count a series of sounds accurately, she is ready to work with sounds in words.

For children this age, teach phonemes in real words and not in isolation. Children need to connect these abstract concepts to something meaningful. They have difficulty mastering meaningless, abstract tasks such as memorizing phoneme–letter associations separately.

All the successful programmes reviewed in Chapter 9 began training with a subset of phonemes, around eight to ten, and restricted word length to two- or three-sound words only. It is not particularly important which phonemes you choose, except to restrict the choice of vowels to this group: /a/, /e/, /i/, /o/, /u/ (bat, bet, bit, hot, but). There are lists of two- and three-sound words at the end of this chapter. Most five-year-olds will not get beyond this level, if they get that far. If a child makes rapid progress, she can move ahead to the lessons for Year 1 children (see next section).

An important finding in the research is that the first phoneme in a word is the easiest to hear, the last phoneme next easiest, and the middle phoneme the hardest. For this reason, the programmes reviewed in the last chapter begin training with the first sound in a word. Most then introduce the last and middle sounds in that order. However, the main goal is for the child to be able to segment (separate) each phoneme in a word, and then blend isolated phonemes back into the word *in the right order*.

Most programmes begin with listening exercises. The child sees a set of simple pictures each representing an object or animal. She says the word in the first picture and listens for the first sound. As she identifies each picture in turn, she is asked to put them together in groups depending on whether they start with the same first sound: *c*at, *c*ub, *c*ap, *or b*ig, *b*at, *b*all. Next, pictures can be sorted on the basis of the last sound (cu*p*, ma*p*, to*p*), and then middle sound (c*o*t, d*o*g, t*o*p). Don't use rhyming endings for these exercises because children will think that two phonemes are one sound. Once children can do this, they can be taught to substitute blank tokens for each phoneme in two- and three-sound words placed in a row from left to right. The final step is to introduce the concept of a 'sound-picture' to teach the child about letters. This term was developed for the Phono-Graphix™ curriculum and solves a number of problems. Children learn that a letter is a 'picture' for one sound. This makes it clear what is being symbolized. Just as *real* objects can be drawn in pictures, so can *real* sounds be drawn as pictures. This terminology helps later when the child is introduced to sound-pictures that have more than one letter. The teacher should say something like: 'Words are made up of sounds. Letters are sound-pictures for each of these sounds. It's just like when you draw a picture of a dog or a house. This is the sound-picture (b) for the sound /b/ in the word "bat".' Show the child the letter or point to it. *Do not use letter-names.*

Some children will need extensive practice with these exercises. Others will move ahead quickly. Detailed lessons on how to introduce phonemes and letters are provided in the next section on Year 1 reading instruction. Information on where to get materials for teaching these skills is provided in the Appendix to this chapter.

Logic

The child should learn the logic that governs this level. This is that the *same* phoneme, no matter where it appears in the word – first, middle, last – is represented by the *same* letter symbol. We learned earlier that young children have trouble with the logic of 'transitivity'. This is where a symbol stands for the same thing no matter where it appears. Children can learn a phoneme sequence in a two- or three-sound word but then be unable to generalize this knowledge to another word containing one or more of those phonemes. Do exercises in which the same phoneme occurs in different positions: bag/cab, mad/dam, pit/top. You can use nonsense words as well: bip/pim, etc. The teacher or parent needs to point out that no matter where a sound is in a word, it is spelled with the same letter, and no matter where a letter is in a word, it stands for the same sound.

Fine Motor Control

The children's section of most bookstores has books for tracing, joining dots, copying shapes, etc. These are good exercises for training a child's ability to control a pencil and to notice visual detail. When a child begins to learn to read, she should also trace and copy letter shapes. *Copying letters helps you see them.* Copying letters in a left to right sequence helps the child organize his thinking about the order of sounds in words and the order of words on the page. Once tracing and copying skill is fairly good, children can write some words from memory: *cat, dog, pig,* and once they can do this, they can write *sound sequences* using the letters they are learning about, saying each sound out loud as they write. They can write what you say from segmented sounds: /c/–/a/–/t/, and from sounds blended into the word: 'cat'. Use wide-ruled paper for this.

Don't waste classroom time letting children scribble, colour in a colouring book, write pseudo letters or letter strings that are not legitimate in English spelling. If a child wants to do that at home on his own, that's fine. The children should learn early on that letters have special and constant forms, and that letters are sound-pictures that stand for sounds in words.

Visual Discrimination and Scanning

These skills will improve the more the child copies letters and words (not scribbles), especially if he sounds out each phoneme as it goes on the page, as described above. The movement of the hand combined with the sound of the voice trains the eye where to look. The sound of the voice combined with the place where you look, trains the hand where to move. (By the way, 'sky-writing', or writing letter-forms in the air – a feature of some reading programmes – doesn't work. To create cross-modal connections like the ones I'm talking about, *two or more* modes must be connected: writing is movement made *visible.*)

Some children may not get far with these skills, and that's perfectly OK. Children are highly variable in their perceptual and motor development at this age, and most will improve noticeably when they are six. What you have done is put them on track, so that when reading and writing begins in earnest, they will have the right logic, and some of the right skills.

Year 1: Teaching the Basic Code

Good reading programmes use materials that correspond to the child's developing expertise in mastering the alphabet code. This does not mean that the teacher should not read interesting stories, teach poetry, or invite children to invent stories that she can transcribe. One innovative teacher I observed published a weekly 'magazine' of individual children's stories. These were not stories the children wrote in undecipherable invented spelling, but stories composed *verbally* that the teacher recorded. The children experienced the power of writing directly, as a true method of preserving their thoughts and ideas. These transcriptions transcended time and space because they were completely intelligible to the whole family. They faithfully preserved what the child *meant* to say.

Teaching the beginning reader is accomplished by keeping to materials and exercises that are mutually reinforcing and complementary. If a child is just beginning to master one-to-one mapping of consonants and simple vowels ('a pig sat in mud'), he or she should not be expected to read text written at a more complex level of logic ('Fido was a friendly dog until he saw a stranger in the yard').

The more compatible the materials (games, readers, stories, worksheets, spelling words) across all three skills: reading, writing, spelling, the faster children will learn and the less likely they will be to develop reading difficulties. The text of traditional children's literature is peppered with digraphs, consonant clusters, phonograms, and irregular spellings, and should be off limits for the child reader at this stage. This does not mean that children's literature is off limits for the teacher or parent at story time. Nor am I proposing that 'big books' should be banished from the classroom. However, the sooner the child masters the alphabet code, the sooner she will be able to read anything in print.

In this section, I have adopted a pragmatic approach. I am assuming that children have not had the advantage of skills training in the Reception class as described above. For most teachers, and for parents who have discovered that something is amiss with their six-year-old's reading skills, this section outlines how to begin from the beginning. Traditional instruction will usually guarantee that the child has learned precisely what he does not need, and precisely what he should not know. By Year 1, children have usually memorized letter-names which can interfere with learning to read and spell. They have been taught lots of 'sight words', setting them up for failure. These children have learned two things:

1. Letter-names are something you chant in sequence and don't help you read.

2. The way you learn to read is to memorize whole words by sight.

The goals of beginning reading instruction are identical to those already reviewed. The difference is that most six-year-olds understand the logic of sequencing and symbolizing. Working in small groups, or with one child, the first step is to begin introducing each phoneme in a word, first by sound alone, and then with its accompanying letter. Consonants and vowels should be interleaved, so that children can begin to read, write and spell simple words. The order in which these sounds are introduced is governed by the difficulty of the mapping logic.

For the Teacher

Because the teacher or parent needs to know how to produce each phoneme correctly, Tables 10.1 and 10.2 are for adults, so that you can organize your thinking. To help you understand how English phonemes are produced, they have been set up in linguistic categories. The categories are based on which parts of the mouth move to make each sound and how the air is released. Consonants can be 'plosive' or 'stopped' (air flow is interrupted, held, and 'exploded'); 'fricative' (expelled with force or friction); 'aspirated' (breathy); or 'continuous' (voicing can be extended). Sixteen consonants can be categorized into pairs because they are produced by the same mouth movements, and vary only because one of the pair is voiced and one is not: /b/ (bat) and /p/ (pat). Stand in front of a mirror, say each sound, and put your hand over your windpipe.

All vowels are 'voiced' (vocal folds vibrate). Vowels differ from one another due to the position of the lips, jaw, and tongue. Linguists have organized the vowels into a 'vowel circle' according to these positions. Vowels adjacent on the circle are harder to tell apart. We have found in the clinic that children have trouble discriminating the adjacent vowels in the sequence /i/, /e/, /a/, /u/, /o/ (bit, bet, bat, but,

TABLE 10.1   Classification of English Consonants

Parts of the Mouth	Voiced	Unvoiced	Air Type
bilabial	b	p	plosive
alveolar	d	t	plosive
velar	g	k	plosive
labial/palatal	j	ch	plosive
labial/palatal	zh	sh	fricative
palatal/dental	z	s	fricative
dental/labial	v	f	fricative
lingual/dental	<u>th</u>	th	fricative
pharyngeal		h	aspirated
labial/velar		w	aspirated
alveolar	l		continuous
velar	r		continuous
Air via the Nose			
bilabial nasal	m		continuous
palatal nasal	n		continuous
velar nasal	ng		continuous
Co-articulated Consonant			
labial/velar		qu (kw)	plosive/aspirated

Latin terms: labia = lips; alveolar = upper gums; velar = soft palate; palatal = hard palate; dental = teeth; lingual = tongue; pharynx = throat; nasal = nose.

hot), set out here in order from the jaw most closed/mouth most smiling/tongue most forward, to the jaw and mouth most open/tongue flat (see Table 10.2). You might want to check this in a mirror. You should be able to pronounce each of these vowels accurately, with slight differences in the position of the mouth and jaw, so that children can hear *and see* the difference between them. Because vowels with similar postures (e.g., /i/ and /e/) sound alike, introduce the vowels further apart on the chart first: /i/ (bit) and /o/ (hot) are the widest contrast; /i/ and /a/ (bat) make the most three-sound words (see Appendix). Diphthongs are combinations of two simple vowels produced in rapid succession, counting as only one vowel in a syllable.

In British English words containing the sound /ah/ are usually

TABLE 10.2   Classification of Simple English Vowels

Sounds	Jaw Position	Word	Lip Posture	Tongue Position
/ee/	close	see	smile	forward
/i/	⎪	sit	smile	forward
	to			
/e/	⎪	get	smile	forward
/u/	↓	but	unrounded	mid
/ah/	open	last	unrounded	back
/o/	open	hot	rounded	back
/aw/	⎪	law	rounded	back
	to			
/oo/	↓	look	rounded	raised
/o͞o/	close	soon	rounded	raised

English Diphthongs

Sound	Word	Combines Vowel Sounds:
/ae/	ate	/e/ + /ee/
/ie/	die	/ah/ + /ee/
/ue/	cue	/ee/ + /o͞o/
/oe/	toe	/u/ + /o͞o/
/ou/	out	/a/ + /o͞o/
/oi/	oil	/oe/ + /ee/

Vowel + r

Sounds	Word	
/or/	for	/or/
/er/	her	/er/

spelled a. This creates a code overlap problem: 'cat', 'last'. Avoid words with /ah/ vowels in these early lessons.

Getting Started

The Basic Code presented at the beginning of this book is illustrated in Table 10.3 in a more convenient form.

The teacher should begin by asking children if they know how they

TABLE 10.3   Letters for a Basic Code Movable Alphabet

Vowels

Sounds	Key Word	Letter(s)
/a/	sat	a
/e/	set	e
/i/	sit	i
/ah/	last	a
/o/	dog	o
/aw/	law	aw
/u/	but	u
/ae/	ate	a–e
/ee/	seem	ee
/ie/	time	i–e
/oe/	tone	o–e
/ue/	cute	u–e
/oo/	book	oo
/$\overline{oo}$/	soon	$\overline{oo}$
/oi/	oil	oi/oy (optional)
/ou/	out	ou
/er/	her	er
/oe/er/	for	or

produce speech. The children need to explore how their mouth-parts move when they talk. Ask them to close their eyes and feel the movement. Draw their attention to particular movements, such as what the lips are doing at the start of these words: 'mut', 'but', 'mit', 'pit'; feel the teeth touch the lower lip in 'fat' and 'vet'; feel where the tongue goes at the start of these words: 'dog', 'log', 'tag', 'nag'. These exercises can be done with the whole class, and then repeated in small groups.

Working in small groups, tell the children you are going to teach them each sound in *their speech*, and how each of these sounds is written. Start with a set of consonants that obey one-to-one mapping (*no digraphs*) and choose those that are easy to model, and easy for the child to feel and hear. Model each sound clearly and insist that the children watch your mouth. The sound /m/ is a good

TABLE 10.3   Letters for a Basic Code Movable Alphabet   *Cont'd*

Consonants

Sound/Letter(s)	Key Word
/b/	bed
/d/	date
/f/	fun
/g/	get
/h/	hot
/j/	jump
/k/	kin
	c̲ as option
	for /k/
/l/	log
/m/	mat
/n/	not
/p/	pan
/r/	red
/s/	sit
/t/	top
/v/	vet
/w/	wet
/x/(ks)	fox
/z/	zip
/ch/	chip
/ng/	song
/qu/	quit
/sh/	ship
/t̲h̲/	them
/th/	thin

beginning because the children can see your mouth posture, feel this in their own mouth, and hear it easily when it is extended – /mmmmmmmmmmmmmmmm/.

HINTS FOR UNGLUING SOUNDS

When you introduce one of these voiced consonants – /b/, /d/, /g/, /j/, /w/ – try and say it *with no vowel attached to it*. Say /b/ and not /buh/. Voicing obviously adds sound beyond the consonant, but keep it as short as possible. Nor should a vowel sound ever be connected to unvoiced consonants such as /h/, /k/, /p/, /t/. Say /p/ (a puff of air) and not /puh/. Only this way can the child learn how to unglue sounds in words. This is the key for using a phonetic alphabet. (The voiced consonants /m/, /n/, /ng/, /l/, /r/, /<u>th</u>/, /v/, /z/ can be extended without a vowel, and so can the unvoiced consonants /f/, /s/, /sh/, /th/.)

When all the children can make the sound you have introduced (/mmm/) both at the beginning and at the end of several three-sound words, introduce the letter that represents it in print as a sound-picture for that sound. You can do this with a movable alphabet, or use a small whiteboard and marker pen. A complete movable alphabet is useful for teaching the Basic Code. If you purchase one, make sure that the digraphs are printed together on the same card, felt or tile (see Appendix). You can make your own movable alphabet out of cardboard covered with self-adhesive plastic.

The word charts at the back of this chapter list two- and three-sound words with one-to-one mapping only. You can use them to set up a sequence of instruction, or purchase curriculum materials organized in this sequence (see Appendix). It's a good idea to introduce the sound /k/ with both spellings <u>k</u> and <u>c</u> because more words are spelled with <u>c</u> than with <u>k</u>.

You should move quickly through the introductory process. Be sure to make it cumulative by incorporating previous information into new lessons. Children will learn this one-to-one logic rapidly and should be able to master a new phoneme/letter combination about every other day or faster. They should have practice, however, to make this stick, at least one hour over a two- or three-day period.

When the child has learned a subset of phoneme/letter relationships, she can begin to learn the important elements of an alphabetic writing system. These are how to segment or separate phonemes in two- and three-sound words into isolated sounds: /c/–/a/–/t/, how to blend sounds back into a word ('cat'), and how to listen for sequences of phonemes in a series of words, a process called 'tracking' or 'chaining'. Some exercises are described below. The child should also write at every step, copying letters in left to right sequence, saying each sound aloud (*not* the letter-name) while copying each letter, and spelling words you dictate, sound-by-sound.

You can buy reading materials (listed in the Appendix) that will complement these early lessons. Read America has stories for the Basic Code level. Some phonics readers are good because they stay with simple three-sound words. This is also true of some of the older phonics readers which may be in your library. A list of them is included at the end of this chapter. Stay with materials that are consistent with one-to-one mapping first before moving on to digraphs.

The child will learn a few 'sight words' *in the context of reading*. These are words which are not easy to decode because their spellings are irregular. Several irregularly spelled words are hard to avoid in stories: a (uh), the (thuh), was (woz), one (won), once (wonce), says (sez). If the child encounters one of these words, simply tell him what it says. Don't explain anything or give a lecture on 'sight words', or insist that he memorize them. There are so few of these words, children will learn them without difficulty. Be sure that he *does* read all the words that are consistent with the Basic Code to this point. *Do not ask children to read books containing a lot of clusters and irregularly spelled words*, no matter how pretty the pictures nor how much 'fun' they are to read.

Actively discourage letter-names. If a teacher asks the class: 'What sound does this letter stand for?' and shows the letter b, she'll get a chorus of 'It's a bee!' She must insist that 'bee' is a letter-name *they will have to forget for now*. Children should be told that letter-names do not help you read or spell. What is important is the *sound* each letter stands for in a word. *Show* them the letter b – don't say its name – and tell them it is a sound-picture for the sound /b/. No matter where that sound comes in a word, it is always spelled with this letter or sound-picture: b.

Lessons should begin with a review of what was done during the previous lesson. This means keeping a record book, especially if you are working with several different groups. The teacher needs to make certain that all children learn to do these exercises independently. Children can gradually be identified as to who is going to need more time versus those who get it immediately.

During this first level, children can practise using a variety of materials. The letters can be traced, copied, or written from memory. Montessori teachers can use sandpaper letters, first traced by movement of a finger and then copied on to paper while saying the sound. Pictures or objects can be used to cue matching to the initial, final, or middle sound, and then the letter for this sound can be printed on paper or in a workbook. Children should copy words, and say each sound as they are writing the letter.

When these exercises become familiar, the teacher or parent should introduce the terms 'consonants', little short sounds that come and go quickly, and 'vowels', sounds that last longer. Children should be told that you can't have a language with just consonants. Tell a story in an imaginary language made up of consonants so they get the point.

Vowels add volume to speech. You can sing and shout with vowels and not with consonants. Use an example of calling a child for dinner, first with the consonants of his name: 'John' – /j/–/nnnnnn/, and then say the vowel sound /o/ elongated. Ask the children which sound John would be likely to hear if he was down the street. If we only had vowels we couldn't have a language either. Illustrate this by telling a story using only vowels. The point of this exercise is to give children a vocabulary to talk about the two types of sounds in words. This lesson should make it clear that most words have both vowels and consonants (exceptions are: I, you, a), and *all words have a vowel*, no exceptions.

This information is very helpful for spelling in creative writing. Children tend to leave vowels out of words when they write. 'The nd' is a common mistake. The child uses the *letter-name* 'en' for the vowel+consonant sounds. If children are taught accurate sound–letter relationships, plus the fact that all words have vowels in them, they would never make these kinds of errors.

Segmenting, Blending, and Tracking

Simple CV, VC or CVC words and nonsense words can be constructed with the movable alphabet in small group exercises with the teacher. Children should watch and listen while the teacher makes the sounds as they are separated and joined into words using the movable alphabet. Begin with very short patterns, and make certain each child can see as you model the changing sounds, left to right (child's view). Next the children can make the sounds as the teacher moves the letters apart and together:

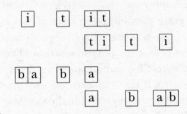

Hundreds of combinations can be made using real and nonsense C V, VC and CVC patterns. Showing children how these patterns can be connected and disconnected helps them to understand how sounds are represented in print. During these exercises the child should touch each letter and say its sound, both when the letters are apart (segmenting) and when they are side-by-side (blending). This technique is very powerful because it focuses the child on left-to-right sequencing as he decodes words, and trains the eyes to look at every letter.

Few children have difficulty hearing isolated phonemes (/b/, /m/, /v/) or making comparisons between them ('Is /d/ the same as /g/?'). The trouble begins when phonemes are embedded in words. 'Tracking' or 'chaining' allows the child to hear that there has been a change made *somewhere* in a sound sequence and to begin to identify where in that sequence the change took place.

The rules of tracking are as follows:

1. Only one phoneme changes at a time.
2. Phoneme changes occur in one of five ways:
   a. Addition: a new sound comes in (tip/stip).
   b. Deletion: a sound went away (tip/ip).
   c. Substitution: one sound went away and another took its place (tip/top).
   d. Repetition: two sounds in the word are the same (tip/pip).
   e. Reversibility: sounds change places (tip/pit).

A tracking sequence can extend anywhere from a single phoneme to a multi-syllable word. Sample sequences are set out below and in the tables at the end of this chapter. The teacher begins by putting out a letter from the movable alphabet facing the child. For groups, each child should have his own set of movable alphabet cards, tiles or felt letters.

The child is told: 'If that is /p/, show me /pi/' (say /i/ 'it'), and the child should bring the letter i into position to the right of the p. The chain proceeds: 'If that is /pi,/ show me /pip/,' the teacher repeating the last word each time before the next instruction. The child, and not the teacher, is responsible for manipulating the letters according to the instructions. For each tracking exercise give the children only the letters they will need for the sequence. In the example below left, they will need a, i, o, b, h, p, p, s, t.

REAL WORDS	NONSENSE WORDS
p	p
pi	pi
pip	pim
pop	pom
hop	dom
hot	dop
hat	dup
at	tup
bat	tut
bit	ut
sit	sut
sip	tus

If a child makes an error or becomes confused, simply back up and repeat an earlier simpler pattern. Keep the sequencing simple if the child has difficulty with complex transformations. The child should touch the letters and say the sounds (*not* letter-names) in left-to-right order to keep the sounds in mind. A child must work just at the margin of his level of competence.

When children write a word, or spell it with a movable alphabet, using spellings that have not yet been taught or discussed, these should correspond to the Basic Code. For example, 'duk' or 'duc' is acceptable for 'duck' until the child has learned about the <u>ck</u> spelling for the sound /k/.

Consonant Clusters

When a child is secure with simple CV, VC and CVC patterns, and most letters for one-to-one mapping have been taught, consonant clusters can be introduced. A chart of the consonant clusters that begin words and end words is provided in Table 11.2 (p. 274). Lists of words with consonant clusters are provided at the end of this chapter. Consonant clusters are *two or more phonemes* and must never be confused with digraphs (one phoneme). At this point in learning to read, consonant clusters must be restricted to those spelled with single letters, those the child has already learned. *Most clusters have only one spelling.* This means the children can take the knowledge they have so far and expand this using the same logic into hundreds of new words.

When children move on to clusters make it clear that double letters stand for only one sound. The double letters <u>ff</u>, <u>ll</u>, and <u>ss</u> occur often at the ends of common words.

Start with two-sound clusters in the initial position: /s/-/l/ '*sl*at' (CCVC). When children are reasonably secure on several different CCVC clusters, move on to two-sound clusters in final position: /n/-/d/ 'sa*nd*' (CVCC), and finally to clusters in both positions: 'grand' (CCVCC). When you use nonsense words in tracking exercises, be sure to keep to the clusters that are legitimate in English, that is, those that are likely to appear in real words. The pair /mp/ is a legitimate final cluster in English ('bump'), but /np/ is not, even though it can be pronounced.

As a rule of thumb, some clusters are much more common than others. Consonant plus /l/ or /r/ are common in initial consonant clusters and are fairly easy to hear, especially by extending or exaggerating the /l/ or /r/ sound in the word. These two consonants follow a limited number of initial consonants: /b/, /f/, /g/, /k/ (c), and /p/ (brim, flat, grip, glad, clap, plan). The /r/ can also follow /d/, or /t/ (drop, trip). The initial /s/ blends with more sounds than any other: /k/, /l/, /m/, /n/, /p/, /t/, /w/ (skip, slam, smell, snap, spin, stop, swim), as well as in triple clusters: /scr/, /spl/, /str/ (scrap, split, strap). However, triple clusters are very difficult for young children to master, especially in final position ('tempt') and come late in speech development. It is not important to teach triple clusters at this stage. Leave them for later.

Final consonant clusters begin with a limited number of consonant sounds, mainly /l/, /n/, /r/, and /s/. Most of these sounds *precede* the following consonants: /d/, /p/, /k/, /t/. Examples for /l/ are 'old', 'alp', 'elk', 'melt'; for /n/ 'and' and 'bent'.

The same kinds of activities described earlier should be used for learning clusters. These include sorting words cued by a picture containing initial or final clusters or both; copying words with clusters; filling in missing letters in a cluster on worksheets (c—ab = crab), writing stories which contain certain words with clusters, and tracking exercises with clusters. (Be careful not to get digraphs, where two written letters represent one sound – ch, ng, sh, th, ck, etc. – mixed up in these exercises.)

When students begin to show facility in mastering clusters in both initial and final positions in a word, they are ready to move on to consonant digraphs.

Consonant Digraphs

Consonant digraphs introduce a completely new logic. The teacher should not begin to work with digraphs until the child is comfortable manipulating, reading and spelling single letters alone and in clusters. The children have so far learned a particular logic, which says, 'Sounds can be represented by one letter: one letter = one sound.' For young children, a sudden switch to a logic that says 'Sometimes two of *these same letters* will represent one sound,' creates a class-inclusion problem in which a symbol is simultaneously in two categories at the same time (see Chapter 8). When the simple logic of one-to-one mapping is secure, then teaching digraphs will go smoothly and quickly.

The remaining consonant sounds in English are:

/ch/ – chair
/ng/ – ring
/sh/ – shut
/th/ (voiced) – them
/th/ (unvoiced) – thing
/kw/ – quit (always spelled *qu*)

Introduce the ck spelling alternative here also. It is a common spelling for /k/ in the final position in a syllable.

Digraphs need a special introduction to explain that two letters make a sound-picture that stands for one sound. If the children are receptive, they may enjoy hearing the story about the people who invented our alphabet. English monks borrowed the letters from the Latin alphabet and ran out of letters because English had a lot more sounds than Latin. Instead of inventing new letters, they just stuck two of the old letters together to stand for the leftover sounds. This is an interesting (true) story and makes the important point that letters are assigned to sounds, rather than sounds being assigned to letters.

To understand that a digraph represents *only one sound*, children have to go back and explore mouth movements, and do listening exercises, to make this point stick. Once the child has become aware of the *sound* /ch/, the teacher can introduce the sound-picture ch written on a *single* letter tile, card, or piece of felt, in the movable alphabet. Do not teach this with two separate letters pushed together. This same procedure is used for the remaining consonants spelled with digraphs. Practice with digraphs proceeds in exactly the same way as discussed earlier. Lists of words spelled with digraphs are found at the end of this chapter.

If you introduce the spelling alternative ck, explain that this is a sound-picture for the sound /k/ at the *ends* of some words.

Redundant Consonants

The letters c, x and q are redundant in English spelling. They stand for sounds that can be spelled with other letters. This is important information for the teacher, but the children do not need to know this. Children will already have learned that the letter c stands for the sound /k/. Later, they will be learning that c is also a spelling alternative for the sound /s/ when it is followed by the letters e, i, or y: cent, city, cypress (the only spelling rule that is completely consistent). The letter x stands for /ks/, spelled in the singular as x (fox) and in the plural as ks or cks: (sharks, socks). The spelling x is also used in the Latin prefix ex, as in 'explode' and 'exact', for /ks/ (eksplode) or /gz/ (egzact), and rarely as /z/ at the beginning of Greek words (xylophone).

The letters qu stand for the consonant sounds /kw/ pronounced simultaneously, and this spelling is always used. You may have a child who notices that /ks/ or /kw/ is like 'two sounds', and that's OK. Just tell her that she is a very good listener to notice this.

Plurals

Introduce plurals after consonants are secure. Plurals are usually spelled s or es even though they sound /z/ or /ez/ most of the time. In fact, the only time that the plural s sounds /s/ is when it follows the phonemes /f/, /k/, /p/, /t/ (cliffs, bricks, caps, cats). Children will need to be taught about plurals (spelled s but sounds /z/) so no one gets confused. Most children have no trouble with this in reading because it doesn't sound right to read words incorrectly: 'panss', 'tubss'. In creative writing, however, they might write a z, which is incorrect: 'panz', 'tubz'.

Vowel Digraphs

So far, the children have learned five vowel sounds and five vowel letters. There are sixteen true vowel sounds in standard BBC English, excluding vowel + r, and the many regional variants. The children should have practised enough consonant digraphs to be comfortable with the fact that two letters can be a sound-picture for one sound. The teacher must be aware that apart from poor phonemic awareness, *vowel digraphs are the single most important cause of reading and spelling problems*. There are so many of them spelled so many different ways. The children must be taught consistent spellings for these vowels (Basic Code) and stay with this long enough for the sounds to be firmly embedded in memory. The key to mastery of English spelling is being absolutely secure on the sounds of the vowels. Some vowels are hard to tell apart and vowel spellings cannot be constantly shifting when these sounds are introduced.

There is no satisfactory way to classify English vowels. Vowels aren't actually long or short, so that's no help. Vowels *are* simple or complex in terms of their sound patterns. Complex vowels, or diphthongs, are two simple vowel sounds pronounced in rapid succession: /oe-ee/

'toil', but our spelling code doesn't mark vowels this way (<u>toeeel</u>), so this is no help either. As there is no solution to this problem, don't try to classify vowels for children, especially do not use the terms 'long' and 'short'. This makes them believe that they should have noticed something about these vowels that they cannot see or hear.

As the teacher proceeds to introduce each vowel sound, she should continue to use all of the techniques described earlier. Children should learn the vowels in the same types of exercises – segmenting, blending, copying, tracking, reading, writing, spelling. Teach the remaining vowels in this order:

E-CONTROLLED VOWEL SPELLINGS
Five vowel letters combine with <u>e</u> to stand for five different vowel sounds. They are introduced next for several reasons.

1. They reuse all five vowel letters the children have just learned, adding the same spelling feature (an extra <u>e</u>).

2. The e-controlled spelling is the most probable (likely) spelling for the vowel sounds /ae/ /ee/ /ie/ /oe/ and /ue/ in common English words. In other words, they are ideal for the Basic Code.

3. They introduce a new principle, in which a digraph can be split apart by a consonant and still work together. The <u>e</u> can 'control' the pronunciation of the preceding vowel *at a distance*. These are the only digraphs like this.

The teacher needs to know that all but one (/ee/) is a diphthong, so she can pronounce them correctly. She needs to know that the splitting off of the <u>e</u> occurs very rarely for the sound /ee/ (seen, queen, theme), *always* for the sound /ae/ (came), and mainly for the rest: time, tone, cute. For these reasons, the movable alphabet should reflect these common spelling patterns: <u>a</u>–<u>e</u>, <u>ee</u>, <u>i</u>–<u>e</u>, <u>o</u>–<u>e</u>, <u>u</u>–<u>e</u> (same, seem, time, tone, cute), with each digraph on a separate tile.

Don't let the child confuse the vowel sound /ue/ (as in 'cute') with /$\overline{oo}$/ ('coot'); /ue/ is a diphthong (/ee-$\overline{oo}$/) and /$\overline{oo}$/ is a simple vowel.

The children should be taught that even though the <u>e</u> is separated from its vowel letter, the sound is the same as if the letters were side-by-side. Do not teach this as 'the e is silent'. Instead, simply say that two letters work together as a sound-picture for a vowel sound.

To illustrate how the e̲ can move to the right, make up lots of these vowel pairs on cardboard and then cut the letters apart, inserting the consonant to spell a word:

| c | ae | k | | c | a | k | e |

Let the children use scissors to cut off the e̲ from its companion vowel, and reassemble the letters in the correct order. Words with e-controlled spellings are listed at the end of the chapter.

Another way to teach the impact of the e̲ on preceding vowels is to transform one word into another using the letter e̲ from the movable alphabet: subtracting and adding it back to make words like: bit/bite, hat/hate, win/wine, pin/pine, etc. There is a list of these words at the end of this chapter.

VOWELS SPELLED WITH O

The next group of vowel digraphs all coincidentally use the letter o̲. These are the sounds /o͞o/ (soon), /oo/ (book), /ou/ (/a-o͞o/; out), and /oi/ (/oe-ee/; oil). The first two are simple vowels; the last two are diphthongs. The difference between the vowel sounds /o͞o/ (soon) and /oo/ (book) is hard to hear, which probably explains why they were spelled the same way. Both vowel sounds are produced by an exaggerated rounding of the lips. The /o͞o/ has the smallest opening. The teacher should ask children to say word pairs contrasting these sounds and listen carefully: soon/soot, boon/book, loot/look, and so forth. Teach each vowel one at a time using all the previous exercises.

VOWEL + R

There are many vowels that combine with /r/. In most British dialects the final r is softened and shortened to /er/. The sound /er/ by itself can be written er̲, ur̲, or ir̲. In one case the r̲ signals a change in the main vowel sound – /or/ is different from /o/ in 'hot' and has multiple spellings: or̲, oar̲, ore̲, our̲, oor̲ ('for', 'soar', 'tore', 'four', 'floor'). To hear these vowel contrasts clearly, stand in front of a mirror and say these word pairs slowly: hem/her; fob/for.

THE LETTER A̲

Two vowel sounds in British English share the Basic Code spelling a̲ (/a/ cat /ah/ fast). You will have to teach this as a 'code overlap'.

However, in many regions the vowel sound /ah/ is not used, and words like 'fast' 'father' 'bath' are pronounced /a/ ('cat'), as they are in the U.S. Use the vowel sounds that are common in your region.

Y VOWEL LETTER

Y is not a consonant as many people think. The letter y is a spelling alternative for several vowel sounds, mainly /ee/ (baby), /ie/ (cry), and /i/ (gym), the most common substitution being for the final /ee/ in multi-syllable words (lucky, plenty, mainly, vicinity). The beginning sound in the word 'yes' is also a *very* brief /ee/ sound (so brief, some people can't hear it), but it can't be spelled ee, or else 'yes' would be spelled: *eees*, 'yellow' *eeellow*, and so forth. The teacher might want to introduce the letter y here because it appears frequently. She should explain that sometimes this letter is a sound-picture for vowel sounds the children already know. Y can be introduced informally when a child asks how to spell a word like 'yes', or 'baby' during creative writing.

Once the children have learned one symbol for every sound in English, they know the Basic Code, the most common spelling for the sounds of the English language. They will also know the alternative spellings c, ck, and y. This sets up an 'Initial Teaching Alphabet' but without any funny letters that must be unlearned. Children can now spell hundreds of words correctly, *and nearly every word* phonetically. When this initial alphabet or Basic Code is secure, it is time to move on to the next step in the logic of learning the alphabet code. Children are now ready for training in mastering the spelling alternatives of English orthography which are introduced in the next chapter.

This chapter provided a brief overview of the sequence in which the sound-to-letter code of our alphabet should be mastered. Depending on the age and aptitude of the child when lessons begin, this sequence should take from about four to eight months to teach. If this doesn't happen, you're either doing something wrong, the child is too young, or the child has a problem you haven't discovered, such as a difficulty with visual tracking. If you're using this approach correctly, any problem a child might have with phoneme-awareness should disappear.

The approach outlined here is compatible with most types of

language arts instruction that are ongoing in the classroom. If taught properly, the children can read stories written in simple prose in Year 1. This method is not, however, compatible with invented spelling, where children are allowed to misspell words without correction and to invent and practise spelling patterns that don't exist in English. This will undo everything the teacher is trying to accomplish.

This does not mean that children should do no creative writing. By the middle of Year 1, children should have a good grasp of the Basic Code, which means they can write most words in English they want to and be able to spell them phonetically. They can do lots of creative writing. Any errors in their phonetic spellings can be checked for confusion they may have about the code so far, and turned into an individual spelling lesson. Spelling lessons should be based upon words that the child uses and that he can read, and not on unrelated word lists.

Word Lists

CV/VC/CVC Words

Consonants: p/b, t/d, k/g, f/v, s/z, j   Vowels: a, e, i, o, u

/a/	/e/	/i/	/o/	/u/
at	bed	bib	Bob	bug
bad	beg	bid	dog	bus
bag	bet	big	dot	but
bat	fed	bit	fog	dug
fat	get	did	got	Gus
gap	jet	dig	job	jug
gas	keg	fib	jog	jut
pat	peg	fig	jot	pup
sad	pep	fit	pop	sub
sag	pet	if	pot	tub
sap	Ted	it	sob	tug
sat	vet	kid	top	up
tag		kit	tot	us
tap		pig		
zag		pit		
zap		sip		
		sit		
		tip		
		zig		
		zip		

C as option for k. C sounds /k/ when not followed by e, i, y:

cab			cob	cub
cap			cod	cup
cat			cop	cut
			cot	

Words ending x /ks/:

ax	ex	fix	ox	
fax	Rex	mix	box	
lax	sex	six	fox	
max	vex		pox	
sax				
tax				
wax				

253

CV/VC/CVC Words *Cont'd*

/a/	/e/	/i/	/o/	/u/
Nasal Consonants (m, n)				
am	Ben	bin	mop	gum
an	den	dim	not	gun
Ann	men	din	on	muff
can	met	fin	Tom	Mum
Dan	mess	kin		mutt
fan	net	kiss		sum
jam	pen	miss		sun
mad	ten	mit		
man		nip		
map		pin		
mat		tin		
nap				
pan				
ran				
Sam				
tan				
Aspirated Consonants (h, w)				
had	hem	hid	hog	hub
ham	hen	him	hop	hug
hat	wed	hip	hot	hum
	wet	hit		hut
		win		
		wit		
Continuant Consonants (l, r; final l usually doubled)				
lad	bell	Bill	log	gull
pal	fell	fill	lot	rub
ran	led	hill	rob	rug
rat	leg	Jill	rod	
	red	lid	rot	
	well	lip		

CV/VC/CVC Words *Cont'd*

/a/	/e/	/i/	/o/	/u/
		lit		
		mill		
		pill		
		rid		
		rim		
		will		

Avoid these types of words for now:

1. '<u>all</u>' endings where vowel sounds /aw/ ('ball').
2. <u>a</u> spellings where vowel sounds /ah/ ('last', 'path').

CVC Consonant Digraphs (a, e, i, o, u vowels)

ch/sh/th/<u>th</u>/

/a/	/e/	/i/	/o/	/u/
ash	mesh	chin	chop	much
cash	shed	chip	gosh	rush
chap	shell	dish	moth	such
chat	them	fish	shop	shut
dash	then	ship		thug
mash		thin		
maths		this		
sash		wish		
shall		with		
than				
that				

/ng/

/a/	/e/	/i/	/o/	/u/
bang		ding	dong	hung
fang		king	long	lung
gang		ring	gong	rung
hang		sing	song	sung
rang		thing		
sang				
tang				

/kw/ (always spelled *qu*)

/a/	/e/	/i/	/o/	/u/
quack	quell	quick		
		quip		
		quit		

255

E-controlled Vowel Spellings

e–e	a–e	i–e	o–e	u–e
eve	age	bike	bone	cube
even	ape	bite	choke	cure
here	ate	chime	code	cute
theme	bake	dice	cone	fume
	base	dime	dome	mule
	cage	dive	dope	mute
	cake	file	dose	pure
	came	fine	doze	Yule
	case	fire	hole	
	chase	five	home	
	date	hide	hope	
	face	hike	joke	
	fade	hive	lone	
	fake	ice	mole	
	fame	kite	mope	
	gale	life	nose	
	game	like	note	
	gate	lime	poke	
	gave	line	pole	
	hate	live	quote	
	jade	mice	robe	
	lace	mile	rode	
	lake	mike	rope	
	lane	mine	sole	
	late	nice	tone	
	made	nine	vote	
	make	pine	whole	
	mane	quite	zone	
	maze	rice		
	name	ride		
	pale	ripe		
	race	shine		
	rake	side		
	rate	tide		
	sale	tile		
	save	time		
	shade	vine		
	shake	while		

E-controlled Vowel Spellings *Cont'd*

e–e	a–e	i–e	o–e	u–e
	shame	whine		
	shape	white		
	take	wide		
	tale	wife		
	tame	wine		
	wade	wipe		
	whale			

Vowel Transformations

e–e	a–e	i–e	o–e	u–e
her-e	at-e	bit-e	cod-e	cub-e
them-e	fad-e	din-e	hop-e	cut-e
	hat-e	fin-e	mop-e	mut-e
	mad-e	fir-e	not-e	
	man-e	hid-e	rob-e	
	pal-e	kit-e	rod-e	
	rat-e	pin-e		
		quit-e		
		rid-e		
		rip-e		
		shin-e		
		tim-e		
		win-e		

Consonant Clusters: Vowel Sound /a/

CCVC	CVCC	CCVCC
blab	band	bland
brag	bank	blank
bran	camp	brand
clad	damp	clamp
clam	fact	crank
clan	lamp	drank
clap	land	flank
crab	lank	gland
crag	pact	grand
cram	pant	plank
drab	ramp	prank
drag	rank	scamp
dram	rant	scant
flab	rapt	spank
flag	sand	stank
flap	sank	swank
flat	tact	tract
glad	tank	tramp
grab		
gran		
plan		
scan		
scat		
slab		
slam		
slap		
slat		
snap		
span		
spat		
stab		
stag		
tram		
trap		

Consonant Clusters: Vowel Sound /e/

CCVC	CVCC	CCVCC
bled	belt	blend
bred	bend	blest
clef	best	cleft
dress	deft	crept
dwell	dent	crest
fled	desk	slept
flex	fend	spend
fret	held	spent
sled	help	swept
smell	jest	trend
sped	kept	
spell	left	
swell	lend	
	mend	
	nest	
	next	
	pelt	
	pest	
	rent	
	rest	
	self	
	send	
	sent	
	tend	
	tent	
	vent	
	vest	
	weld	
	wend	
	went	
	west	
	zest	

Consonant Clusters: Vowel Sound /i/

CCVC	CVCC	CCVCC
brim	dint	blimp
cliff	disk	blink
clip	film	brink
crib	fist	brisk
drip	gift	crimp
flip	gild	crisp
flit	gist	drift
frill	hilt	drink
glib	hint	frisk
grid	jilt	glint
grill	kiln	primp
grim	kilt	print
grin	kink	skimp
grip	lift	spilt
grit	lilt	stilt
prim	limp	stink
skid	link	stint
skiff	lint	twist
skill	list	
skim	milk	
skin	mink	
skip	mint	
skit	mist	
slid	rift	
slim	rink	
slip	risk	
slit	sift	
sniff	silk	
snip	silt	
spill	sink	
spin	tilt	
spit	tint	
stiff	wilt	
still	wind	
swim	wink	
trill	wisp	
trim		
trip		
twin		

Consonant Clusters: Vowel Sound /o/

CCVC	CVCC	CCVCC
blot	bond	blond
clog	cost	frond
clot	fond	frost
crop	golf	
cross	honk	
drop	loft	
frog	lost	
slot	pomp	
stop	pond	
trod	romp	
trot	soft	

Consonant Clusters: Vowel Sound /u/

CCVC	CVCC	CCVCC
blub	bulk	blunt
bluff	bump	brunt
club	bunk	crust
drug	bust	drunk
drum	cult	grump
fluff	cusp	plump
glum	duct	skulk
grub	dump	skunk
gruff	dunk	slump
plug	dusk	slunk
plum	fund	spunk
plus	gulf	stump
scuff	gulp	stunk
scull	gust	trump
scum	hump	trunk
slug	hunk	trust
slum	hunt	
smug	husk	
spud	jump	
spun	junk	
stub	just	
stuff	lump	
stun	musk	
	must	
	pulp	
	pump	
	punk	
	punt	
	rump	
	runt	
	rusk	
	rust	
	sulk	
	sunk	
	sump	
	tuft	
	tusk	

Examples of Tracking Sequences

Teacher begins by setting up the chain, or by the statement 'Show me—', followed by, 'If that is—, then show me—.' An example of a simple chain would be, 'Show me /ip/. If that says /ip/, show me /bip/.' Use nonsense as well as real words for this exercise.

Simple	Complex
ip	ab
bip	tab
bep	bat
ep	bit
up	it
vup	et
vut	te
vuz	tek
suz	ket
siz	kat
diz	kap
dip	kop
fip	sop
fap	sap
hap	tap
hag	pat
bag	pet
bug	pe
bog	ep
fog	up
dog	ups
dig	us
dif	tus
if	stu
it	stuf
sit	stup
zit	step
zip	stap
zap	sap
gap	pas
gop	past
top	vast
op	vest
po	vet

Appendix: Reading Programmes and Curriculum Materials

Beginning Reading Programmes

Sound Foundations by Byrne and Fielding-Barnsley. (Peter Leyden Educational, Sydney, Australia.)

Phono-Graphix™: Reading Fundamentals and *Classroom – Grades 1–3* (Read America Inc., 370 Whooping Lane, Suite 1142, Altamonte Springs, FL 32701, USA. Tel: 00 1-352-735-9292; fax: 00 1-352-735-9294). *Phono-Graphix™* has been adapted for British students.

READING PROGRAMMES FOR PARENTS AND HOME-SCHOOLING

Reading Reflex (Carmen McGuinness and Geoffrey McGuinness, Read America, Altamonte Springs. British edition 1998.)

Early Readers for Home and Classroom

Allographs I: Sound Search Stories by D. McGuinness (SeaGate Press, PO Box 563, Sanibel, Florida 33957, USA). British edition available.

Phono-Graphix™: Story books and coded text readers (Read America, Altamonte Springs). British editions available.

Old phonics readers. Try the library. The following have controlled vocabularies and spellings:

Reading with Phonics by Hay and Wingo. (J. B. Lippincott, 1954.)

Lippincott Readers by McCracken and Walcutt. (J. B. Lippincott, 1963.)

Let's Read: Part 1 by Bloomfield and Barnhart. (Self-published, 1963.)

Merrill Linguistic Readers by Fries, Fries, Wilson & Rudolph. (Merrill Books Inc., 1966.)

Carden Reading Method: Grade 1, Book 1. (Mae Carden Inc., 1967.)

The Royal Road Readers: Book 1 by Daniels and Diack. (Chatto and Windus, London, 1962.)

Curriculum Materials

'Alphaboxes' in cardboard or felt; overhead transparencies; an audiotape of forty-two sounds (British version available); games – 'Sound Bingo' and 'Sound Memory', graded levels. (Read America, address as above.)

....

CHAPTER 11

Mastering the Advanced Code in Reading, Writing, and Spelling

Once a child has mastered the Basic Code, as described in the previous chapter, he has learned the *most probable* spelling alternative for every sound in English. The next step is to add the remaining less probable spelling alternatives to this code. A child cannot understand the logic of our spelling system unless and until the foundation of the Basic Code is secure.

Spelling is more difficult than reading because it is entirely a sound-to-print activity. First, you have to think of the words you want to write, hear the order of each individual phoneme in those words in your mind, and then transcribe those phonemes into a letter-by-letter representation on the page. This is opposite to reading, where the translation is from print back into sound. In reading, the printed text provides reminders or clues of how to decode, and the context of the story adds further information. In spelling there are no clues. You begin the task of writing facing a blank page. Initially, the process is tedious, sound-by-sound-by-sound. Ultimately, it becomes automatic and words and phrases are mentally regrouped and transcribed on to the page as units or chunks of sounds.

If every English word was spelled according to the Basic Code, this chapter would not need to be written. But as English spelling has multiple spelling alternatives for the same phoneme, this adds a further processing step. Images of letter-patterns have to be stored in memory in such a way that the reader and speller knows *which* pattern fits with *which* phoneme into *which* word. Unless there is some type of probability structure stored in memory about these patterns, every spelling of every word would have to be memorized separately – in other words, randomness or chaos.

Certain types of information help organize memory and reduce the memory load. This is information about how words and word parts can be classified so that there are clues about which spelling alternatives are more or less probable. This classification process is known as orthography. For example, the final /ee/ sound in multi-syllable words is spelled mainly y (baby) and sometimes ey (monkey) and rarely ee (jamboree). This does not mean that children should learn this as a 'spelling rule', because memorizing rules is not only inefficient, it doesn't work. Even when children can memorize rules, research has shown that they never apply them when they read or spell. Instead, spelling 'tendencies' or 'expectancies' must become part of tacit knowledge through *use*, so that they are stored in memory effortlessly.

The structure of our spelling system is set out in a spelling programme I designed, called Allographs™, a name derived from 'all graphs', or all possible spellings. Allographs was developed in response to a client's insistence that 'spelling is completely random'. Mike's story is informative. He had suffered injuries in a car crash that left him permanently disabled. He could not continue in his job because of its heavy physical demands, so he returned to university to train for another career. Mike is highly intelligent but suffered incredibly in his courses because he couldn't spell. He couldn't take notes that he could read. He couldn't write exams that the professor could read. He came to every exam with a bulky electronic spell-master that dramatically slowed down his performance, as he had to feed every third or fourth word into the machine. When Mike wrote a paper he always got As. On exams he usually got Cs, not because he couldn't remember the material, but because he ran out of time and patience.

Mike heard about the work I was doing with poor readers and came to ask for help with his spelling problem. But Mike had more than a spelling problem: he had an attitude. He protected his self-worth with an unassailable defence about why he couldn't spell. At every session he would arrive with a list of words he had heard the previous week that were spelled irregularly. He became more and more expert at this as we began to work together. The more he improved in his awareness of spelling patterns, the more he noticed spellings with rare patterns. I told him that experts had determined that more than 80 per cent of English spellings were regular. He was convinced this was incorrect and started compiling more and more lists of irregularly spelled words to prove that the experts were wrong. Mike was deaf to my argument that in order to learn to spell, you must focus first on what is regular. By paying attention *only* to what is irregular, you have to remember every word as a unique visual pattern.

Memory is efficient when it is organized on the basis of what is most likely rather than what is most unlikely. The human brain is particularly adept at storing recurring patterns, and very inefficient at remembering randomness (this is one of the primary differences between the human brain and a computer). Mike's strategy, however, blocked his brain from organizing predictable, recurring spelling patterns, with the result that nothing could ever be retrieved from memory.

I took this as a challenge and decided to prove to him that spelling patterns were non-random. I began by looking at all the spelling books that were available in classrooms or in the library. Everything I saw was indeed random (Mike was right!), and I had to abandon this effort and start from scratch. If spelling was non-random, the only way to demonstrate this would be to find every spelling alternative for each of the forty-three phonemes and phoneme combinations in English. Next, I had to find every common word that was spelled with each particular spelling variation. Although the task was clear, the way to execute it was not. There is no simple way to look up this information either in a dictionary or anywhere else. (See Note 7, Chapter 5.)

After several months of work compiling a sound-to-print dictionary, I had a basic framework sufficient to demonstrate the probability structure of the code for English spelling. (The final version of the spelling dictionary took much longer.) Mike was convinced, and as he became less defensive and began to learn to spell, we could even joke about his dogmatic belief system. One day I asked him if he knew when his spelling problems began. He remembered vividly that when he was seven, he saw that most of the spelling words he was given each week did not 'play by any rules'. That is, they did not fit with any rudimentary phonics he was being taught in reading lessons or any other kind of logic. He pointed this out to the teacher and was not given a satisfactory explanation. At that moment, he decided that as spelling 'made no sense', he would not bother learning to spell at all. Instead, he became an 'anti-speller', committing about twenty-five years of his life to a belief system created by a seven-year-old! If there is any doubt that a child's logic is important to learning, Mike is living proof to dispel that doubt.

Shortly after my work with Mike (who learned to spell and completed graduate school with honours), my students and I began doing observational research in first-grade classrooms. These transcriptions illustrate why so many children have problems learning to spell. Here are minute-by-minute notes from a classroom exercise in spelling:

> The lesson begins at 8.32 a.m.
>
> 'Today we're going to learn a new spelling list which has words that share the sound /ee/, like long /ee/ or short /ee/.' [Writes on the board *eat*.]
>
> 'Some of you might spell this /ee/, /tee/ [writes on board *et*] which is OK for your spelling, but now you should remember that it's /ee/, /ae/, /tee/. Next, we're going to learn the short /ee/ sound, like in the word /hed/.' [The word *head* goes on the board.]
>
> Asks a student to write the word *bean* on the board. Asks another student to write the word *instead* on the board. Next, introduces the bonus word 'leprechaun'. Children get a list of spelling words. They chant in unison. They spell words out loud in unison with letter-names: '/ar/, /ee/, /ae/, /dee/ – read.'
>
> The lesson ends at 8.44 a.m., twelve minutes later.

This example is by no means unusual. The children will have spent twelve minutes in an entire day, and perhaps an entire week, with this so-called 'spelling' exercise. This may be the only explanation they will ever get about the vowel sound /ee/ or the vowel digraph ea.

Let's dissect what the teacher was actually doing:

1. She begins by telling them a lie, that everything in their spelling list has the sound /ee/, when half of the words contain the sound /e/ (bed).

2. She makes the sound /ee/ and writes the digraph ea with no explanation about why the sound /ee/ is spelled this way, or why two letters are used for one sound instead of one letter. She is actually introducing a letter pair (digraph) and not a sound. The letters ea, in and of themselves, do not 'sound' anything.

3. She says and writes that e̱ ṯ (letter-names) is an 'OK way to spell'. In fact, she uses letter-names instead of phonemes to 'spell' *eat* to the class: 'ee-ay-tee'. This gives them the impression that 'eat' has *three* sounds (actually there are *four* in her version – /ee/, /ae/, /t/, /ee/) instead of two (/ee/, /t/), and that 'eat' is spelled this way by chance.

4. She tells them that they are going to learn a 'short /ee/ sound'. There is no such thing as a short /ee/ sound. She then uses an example of a word containing the vowel sound /e/ ('head') which is *not* the sound /ee/.

5. She alternates back and forth between words that contain the sounds /ee/ and /e/, the only common denominator between them being the vowel digraph e̱a̱. This destroys any chance for the child to infer a connection between a phoneme and its spelling.

6. Next comes 'leprechaun', presumably because they had been told a story about one. The word does not contain the sound /ee/, does not contain the vowel digraph e̱a̱ as a spelling for /e/, but *does* contain the main way to spell the sound /e/ (which is e̱), something she didn't teach. This word is much too difficult for this age, and reinforces visual memory as a way to learn to spell.

7. Students end the lesson by spelling the words out loud using letter-names. This reinforces learning that letter-*names* is the most important thing to remember. Letter–sound correspondences are never mentioned.

We have many examples like this one, taken from three different schools and seven different classrooms. It is obvious when reading through these notes that this teacher has no idea what she is doing; no idea how to teach a phonetic alphabet; and that the children would probably be better off if she didn't even try. The only thing she has succeeded in doing in this lesson is to confuse the children about how to spell words. She gives them the impression that everything must be memorized visually, because this is the only coherent perceptual experience that connects with what she described.

Teaching spelling with the correct logic, from sound-to-print, avoids this kind of confusion. The lesson just described should have been three separate lessons. The first lesson should have gone like this: 'There are two main ways to spell the sound /ee/. One you will already know because it is the Basic Code spelling: e̱e̱ (feet). Now we're going to learn a second way to spell the sound /ee/ which is e̱a̱ (each).' Next, children need practice in using this information. They can write stories using words that sound /ee/, fill in worksheets with these sounds and spellings, and so forth.

The second lesson should have been that there are 'two main spellings for the sound /e/'. One they already know as the Basic Code spelling: e (bed), and the second most common is ea (head). They also learn that the spelling e is used most of the time. Again, the children engage in activities using this information. When this foundation is established, the third lesson begins. The teacher points out that the digraph ea is used for *both* the /ee/ sound and the /e/ sound (an example of code overlap), and that the ea spelling is used much more often to spell the sound /ee/ than it is to spell the sound /e/.

These three steps make the logic clear. There is no confusion about what is being taught. The child's task is clear as well. She knows that she must learn which spelling alternative is used for a particular sound in a particular word. She *does not learn* that she has to memorize the spelling for every single word in the English language separately.

For the remainder of this chapter I want to outline how reading and spelling should be taught at this level in schools, and show along the way how learning to spell can be fun.

Allographs™ *in Practice*

Allographs consists of a child's spelling dictionary, a teacher's manual with sixty partially scripted lesson plans and an activity guide, plus worksheets and stories for most lessons. In the spelling dictionary all possible spellings for all common English words are organized by phoneme. The information is sequenced by initial and final consonants, initial and final consonant clusters, and vowels. Allographs I contains one- and two-syllable words. Allographs II contains two- to five-syllable words; lessons on compounding, prefixes and suffixes; and spelling patterns for words borrowed from Latin and Greek. In this chapter, I discuss Volume I, which is suitable for children from the end of Year 1 to junior school. It is also suitable for anyone, up to and including adults, who has not learned the spelling code.

The major goals of learning to read and spell with Allographs are as follows:

1. To use a phonetic strategy to look up sounds in words. This has the important function of reinforcing the correct strategy.

2. To connect spelling to the sound-based strategy used in learning to read. Reading and spelling are integrated.

3. To learn which spelling alternatives are most or least probable. When in doubt about spelling a word, start with the most probable spelling first (Basic Code). Check the result with visual memory to see if it looks right. If it doesn't, try the next most probable, and so forth.

4. To isolate which spellings are irregular and must be memorized by sight.

5. To learn all this effortlessly via *controlled exposure*, by the correct sequencing of spelling training and by being able to *look up sounds in words*. The Allographs dictionary contains over 3,000 words (about 70 pages) and can be used easily by most children in Year 2 as a reference resource. It is far easier to use than a conventional children's dictionary.

The dictionary is organized into three sections, which are colour coded. The book begins with summary charts of spelling alternatives for initial and final consonants, consonant clusters, and vowels, as illustrated earlier and reproduced here for convenience. After the charts come word lists with sounds that have alternative spellings. There are separate lists for consonants that begin words and for consonants that end words or syllables. This is followed by the vowel section, which is the largest section. Each page (or pages) is devoted to one vowel sound. All common words with that sound are set out in columns under each spelling alternative. The spelling alternatives are ordered from left to right in order of probability (most to least likely), and the words themselves are set out alphabetically down and across the page.

Initial Consonants

First, children are told that sometimes there are different spellings for sounds than the ones they have learned so far, and that these are called 'spelling alternatives' or 'spelling options'. Lessons begin with the twenty-two *initial* single consonants in the following order:

1. Consonants with only one spelling (12) – a review of the Basic Code.

2. Consonants with two different spellings (6).

TABLE II.I   Single Consonant Spelling Alternatives

Sound	Key Word	Word Beginning			Word Ending			
b	big	b			b			
d	dog	d			d			
f	fun	f	ph		f	ff	ph	gh
g	got	g	gu	gh	g	gue	gg	
h	hot	h	wh		—			
j	job	j	g		ge	dge		
k	kid	c	k	ch	k	ck	c	
l	log	l			l	ll		
m	man	m			m	mb	mn	
n	not	n	kn	gn	n	gn		
p	pig	p			p			
r	red	r	wr		r			
s	sat	s	c	sc	ce	se	ss	s
t	top	t			t	bt		
v	van	v			ve			
w	win	w	wh		—			
x /ks/	tax	—			x			
z	zip	z			se	ze	zz	s z
ch	chin	ch			ch	tch		
ng	sing	—			ng			
qu/kw/	quit	qu			—			
sh	shop	sh			sh			
th	thin	th			th			
<u>th</u>	then	th			the			

Spelling alternatives are ordered by most to least likely.

3. Consonants with three different spellings (4).

Most consonant spelling alternatives are *digraphs*. New consonant digraphs in this group are: /f/ <u>ph</u> (phone); /g/ <u>gh</u> (ghost) and <u>gu</u> (guard); /k/ <u>ch</u> (chaos); /n/ <u>gn</u> (gnat) and <u>kn</u> (know); /r/ <u>wr</u> (write); /s/ <u>sc</u> (scene); /w/ <u>wh</u> (which). (Rare digraphs (<u>pn</u>, <u>rh</u>) aren't taught here.)

TABLE 11.2 Consonant Clusters

Beginning Clusters	Spelling Alternatives	**Ending** Clusters	Spelling Alternatives
bl br			
dr dw		dth	
fl fr		ft fth	
gl gr			
kl kr	**cl cr** chl chr	(kt)	**ct**
		ld lf (lj) lm ln lp lt lch lsh lth	**lge**
		mp mpt (mf)	**mph**
		nch nd (nj) nt nth	**nge**
pl pr		pt pth	
		rb rc rd rf rg (rj) rk rl rm rn rp rt rch rsh rth rve	**rge**
sk skr sl sm sn sp spl spr st str sw squ	**sc** sk sch **scr**	sk sm sp st	
tr tw			
		xt (ngk) (ngkt) ngth	**nk nct**
shr thr			

Clusters in brackets are never spelled this way. Optional spellings in bold are the most likely (or only) spelling.

TABLE 11.3 Vowel Chart

Sound	Key Word	Spelling Alternatives (in order of most to least frequent)						
		1	2	3	4	5	6	7
a	had	a						
e	bed	e	ea	ai				
i	it	i	y	ui				
o	dog	o	a					
aw	law	aw	au	a	ough	augh		
ah	father	a	ar					
u	but	u	o	o–e	ou			
ae	made	a–e	ai	a	ay	ei	eigh	ey
ee	see	ee	ea	y	ie	e	e–e	ey
ie	time	i–e	i	y	igh			
oe	tone	o–e	o	oa	ow	ou	ough	
ue	cute	u–e	u	ew	eu			
oo	look	oo	u	ou				
o͞o	soon	o͞o	u–e	ew	u	ou	ui	
ou	out	ou	ow	ough				
oi	soil	oi	oy					

Vowel + r

er	her	er	re	ur	ir	or	ear	ar
or	for	or	ore	oar	our	ar		
e + er	bare	are	air	err	ear			

In a sequence of lessons, corresponding to the level of difficulty, children create their own spelling notebooks with words they choose. Every lesson has activities, worksheets, and humorous stories in rhyme to allow the child to practise new information.

Initial Consonant Clusters

Following lessons on single consonant spelling alternatives, children move on to review the twenty-eight initial consonant clusters. They are reminded that clusters are two or more single consonants in a row, and that most are spelled in Basic Code which they already know. The exceptions are rare and mainly involve Greek words. The spelling alternatives are: <u>cl</u>, <u>chl</u> (clap, chlorine); <u>cr</u>, <u>chr</u> (cream, chronic); and <u>sc</u>, <u>sk</u>, <u>sch</u> (scum, skunk, school). Children do not use many Greek words at this stage, and so only the last group is important: <u>sc</u>, <u>sk</u>, <u>sch</u>. The teacher must point out that <u>sc</u> is also a digraph for /s/ in 'scene', but *two* consonants (/s/ and /k/) most of the time, as in the word 'scare'.

Every child has a copy of the Allographs dictionary and can check the spellings on the charts or in the word list sections, depending on the task he is assigned. For example, children are taught that words that begin with the sound /r/ can be spelled two ways: <u>r</u> and <u>wr</u>. Later, a child may be writing a story about the time he fell and broke his wrist. If he can't remember how to spell 'wrist', he can check the Initial Consonants Chart at the front of his dictionary and find that there are two ways to spell words beginning /r/, either <u>r</u> or <u>wr</u>. At this point he can write this both ways to see what 'looks right' (*rist* or *wrist*). If he is still uncertain, he can turn to the colour-coded 'Word Beginnings' section and look up the words that begin with the sound /r/. The Word Beginnings section is *only two pages* long, as it only lists words with alternative spellings. Most initial consonants are consistent with the Basic Code.

Table 11.4 illustrates page two of Word Beginnings. Under the sound /r/, the child learns that all words beginning with this sound are spelled <u>r</u>, *except* for the words listed. The child knows that if he *doesn't* find the word 'wrist' here, it will be spelled with the letter <u>r</u>. Note that while the child is looking up 'wrist', he is also systematically searching through every common word that starts with <u>wr</u>. There are only twenty-two of them and only about fourteen that the child is likely to use. Looking through this list increases his familiarity with the words spelled <u>wr</u>, so his brain will begin to remember them without practice or conscious effort.

TABLE 11.4 Allographs™ Dictionary: 'Word Beginnings', p. 2

Sound /s/ (Key word: see. Spell s except:

c(e)	cease, cedar, cede, ceiling, celebrate, celery, celestial, cell, cement, cent, centennial, centre, cent— (100), central, century, ceramic, cereal, ceremony, certain, certify
c(i)	cider, cigar, cigarette, cinch, cinder, cinema, cinnamon, cipher, circle, circuit, circulate, circus, cite, citizen, citrus, city, civic, civil
c(y)	cycle, cyclone, cylinder, cymbal, cynic, cypress, cyst
sc	scene, scent, science, sceptre

Cluster /sk/ Key word: skip. Spell sc except:

sk	skate, skeleton, sceptic, sketch, skew, ski, skid, skiff, skill, skim, skimp, skin, skinny, skip, skirt, skit, skull, skunk, sky
sch	scheme, scholar, school, schooner

Sound /w/ Key word: wet. Spell w except:

wh	whale, what, wheat, wheel, wheeze, when, where, whether, which, whiff, while, whim, whine, whip, whirl, whirr, whisk, whistle, white, whiz, whoa, why

---

Sound /r/ Key word: rug. Spell r except:

wr	wrack, wrap, wrath, wreath, wreck, wren, wrench, wrestle, wretch, wriggle, wring, wrinkle, wrist, writ, write, writhe, wrong, wrote, wrung, wry

---

Final Consonants

There are twenty-one final consonants and forty-eight final consonant clusters that close syllables. Some final consonants and all but three of the final clusters are different to those in initial position and need extra lessons. Final consonants should be taught in the following sequence:

1. Consonants with only one spelling (10) – a review of the Basic Code.

2. Consonants with two spellings (3). The alternative spellings are rare: /g/ gue (vague), /n/ gn (sign), and /t/ bt (debt).

3. Consonants with more than two spellings (4). One group has few words: /m/ m, mb, mn, mme (sum, dumb, autumn, programme); but the other three need extensive practice: /f/ f, ff, gh, ph (gulf, cliff, laugh, graph); /s/ s, ce, se, ss (gas, race, mouse, dress) and /z/ z, s, se, ze, zz (quiz, his, rise, freeze, buzz).

4. Consonant spellings controlled by the preceding vowel sound (4). An example is final /ch/ which is spelled ch unless it follows the vowel *sounds* /a/, /e/, /i/, /o/, /u/, when it is spelled tch (branch and brooch, but batch and botch).

5. Final consonant clusters. All have only one spelling (48) – a review of the Basic Code.

The forty-eight final consonant clusters are all spelled in Basic Code with no spelling alternatives. It helps a child enormously to know this, because there is no way to misspell them. There is one source of confusion. Six final consonant clusters can be confused with the spelling for the past-tense verb ed in all clusters ending in the sounds /d/ or /t/. These words sound exactly alike: pact/packed, past/passed, bend/penned, etc. It is much easier to spell these words correctly if you know whether or not the word is a past-tense verb. This can be turned to good advantage by teaching these final clusters simultaneously with a lesson on past-tense verbs.

During these lessons, children also begin to learn about multi-syllable words. They learn, for example, that initial and final consonants and clusters are 'initial' and 'final' for single-syllable words and can also appear in the middle of multi-syllable words. For example, the sound /f/ spelled ph, can appear at the beginning of a word – 'phone'; in the middle – 'dolphin'; and at the end – 'graph'.

Multi-syllable work continues in the last lessons in Allographs I. The final consonants section ends with the introduction of the schwa + /l/ words. A schwa is an unaccented /uh/ sound in multi-syllable words. This is a perpetual problem in English spelling, because the schwa can be spelled so many ways: *a*bout, c*o*nfuse, import*a*nt, ben*e*fit, sens*i*tive. About 250 multi-syllable English words end in the sounds /ul/, as in: table, uncle, symbol, tribal, gavel, awful. The spellings are not consistent, but they are predictable by the consonant that *precedes* the schwa. For example, words that end in the sounds /bul/ are much more likely to be spelled ble than any other way: table, but *not* tabul, tabel, or tabol. Words ending in /vul/ are more likely to be spelled

<u>vel</u>: marvel, novel, travel, etc. For this reason, this group of words is organized alphabetically by the consonant sound that preceeds the schwa + /l/. A page from this group is shown here.

TABLE 11.5　Word endings

Sounds /ul/ (key word: apple).	
Sounds/spellings	*Words*
/b/	
bal	tribal
bel	label, libel, rebel
bol	symbol
ble	able, amble, babble, bauble, Bible, bramble, bubble, bumble, cable, cobble, crumble, double, dribble, edible, fable, fumble, gable, garble, gobble, hobble, horrible, marble, mumble, nibble, noble, ogle, pebble, possible, ramble, rumble, rubble, sable, scribble, sensible, stable, table, terrible, treble, trouble, tumble, wobble, visible
/c/	
cal	rascal
cle	miracle, uncle
kle	ankle, sprinkle, wrinkle
ckle	buckle, chuckle, cockle, crackle, fickle, knuckle, pickle, tackle, tickle, trickle
/d/	
dal	bridal, medal, pedal, scandal, tidal
dle	bridle, bundle, candle, cradle, cuddle, curdle, dawdle, fiddle, fondle, girdle, griddle, huddle, hurdle, ladle, meddle, middle, muddle, noodle, paddle, poodle, puddle, saddle, straddle, swaddle, swindle, trundle, waddle
/f/	
fle	baffle, muffle, rifle, ruffle, shuffle, sniffle, truffle, waffle
ful	awful, bashful, beautiful, careful, dutiful, faithful, graceful, grateful, hateful, helpful, hopeful, restful, wonderful
/g/	
gle	beagle, eagle, gaggle, gurgle, jiggle, struggle, wiggle, wriggle

Vowel Spelling Alternatives

Vowel spellings cause the most difficulty in both reading and spelling. Using Allographs avoids confusing the child, reinforces the correct skills and integrates them. The vowel sounds are set out in four major groups, as shown earlier in Table 11.3.

First come the sounds /a/, /e/, /i/, /o/, /aw/, /ah/, /u/, followed by /ae/, /ee/, /ie/, /oe/, /ue/, then /oo/, /o͞o/, /ou/, /oi/, and the vowel + r group. This is the same order in which the vowels were learned originally.

In the Allographs dictionary, each vowel sound is represented on a page or a series of pages. Words containing that sound are listed under each spelling alternative from left to right across the page in order of the most to least probable spelling. Words are listed in alphabetical order down and across the page. The order of the alphabet is highlighted in bold in the margin, so the child also learns about alphabetical order and must use this order to look up words and how they are spelled. When children reach this stage in Allographs, it helps to have an alphabet chart on the wall (lower-case letters only).

A particular advantage of this approach is that the spelling alternatives that overlap two or more sounds (code overlap) never get mixed up. This avoids the confusion that the teacher created in the example. Allographs shows the child clearly where and how often the <u>ea</u> spelling alternative (and any other spelling alternative) is used. A page for the sound /e/ (bet) is shown in Table 11.6. The child can see immediately that <u>ea</u> and <u>ai</u> are less likely spellings for the vowel sound /e/ (bed), and that <u>e</u> is the most likely spelling for this sound.

The teacher's manual has several scripted lessons for every consonant or vowel sound with more than one spelling. These lessons involve the child in thinking about sounds in words, using this information to solve interesting puzzles or problems, and reading and writing exercises. These can be conducted as a class activity, small group activity, or individually in the classroom or at home. One of the tasks the children most enjoy is searching for a target sound in stories that feature one sound. The child has a worksheet or a story with lots of words containing a particular sound. The child's task is to locate all the words with the target sound and underline them. Next, the child copies these words on to a worksheet, underlines the spelling for that sound and copies the spelling in an adjacent column. Here is an example of a Sound Search story, featuring the sound /ie/.

NIGEL THE NICE

Nigel the Nice was a knight. He was quite a sight in an iron suit that was too bright. Nigel was mild. He was kind. He was nice. But Nigel took flight when he saw the other knights fight.

'Fie on you Nigel,' said King Idle the Wise. 'Get out of my sight. Fly to the wild and find Sir Guy. He might die from tiger's bite.'

Nigel had too much iron on to climb or hike, so he had to ride his bike. He cycled miles under the hot sky to Igo-Ego in Bye-um-Byes, with his visor over his eyes. He began to cry. He felt he'd die and never arrive alive.

Byron the Lion heard his sighs.

'Sire, you must be on fire. You're about to fry. I'll get some pliers. We'll pry open your fine bright iron, so you can survive.'

Nigel, free at last, saved Sir Guy and got a prize. He took a wife and stayed in Bye-um-Byes for the rest of his life.

(Who said that controlled curriculum materials had to be boring?)

There are many activities and games set out in detail in the Allographs teacher's manual. Here are some examples:

1. Search real text for a target sound.

2. Look up words in the Allographs dictionary, using the game I-spy. ('I spy words ending in the sounds /ie/-/t/[ite] spelled <u>ight</u>'.)

3. Sound Search: look for a particular sound or sounds in the Allographs dictionary that have more than one spelling. ('Find all the words that have the final sounds /aw/-/l/ in them and write each one under its spelling alternative – <u>al</u>, <u>ol</u>, <u>awl</u>' [all, doll, crawl].) This provides a concrete example of the probability of a particular spelling.

4. Spell Sort. Children sort a list of words with the same sound into separate spelling alternatives. The words in the list follow the probability structure set up in the dictionary. When the child is finished, she can see (and count) how many words are under each spelling. This provides a concrete experience of how likely it is for a particular sound to be spelled a particular way.

5. Vowel-controlled Sort: this is used to teach final consonant spelling alternatives that are controlled by the preceding vowel sound, such as ch/tch, ge/dge (branch/batch, huge/hedge).

TABLE 11.6

Sound /e/ (key word: bed).
Spelling Alternatives

	e	ea	ai
a			again
b			bargain
	bed		
	bell		
	belt		
	bench		
	bend		
	bent		
	best		
	bet		
	better		
	bled		
	blend		
	bless		
	blest	bread	
		breast	
		breath	
	bred		
c			captain
	celery		
	cell		
	cent		certain
	check		
	chest		
	clef		
	cleft		
	clench		
	clever		
	crept		
	crest		curtain
d		dead	
		deaf	
		death	
	debt		
	deck		

TABLE 11.6 *Cont'd*

Sound /e/ (key word: bed).
Spelling Alternatives

e	ea	ai
deft		
den		
dent		
desk	dread	
dress		
dwell		

6. Creative writing: write a story or poem based on a sound. Allographs is organized so that words that rhyme or start with the same initial sound can be easily located in the lists.

7. Parent or teacher writes little stories for individual children or for the class based upon a sound, like 'Nigel the Nice', which couldn't have been written without Allographs.

8. Games using the Allographs tables and charts:

a. How many words can you think of starting with the sound /f/? Is there any other way to spell words starting with this sound? What are some of these words?

b. How many words can you think of that end in the sound /ch/? How many ways to spell this sound? After several words have gone up on the board, children can look up others in Allographs to see how many they missed.

c. How many words use the spelling ie for the sound /ee/? What are those words?

9. Spelling: individual spelling exercises based on a child's spelling errors in creative writing. Children can correct their own errors by looking them up.

10. Spell-check: children can use Allographs to write stories and poems, and check spelling as they go.

11. Children can help each other spell by showing other children how to look up sounds in words. Children with good phonemic awareness can easily help those with weak phonemic awareness.

In addition to the child's own copy of the Allographs dictionary, it is helpful to have a large chart containing the vowel spelling alternatives on the wall, similar to the one shown in Table 11.3. The children can glance at the chart when they write and immediately try out various spellings to see how they look in a word.

These spelling materials and exercises make it possible for a child to write creatively and at the same time avoid practising spelling errors or spelling patterns that don't exist.

Remember that teacher who said to her class that e̲t̲ was an OK way to spell 'eat'? It's *not* OK. Children who are taught correctly and in the proper sequence know that e̲ t̲ would never be a likely option to spell 'eat', and that e̲a̲t̲ is the most likely option for 'eat'. Why withhold this information from children and cause them to make errors?

Code Overlap

Code overlap refers to letters that stand for more than one sound, such as o̲u̲ in 'soul', 'soup', 'out', and 'touch' and a̲ in 'sat' and 'past' (BBC English). Code overlaps create a problem in decoding (reading) more than they do in spelling. Code overlap needs to be addressed in reading exercises, especially when new vowel sounds are introduced. Code overlaps are less of a problem with consonants because they occur in rarer spellings and can be dealt with quickly: gh stands for /f/ in 'tough' and /g/ in 'ghost'. Vowel letters and digraphs are a particular problem in reading because the reader must decide which phoneme a particular letter-pattern stands for.

Here is an illustration of an exercise to teach a code overlap. The sound /oe/ has the alternative spellings: o̲–e̲ 'tone', o̲ 'go', o̲a̲ 'goat', o̲w̲ 'slow', o̲u̲ 'soul' and o̲u̲g̲h̲ 'dough', and there are multiple overlaps in this group. The first spelling, o̲, overlaps with the Basic Code spelling for the sound /o/ (dog). The Phono-Graphix™ curriculum and *Reading Reflex* (the home-based version) have games and exercises to sort words and spell words with letter-patterns that overlap two, three or more sounds. Here is an example of an overlap exercise:

> Sort the words into two groups based on the sound that the letter o̲ stands for in these words. (This can be done on worksheets or with word cards.)

hot sold dog block ghost roll across hello dolphin stroll told profit post radio robin yolk

A more complex version adds a third way to sort words that are spelled o but sound /u/ (as in 'cut'). This would expand the list to include words like front, brother, ton, wonder, other, son, month.

Sight Words

Sight words were originally defined as words with such irregular spellings they had to be memorized 'by sight'. Later, memorizing *all* words by sight became the major mode of learning to read in read-for-meaning approaches, especially look-and-say. Phonics programmes and most reading textbooks today advocate teaching a large group of 'sight words'. Here, the rationale shifts to the 'getting started' theory. Children should learn sight words, it is claimed, because they can start reading right away, and this is motivating. In Britain, there is a belief perpetuated by teacher-training institutions that ultimately all words are recognized by sight, and the goal of every young reader is to increase his 'sight vocabulary'. The early chapters showed clearly that this is impossible.

Teachers are trained to teach sight words either prior to learning some phonics, or concurrently with learning phonics and 'real books'. Teaching sight words this way can have profoundly negative consequences on the child's fragile understanding of the alphabet principle.

All reading programmes have to deal with sight words, in the original meaning of the term. I am advocating two things: teach only *real* sight words, words that are undecodable, and teach them in the context of reading stories or in creative writing. Children readily accept that some words have 'funny spellings' (especially if you tell them), which they will learn easily by sight. This does not mean that special drill and practice should be devoted to sight words.

When children learn the advanced level of the spelling code, they will be exposed to words that cannot be classified into a spelling alternative because there are too few words to constitute a category. In Allographs, on the final page of the word lists for the sound /e/, two words are listed together: 'friend' and 'leopard'. In these words, the sound /e/ is spelled ie and eo. As it doesn't make sense to teach two more spelling alternatives for just two words, these are taught as 'exceptions' (sight words).

It is interesting that children up to about the age of eight don't agree with this solution. Remember, young children are concrete thinkers and actively categorize things. They think that <u>everything</u> can be and should be classified, even if a category contains only one or two of something. Thus, there should be a spelling alternative <u>ie</u> for the sound /e/ in 'friend' and a spelling alternative <u>eo</u> for the sound /ee/ in 'people', and <u>cht</u> for the sound /t/ in 'yacht', and <u>ew</u> for the sound /oe/ in 'sew', etc. They don't like it when things are ambiguous.

The goal in Allographs was to establish a balance between the number of spelling alternatives for each phoneme the child needs to master, and the number of 'exception' words that should be memorized by sight.

I want to spend some time discussing 'sight words' as they are typically taught in classrooms or by reading specialists. I will take as an example sight words from a well-known reading textbook for teacher training. The list was compiled from sources dating back to the famous Dolch sight word series published in 1936. This list was described as containing about 100 'high-frequency words' with 'irregular spellings', plus another group of common words. The children were supposed to memorize these words by sight so they could say them automatically 'within a second'. The teachers were instructed to concentrate on teaching these words during the first two or three years of school.

There are 165 words in the list. I will eliminate the word 'wanted' because the root word 'want' is already in the list, and also the abbreviations for Mr and Mrs. Of the remaining 162 words, 57 (35 per cent) are spelled completely phonetically in Basic Code. Examples are: that, it, for, with, made, at, or, out, etc. Decoding these words should be effortless if the child has been taught correctly. Why then should these words be memorized by sight when they can be decoded in the usual way? This gives the child the impression that these words are somehow different and are 'spelled funny' when they're not.

Another large group of words, forty-eight of them to be exact, are all spelled with a common spelling alternative. In other words, these are *highly probable* spellings. These words are set out below with an explanation about how and why the spellings are common.

TABLE 11.7 Sight Words

anything	give	great	Mrs	says	very
and	at	when	about	time	than
a	could	group	night	should	want
because	do	have	nothing	some	water
in	be	can	out	has	first
again	does	head	of	something	was
is	this	use	then	look	called
almost	done	knew	brother	the	were
another	door	heard	on	sometimes	wanted
that	or	an	them	more	oil
always	buy	know	off	their	what
it	had	each	these	write	its
any	enough	light	one	they	where
are	four	only	long	who	thought
he	by	which	so	go	now
been	from	dog	other	there	father
for	but	she	her	see	down
both	friend	many	own	through	goes
brought	full	might	people	to	work
as	words	how	make	number	day
house	don't	money	put	together	you
with	not	if	like	no	did
city	live	mother	right	today	would
come	gone	Mr	said	two	your
his	all	will	him	way	get
year	they're	school	our	there's	once
I	we	up	into	my	find
made	may	part			

'about'. The schwa (unaccented /u/ sound) in the initial position in a word is almost always spelled <u>a</u> (again, around, above, amount, ahead). The spelling <u>ou</u> is the Basic Code spelling for the sound /ou/.

'all, almost, always, call'. This is an example of an 'l-controlled' vowel spelling where the letter l causes the vowel letter a to stand for /aw/, with very few exceptions ('pal').

'another, brother, among, mother, other'. The spelling o is a common spelling for the sound /u/ (cup), as has already been shown, above.

'come, done, money, some, something, sometimes'. The spelling o–e is the third most common spelling for the sound /u/.

'by, buy, my'. Final sound /ie/ is commonly spelled with the letter y in one-syllable words (cry, fry, fly).

'almost, both, don't, go, most, no, only, so'. The spelling o is the second most common way to spell the sound /oe/.

'know, own'. The spelling ow is the third most common spelling for the sound /oe/ (low, grow, blow, show).

'find, I'. The spelling i for the sound /ie/ is the second most common spelling (mind, child, kind, etc.).

'first'. The spelling ir for the vowel sound /er/ is one of the three common spellings for this sound (er, ir, ur).

'full, put'. The sound /oo/ (book) is spelled two ways. This is one of them (pull, bull, etc.).

'head'. The sound /e/ is mainly spelled two ways. This is one of them.

'knew'. The spelling ew is a common spelling for the sound /ue/ (dew, new, few, stew); kn is always pronounced /n/. There are fourteen words with the kn spelling.

'light, might, night, right' (the author forgot 'sight', 'tight', 'fight', etc.). Most words that end in the sounds /ie/–/t/ are spelled ight. The spelling igh is the third most common spelling for the sound /ie/.

'more'. The spelling ore is the second most common spelling for the sound /or/.

'school'. The spelling oo is the Basic Code spelling for the sound

/o͞o/. The digraph <u>ch</u> is one of three possible spellings for the sound /k/ and is used only for 'Greek' words beginning /k/ or /sk/ (chlorine, scheme).

'these'. The spelling <u>e–e</u> is the fifth most common spelling for the sound /ee/ (theme, eve, recede, etc.).

'they', 'way'. When a word ends in the sound /ae/, these are the two main ways to spell it.

'brought, thought'. The phonogram <u>ough</u> is usually pronounced /aw/. (The author left out the nine other common words spelled this way.)

'want, water' (the author left out wad, waffle, wan, wand, wander, wash, was, watch). This is a w-controlled vowel spelling. When <u>w</u> precedes <u>a</u>, this usually makes the letter <u>a</u> stand for /o/.

'as, has, is, his'. Final <u>s</u> sounds /z/ in these words, which is common. Final <u>s</u> is pronounced /z/ in *all* plurals that don't follow the consonant sounds /f/, /k/, /p/, /t/ (bees, days, words, bags, tables, chairs, cars, trains, etc.). In a child's vocabulary, this would be about 3,000 words.

'be, because, he, she, we' (the author forgot 'me'). <u>e</u> is a less probable spelling alternative for the sound /ee/. It doesn't occur in many words, but it is common in high-frequency words (words that occur often in print). It also includes a group of common prefixes: pre-, be-, de-, e-, re-.

We have now eliminated about 70 per cent of the sight words. This brings us to the next group, those with less probable spellings.

'four, your'. This is a less-common spelling alternative for the sound /or/. But six other words are spelled this way, like 'pour' and 'source', making <u>our</u> a spelling alternative for /or/.

'they're'. This is a contraction of 'they are'. It is unusual but phonetically regular.

'heard'. This is the least-common spelling alternative for the vowel sound /er/. This group includes eight common words (pearl, search, etc.), making <u>ear</u> a spelling category.

'work'. This represents another group of w-controlled vowel spellings. When the letter w precedes or this changes the pronunciation to /er/, as in 'world', 'worry', etc.

'you, group'. The initial letter y *always* stands for /ee/ when it precedes a vowel (yes, yellow, etc.), and the digraph ou is a spelling alternative for the sound /$\overline{oo}$/.

This leaves us with 37 of the original words:

a, are, could, do, does, door, enough, father, friend, give, gone, great, have, into, live, of, once, one, people, said, says, should, the, their, there, through, to, together, today, two, very, was, were, what, where, who, would.

The children would argue that these can be classified, and the list reduced further. The words with the sound /oo/ spelled *ou* ('could', 'should', 'would') could be a category, as could 'great', plus 'break' and 'steak'; and 'door', plus 'floor', and 'poor'. They would also argue that 'to', 'two', 'do', and 'who', should be a group where the letter o represents the sound /$\overline{oo}$/. Also, there is no need to memorize the word 'to' and then memorize it all over again in compound words like: 'into', 'together', 'tomorrow', and 'today', and so forth. (In the US the pronunciation of 'father' is unusual. But in Britain the letter a is a common spelling for the sound /ah/, for instance, in 'grass', 'past', and 'bath'.)

If we follow the children's thinking, this eliminates twelve more sight words from the list.

This reduces the list to very few *true* sight words, in the sense that the spellings are so irregular and unpredictable that they cannot be decoded. But the point of this exercise is to show something else. *If* it was a good idea to teach sight words because of 'irregular spellings', then *most of the true sight words are missing from this list.* Furthermore, if the words 'I' and 'kind' are supposed to be sight words, then what about all the other words with this spelling, such as behind, bind, blind, child, Christ, climb, find, grind, iron, lion, mild, mind, pilot, pint, quiet, sign, silent, triangle, vibrant, wild, wind – and about a hundred more?

If all words ending in the sound /z/ spelled s are 'sight words', then about 50,000 plural words are missing.

I hope this exercise has not been too tedious. The purpose is to illustrate that 'experts' in the field of reading, those who write the textbooks and curriculum that many classroom teachers try to rely on, *do not know the English spelling code*. They have never bothered to work it out. Teachers all over the world teach 'sight words' based upon lists like this one. This is very scary, because if authors of textbooks don't know the code, then teachers can't learn the code, and if teachers don't know the code, then children can't learn the code. If the child can't learn the code, the child can't learn to read or spell.

Multi-syllable Word Level

Over 80 per cent of English words are multi-syllable words, though the words that are used most often are only one syllable long. As was seen from the examples, children get introduced to many two-syllable words in Allographs I. In Allographs II, they begin to learn more complex words through 'multi-syllable word-building'. These include compound words ('greenhouse'); common root words which take prefixes and suffixes ('unhappy', 'happier'); and roots, prefixes and suffixes borrowed from Latin and Greek ('information', 'symbol').

The multi-syllable level needs considerable attention and there isn't space here to discuss this in any depth. Two auditory skills are involved:

1. The ability to segment words into syllable units. This is easy for almost everyone as we learned from the research in Chapter 9.

2. The ability to decode phoneme-by-phoneme *within* each syllable unit and remember the phoneme sequences in the right order, and to encode (spell) each syllable, chunk by chunk. This is hard for everyone.

Children can become overwhelmed at the multi-syllable level because they see a very long word and don't know how to attack it, break it apart, and reassemble it. At the multi-syllable level, everything must slow down. The children need practice in verbally isolating syllables in words, and putting syllables together into words. Start these lessons with children's names, because this is motivating: Jenn-i-fer, Al-ex-an-der, Jon-a-than. Do this verbally. Don't have children clap, because they can't hear anything when they're clapping.

These lessons are followed by a two-step process: isolating a syllable in a word and analysing its phoneme components; then going on to the next syllable and doing the same thing, keeping track of the *order* of phonemes across all the syllables in the word. Let the child decide where the syllable boundaries come. There's no absolute right or wrong way, despite what the style manuals say. Thus, a child could tackle the word 'comforting' in one of two ways:

/k/ /u/ /m/——/f/ /or/——/t/ /i/ /ng/
/k/ /u/ /m/——/f/ /or/ /t/——/i/ /ng/.

The final stage of multi-syllable work introduces the last level of logic, which cannot be taught using a strict phonetic approach. These are the Latin suffixes which don't conform to any of the English spelling patterns introduced so far. Latin prefixes, by contrast, are usually spelled phonetically (un, in, re, de, sub, ab, ad). Latin suffixes must be taught as a special group in which a set of letters (a phonogram) represents more than one sound. The suffix /shun/ tion is a case in point. There are thousands of words ending in the three sounds /sh/ /u/ /n/. There are over 500 words spelled ation alone, such as 'nation', 'information', 'investigation', and so forth. The suffix /shun/ is spelled seven main ways: tion (nation), cian (musician, electrician), cion (suspicion), sion (aggression, tension), cean (ocean); plus shion in two words (fashion, cushion). The phonemes /sh/ and /u/ in these Latin suffixes can *each* be spelled several ways. The sound /sh/ can be spelled ti (nation), ci (musician/suspicion), ssi (aggression), shi (cushion), sci (conscious), ch (machine); and the vowel sound /u/ as o (tion), a (cian), and ou (ous). It is far more practical to teach /shun/ 'phonograms' than to memorize nine new spelling alternatives.

The child learns that tion, cian, cion, sion are the main ways to spell /shun/ when these sounds come at the end of a multi-syllable word. And there are further clues: tion is by far the most probable spelling of the four; cian is for an occupation or person; cion is infrequent; and the tion/sion distinction is often determined by the spelling of the root word – vacate/vacation; aggress/aggression. This approach also works well with code overlaps, because entire phonograms can 'overlap' more than one sound unit: sion stands for /shun/ in 'aggres*sion*' *or* /zhun/ in 'vi*sion*'; tion can be decoded as /shun/ or /chun/ (question).

Comprehension

There are no special comprehension exercises at this level. Standard comprehension approaches will work fine with this programme (finding the storyline, getting the main idea, retelling the story in the child's words, etc.). It turns out that comprehension exercises during early reading instruction matter less than one might think, though, of course, interpretation of text is critical for enjoyment of reading.

The highest predictor of a child's comprehension score on a standard reading comprehension test is a measure of decoding skill, the ability to read one word at a time *out of context*. This means simply that if you can understand the meaning of spoken language, you should be able to understand the meaning of written language. And the only way you can understand the meaning of written language is to be able to decode it accurately and fluently.

According to Australian researchers Brian Byrne and A. Gates, reading comprehension can be predicted completely by two measures: nonsense-word decoding accuracy and speed. They followed 159 children in Years 2 and 3 (seven and eight years old) over one year. Accuracy was more important than speed, because slow but accurate decoders could still comprehend what they read, whereas rapid, inaccurate decoders could not. Most reading textbooks that teachers rely on say just the opposite.

The truth is that fluency *follows* accuracy and does not precede it. So the teacher who says: 'Don't sound it out. Don't slow down. Read it faster or you won't understand it,' isn't helping the student who has decoding problems, and this student won't understand what he reads. Simply 'reading faster', or practising to be 'fluent', without understanding the code, doesn't improve reading or comprehension.

Similar findings were reported by Connie Juel and her colleagues in Austin, Texas. They followed 129 children over the first two years of school, from early first grade to the end of second grade (ages six to seven). They measured the children's phonemic awareness, decoding skill, listening comprehension, IQ, and various measures of writing, reading, and spelling at the beginning and the end of the study. Reading comprehension across the two years was strongly predicted by reading and spelling *isolated words*, and these in turn were predicted by decoding accuracy, which, in turn, was predicted by phoneme-awareness. Reading and spelling isolated words correlated to reading comprehension across the age range at .69 to .84. By contrast, listening comprehension, the ability to understand the meaning of what someone said, was not highly predictive and nor was vocabulary (correlations around .37–.44), which is a very interesting finding. This means that in order to understand what you read, you must be accurate and fluent in decoding it, *more than* whether you understand the meaning of natural spoken language (the opposite of what 'real books' advocates claim).

Research showing the connection between comprehension and simple decoding is now substantial, and studies like these have been replicated many times, using different subject groups and different tests. The Connecticut Longitudinal study group recently published the correlations between decoding accuracy and reading comprehension. The correlations are very large and consistent at each grade (.89 in first grade). But, more important, they are consistent *over time*. Ninth grade (age fourteen) comprehension scores can be predicted by decoding accuracy at every grade from second grade (age seven) onward, at around .60.

The research clearly shows that accurate and fluent decoding skills underpin everything that follows. And while traditional comprehension activities, such as 'finding the main ideas', answering questions about specific information, and writing summaries, are important and useful activities, they will not have any impact on a child's comprehension unless the child is decoding accurately and efficiently.

Writing

When children start to feel confident with the mechanics of writing letters and words, it's helpful (and interesting for the child) to copy sentences or passages of printed stories. This gives the child a feeling of pride and accomplishment, and begins to train the various technical aspects of writing itself, such as manual left to right sequencing, leaving spaces between words, capitalizing and punctuation. The children need this experience, otherwise their creative writing will not be legible.

When children write stories on their own, the teacher should be watchful about how words are spelled. This does not mean that everything needs to be corrected, but rather, misspelled words can provide important information about whether the child is progressing appropriately in learning sound-to-letter correspondences. Words that the child should be able to spell based on what has been taught, or misspelled words that are 'impossible' spellings (non-phonetic transcriptions), can be circled or underlined. These provide a useful list for spell-checking using the Allographs dictionary. The spellings can be corrected on the same page. Children should not be taught to spell from word lists unrelated to the stories they are reading, and should never be asked to spell words they cannot read, or at a more advanced level than their current knowledge of the spelling code.

Once the child has succeeded in presenting a reasonable approximation to a correctly spelled piece of creative writing, this should form the basis for an anthology book of that particular child's work. The selection by the teacher of the child's best work again motivates the child to want to succeed. Work that is chosen for an anthology should have all spelling errors corrected. Whether the child chooses to recopy the story or leave the corrected spellings on the copy, is unimportant and should be the child's decision.

Invented Spelling

Before ending this chapter, I want to say a few words about invented spelling. Remember, this is a method of teaching creative writing which is supposed to allow the child to 'discover' our spelling system on his own. When invented spelling is used in conjunction with a 'real books' philosophy, the teacher believes she should never interfere, or ask the child to correct anything that he has written. (As children are supposed to develop an awareness of the alphabet code through discovery, if you interfere it isn't 'discovery'.) There is no evidence whatsoever that it's *better* for a child to 'discover' the code unaided than to be taught the code directly, and overwhelming evidence to the contrary (see Chapter 9).

This does not mean that children should never do creative writing until they can spell every word correctly – far from it. Beginning readers should be encouraged to write freely and to spell words they don't know by the closest approximation. Once they know the Basic Code, they can spell everything phonetically, so that anyone can read it. However, this doesn't mean that their spelling errors are off-limits to the teacher. These errors can be very helpful in providing feedback to the child.

Unfortunately, this is not the way that 'invented spelling' is used in many classrooms. In fact, we have never seen it used this way in any classroom in Florida that we have observed. Instead, the teacher teaches nothing and the child 'invents' his own version of a writing system. This 'invention' is so unstable that it changes from word to word, and from line to line, except for those words that have been memorized by sight.

Inventing non-existent phoneme-grapheme combinations is one thing, but spending valuable time practising them is quite another. The main thing that 'pure' invented spelling offers the child is the certainty that he will spend hours practising errors, because there is no way the child can self-correct his mistakes. Further, our observations also show that one of the claims for invented spelling isn't valid either. This is the claim that children are 'free' to be creative if they are never taught to spell, and that even if adults cannot read what a child writes, the child can. When we asked six-year-olds to read to us what they had *just* written, minutes earlier, many of them made up completely different words (assuming we could translate it in the first place). Let's take this example which was written sufficiently clearly for us to transcribe: 'I just love mukes speshle babesg uus.' Notice first that the child is practising writing letter sequences that do not exist in English: shle sg uu. The first three words were learned by sight, so the child gets the first words correct, but reads: 'I just love cats because they are nice.' Children frequently stared up at the ceiling as they 'read' to us. If the teacher wants the children to be 'creative' before they know enough of the spelling code to write something that can be read, then why not have them tell stories out loud which she could transcribe? No one should ever be encouraged to write misspelled gibberish he cannot read.

In the following chapters we take up the issue of remedial teaching, the emotional consequences of reading failure, and what programmes look like that can bring a child or adult up to the appropriate age level in a short space of time and allow an illiterate adult to read on his own for the very first time.

Appendix: Spelling Programmes – Home or Classroom

Allographs™ *I*, designed for ages seven to nine. Spelling patterns for the English and French layers of the language, up to two-syllable words. Includes child's spelling dictionary; teacher's manual and lesson plans: worksheets; and sound-search stories in three volumes. (SeaGate Press, PO Box 563, Sanibel, FL 33957, USA. Tel: 00 1–941–472–4515; fax 00 1–941–472–4513.) British supplement available.

Allographs™ *II*, designed for ages nine to eleven. Multi-syllable word-building. Exercises for compounding, prefixes, suffixes, and the Latin and Greek layers of the language. Includes teacher's manual, lesson plans, and workbook. (SeaGate Press, details as above.) British supplement available.

CHAPTER 12

Helping Those Who Didn't Make It

The saying 'an ounce of prevention is worth a pound of cure' is more relevant to reading instruction than to any other sphere of endeavour. Reading skill affects almost everything we do. It determines how we learn, what we learn, whether we can pass exams, gain entrance to university, or hold down a job. Reading skill is essential to every school subject, including mathematics. This chapter is about that 'pound of cure', and the emotional consequences of reading failure for adults, for children, and for their parents. It is written mainly for parents of children with reading problems, adults with reading problems, and reading specialists who work with poor readers.

To understand the plight of the child or adult who has problems learning to read, imagine that your youngster has joined a neighbourhood cricket club. They are being coached by a local dad who doesn't know much about the techniques of the game, but who has some very strong opinions about how to coach batting. He tells his young charges to be certain to keep their weight on the back foot as they strike the ball, and for good measure, to close their eyes just before the ball hits the bat. He has developed numerous exercises for teaching these techniques. His reasoning sounds plausible to the children and even to most of the parents. For instance, he tells them that 'anchoring your weight on the back foot keeps you balanced, whereas moving into the ball and shifting to the forward foot alters the plane of the bat'. Furthermore, he has read somewhere that the ball moves too swiftly for the eye to track it all the way to the bat. Thus, closing your eyes at the last minute makes you more accurate than leaving them open. He can produce a very convincing set of arguments for these beliefs. Of course, they are simply nonsense, as anyone who has ever played cricket can tell you.

Most children who are instructed in these ridiculous exercises will be miserably inept at batting. Staying on the back foot means that you are off-balance and can't transfer your weight to and produce any power. Taking your eye off the ball means that you are likely to miss a googly or an off-break. How will the children respond to this kind of training? Take those who have innate natural talent. Some may have marginal success when following these instructions, because their bodies can compensate even when off-balance. More independent children will just ignore what the coach is saying, because it feels so wrong, and because they observe that great players on TV do neither of these things. Others, less assertive and anxious to please, can have their talent temporarily derailed and lose interest in the game.

Later on, these children may get a new trainer or join the school cricket team. Now they will have to learn to do the exact opposite of what they had been taught. This involves unlearning the habits they have developed and acquiring new habits. Because the two physical actions are mutually incompatible, this is a difficult and frustrating experience.

Here, in a nutshell, is the predicament of every child or adult with reading problems when they come for remedial help. For many poor readers, their inadequate skill has been *caused* directly by bad methods in the same way that the well-meaning dad taught bad batting habits. Others may have developed their own strategies or habits by themselves. These habits of mind cannot be visually inspected like the physical act of hitting a ball, however. Chapter 2 reviewed the various strategies that children typically adopt when reading instruction is absent or confusing. Remedial reading instructors must always test for strategies before training sessions begin and be certain to monitor this throughout remedial training. (See 'Do-it-yourself Diagnostics' at the end of this chapter).

Parents as Motivators

The motivation and determination of parents of children with severe reading problems are critical to the success of the remedial process. Hopefully, this may change when teachers have more knowledge and better training. Parents often have to fight the system to get testing and help for their child, monitor this help on a daily basis to judge its worth (assuming they get it), and fight the system once more when they find it's not working, which is frequently the case. Their next task is to locate a reading specialist who knows what he or she is doing. This is especially true for those children with auditory or visual processing difficulties that must be corrected *before* the child can learn to read. Unfortunately, there are few good reading specialists who can give such special treatment.

Parent motivation continues to be vital to the success of any ongoing remedial help. Children have to be delivered to the reading specialist. This must take precedence over tennis lessons, gymnastics, horse-riding, family holidays, and so forth. Parents need to recognize the commitment involved when they begin a series of sessions for their child. When the child is changing bad habits and developing new perceptual skills, the training must be ongoing and consistent. One solution to maintaining gains, used by the Lindamood–Bell clinics, is daily 'intensives', where the child rotates through various teachers for several hours each day for about a month. Intensive training makes it possible to introduce new techniques at the same time as preventing the recurrence of old bad habits. The child doesn't have days or weeks to slip back into what he was doing before. Another solution, adopted by Read America, is to involve parents in the training process itself and to provide fail-safe homework materials so that progress is maintained from one weekly session to the next and can continue long after sessions have been completed.

Parents' Emotions

Parents' emotions are sometimes even more important than the child's in producing a successful outcome. Parents come to a reading specialist with a variety of mixed feelings. These are largely the result of their lack of knowledge about the complexities of reading and frustration with the school or with the child. It is important for a remedial teacher to be aware of parents' thoughts and feelings about their child's situation. Sometimes people can hold quite incompatible beliefs.

One common assumption is that 'reading is easy because it's something everyone does', especially if the parent is an expert reader. (If a parent has had trouble learning to read, she will have much more sympathy with her child.) This assumption is in conflict with the reality that the child isn't reading. 'If reading is easy and everybody can do it', this means that her child is failing at something 'easy'. Parents search for reasons to explain how this could happen. Maybe their child has low intelligence or has something wrong with his brain. Another possibility is that their child is too lazy to learn to read. This belief can be reinforced by teachers who tell parents that their child 'isn't trying', or 'isn't paying attention'.

Early in the process, the reading specialist needs to find out what the parents believe about their child's reading problem. Sometimes she or he may have to convince parents that many of these beliefs are in error. For example, reading is *not* easy, as the preceding chapters have shown. Most children, even those whose reading is average for their age, do not read phonetically. Contrary to what the classroom teacher may have suggested, children with reading problems have tried very hard. Every child wants to learn to read. If children stop 'paying attention' or stop 'trying', it's because reading is too difficult for them, not because they don't care. We know that reading is not a biological property of the brain and so there cannot be damage to a 'reading centre' in the brain. Furthermore, if there was damage to such a centre, remedial help wouldn't work!

Parents have a range of emotional reactions to this new information. Some experience a sense of profound relief that their child isn't brain-damaged or 'stupid'. Often this information confirms what they already know about their child, that he is intelligent and highly motivated. This relief can sometimes turn into anger that is directed to the school system or to the child's previous teachers. The anger grows in proportion to the number of years they have spent trying to get help from the school and is fuelled in proportion to the child's progress in learning to read during reading therapy. Parents have said to us: 'If you can teach my child to read, why can't his teacher?' 'If you know these methods that work, why doesn't the school system know them?' These are legitimate questions that are hard to answer because they involve a discussion of experimental research, a detailed background about the remedial method we're using, and a brief historical account of why we are where we are. (Parents' questions and concerns have been one of my major motivators for writing this book.)

Sometimes parents lose faith that their child can be helped. My colleague had the following exchange with parents who had recently moved into town. The parents had been visiting various schools in the district. My colleague ran a private school that specialized in both classroom and remedial treatment for children with reading problems. The programme had a documented history of success with children with severe reading problems. Children's lives had literally been turned around at this school.

The parents stated that their child had a serious reading problem and they were looking for the right school. My colleague assured them that their child would learn to read, and that she specialized in teaching children with severe reading problems to read. She said to the parents, 'Don't worry, we will teach your child to read.' This appeared to make the mother furious. She responded with words to the effect that their child would never learn to read, that he was 'dyslexic', and that my colleague didn't know what she was talking about because 'our child has been tested by experts'. They left the school abruptly, never to be seen again. In psychological terms, this reaction is known as 'cognitive dissonance', in which the amount of time, effort and money spent to accomplish something (in this case the diagnosis 'incurable dyslexia' from 'experts') is in direct proportion to the intensity in defending one's opinion against contradictory information.

This brings us to another common misconception on the part of parents and also many reading specialists. This misconception derives from a 'nominal fallacy', the belief that naming something explains it. Many people hold the belief that you can 'have dyslexia' as if it was a brain disorder or disease. I have already discussed the fact that 'dyslexia' simply means 'reading poorly' and has no valid diagnosis. But there is a reason why the notion of a 'brain-damaged' model of reading failure, such as that implied by the term dyslexia, is comforting to parents. Many of them have been searching for years for answers to why their child has a reading problem. It is often more acceptable to believe that their child is unique and has a special reading disorder than to face the fact that their child has lost years of education because of poor reading instruction.

The Client's Emotional Reaction to Reading Failure

People have various reactions to reading failure. These can range from outbursts of highly aggressive behaviour and subsequent hospitalization to mute passivity and depression. The reading specialist has to be able to deal with every type of emotional reaction to reading failure, otherwise she cannot convince the child or adult to trust her, and nothing can be accomplished. Making the client feel safe and establishing trust is the first step towards a successful remedial intervention.

Reading problems cause major emotional problems which increase in intensity the older the child becomes and continue throughout adult life. This is because reading is unavoidable and the poor reader believes that 'everyone else can read except him'. Children are reminded of their shortcomings on a daily basis and there is no escape. When the object of loathing cannot be avoided, there is intense distress. All children want to learn to read. When they come up short in comparison to their classmates, this causes an incredible sense of failure. What children want most is to show that they are competent in all areas in which their peers are competent. When a child cannot do this, there are four main ways to respond to the distress.

Anger/Acting Out

Frustration causes anger. If someone is repeatedly teased he will ultimately retaliate by losing his temper. If you are required by law to sit for five or six hours every day in a classroom where you cannot do the work, this is the ultimate frustration. Because anger against an adult, especially in classrooms, is unacceptable behaviour, only the very daring or desperate will actually display overt aggression. Children can redirect their anger into more covert ways of getting back at the teacher or getting even with the school which they blame for failing them (with some justification).

All sorts of minor misdemeanours can be perpetrated which contribute to making the teacher's life miserable. A youngster can wander around the room at inappropriate moments and feign surprise when reprimanded: 'I was just looking at the rabbit!' They can throw paper balls, tell jokes to their neighbours, tease other children, and so on, which gains them some attention and potential respect from their classmates. This compensates for their academic shortcomings which are known to *everyone* in the class. Make no mistake, children keep score. They always know how everyone else is doing, no matter how hard the teacher tries to disguise this, such as labelling reading groups 'Swallows' and 'Robins'. Children will tell you in the blink of an eye that 'I'm in the Robins, that's the good reading group, but my friend Sarah is in the Kingfishers, because she can't read.'

One day I was walking with eight-year-old Mark from the classroom to the testing room. To make conversation I asked him, 'I suppose you're a good reader. Do you like to read, Mark?'

Mark replied without pausing for breath, 'I've read five more books than Joe already this term, and he used to be the best reader in the class, but now I am.'

Being the class clown or the class nuisance is a benign way of expressing anger, but the motive is anger none the less. Other children act out in much more destructive ways. We tested a child at our reading clinic who had severe reading problems. His mother was so distressed with him that they were scarcely on speaking terms. He had been in continuous trouble at school. The child was brought to two sessions, but before he came to the third, he stood up on a table in the middle of the school cafeteria and began screaming at the top of his voice. He was subsequently hospitalized. I can't finish his story, because we never saw him again.

Another child expressed her anger and anguish in a different way. Susie began to act bizarrely at school, paying no attention whatsoever to anything anyone told her to do. She interfered in other children's work. She bossed them around. She used her body in provoking and inappropriate ways, sticking her feet up on her classmate's desk and tipping over chairs. She was diagnosed 'mentally retarded' by the school psychologist because she wouldn't respond during testing. Her mother came in despair, seeking our help.

Testing was impossible. Feet went up on the table and the test materials were scattered across the room. She never made eye-contact at any time and sat backwards in the chair for much of the session. Her behaviour was nearly autistic. Eventually, all that could be done was to try to connect with her in some kind of conversation, and even this was difficult. Working with Susie continued to be a problem throughout the first few sessions, until she began to trust the teacher and began to try. Fortunately, she had a sense of humour and could be reached through humour. Susie, who was taught by my colleague, is now a perfectly normal and delightful child. She's popular with both adults and children, and is reading at her age level.

These examples are not untypical. Well over half of the children with behavioural problems and attentional problems, and 90 per cent of juvenile delinquents, have serious reading difficulties. Susie is a reminder that children can literally be driven insane by what goes on in our schools. We often wonder what would have happened to Susie if her mother hadn't persisted and found us. By now she would be in a classroom for the 'mentally retarded'. She would be reading nothing and would have become a burden on her parents for the rest of her life. There are thousands of children like Susie who are lost for ever in special classrooms. When you see the consequences of this first-hand, it makes you aware of the cruel treatment that some schools can mete out to youngsters in need.

Fear

Fear is the opposite of anger. It is the reaction of children or adults who desperately want to please and haven't the guile or gumption to impose their personality on others through acting out. Ultimately, these people can develop what is called 'learned helplessness', a profoundly debilitating condition in which they come to believe that they need help in every phase of their life. This reaction poses a different kind of problem for a reading specialist in attempting to gain the trust of someone who is afraid that no one can ever make him self-sufficient.

Putting anything in print in front of someone like this causes instant panic, and the specialist needs to proceed slowly and cautiously, always being sure to begin each session at the place where the client experiences some comfort and sense of control. I am always particularly emphatic to parents about children who manifest these symptoms that they should not under any circumstances put any pressure on their child to read to them until the remedial teaching has progressed substantially. I also try to get parents to convey this message to the classroom teacher.

Fearful children and adults often have a finely developed ability to manipulate anyone who tries to teach them. Experience in classrooms has taught them that there is only one answer to any question, and their task is to find that right answer. They do this by a subterfuge that involves asking a question when they are given a question. They become adept at reading people's expressions, searching their face for clues that they are on target.

Eva's case epitomizes this type of emotional response. She was a woman in her late twenties who had a severe speech defect that made her seem unintelligent, and whose self-esteem was at zero. Her reading age was twelve, but even this was based on untimed tests which she took for ever to complete. She had had years of speech therapy and years of remedial reading classes. Having been diagnosed learning disabled, she was currently struggling through a Community College with a 'tutor' (paid for by the taxpayers) who helped with her written assignments. Eva gradually revealed that she had more or less manipulated this tutor into writing large portions of her essays. I spent considerable time convincing her that her life would be unmanageable if she had to conduct the rest of it with a tutor at her elbow!

As we began to work, she would take her eyes off the materials and stare into my face. If I asked her, 'Which sound went away?' she would reply with a question, 'The /b/?' and quickly scan my face for a clue to whether she was right. If I replied, 'Are you sure?' she thought she had made a mistake and immediately substituted another question using another sound – 'The /e/?' After a while my constant reminder: 'You won't find the answer on my face,' became a standing joke between us. It took her months to stop doing this.

Eva learned to read at the appropriate level for her age and improved her speech to the point where she sounded completely normal, which made her brother from out of state burst into tears when he telephoned her to wish her Merry Christmas. She had a successful interview for a job at a local bank and moved into her own apartment. She no longer needed her tutor and was writing her own essays and getting all As by the end of our thirty-five sessions.

Depression / Withdrawal

Clinical descriptions of psychological distress can be ranked on an energy continuum. A person who is filled with anger/hostility has a much higher energy level than someone who is afraid (anxiety), which is, in turn, a higher level than sadness or depression. Some clinicians believe that prognosis in psychotherapy depends on the level of energy, and that people with extremely low levels of energy are much harder to treat. Depression is close to psychological 'death'. People who slip into a clinical depression can withdraw completely from human interaction.

Children or adults who have reacted with depression to their reading problems are difficult to teach for just this reason. Some are so depressed and withdrawn that they are nearly mute, staring into their laps and mumbling inaudibly only when spoken to. It's exhausting to work with such clients because the specialist feels obliged to provide energy for the client as well as herself. This is like pouring water into a cup with a hole in it. Depressed people extract energy from everyone around them, but this does little to improve their condition. To deal with this type of client you must attempt to fix the 'hole'. This means setting clear goals and doing exercises in self-awareness. The more the specialist attempts to take responsibility for the client, the less responsibility the client will take to remedy the situation. People whose depression is based *solely* upon their reading failure need a remedial programme that involves more ongoing support, such as more frequent sessions and activities where the clients can estimate their progress – 'Look how far you've come!' This keeps them from slipping into apathy between sessions and keeps the goals in focus. If depression appears to be due to other causes, this type of client should be referred to a suitable professional for psychological treatment.

Intellectualizing

A highly intelligent child or adult can intellectualize their reading problem. We have already seen how Mike decided not to learn how to spell, because 'spelling made no sense'. Many very bright youngsters know they are clever because they are able to learn quickly and remember everything they hear or see. They usually get a lot of positive feedback from their parents about their abilities. When it transpires that they have difficulty learning to read, they can invent some extraordinary kinds of rationalizations about this deficiency to protect their self-worth. These children can be challenging to work with because the teacher constantly has to outwit them.

Bobby was six-and-a-half and had decided to stop reading altogether when he was brought to me for testing. His mother and father were both very concerned and both seemed motivated to get help for him. Bobby had an impenetrable set of logical arguments about why he didn't need to learn to read. He was quite a talented artist. He argued that as he was going to be an artist, artists didn't need to learn to read. After all, they never had anything to do with the printed word. I reasoned that if he was ever commissioned to produce a work of art, he would need to sign contracts and be able to read them, otherwise he could be cheated. He disagreed and said that he would only deal with honest people, and their contract would be a handshake. Furthermore, when he got famous (which was sure to happen), he would hire someone to deal with all the paperwork.

We had many similar discussions, which, of course, were deliberate time-wasting ploys that Bobby enjoyed. In addition to his many intellectual arguments about not needing to learn to read, he had scores of premeditated behaviours to distract me from the task at hand. He would smuggle strange objects into the session and then begin to pull them out of his pockets at various intervals. His high intelligence extended to a masterful ability to manipulate adults, especially his mother. (If he came to a reading session, he got a treat.) I pointed this out to him on one occasion and he just grinned.

Obviously, I genuinely liked Bobby and we had a great rapport. He also liked coming to sessions but not to learn to read. We would rarely work longer than about five or ten minutes before the fun and games began.

There was a more important aspect to this case. Bobby had a hidden agenda behind his manipulative games that he was too young to be aware of. When Bobby's parents were first interviewed, I asked whether there was anything in his life that was upsetting him, because his test scores revealed that there was basically nothing wrong with him. He had no deficits in any subskills related to reading. His mother hastily responded that everything was fine. His father, on the other hand, pointed out that Bobby had just lost a favourite grandparent and that his other favourite grandparent was in hospital at that moment. Bobby went to visit every evening. (This grandparent subsequently recovered.) Then the father confessed that he and his wife were in the process of separating for the third time. Yet the mother had stated that 'nothing was wrong'.

Some time after we had been working together, Bobby returned from a month-long trip to visit his dad, the third separation now being under way. Bobby's first remark came immediately after we began to work. He told me that the whole time he was with his dad, 'he didn't make me read one word'. Suddenly I saw a purpose in Bobby's behaviour. He could hold his parents together by virtue of his continuous failure to learn to read. This upset was their common interest and it focused their attention on him. His dad could 'punish Mom' by telling Bobby he didn't have to read when they were together, knowing Bobby would convey this information, just as he did to me. Mom, who was trapped in the game, was practising denial that anything in their family life was affecting Bobby. It's not surprising that I was having little success, because I became an unwitting pawn in this game. Although Bobby certainly had a minor reading problem that could easily have been helped, he didn't need a reading specialist so much as an astute family therapist.

Intellectualization plus denial is common in the adult poor reader, as we saw with Mike in the last chapter. These are people who can read, but very badly. They have poor decoding skills and have to reread the same passage over and over again. They also have serious spelling problems. However, they will fight everyone who tries to help them in order to protect their self-worth: 'I don't really have a reading problem, I just don't like to read.' 'I don't really have a reading problem, I'm just a slow reader.' They also worry that their fragile grasp of the written code could be undermined by being taught a new method. They could be worse off than before. ('Better the devil you know.') There is some justification for this concern, as many poor readers have been in remedial reading programmes already with no measurable outcome. It is hard to convince these people that there are programmes that really work, something you need to be aware of if this description fits a family member. It is also something a reading specialist needs to be aware of when a surly client is dragged in protest to their office.

Incidentally, families often don't know how serious a reading problem is for an adult member of the household. Here is a trick you can use to find out. If you find something interesting in a magazine or newspaper while you're in the same room, toss it to them and say: 'Have a look at this! This is amazing!' The first thing a poor reader will do is to put the magazine or paper down somewhere, on the coffee table or the floor. Then he will say something like: 'I'll read it later,' or 'Why don't you tell me what it's about?' or 'I'm just about to (a) watch TV, (b) mow the lawn, (c) go for a walk.' This may be true, so repeat this experiment a few times. If these reactions occur each time, you know there is a problem.

This is a glimpse of the many kinds of additional issues that adults and children can bring to a reading specialist. I have given examples of relatively severe cases, and most people will not have such debilitating emotional reactions to reading problems. Children with minor deficiencies can be helped fairly quickly and because they see gains almost immediately, are easy to work with. Even in the more severe cases the psychological distress will diminish as soon as the client begins to see progress and trusts the teacher. However, when these symptoms do not disappear, or when a client devotes his entire energy to game-playing, as Bobby did, it is usually a sign that something else besides reading needs to be addressed. Because a reading specialist is not really in a position to recommend other forms of treatment, she is often in a difficult position with certain clients and must handle the situation with great tact.

The Remedial Environment

The School

In an ideal school no child would ever need remedial help. Some children might take longer to learn to read than others, but everyone would learn by the right method. Hopefully, one day, remedial reading specialists will become an extinct species and the schools will at last take on the job of doing what they are supposed to do, teaching all children to read. Until that time, there are millions of children who need help now and who cannot roll back the clock and start anew. Here is a brief outline of a model remedial programme that should be implemented in every primary school.

1. Each school would employ a reading specialist. This person should be trained in how to test and diagnose reading subskills. She would have an understanding of child psychology and be aware of the types of emotional problems created by reading failure. She would know how to use methods like those described in this book.

2. The specialist would have her own quiet and self-contained space, big enough to work with children in small groups as well as individually.

3. The specialist would coordinate each child's curriculum with the classroom teacher. This would include separate stories, books, and worksheets, so that the child's time in the classroom was productive instead of being wasted.

4. The specialist would have regularly scheduled meetings with the parents and advise on homework and reading activities appropriate for each child.

5. The specialist would meet with the school psychologist or other professional to discuss children with special emotional problems.

Private Tuition

A key issue for parents and for reading specialists in private practice is that parents have no knowledge about how to evaluate a reading specialist or a particular method. One of the main goals of this chapter is to provide information that will enable people to make an informed choice. Specific information on how to find a reading specialist is provided in Chapter 13. The layperson tends to equate specialists with 'tutors', and doesn't understand why she should pay higher fees to specialists in private practice. A specialist is a professional and needs to pay rent, staff salaries, miscellaneous office expenses and still make a living. A reading specialist using a good reading method will teach a child to read correctly in a short space of time, so that he can function to the maximum of his potential.

The atmosphere of the specialist's private office is critically important. The work area should be quiet, peaceful and uncluttered. Nothing should distract from the task at hand. Children should be made aware that what they do in this environment is a serious matter, and that this is a special place where they will learn to read. For these reasons it is not a good idea for the specialist to teach children in her home (unless there is a self-contained office). This blurs the boundaries between the professional and the client, and can create a situation where misbehaviour is more likely to occur.

I once agreed to test a child who lived in the neighbourhood in my home. The clinic was about thirty minutes' drive away, so going there was inconvenient for both of us. I had about ten seconds to say 'Hello, Johnny,' and then Johnny took off, running from room to room, up and down stairs, opening doors and cupboards, while his mother did nothing except to utter the unbelievable remark: 'He doesn't usually act like this.'

Diagnosing the Problem

Mandatory Tests

Parents need to be informed about which kinds of tests are useful for diagnosing a reading problem and which are not. They also need to know that a reading specialist who does not use diagnostic testing is not doing her job properly.

No type of intervention should begin until the reading specialist has a profile of the client. Without this profile, she doesn't know where to attack the problem precisely. For example, a child or adult may have good phonemic awareness, understand the phonetic code perfectly in isolation, but be unable to apply this code when reading text. This would direct the specialist to focus more on blending and segmenting activities than on teaching phoneme-awareness and sound–letter correspondences.

It isn't necessary to spend weeks or months waiting on the school system for special testing in order to determine whether a child needs remedial help. A simple reading test will reveal whether a child is reading below their age level. Other straightforward tests are all that are required to pinpoint specific weaknesses in perceptual or cognitive abilities that affect reading. The following five tests are the most useful in determining a diagnostic profile and apply equally to children and adults (examples are given at the end of the chapter):

1. A standardized reading test that has the following properties: isolated word recognition and nonsense-word decoding (word attack). Word recognition errors should be phonetically transcribed so the child's predominant reading strategy can be determined.

2. A test of phoneme-awareness: the client is asked to listen to a word or nonsense word and then to manipulate (reverse, add, delete) phonemes in the word.

3. A test of phoneme segmentation: the client hears a word and has to isolate (separate) each phoneme one at a time in sequence.

4. A test of blending: the client hears a series of isolated phonemes and is asked to blend them into a word.

5. Code knowledge. Letters or letter-patterns from the spelling code are listed and the client has to decide how these would sound if they appeared in a word.

The purpose of the testing is to rule in or rule out certain processing problems that will affect the speed at which recovery will occur, as well as specific problem areas that the specialist needs to be aware of.

The reading test will give a rough idea of the child's reading age. The nonsense-word reading test measures pure decoding skill and reveals whether or not the client has any ability to decode phonetically. The client's reading strategy will be determined by the phonetic transcriptions of errors in the word recognition reading test.

Phoneme-awareness test scores will reveal whether the client has a problem hearing and manipulating phonemes when they are embedded in words. Two tests are normed (i.e., they've been tested on hundreds of children and scores fit a normal distribution curve). These are the Lindamood Auditory Conceptualization test (Lindamood and Lindamood, 1971) and the Auditory Analysis Test (Rosner and Simon, 1971). Neither test is recommended for children younger than six, and the logic can be too difficult for some six-year-olds. Poor performance on either of these tests will direct the specialist to intensive training in phoneme-awareness.

Segmenting tasks, in which the client has to separate each sound in a word ('Say each sound in the word "frog"'), illustrate the ability to analyse the sound sequences in words. Blending is the subskill that allows the client to put the sounds back together. It is common for poor readers to have one skill and not the other.

Optional Tests

1. A sample of the client's writing is a powerful aid in determining the degree of their confusion about the spelling code. For older children and adults it is useful to ask for a page of written work with spelling *uncorrected*. This is one way to identify the poor speller who might score well on the diagnostic tests. It is also useful later, when reading, spelling and writing have improved, in order to illustrate the improvement to the client.

2. Reading fluency. It is useful to measure how long it takes to read a standard passage, as a base for later comparisons. Although this gives the reading specialist little diagnostic information, it can be a big help in motivating the client during the remedial process.

3. Reading comprehension tests have little predictive value for diagnostic purposes. I have had clients take forty-five minutes to read twenty-five single-sentence passages and score almost perfectly on these tests. However, for adult clients, a comprehension test can be informative. It provides a vivid impression of the effort it takes for a poor reader to extract any meaning from what she reads. If the first ten or twenty items are timed, this provides a useful measure of improvement in later sessions. Finally, it will expose the rare fluent decoder who doesn't process the *meaning* of (comprehend) what he reads, indicating that comprehension itself may need special attention.

4. A spelling test can be useful for children aged eight and above. A 'spelling recognition' test (where the client chooses among possible spellings: clene, clean, cleen, clien) is essentially a reading test and should be avoided. A spelling dictation test should be given instead. The Wide Range Achievement spelling subtest is used most often in research and in many clinical settings (though it has some problems). A new spelling dictation test has been developed by Pro-Ed which provides separate scoring norms for phonetically regular and irregular words. Unfortunately, we do not have good spelling tests with sufficient range and good psychometric properties.

The Testing Climate

One day I was visiting a friend's clinic and observed a child being tested who was unable to focus on the task at hand for any length of time. He kept turning around to look at the door behind him and constantly squirmed uncomfortably in his seat. Fortunately, my friend was a sensitive person who bothered to ask him what was wrong. He was simply worried about when and whether his mother would return for him, and if she had been told what time he would be finished. Once reassured, he immediately settled down to focus on the test.

Someone else, sticking strictly to the test manual, might plunge ahead and write in her notes: 'hyperactive behaviour, attentional problems?' I have seen people who should know better rush through testing, disregarding the emotional and physical state of the client. Children and adults arrive straight from school or work and may need to go to the bathroom or get a drink. These are routine courtesies that a specialist should extend. It sets the climate for testing in that the child or adult feels the tester's concern for her well-being.

The specialist should reassure clients that they will be given very few tests and none will be done to a time limit. Clients (and parents) often come to a testing session in a state of anxiety and even panic. Many have been tested over and over again with little outcome except humiliation. They need to know that the specialist is going to teach them how to read and not just send them back into the void. The purpose of the tests is not to upset them but to provide a set of guidelines for the remedial process.

Testers should *never* let a client continue if he has misunderstood the test instructions. The purpose of the tests is *not* to determine whether or not the client understands test instructions. The purpose of testing is to get a true measure of ability. Even when clients have been told that reading tests are untimed, they frequently rush ahead, scarcely looking at the words, to impress the tester with their speed. They should be told to slow down and be reminded that the test isn't timed. When transcribing errors, this is all the more important. A similar problem occurs in the nonsense-word reading test. Clients start to invent real words for each example, reading 'bif' as 'bit'. They should be stopped and the instructions repeated. The purpose of the test is to force them to try to decode, so that the specialist has some idea whether or not they have any decoding skill.

Communicating Test Results

Many parents with a child who has been tested by the school system have experienced being handed a fistful of incomprehensible charts and tables and/or a jargon-laden narrative that provides them with absolutely no information whatsoever. I have interviewed parents who have arrived with folders full of years of test score results, charts, and reports, most of which made no sense even to me. The purpose of these reports seems to be to obscure what is actually wrong with the child.

A remedial reading specialist and the special educational needs staff at school have a duty to the parents of a poor reader, to communicate clearly and unambiguously the test score results with either a verbal or written explanation in plain English. They must be able to state the reason why the test was given. They must be able to state how *that particular test* defined a specific problem that affects reading or spelling, and how that problem is manifest. They must be able to tell the client or parents how the intervention they plan will help the child, based on the diagnostic test scores, how this will be measured, and finally, *how long this intervention will take*, based upon the severity of the problem. A good reading specialist can give you a broad time estimate over the phone based upon their experience, and a fairly accurate time estimate after testing. Never trust anyone who says they have no idea how long it will take (or how much it will cost). If someone tells you this at your child's school, seek outside help immediately.

What a Good Remedial Reading Programme Looks Like

In Chapter 9, I reviewed the research into new approaches to teaching reading. Many of these studies were short-term experimental programmes or programmes for younger children. Here, I will describe a remedial reading programme that works for everyone, and meets the following requirements for an effective reading method:

1. Published, peer-reviewed research that indicates large and consistent gains.

2. Uses phonemes as the basis for teaching the alphabet code. Includes most or all of the spelling code.

3. Works for *everyone* at all ages – no one fails.

4. Works quickly. It should take no longer than twenty-four hours of lessons to teach anyone to read.

I wish I could tell you about hundreds of good remedial programmes, or even ten or five, where you could be certain that your child or family member would learn to read, but I can't. This is not to say that there aren't good remedial programmes in the schools or the private sector. The problem is that most reading specialists do not do scientific research. This means that one has to rely on the reading teacher's belief that her programme works, and without published information, it's very difficult to find out about good programmes. One of the goals of this chapter is to present a successful programme in sufficient detail that you will be able to evaluate a reading programme that's on offer to you.

Parents should be aware that traditional phonics programmes don't get any better when transported to the reading specialist or to the special education classroom. They have the same shortcomings they do in the regular classroom and don't miraculously improve simply because the child is working one-to-one with a specialist. Phonics programmes do not teach phoneme-awareness, nor do they teach the correct logic for the alphabet code. Some reading teachers in private practice have told me that they have had more success after providing phoneme-awareness training *prior to* teaching phonics. This may be so, but this still does not eliminate the cumbersome and time-consuming instruction required by phonics logic in order to teach the entire spelling code.

That remedial teaching is an unsolved problem in the school system has been documented by Steven Truch, formerly a consulting school psychologist in Alberta, Canada. He did a survey of special education teachers and asked what percentage of the children graduated back into the main classroom. The answers ranged from zero to an optimistic 20 per cent. Most teachers estimated 0–10 per cent. Robert Slavin and his colleagues in the US report that special education fails most of the time in the inner-city schools where their research has been ongoing for over a decade. Unfortunately, there is no information on the impact of special education on British children in the classroom or otherwise.

I have already discussed the elements of a good reading programme in Chapters 10 and 11. The first key component is training in phoneme-awareness. Phoneme-awareness begins with the identification of all the phonemes in the language (not just some of them). Then the student must be trained in these skills: auditory analysis, or the ability to manipulate phonemes in words (remove, insert, or reverse sounds); the ability to segment words into isolated phonemes and blend isolated phonemes back into words. *All three skills are equally important* and do not necessarily go together. That is, a child can have good segmenting and poor blending, or poor phoneme-awareness. Variable performance on these three skills is not uncommon.

A good remedial programme differs in two fundamental ways from the classroom programmes outlined in Chapters 10 and 11, though the overall philosophy is the same. First, it requires individual one-to-one training, which is critical for anyone with a reading problem. Each client must be monitored closely, and all errors dealt with immediately. The client has already lost valuable time (usually years) and cannot afford to waste any more.

Small group instruction is considerably less effective. The reading specialist has to shift her focus of attention constantly from one pupil to another. Children tend to misbehave in small groups and distract one another from the task at hand. Children prompt each other with answers instead of waiting their turn. Children and adults alike are embarrassed about their reading difficulties and less likely to be forthcoming when asked to try something new in a group of strangers. Many adults have emotional problems or serious life problems that they cannot share in a group setting. This lesson learned from clinical practice is important for the special education teacher working in schools. She cannot teach reading successfully to a class or group of children with serious reading problems.

The length of time remedial teaching takes is determined by the *total* amount of one-to-one time spent with each individual client. So for small groups you can multiply the amount of time required for an individual by the number of children in the group. This also applies to the *frequency* at which the training takes place. Four hours of work a week is as effective as four hours a month. Beyond this (four hours per year) the rule breaks down. The goal of remedial teaching is to train missing subskills, eliminate incorrect strategies and replace them with correct ones, teach the complete code, and prevent what is gained during sessions from being lost over time and the client slipping back into old habits.

The second difference between remedial programmes and the classroom approach described earlier, is that they are rapidly speeded up in information content. In part, this is because the child or adult has the entire focus of the teacher for the training period, but also because classroom or early home instruction has the luxury of time. The classroom programme outlined earlier is ultra conservative because it must be taught in small groups or to the whole class. It was designed so that no child can fall through the cracks. A remedial programme hasn't the luxury of time. Changes must be made fast. Clients have to see progress happening in real time, otherwise they become discouraged and apathetic. After all, many of them have been through this process before, with no measurable results.

Read America has developed the first comprehensive clinical reading programme that takes advantage of all the research reported in this book. The central philosophy and guiding principles of Read America's Phono-Graphix™ stemmed from the research described in Chapters 7 and 8, including our own research at the University of South Florida. (Chapter 9 includes our research findings and a summary of the programme.) Phono-Graphix™ incorporates these principles:

1. A true linguistic programme in which the phoneme is the basic unit for teaching the writing system.

2. Comprehensive training in phoneme-awareness, phoneme segmenting and blending.

3. A detailed analysis of the structure of the English alphabet code (spelling alternatives/code overlaps). This is the organizing principle for an extensive curriculum.

4. Knowledge about the cognitive and intellectual development of the child, and the applied testing of this knowledge. Management of the complexity of the code through carefully sequenced lessons, one type of logic at a time.

5. Eliminate letter-names, all exercises or language that conflict with the logic of the code, or that add an unnecessary memory load. Keep strictly to the motto: 'Teach nothing that must be discarded later on.' Create a reflex response to the print code by instilling the appropriate strategy through repetition.

6. Involve the parent or adult mentor directly in homework so that she has a positive role and can maintain gains between sessions and after sessions have ended.

Phono-Graphix™ was developed to teach every important skill necessary to read and spell, and to teach them as rapidly as possible. Local clients participate in a one-to-one twelve-hour programme. The maximum time taken to date is twenty-four hours (one adult client). The hour-long sessions are held weekly and a family member supports the client in one or two hours of homework each week using specially designed curriculum materials. If the client is coming from a distance, he or she is taught in 'intensives', and these are set up according to the needs of the clients and their families. A two-hour session, plus one hour of homework per day, is optimum. This programme takes six days.

From about the age of seven on, gains made on standardized reading tests have been found to be the same whether the client is taught over twelve weeks or in intensives over six days. Six-year-olds tend to get slightly lower gains in intensives than in weekly sessions. Improvements in reading age range from one to four years depending upon the age of the client.

The programme and curriculum materials are set up in three levels. These levels would roughly approximate to what a child would learn if he was taught to read properly in the first place. However, not every level is necessarily taught to the poor reader. On the basis of diagnostic testing, each client begins at a level, or at a place within a level, most suited to his ability and knowledge.

Level 1 covers the Basic Code – one-to-one mapping only (one sound = one letter); *no digraphs*. Skills training covers phoneme analysis, segmenting, blending, reading, and spelling. These skills are mastered in simple three-sound words and words containing consonant clusters.

Level 2 is the Advanced Code. The first part of this level includes consonant digraphs. Next come vowel digraphs, followed by phonemes with multiple spelling alternatives (one-to-many mapping). All but the rare spelling alternatives are taught. Code overlap (many-to-one mapping) is integrated with teaching spelling alternatives. The advanced code level is the most extensive in the programme and continues to teach segmenting, blending, reading coded text (where digraphs and phonograms are emphasized by special type), analysis of text through 'sound search' worksheets and stories, and in spelling and writing.

Level 3 teaches multi-syllable words up to five syllables long. Clients are trained to build words by syllable and to decode by syllable, reducing long words to manageable chunks. They do this by analysing phoneme sequences within syllables and reassembling syllable chunks into a word.

There is a curriculum of hands-on materials for each of the levels. There are picture cue-cards with 'sound-picture' cards to construct the word in the picture. There are phoneme analysis cards for phoneme-awareness training, and over 1,000 word cards. All materials are organized *by phoneme* except for code overlap exercises and Latin suffixes. Story series in coded text were written for three age groups and for adults. There are also 250 worksheets and several games.

The curriculum is organized according to the child's age or skill *and* according to the mapping logics involved. The client learns all possible spelling alternatives and all possible code overlaps in more than one thousand words. Consistent spelling patterns are taught as 'tendencies' or 'expectancies' and never as 'rules' (the sound /ae/ tends to be spelled ay at the ends of words and sometimes ey). These tendencies are taught by *exposure*, by sequencing the materials so that the client discovers these patterns during controlled exercises.

The homework materials consist of a packet of over 250 worksheets, stories and games designed to reinforce the teaching sessions. Each client's packet contains materials from the place where the client begins in the programme through the remainder of the curriculum. The materials are constructed to promote the correct strategy. This packet becomes the property of the adult mentor or client. (All the parents who replied to an anonymous follow-up survey reported they were still using the home materials.)

The diagnostic tests allow one to begin sessions at the point in the curriculum most appropriate to the client's level of skill. No time is wasted teaching what they already know or can do. For example, if a client has very poor phoneme-awareness, he will begin at Level 1 auditory processing training. If a client has good phoneme-awareness, he skips this level altogether. However, segmenting and blending are practised at all levels, as can be seen in the examples below.

In remedial settings where most clients are older, progress can be speeded up by interleaving the levels of logic, providing the logic is always made clear. Vowels spelled with digraphs can be introduced together with lessons on spelling alternatives, and followed immediately by sessions on code overlaps where necessary.

The teacher needs to keep the client actively engaged at all times, mentally and physically, and also to keep the questions and explanations to a minimum. Much of the success of the programme is due to *how* the clients' errors are handled, so they understand clearly and quickly what they did wrong and how to correct it. When the client makes an error, she is informed immediately of what she did.

For example, a child is asked to do a tracking exercise as described in Chapter 10. She is told to change the word 'cot' into the word 'pot', using letter cards. She has chosen the wrong letter, the letter m.

The teacher says, 'That says "mot". We want "pot".' The teacher says the whole word without segmenting the sounds and points to each letter in turn as she does so. If after a few tries, the child does not make the correct change, then the teacher segments each sound.

'We need to make "cot" say "pot": /p/-/o/-/t/.' The teacher points to each letter the child has placed in sequence as she says this. The child can see the mismatch between what she hears (/p/) and the letter she has chosen (m) and she will be successful at this step.

In another example, the client reads a word, segmenting each sound accurately. When asked to blend the sounds together to make the word, she blends them incorrectly: '/m/-/a/-/p/ – cap.'

The teacher says, 'You said all the right sounds, but when you blended them you read "cap".' (The teacher points to each letter in turn as she says the word.)

'If this was "cap", then this [points to m] would be the sound /k/. But it isn't. It's /m/. Try again please.'

The combination of clear language, a carefully sequenced logical structure, and the extensive controlled exercises, produces progress that is so rapid it is almost immediately noticeable to the client. This, along with the variety and novelty of the materials, maintains the client's interest. Through clear and helpful explanations, the client learns exactly what he did, and why, and what to do next. In a short space of time, he is able to self-correct his own errors and become an independent reader and speller.

A Special Note on Reading Clinics

In America, reading clinics are a booming cottage industry, with as many as twenty or thirty clinics in each major city. Many are excellent because good reading specialists keep up to date with the reading research, travel extensively to workshops, and are constantly on the lookout for better and better programmes. In Britain, there is nothing like this, and the situation is exceedingly bleak. In calling round to specialists and tutors in Britain, I frequently encountered people who did not even know what method they were using. Typically, these people tried a little bit of everything and 'tailored the method to the child's learning style', a recipe for failure. I know that there are good private reading teachers, because parents have told me about them, but they aren't easy to find. To help you with this problem, I have provided guidelines in the next chapter for how to find and evaluate a good reading specialist.

In addition to the *Yellow Pages* for sources of help, you might also want to call the British Dyslexia Association (0118 966 8271). The issue of 'dyslexia' as a valid diagnosis notwithstanding, this organization is committed to helping children learn to read. They may be able to recommend someone in your area. The closest you will get to the best of the American methods is to look for a highly structured, systematic phonics programme. That is your safest bet for now.

If you have no success, you might want to contact Read America in Orlando (tel: 00 1-352-735-9292; fax 00 1-352-735-9294). They publish a British version of *Reading Reflex*, a home programme for parents to use with beginning readers, and for children who are falling behind. They also publish a British version of the Phono-Graphix™ programme for the classroom and reading specialist, and also will be scheduling training for reading specialists in Britain. If your child or family member urgently needs help now, it may be worth two cheap airfares and an inexpensive motel room, for the guarantee that your child or family member will learn to read in approximately one week of intensive sessions.

Do-it-yourself Diagnostics

The following tests are designed for parents and teachers to evaluate a child. They will provide information on the child's reading skill, reading strategy, phonemic awareness, and knowledge of the advanced spelling code. These are not standardized tests, but they have been used in research and in the clinic. If a child is having trouble on any one of these tests, you need to seek further advice from a professional, or teach the child yourself based upon the information provided in Chapters 8, 9, and 12.

Word Recognition and Strategies Test

Write the words listed below on white 3 × 5 in (8 × 13 cm) cards, three words to a card, in large lower-case letters. Number the cards on the back from 1 to 15.

Hold up each card, or hand it to the child, and ask him to read each word carefully. There is no time limit.

This is also your scoring sheet. When the child makes an error, record *what he said* in the spaces provided (any spelling will do).

1. no	16. then	31. plate ....
2. an	17. says	32. warm ....
3. be	18. feet	33. blow ....
4. sat	19. clock	34. funny ....
5. bed	20. here	35. river ....
6. fox	21. cold	36. break ....
7. book	22. house	37. shout ....
8. to	23. dear	38. could ....
9. bag	24. log	39. honey ....
10. them	25. said	40. melon ....
11. see	26. time	41. watch ....
12. good	27. new	42. exam ....
13. dry	28. uncle	43. blue ....
14. hot	29. sheet	44. answer ....
15. gas	30. anyone	45. believe ....

Scoring the Test

Approximate placements are shown for reading all or most of the items correctly.

Items 1–6	Beginning Year 1
Items 1–15	Middle Year 1
Items 1–30	Beginning Year 2
Items 1–45	Middle Year 2

Assessing Strategies

Pure Guessing

Child guesses a real word that has no connection to the word either in letter–sound correspondence or in word length.

Example: 'no' is read as 'fun' or 'look'

Modified Whole-Word Errors

Child decodes the first letter or letters correctly and guesses a real word with attention to word length and shape.

Examples:	no	as 'not'
	sat	as 'say'
	them	as 'this'
	good	as 'great'
	clock	as 'clover'

Part-Word Errors

Child tries to break the word down into 'sound bites'. Typically reads nonsense words and reuses letters.

Examples:	them	as 'the-hem'
	clock	as 'cloawok'
	sheet	as 'she-heat'
	anyone	as 'an-yunee'
	plate	as 'play-ate'

Orthographic Errors

Child reads phonetically, letter by letter from left to right but decodes many letters incorrectly.

Examples:	here	as 'her'
	house	as 'huss'
	dear	as 'dar'
	uncle	as 'unclee'
	plate	as 'plat'

Phonetic Errors

Child reads a phonetically probable rendition of the word, but misreads word.

Examples:	no	as 'naw'
	says	as 'saize'
	house	as 'hooss'
	anyone	as 'anyoan'
	blow	as 'blou'
	honey	as 'hoany'

The strategies are set out from the worst to the best. Code each error into the highest possible strategy. Example: 'her' may have been a guess, but is also a phonetic decoding.

To estimate your child's predominant strategy or strategies, count each *type* of error and divide this number by the total number of errors. This will give you percentage of each type of strategy error.

Children with a year or two of reading instruction should be making mainly orthographic or phonetic errors. If this is not the case, you may want to get outside testing and remedial help or teach the child yourself.

Instructions for the Nonsense-word Test

This test can be used in two ways. If you use it both ways, be sure to give the reading test *first* and the word repetition *last*.

Nonsense-word Repetition

Screening test for possible speech problem. Suitable ages: four to eight. (Three-year-olds can do this test but a poor score doesn't mean anything.) If the child scores below average, you may want to get proper testing by a speech therapist.

Tell the child you are going to play a game by saying words in 'Martian'. His job is to repeat back the word exactly as you said it. Be sure to practise first so you can read each word fluently. It doesn't matter if you do not pronounce it correctly, but it *does* matter that the child repeats it exactly as you have spoken it. If he does, then score it correct.

The average scores for ages four to seven are as follows:

Four-year-olds:	15–20
Five-year-olds:	20–30
Six-year-olds:	30–35
Seven-year-olds:	35–40

Nonsense-word Decoding

To use this as a decoding test, print words on 3 × 5 in (8 × 13 cm) cards, three words to a card, in large lower-case letters.

There are no norms for this test. Anyone who knows the code can read every word because they are phonetically regular. However, this would be unusual, even for many adults. Younger children (ages six to eight) will not be able to read many of the multi-syllable words. This test will give you information about whether or not your child has any idea about how to decode our writing system.

Nonsense-word Test

1. dap ....
2. fim ....
3. pob ....
4. tad ....
5. bek ....
6. seef ....
7. kug ....
8. doif ....
9. kibe ....
10. boosh ....
11. chuj ....
12. fowp ....
13. thev ....
14. woamp ....
15. feench ....
16. nempt ....
17. barng ....
18. gleth ....
19. straimp ....
20. droiper ....
21. bloamite ....
22. strōōkle ....
23. varthip ....
24. roilesh ....
25. quomple ....
26. lomramp ....
27. chowmerg ....
28. sharlfen ....
29. groithek ....
30. zichong ....
31. kagpeb ....
32. vifthung ....
33. distroamber ....
34. sizchullen ....
35. meminum ....
36. jozipesh ....
37. zotrempering ....
38. chibbyreenom ....
39. quodistelpab ....
40. rinpohacherfelp ....

Blending Test

Do not allow the subject to see the test. Tell the subject that you are going to say some sounds. He/she should tell you what word it sounds like. Sit near enough so the subject can hear you clearly and see your mouth. Explain that you can say the sounds only once and he/she should listen and watch carefully. Say each sound in the first word, with a one second interval between each sound – 'p', 'i', 'g'. Do not repeat the word. Write down the first response.

Part One		Part Two	
p i g	....	f r o g	....
b u g	....	g r a ss	....
h a t	....	s t i ck	....
p i n	....	p r i n t	....
r a t	....	c r u n ch	....
b ir d	....	p l a n t	....
sh e ll	....		
f i ve	....		
b oa t	....		

Interpretation of Scores

Less than a perfect score on part one indicates that the subject has trouble blending or pushing together the sounds in three-sound words.

Less than a perfect score on part two indicates that the subject has trouble pushing together sounds in four- and five-sound words.

Phoneme Segmentation Test

Do not allow the subject to see the test. Explain that you will say all the sounds in the word dog. If the subject offers a letter name say, 'That's a letter. What's the sound?' If he/she persists in responding with letter names, mark those responses wrong. Put a check for each correct answer in the corresponding space. If he/she omits a sound mark it wrong, e.g., 'frog' = 'f' 'o' 'g'. You would mark these responses like this ✔ ✗ ✔ ✔. If he/she gives the wrong sound, mark it wrong, e.g., 'frog' = 'f' 'r' 'a' 'g'. You would score these responses like this ✔ ✔ ✗ ✔. If he/she blends two sounds together mark both sounds wrong, e.g., 'frog' = 'fr' 'o' 'g'. You would score these responses like this ✗ ✗ ✔ ✔. 'f' 'ro' 'g' would be marked like this ✔ ✗ ✗ ✔.

Part One		Part Two	
dog	....	frog	....
hat	....	black	....
pin	....	nest	....
pot	....	trip	....
rat	....	milk	....
nut	....	drum	....

Interpretation of Scores

40+ = good   36–39 = low moderate   under 36 = poor

Did they:

Offer a letter-name more than two times, e.g., 'dog' = 'dee' 'oe' 'gee' ? The subject may not understand that letters are symbols for sounds, and may be trying to recall the sound of the letter by thinking of the letter-name, an unnecessary step requiring a translation.

Omit vowel sound or chunked it to a consonant sound two or more times, e.g., 'dog' = 'd' 'g' or 'do' 'g' or 'd' 'og' ? The subject may be connecting a vowel sound to each consonant and may need training in the pronunciation of consonant sounds.

Chunk consonants together or omit one of them more than twice, e.g., 'frog' = 'fr' 'o' 'g' or 'f' 'o' 'g'? The subject may be having trouble isolating the separate sounds in words, causing him/her to leave sounds out and add sounds that aren't there.

Repeat the wrong sound two or more times, e.g., 'frog' = 'f' 'r' 'a' 'g' ? The subject may have a low auditory memory.

Auditory Processing

Do not allow the subject to see the test. Ask the subject to say the word pig. Now ask for pig without the sound 'p'. If he/she has trouble doing this, offer an example. Say, OK, if I wanted to say 'dog' without the 'd,' it would be 'og'.

Part One

Say **pig** without the 'p'	.... (ig)
Say **pog** without the 'g'	.... (po)
Say **sip** without the 's'	.... (ip)

Part Two

Say **stop** without the 's'	.... (top)
Say **nest** without the 't'	.... (ness)
Say **flag** without the 'f'	.... (lag)

Part Three

Say **plum** without the 'l'	.... (pum)
Say **best** without the 's'	.... (bet)
Say **grill** without the 'r'	.... (gill)
Say **lost** without the 's'	.... (lot)

Interpretation of Scores

8+ = good   5–7 = moderate   under 5 = poor

Were they:

Unable to score correctly on all of the first three test items? Subject is experiencing difficulty segmenting and isolating single sounds in simple words.

Removing the adjacent consonant to the target sound in part two or three, e.g., flag without the 'f' = 'ag'? The subject is experiencing difficulty segmenting individual consonants.

Unable to perform (no correct responses)? The subject is having difficulty understanding the nature of sounds in words.

© Copyright Read America, Inc.

Code Knowledge Test Key and Interpretation

This page is the key for the code knowledge test on the next page. Use the next page as the cue sheet for the test. Do not let the subject see this page. After each sound is an example of a word or words containing that sound in case you are uncertain of the sound that the letter(s) represents. For example, the <ie> in the last column can represent the sound 'ie' as in the word die, or 'ee' as in the word chief. Begin by pointing to the first letter and asking: 'If you saw this in a word, what sound would you say?' If subject says a letter-name, you say: 'That's a letter. I want to know what it stands for.' If subject continues offering letter-names, mark these answers incorrect. Only sounds are correct answers. Keep track of the number of correct and incorrect responses.

__b	boy	__y	yes	__oa	boat
__c	cat		happy	__ow	now
	city		fly		snow
__d	dog	__z	zipper	__igh	night
__f	fat	__i	rip	__eigh	eight
__g	got	__e	net		height
	gentle	__a	mat	__ay	play
__h	hop	__o	mop	__ie	die
__j	job	__u	nut		chief
__k	kid	__sh	ship	__aw	saw
__l	lap	__ch	chip	__ee	seen
__m	mop	__th	this	__ey	key
__n	nod		Thursday		they
__p	pat	__ck	duck	__ue	blue
__r	rat	__qu	quick 'kw'	__ew	few
__s	sat	__ce	nice	__au	August
__t	top	__ai	rain	__oo	wood
__v	give	__ou	out		moon
__w	with		group	__ui	suit
__x	fox 'ks'		touch	__oy	boy
	exit 'gz'	__ea	each	__oi	soil
			steak		
			bread		

Interpretation of Scores

(Multiply score by two to arrive at the percentage of correct answers)

	good	*moderate*	*poor*
Six years old	60–100%	50–59%	under 50%
Seven years old	70–100%	60–69%	under 60%
Eight years old	80–100%	70–79%	under 70%

For older children and adults use the eight-year-old values.

Code Knowledge Cue Card

b	x	oa
c	y	ow
d	z	igh
f	i	eigh
g	e	ay
h	a	ie
j	o	aw
k	u	ee
l	sh	ey
m	ch	ue
n	th	ew
p	ck	au
r	qu	oo
s	ce	ui
t	ai	oy
v	ou	oi
w	ea	

CHAPTER 13

What Parents Can Do

Parents have many questions that range across a broad spectrum of issues, from how to teach subskills to pre-school children to how to find remedial help for a child in trouble. Family members and friends of adults with reading problems also have questions. In this chapter, I will do my best to answer the many questions people have asked me over the years.

Parents all want to know when a child should begin reading and when to intervene if they suspect there is a problem. The simple answer is that it is never too late to teach anyone to read, and that there is no special time to begin teaching a child to read. Children in Scandinavian countries learn to read two years later than children in most other European countries. This works fine because parents are under strict orders to do nothing in the home prior to the time the child begins school, and they willingly comply. It also works because most schools are doing their job. Finland, Sweden and Norway have the highest literacy rates in the world.

But Scandinavian children, like children in Germany, Spain, Italy and France, learn a more straightforward alphabetic writing system. Because our alphabet is so complex and causes so many problems when it is taught incorrectly (which is most of the time), parents in English-speaking countries are justifiably concerned about whether their child will learn to read.

So the issue is really more subtle than when to begin to teach reading or when to begin to worry. The issue is rather that because inappropriate teaching methods are the norm, the child can easily develop incorrect decoding strategies. The more these strategies are practised, the worse things become. A parent can intervene either preventively before this happens, or after the fact. Parents need to be aware that *if* a child is in trouble, they must seek help immediately. The longer the child practises reading and spelling using the wrong strategy, the further he will fall behind his classmates. All the evidence shows conclusively that poor readers *do not catch up* simply because they get older. Don't believe any teacher who tells you this.

The Pre-school Child

Let's begin at the beginning. What can parents do to help rather than hinder their child's progress in learning to read? The answer can be divided into three categories: what is helpful, what is harmless and what is harmful.

Helpful Activities

Talk to your child, even if you're just expressing out loud your thoughts about what you're doing or thinking. An amazing study was carried out in the US by Betty Hart and Todd Risley. They studied forty-two families from three social groups and recorded how mothers spoke to their infant children during the first two and a half years of life. They recorded everything that was said to each child for one hour per month. The average number of words addressed to the child ranged from 1,500 to 2,500 per hour in homes classified as 'professional', 1,000 to 1,500 in the middle-class homes, and 500 to 800 in the homes of single mothers on welfare. By the age of three, it was estimated that children in professional families had heard nearly 35 million words, middle-class children just over 20 million words, and children of welfare mothers around 10 million words. These differences were found even though welfare mothers spent more time overall in the same room with the child.

The speech addressed to the child also varied in terms of the richness of vocabulary and style of speaking. Mothers in the professional group used a more complex sentence structure, a richer vocabulary and a highly affirmative feedback style: 'that's right', 'that's good', along with a more positive tone of voice. Welfare mothers, in contrast, often used a negative tone, and lots of explicit disapproval: 'stop that', 'don't spill it', 'don't do it that way'. Welfare mothers, however, did not differ in any other measures such as affection, concern for their child, the cleanliness of the home, and appropriate reactions to a child in need. Nor was race a factor in any of the data.

The various measures of the mother's speech, taken together, were highly correlated to the child's language skills later on, to vocabulary development, to vocabulary use, and to standardized measures of IQ, vocabulary, and language use. These relationships were much more powerful when based solely on parenting speech style than when correlated to socio-economic status. The correlations between the mother's speech output and style and the child's later verbal and intellectual ability were high at age three and also at age nine (correlations ranged from .74 to .82).

We saw earlier that vocabulary and IQ are not strong predictors of reading success, though British researchers have found them much more so than researchers in other countries. The major problem of the poor reader is weak or absent phonemic awareness, and a lack of knowledge of the English alphabet code. However, when children do learn to read spontaneously, or are in situations where phoneme-awareness *is* taught and the appropriate method *is* used, then vocabulary becomes much more important. Reading accuracy and fluency are enhanced if the word you are decoding already exists in memory. This is obvious in the difficulty people have in decoding strange words like those in 'Bad Fruit' in Chapter 2. Also, as discussed in Chapter 11, decoding accuracy and fluency are the main predictors of reading comprehension.

Read to your child. Reading to your child has lots of spin-offs for teaching pre-reading and early reading skills. It familiarizes children with the format of books. There are pages that turn in a fixed order. It familiarizes children with the print code, at least if the parent points this out. For example, the parent can trace along the text with a finger as she reads, training the child that our print code goes in rows from left to right and from top to bottom down the page. She can begin to train early awareness of how our alphabetic writing system works, by pretending to have trouble reading a word – 'Oh, let's see. Let's sound this word out'. The mother points to each letter or letter-pair (digraph) and says each sound separately: /f/, /r/, /o/, /g/, and then blends it into the word 'frog', moving a finger swiftly under the letters in the

337

word as she blends the sounds together. Be sure the child sits beside you and can see what you're doing. The child learns that letters are ordered from left to right in a word, that letters stand for sounds, that words are made up of these sounds, and that sounds in words can be broken apart and put together.

In addition, the child also learns all the other important aspects of language and literature, such as new vocabulary; that stories have a beginning, middle and end; that stories can be made up, and so forth. Parents can enhance comprehension and awareness by asking questions like: 'Why did the baby dinosaur have to wear a coat?'

Encourage pre-writing skills. Get materials from the stationer's or supermarket so that the child can begin to practise tracing, and connecting dots, in order to develop manual control over a pencil, pen, or crayon. Let the child write with imaginary writing – 'Why don't you write a letter to Grannie, and draw her a picture?'

Harmless Activities

The research evidence shows clearly that rhyming activities do not have any effect on learning to read as scientists once thought. The rhyme component of a word contains more than one sound. It consists of the final vowel sound plus any consonants that follow it. Multi-sound units, such as the rhyme, are not the basis for an alphabet code, so teaching rhymes specifically is a waste of time. Pointing them out in structured lessons, where rhyming patterns and 'word-families' are taught as a basic decoding strategy, is actually detrimental. ('The letters ay-tee sound /at/ in "the cat sat on the mat".') Instead, the child should learn that the *sound* /a/ is spelled a anywhere in a word, and the *sound* /t/ is spelled t anywhere in a word.

This doesn't mean that children shouldn't learn nursery rhymes, poems, and songs, and use word-play. It's something young children enjoy very much. Remember the finding that Pig Latin correlates with reading skill? If you want to teach a word-play game that actually might be beneficial, this is a better choice, because it involves picking off a single phoneme from the front of a syllable and putting it at the end: Oo-day oo-yay ikelay eadray-ingay? [Do you like reading?]

Harmful Activities

One of the most harmful things you can do is to force children to do reading activities they don't want to do. Children are highly active learners, and they decide what they want to learn at any moment in time. And so they should, unless their particular activity is harmful to someone or something. (My son, aged two, used to tip over furniture from various angles, to see 'if it would break', as he explained it to me; an experiment on the force of gravity on falling objects. After a while I could intercept him in this activity by listening for grunting noises.)

You should know the other harmful activities by now. The first is teaching letter-names; forcing your child to memorize and recite the alphabet; having him read ABC books and memorize the names of capital and lower-case letters. You can teach the alphabet a much better way, should the child show any interest. Begin with simple words in lower-case letters and *say the sound each letter stands for as you write it or point to it* – /d/, /o/, /g/ – not its letter-name. If your child's nursery teacher is teaching letter-names, you'll just have to live with it, or ask her to stop.

Teaching letter-names is more benign than teaching whole words by sight, which sets up completely the wrong logic. If your child recognizes a word, points, and says, 'that says "dog",' find out how she did it.

Don't shriek, 'Oh! She's reading!!'

Ask her to show you what cues she was using. If she can't do this, then you show her. Say something like, 'That's right. How did you know that? Can you tell me what you *see* that makes you know it says "dog"?'

If she can't do this, other than to say, 'It starts with a dee', or 'I just know it does', then prove to her it does.

'Let's prove that it says "dog", shall we? The first letter is for the sound /d/, the next letter is for the sound /o/ [say /o/ not /oh/] and the last letter is for the sound /g/. Let's put it together: /d/-/o/-/g/ – "dog". Aren't you a clever girl to work that out!'

As a general principle, pre-school children are better off learning *nothing* about reading, than learning something that is detrimental to the reading process. If they don't want to have anything to do with

339

activities related to learning to read, then so be it. Doing nothing is not going to hurt them.

The Reception Class

'What should my child be learning when she starts school?'

Oh dear. Here is where the problems begin. Your child should be doing everything described in the first sections of Chapters 9 and 10, but odds are that she will be doing none of these things. Instead, she will be learning letter-names and sight words.

The first thing you have to do is find out from the teacher what she intends to teach the children. Then you have a choice. You can ask the teacher to leave your child out of the lessons, which is not easy for her to do. You can take your child to another school, but chances are nothing will be different there. (A Montessori school is the safest place to go.) You can teach your child at home *and* send her to school, and hope that you have more influence over your child's thinking than the teacher does, because what you will be doing is directly opposite to what she is doing. The final option is to take your child to a good reading specialist, but few take children this young.

I can't help you make this decision, but I can give you some idea of what to teach at home.

If you find out that the teacher is actively teaching the wrong things, then you have to create a pact with your child *if and only if* your child finds this a problem. If your child says something like, 'Mrs Bowers doesn't do it this way,' you reply, 'Never mind what Mrs Bowers is doing, we are going to learn to read the proper way.'

If this issue doesn't come up, then just ignore it. More subtly, you can also ignore your child's developing skill in reciting the alphabet, and pointing to letters and saying their names. Don't give any praise or reinforcement for these behaviours. Give her the *sound* the letters stand for instead: 'Yes, that letter is for the sound /b/.' If your child is learning 'sight words', then go through the routine I showed you above, *especially* with words that are phonetically regular. If they are not, and they are truly 'sight words' like the words 'the' (thuh), 'one' (won), 'of' (ov) (see Chapter 11), then say nothing.

If you are serious about teaching your child at home, you will need to work with the exercises in Chapter 10 and/or get one of the programmes or sets of materials described in the Appendix to that chapter, such as the British edition of *Reading Reflex* (the only complete parent programme that teaches all elements of reading correctly). Also, purchase a good audiotape of English phonemes.

The materials should train the child in left-to-right sequencing, symbolizing (that symbols can stand for something else), and how to segment sounds and blend sounds into words. Any type of more complex auditory analysis (such as segmenting clusters like /b/, /l/, /a/, /k/) is too difficult at this age. Begin by teaching around eight to ten sounds in CV and CVC words like those at the end of Chapter 10. Teach initial sounds first and show the child the letter that stands for that sound. You can also create little phrases and stories from the word lists.

Go slowly and don't force the issue, because young children are extremely variable in their aptitude for these tasks. Some children will just take off and start reading, others will struggle and want to give up. Be patient.

Year 1

'When can I discover if my child is learning to read or not?'

A six-year-old should be able to read simple stories by the end of the school year. Around the middle of Year 1 he should be able to read many simple words, especially three-sound words like those listed at the end of Chapter 10. He should be able to write his letters correctly, even though the handwriting leaves something to be desired. He should be able to spell his name and also common, phonetically-regular three-sound words.

If none of this is happening, then start to become concerned. Ask your child to read simple text to you. Listen to what he is doing, and reread Chapter 2 to see if he is using a bad strategy. Be very suspicious if he is spelling like Tommy in Chapter 1. If your child can't read a word by the middle of Year 1, you need to take action. Get him to a good reading specialist, or try to teach him at home. The longer the reading problem continues, the further behind your child will become. There are simple tests provided at the end of Chapter 12 to check on his strategy, phoneme-awareness and decoding skills, and later in this chapter I will show you how to find a good reading specialist.

After Year 1

'Does my child have a "learning difficulty"?'

Well, the problem with this question is that you're never going to know until the child is about one to two years below age norms, at which point he gets tested, diagnosed as having a learning difficulty, and put in a special classroom, or visited in the main classroom by the special educational needs teacher or support assistant. And of course, as you are already aware, *there is no such thing as a 'learning difficulty' anyway* (see Chapter 7). If you wait for a diagnosis, the earliest most children can be diagnosed is around the age of seven or eight, because this is the first time that a child of average intelligence can be far enough below age-norms in reading. This means that he will have lost more than two years of school, and will go on losing ground in most special education programmes. You also need to be aware that most local authorities do not have sufficient funds to give effective help to poor readers.

The dilemma for many parents is in the grey area between the end of Year 1, when parents recognize there is a problem, and waiting and hoping for the child to qualify for special educational needs support. Start by giving the screening test battery at the end of Chapter 12. If your child has problems on any of these tests, my advice would be to get him tested by a good reading specialist or by an educational psychologist in private practice. Chances are you will not be able to get appropriate testing at the school unless the child has severe difficulties, acknowledged by all. But you could try. Local Education Authorities vary enormously in the amount of money they spend on special educational needs.

Educational psychologists in private practice are trained to give tests and write reports summarizing the test results. By and large, they are not trained as diagnosticians and usually cannot give remedial help to the poor reader. If they could, they would be much more likely to give tests with greater diagnostic value. They can tell you that your child has a reading problem but not why, or what to do about it.

Educational psychologists in private practice tend to be expensive, and this is sometimes as a result of testing overkill. It is often difficult to get only a reading test, which is what you need initially. You can make a few phone calls and see if anyone is willing to do this. Ask for tests which measure 'word recognition' and 'nonsense-word decoding' (word attack). These are the best tests to show whether your child is reading below age-norms. If the psychologist also administers a phoneme-awareness test, such as the Lindamood Test of Auditory Conceptualization, Rosner and Simon's Auditory Analysis Test, or Bruce's phoneme-awareness test, then ask for this also. In my experience, it is rare for an educational psychologist to give any of them.

Nevertheless, a good educational psychologist can screen for many other problems, such as cognitive deficiencies like poor memory, weak vocabulary, auditory and visual perceptual difficulties, problems with fine-motor coordination, speech dysfunction, and so forth. If you suspect any of these problems, then it will be a good idea to have a complete test battery. An educational psychologist is also one of the few professionals who is qualified to give an intelligence test. (They may suggest your child is 'dyslexic'; the important thing then is to find a reading specialist with effective teaching methods – avoid any who use the 'dyslexia' label as a cop-out for failing clients.)

Another option is to phone a local reading specialist. Look under 'Educational Services' in *Yellow Pages* to find someone who will give a reading test (many call themselves 'dyslexia specialists'). Some reading specialists, especially those using the small-group tutorial model, don't do any testing at all. Tell them that you want your child tested for age-level placement on 'word recognition' and 'word attack' *only*. Be sure to ask how much it will cost before you make an appointment. Testing should take about thirty to forty minutes. Information from both tests is equally important.

If your child is not at age-level on one or other of these tests, then you will need to schedule more testing and proceed through the inquiry process set out later in this chapter, or attempt home intervention. If your child is only marginally behind you can teach him yourself. Follow the methods set out in Chapter 10.

If your child is reading a year or more below age norms, or has serious problems in any one of these areas: phoneme-awareness, segmenting, blending, code knowledge; then I would advise you to get outside help. It will be much faster, more effective, and will cause far less friction between you and your child.

If, after testing, you find out that your child scores normally or above age norms in reading but is still having problems in school, then you will need to address other issues. Is there a family problem the child is not coping with? Are there other problems that would affect school work, such as difficulty with handwriting, or a conflict with a particular teacher? Arrange to see the classroom teacher and ask her to pinpoint specifically the weaknesses your child has. Don't accept vague statements like, 'He just isn't paying attention; I think he's dyslexic/developmentally delayed/emotionally disturbed', *or* 'isn't motivated to learn', *or* 'never finishes his work'. There could be twenty reasons why he isn't paying attention, isn't motivated, or doesn't finish his work. One reason could be boredom. You want specific information:

'His handwriting is illegible and it takes him for ever to write anything.' (Find a tutor who specializes in penmanship and fine-motor control, or teach him yourself.)

'She reads all right, but she can't spell.' (Get her tested by an educational psychologist and get remedial help. If she can't spell, she doesn't understand the code.)

'I sometimes wonder if she can hear properly, because when I ask the children to do something, she behaves as if she hasn't heard a word.' (Get her hearing tested.)

'He finishes his work correctly in about five minutes and just stares out the window, and recently he's stopped doing work altogether.' (Ask if he can be given more challenging work, or change schools.)

In Chapter 7 I reviewed evidence to show that speech difficulties affect reading. Speech problems need remedial help, especially when they persist past the age of four. Take your child to a speech therapist. If you can't see any significant progress, change therapists.

A minority of children have visual problems. If your child gets tired while reading and keeps rubbing his eyes, then he might need glasses. If he reads in funny postures, looking sideways at the print, and complains that he can't see, he may need to be tested by an optometrist who specializes in diagnosing and treating problems with binocular fusion and tracking. These children may be able to read isolated words on a reading test but not to do sustained reading activities because the print is constantly going in and out of focus. (See the section on vision in Chapter 7.)

If Your Child has been Diagnosed with Learning Difficulties

The immediate and urgent question you must ask is whether or not your child has made any progress. If your child has been diagnosed as having special educational needs and is receiving remedial teaching, then she should show noticeable improvement within six months. She should be back on track, reading at the appropriate level, in one year *at the latest*. If this isn't happening, get help fast somewhere else. Although some special education programmes are excellent, most are not.

If your child has been diagnosed with learning difficulties and you are going to see his special education teacher or school psychologist, then you need to know the answers to the following questions:

1. How far is my child reading below age-level?
2. Which diagnostic tests were given?
3. What skills do these diagnostic tests measure?
4. What effect do these skills have on learning to read and spell?
5. What methods are you using to remedy my child's reading problem?
6. Which diagnostic tests did you rely on to set up an individual educational plan or statement of special educational needs for my child?
7. What is the scientific evidence that your reading method works? Could you provide me with published reports on this research?
8. How long will it take you to teach my child to read?

If you're unhappy with any or all of the answers to these questions, take your child to an outside reading specialist immediately, or read the earlier chapters carefully and try to teach your child yourself. If the school psychologist and the special education teacher do not know why they give certain diagnostic tests, or how these tests would predict progress in a specific reading method, or how long it will take to teach your child to read, they don't know what they are doing and can't teach your child to read. If they can't cite research evidence in support of the programme they are using, they don't know why they are using it.

The Adult Poor Reader

The adult poor reader can be someone who has made do with an extremely ineffective strategy, or someone who gave up long ago and can't read a word. Most adult poor readers will not be reading this book. The motivation to get help has to come from the outside, from a family member or friend who insists that help really exists and that they can be taught to read.

Here, I am not describing someone who somehow missed out on reading instruction, or an immigrant who speaks another language. These people will probably do well in a community-based adult reading programme. I am talking about people who didn't miss out, and who will *not* be fine in an adult reading programme. Someone needs to reach out to these people, *if* you can find them, because, often, they develop ingenious means for disguising their disability. Others are in denial that they have a reading problem, as we saw earlier. In the American Adult Literacy Survey reported in Chapter 1, 75 per cent of the adults classified as 'functionally illiterate' told testers that their reading skills were 'good'. Adults with reading problems are often reluctant to get help and need to be reassured that help will actually make a difference. Let them know they are not alone. Twenty-one per cent of Americans and 22 per cent of British people are functionally illiterate, many of them highly intelligent. Read them the book *The Teacher Who Couldn't Read* by John Corcoran, so they can see they're not unique and that remedial teaching really does work.

Finding a Good Remedial Specialist

First, reread Chapter 12 so you will have a clear idea of what a good remedial reading programme looks like. If a similar programme is offered in your school as part of special education instruction, *say a prayer of thanks!* I know first-hand that there are excellent special education programmes and instructors, but they tend to be the exception. If your special education services do not match up, or if you have a child working with a support assistant but making no progress, you will have to go outside the school system for help. Don't waste any time.

Sources of Information

The best source is someone else who has had successful remedial help for him or herself or for a child. But this information can be hard to come by. Adults are humiliated by their reading problem and won't talk about it. Parents can be embarrassed about their child's reading problem and often reluctant to mention it because they blame themselves. If a parent does recommend someone, you need to ask for specific information about *how* her child was helped. She should be able to tell you the actual gains her child achieved, how long it took, any changes in status (no longer considered to have learning difficulties, for example) and improvement in school marks, behaviour, and attitude towards reading. Sometimes a parent will recommend someone who actually never helped her child. Instead, she got a diagnosis of dyslexia, plus the information that it could take years for her child to learn to read and still never be 'cured'. This may have made her feel better, because parents feel guilty when their child can't read, but it did nothing to help her child. Getting this kind of 'diagnosis' gets some parents off the hook.

The classroom teacher or special education teacher at the school can be helpful in recommending someone, but again you will need to be cautious. Most teachers care enormously about children, and their attitude is one of selfless concern; if they have had experience with a good reading specialist, they will gladly share it with parents. Some teachers, however, are threatened if an outsider can teach a child to read when they have failed, and will be less forthcoming, or even negative, about getting outside help. We have found this to be the case as well with some teachers in special education, particularly if they are having little success. A successful reading specialist threatens their job and prestige. It also brings the wrath of the parent down on their head if the child has spent a year or more working with them with little or no improvement.

For additional sources, see 'A Special Note on Reading Clinics', p. 323.

Evaluating a Remedial Specialist

Gather whatever information you can and then begin to interview remedial reading specialists by telephone. They are listed in *Yellow Pages* under various headings, such as 'Educational Services', 'Dyslexia', and 'Tutoring'.

Write out the questions listed below on a notepad with space for answers. Don't expect a receptionist to be able to answer them. Ask to speak to the specialist. Begin by telling them something about your child, spouse, relative or friend – his/her age, whether or not he/she has been tested, and your specific concerns about reading, spelling and writing. Then ask these questions in this order:

1. Could you tell me a little bit about your programme? What method do you use? [If they give you the name of a programme: 'We use Reading Recovery', and expect you to know what they mean, ask for more information.]

2. Do you see people in individual or small group sessions?

3. How long does each session last?

4. How many sessions per week do you recommend?

5. How long does the training take overall? [The answer may be in hours or in weeks or months.]

6. What kinds of gains should I expect to see? Will my child be reading at age level by the end of training?

7. Do you do any diagnostic testing? What kinds of tests do you give?

8. How long does this testing take?

9. What does it cost?

10. What does the training cost?

11. Do you give out names and phone numbers of satisfied customers?

12. (If you are calling about an adult.) What is your success rate with adults?

13. How soon could you schedule my child (friend, brother, etc.) if I decide to do this programme?

Then say 'thank you very much' and hang up. Here's what you are looking for:

Every good reading specialist should be able to give you a clear idea of the method they use. Let the person keep talking. If you don't understand, say so. If they can't explain it to you in plain English, they won't be able to teach it. *Never* send your child to a reading specialist who teaches 'sight words' or tells you that he tailors the reading programme to the child's 'learning style'.

Avoid programmes that use small group instruction, especially if your child (spouse/ relative) has serious problems. Use the answers to questions three, four and five to compute how long it is going to take. Thirty hours should be the absolute maximum for children. Multiply this by the answer to question ten if they give you an hourly rate. This will give you the total cost. Some specialists give a discount for sessions within a fixed time period. Often this makes it well worth paying up front, especially if you are impressed by the specialist.

Be suspicious if they have no idea about gains. Clients have told us about a local reading specialist who charges £3,000 'no matter how long it takes'. This is £30 an hour for 100 hours! Be equally suspicious if they give you exact information about gains for your child. Reading therapy can be unpredictable. Gains can only be approximate. A responsible reading specialist will give you approximate figures, or figures for the majority of their clients. They will also tell you that they will be able to predict more accurately after diagnostic testing.

If the answer to question seven is that they do not do diagnostic testing, this is a strong negative. If they give too many tests, this is another strong negative. You don't need testing overkill to diagnose a reading problem.

A good reading specialist has no hesitation in giving out telephone numbers of satisfied customers. They will also be able to provide you with personal statements that former clients and parents have made about their impressions of the programme, and perhaps send you a brochure describing the programme.

For adults, it is more difficult to predict how long remedial teaching will take. Some adults are motivated and make rapid progress. But for those who have spent the better part of their lives with no experience of the printed word, bringing the adult reader up to an adult reading level takes time. Also, some adults are likely to bring emotional baggage to the sessions which can slow down the remedial process. Some are depressed, or believe they are stupid, or take up time relating life experiences. Although adults usually make striking gains in a good programme (four years' gain or more is not uncommon), those who begin as non-readers may still be reading only at the nine- or ten-year-old level at the end of sessions. What they need next is *practice* and support, plus help with more practical skills like writing letters, reading and interpreting fiction, and reading material with technical language. Reading specialists will supply this help, but it can be given equally effectively by a family member.

Finally, question thirteen on the list gives you information on whether there is space available now for your child, relative or friend.

If all the answers are reasonable, you will be very lucky, and the next step is to schedule testing and meet the person who will be seeing your child, if possible. Often the person who does the diagnostic testing is not the person who will be working with your child. Ask to meet this person even if it's just for a minute.

More likely, the answers to the questions will be variable, some pluses and some minuses, and you will have to weigh these carefully. If it is a great programme, with superb results, you may have to pay for expensive testing. If everything looks good, and testing fees are reasonable, you may have to be satisfied with small group instruction. If there are too many negatives, you might want to consider travelling to the Read America clinic (see 'Special Note', p. 323). Work out the costs carefully, because a programme that takes one or two years to help a poor reader can cost more than two cheap airfares, a motel room, and one week of training. At least you will be sure ahead of time that your child, spouse or relative will learn to read, and you won't waste any more of your child's valuable time in the classroom.

CHAPTER 14

Is Anyone in the Schools Listening?

Now that we have the answers to teaching all children to read, you might think that the Department for Education and Employment, the Office for Standards in Education (Ofsted), the School Curriculum and Assessment Authority (SCAA), university departments of education, school heads, classroom teachers, special education teachers, and curriculum specialists, will rush to adopt these excellent programmes. Dare we hope that the system can change? Let me tell you a story.

Once upon a time there was a company called XYZ Company. It was entirely funded by the taxpayer and had no competitors. For over 100 years, it produced products with serious flaws. The product fail-rate in some factories was as high as 50 per cent. Laws decreed that everyone had to have this product, so you couldn't refuse to buy or shop elsewhere. Not only was there a high fail-rate, but the manufacturing process itself was toxic. It destroyed millions of people's lives. They were unable to get or hold a job, to participate in higher education, to get off the dole, and many were sucked into a life of crime. These additional problems cost taxpayers millions more pounds for special welfare programmes, police, prisons, inmate costs, legal costs, etc.

XYZ Company worked with legislators and local officials to try and fix things and got more funding for product recall schemes ('we care'). They trained product recall specialists, complete with a fleet of administrators. The product fail-rate of the Recall Division of XYZ Company was close to 90 per cent. Additional product recall schemes were initiated at more expense to the taxpayers and took over space belonging to other institutions like adult education centres, public libraries, and local community centres.

XYZ Company is still in business. No one can shut this company down, replace it with anything better, or do anything to fix it. XYZ Company owns you. Its local Board of Directors demands taxes on your property. Its national Board of Directors demands taxes on your income. If you don't pay up you could be thrown in gaol.

For over 100 years, XYZ Company had two standard answers for critics, (1) 'There is nothing wrong with our product' and (2) 'We have a chronic shortage of cash'. Meanwhile, ABC Company down the road can take the same raw material and turn out a product with no flaws. They can do this much faster at far less cost, *and* their manufacturing process is completely non-toxic. So why not purchase products from ABC Company? Well, you can if you're rich. But most people aren't rich. Their spare cash goes to pay XYZ Company.

When you look at state education this way, you can scarcely believe this story. Imagine owning a company like this:

> Customer required by law to purchase your product.
> No competition.
> Unending source of free capital.
> No product guarantee.
> Not accountable to its customers.
> Cannot be sued for product failure.
> When critics demand accountability, resorts to subjective assessments, misrepresenting the truth.
> As many administrators as workers, earning much higher salaries.
> Worker training has little or no relevance to on-the-job skills.
> A 50 per cent turnover of workers every three years is common.

Now add these other ingredients and stir:

University departments of education contribute directly to the toxicity problem by ignoring the scientific research, or by failing to recognize what is scientific research and what isn't, and by failing to incorporate important new discoveries into teacher training programmes. This creates a void into which education publishers rush to the rescue of poorly trained teachers by providing the only coherent curricula available. These curricula don't look much like the reading programmes discussed in this book. They tend to come in two main flavours: 'eclectic chaotic' and 'eclectic sequential'. 'Eclectic chaotic' derives from the belief that a little bit of everything at each step is better than just one thing. We saw the consequences of this in Chapter 9 when 'Success for All' departed from its basic floor plan, and began teaching look-and-say, phonics, and 'real books' all at once. 'Eclectic sequential' is an attempt to sequence every known reading method (except the right one) in some kind of order. This order mirrors what children do when they are forced to teach themselves to read. Children are taught sight words, syllables, syllable fragments ('word-families', 'onset-rimes'), along with liberal amounts of the 'real books' approach. When children are thoroughly confused, they are taught the 'sounds of letters' along with spelling rules and lists of spelling words they can't read. This sequence takes three to four years.

Education publishers really can't be blamed for this, because they can only produce curricula that teachers and schools will buy. Teachers have been indoctrinated during four years of training into believing that eclectic approaches are the only solution. Not only this, but important people higher up the system suffer from the same mistaken belief. Here are quotes from four top education officials:

> 'The truth is that there is no single method which should be taught, and there never will be any simple, failsafe approach, which, if adopted in classrooms across the land, would result in all our children learning to read.' (Jim Rose, Ofsted Director of Inspections)
>
> 'There is no single successful method. Teachers should recognize individual differences in children, using a range of methods and strategies.' (Peter Daw, LEA English Adviser)
>
> 'There are three methods to teach reading: phonics, look-and-say, and 'real books'. Teachers use all these methods and work out which suits a particular child at a particular stage.' (Anne Barnes, General Secretary, National Association for the Teaching of English)
>
> 'The Chief Inspector of Schools and other experts agree that teaching reading successfully demands a mixture of strategies.'
>
> (All quotes are from May 1996 editions of *The Times*.)

Even assuming that any of these remarks was remotely near the truth, how on earth is a teacher supposed to decide *which* of these 'strategies' to use for *which* child at *which* 'stage', given that no one else has any idea?

If, by some miracle, a scientifically proven reading curriculum was adopted by the schools, teachers would need extensive retraining. This would entail workshops and ultimately a complete overhaul of education departments in nearly every university. This isn't going to happen in the foreseeable future. The trend has been, and continues to be, to keep shifting the emphasis between known methods and avoid anything explicit or rigorous in teacher training. This is why education is continually losing ground, a process known as 'dumbing down'. Half-baked ideas, and gross misrepresentation of other people's work are standard fare for trainee teachers. Currently Britain is embarking on a 'back to phonics' campaign – assuming anyone knows what this means.

'Invented spelling' is a prime example of the misuse of other people's ideas. Supposedly based on Montessori's 'discovery learning', invented spelling is devoid of everything that Montessori stood for, including her valuable observations and insights about how children learn. Gone is the important work on subskills that make discovery learning possible. Gone is Montessori's fundamental point that children must practise only with materials that promote *error-free performance*. In his book on Montessori, John Chattin-McNichols points out that there is a profound difference between error-*free* repetition and error-*filled* repetition: 'Error is information only if it is correctable – otherwise it *becomes* the information.'

Montessori was in the classroom every day. She developed her methods from years of observing how children learn. All good teachers know what works and what doesn't. Teachers see first-hand that what they were taught in their training has little practical value, and that much of it doesn't even make sense. It is unlikely this is going to change in a hurry, phonics or no phonics. In our research and our teacher workshops, we have heard teachers complain that they were taught next to nothing about how to teach reading. They learned a lot of theory which had little applied relevance, and were given nothing practical to do to teach reading effectively.

The same state of affairs was reported by the National Foundation for Educational Research (NFER) in their 1993 ground-breaking assessment of teacher training in Britain. Teachers' major complaint was that there was little connection between what they were taught, what they actually observed going on in classrooms, and what they knew how to *do* when they began teaching themselves. Only 32 per cent of beginning teachers were confident of knowing how to teach reading. Twenty per cent of new teachers reported they were taught 'little' or 'nothing' about *any* reading methods; and 60 per cent were taught 'little' or 'nothing' about phonics. The majority were taught about 'real books', which isn't a method.

When we do research in schools in the US, teachers frequently ask: 'Could you test this child? I have no idea whether she has a reading problem or not.' A teacher who attended one of our workshops came up to us afterwards with this story. Dissatisfied with reading instruction during her undergraduate training, she subsequently completed a master's degree in 'Reading Instruction'. When she finished this programme she still didn't know how to teach reading. She told us she had learned more in our four-hour workshop than in *six years* of teacher training at university.

In the US, the glue that holds the system together is money and power, creating a strange company of bedfellows such as educational publishers, politicians at the state and local levels, and the teachers' unions. The National Education Association (one of two teachers' unions) has two million members and collects dues of approximately $750,000,000 each year. The NEA has recently become a bank and an insurance company. The NEA has been described as the only union in America that has a seat in the President's cabinet. If the NEA actually represented its members' interests and desires, then this might be forgiven, but it never polls its members about anything.

In Britain, these forces are compounded by extremist political agendas which permeate every level of the system, which is just as top-heavy, bureaucratic, and militant as it is in the US. Melanie Phillips has documented the extraordinary efforts of top-level civil servants at the DES to subvert the government in order to maintain their power-base and justify their existence by taking control over every aspect of British education. It was this group of bureaucrats who foisted a National Curriculum on the schools. The National Curriculum was the unintended consequence of the government's attempt to introduce uniform standards in English, mathematics and science (discussed in Chapter 6).

The National Curriculum is testimony to an unwritten law that when politicians try to fix state education, the outcome will be worse than if they had done nothing at all. William Bennett, Education Secretary in President Reagan's cabinet, coined the term 'the blob' for the education establishment. He believed that nothing could transform

US schools short of abolishing the blob. In Britain, this would correspond to the Department for Education and Employment, Ofsted, the SCAA, university departments of education, teachers' unions, and LEAs, including curriculum specialists and advisers. The blob stands in between any direct communication between the voters (parents), classroom teachers and their government.

When the Thatcher government attempted to implement national standards, the Education Secretary, Kenneth Baker, not knowing personally how to do this, turned over to the then Department of Education and Science, HMI and curriculum specialists (who operated under what became the National Curriculum Council) the task of putting the government's ideas into practice. Given that the education establishment around the world tends to be allergic to science and scientific facts, specialists already in the system are most likely to implement the status quo, and least likely to do anything really important – such as *make it possible* for every child to learn how to read. If they already knew what they were doing, they wouldn't need a government mandate to do it!

The National Curriculum

The end product, the National Curriculum, consists mainly of a list of books to accompany the nine subject areas which must be taught from primary school on, along with guidelines for classroom time to be spent on each subject. These are English, maths, science, history, geography, art, music, PE, and religious instruction complete with 'daily acts of corporate worship', an extraordinary list for children who can't yet read! Classroom teachers complain that this leaves no time for teaching reading, spelling and writing. Further requirements for testing, record keeping, and filing reports, waste even more time.

The National Curriculum is not a curriculum. A curriculum is something that teachers can *use*. A curriculum can be transported directly into the classroom. 'Reading schemes' are curricula. Instead, the National Curriculum requires a fleet of translators at each level of the bureaucracy. Administrators and curriculum specialists second-guess each other down the line. By the time this gets to the classroom teacher and finally into the classroom, it bears little resemblance to what might have been intended, because it was never clear what was intended. To look at this process in more detail, I want to illustrate how the National Curriculum guidelines for reading instruction were translated to classroom teachers by one LEA.

The 1992 National Curriculum Guide provided a list of vague goals to be achieved during Key Stage 1 (ages five to seven):

Know conventions of print.
Know about the alphabet system.
Be aware of the patterns of sounds and ways symbols correspond to those sounds.
Read a growing number of words accurately and quickly.
Use syntactic and contextual cues to check and confirm meaning.

Translation: LEA curriculum advisers and teachers must determine *on their own* what the conventions of print are, what the alphabet system is, and work out the mapping relationship of sounds and symbols. The ability to 'read words accurately and quickly' is merely a definition of 'reading', but there is no mention of how this is to be achieved. The list ends with homage to 'real books': guess words by syntax and context cues.

Further recommendations for teaching 'phonics knowledge' were published by the Department for Education and Employment in the National Curriculum for Key Stage 1 (1993) and include these goals:

Recognize sounds of spoken language and develop phonological awareness.
Recognize alliteration, sound patterns and rhyme and relate these patterns to letters.
Recognize syllables in multi-syllable words.
Identify initial and final sounds in words including rhymes.
Identify and use a comprehensive range of letters and sounds, including combinations of letters, blends, digraphs; and pay attention to their use in the formation of words.
Recognize inconsistencies in phonic patterns.
Recognize that some letters do not produce a sound themselves but influence the sound of others.
It is also recommended that the vocabulary of words recognized 'by sight' should gradually expand to a large number of words.

Translation: A child should 'recognize' all possible letters and groups of letters that stand for all possible elements of 'talk', rather than learn about *phonemes in speech*, which is what an alphabet code is written for. These are to include: initial consonant, rhyming endings, sound blends (which are confused with digraphs), syllables, and syllable fragments. But the ultimate goal is reading whole words: increasing a sight word vocabulary (which this book has shown is impossible). As to which 'inconsistencies in phonic patterns' the student is to become aware of, this is unspecified. Nor are we enlightened about *which* letters influence the 'sound' of other letters, except to note that the authors of these recommendations seem to think that letters actually 'produce' sound, and that other letters assist them in 'producing' sound!

Given this muddle, here is one effort (circa 1995) of a large LEA to make any sense of it. They begin by largely ignoring everything and proceed to organize their recommendations into a three-part typology straight out of Kenneth Goodman's 'real books' framework. The guidelines open with a statement of the overall philosophy: 'In the teaching of reading it is essential to use meaningful texts which conform to the normal patterns of written English, not artificially constructed language.' [No controlled vocabulary – so important for the beginning reader – allowed.] 'Readers use several cueing systems simultaneously and *automatically*.' [Italics mine. We have seen over and over in this book that they do not.]

The 'semantic strand' begins: 'The most effective teaching of reading is that which gives the pupil the various skills s/he needs to make the fullest possible use of context cues in searching for meaning.' [Maximum guessing is the goal.]

In discussing the 'syntactic strand', the authors betray their confusion about the word 'syntax'. The opening words are: 'We are now much more aware of the role of prediction in text processing. Readers interact with the text, constantly scanning it for meaningful connections.' [They are constantly scanning because they can't decode!]

The third goal is 'phonological knowledge and word recognition'. This section begins: 'The learning of sound–symbol correspondences should take place in the context of whole word recognition and reading for meaning.' (This is a quote from the 1975 Bullock Report, which shows how long the 'real books' ideology has held sway.) There are twenty-two recommended activities in this section. Almost all involve exclusively *visual* activities in which the child is supposed to memorize letter shapes, letter-names, search for letters and letter strings in text, and recognize sight words. Allusions to 'sounds' (phonology) usually occur in the context of a visual activity, for example, 'Draw attention to words, letters and sounds.' No information on *how* to draw attention, or to *which* sounds in *which* order is provided. Teachers are instructed to 'help children understand the relationship between letter-names and sounds'. This assumes there *is* a relationship between letter-names and sounds, which, as you know by now, there is not.

Rhyming games are recommended under all three strands (semantic, syntactic, phonological), indicating considerable confusion about these terms. While rhyming games are fun and interesting for young children, rhyming exercises have nothing whatsoever to do with semantics, syntax, or the phonemic basis for the alphabet code. Nor does rhyming ability predict reading and spelling skill, as we saw in Chapter 7. Unless these games are connected to a genre (poetry), they really have no place in the classroom. Mum can play rhyming games. We don't need to pay teachers to do it.

At the point where a child is becoming a fluent reader, it is recommended that the teacher present examples of letter strings that 'make the same sound' and those that 'make a different sound'. It isn't clear whether curriculum specialists actually believe that letters 'make sounds', or if they use this language as a convenient shorthand for teachers. Whichever is true, there is a lack of awareness of the importance of clear, unambiguous language when communicating something this complex to teachers and ultimately to their students. No information is provided on how to teach these letter-string/phonological correspondences, nor *which* letter strings should be taught, nor in what order.

The remaining recommendations provide a good set of goals for teaching basic language skills, developing reading comprehension, teaching children how to analyse different aspects and types of text, and providing children with some exposure to various genres. There is also an extensive list of books for the classroom library. All this is commendable. However, the directives of the various curriculum manifestos betray a singular lack of knowledge about children. Nine subject areas are beyond the capacity of very young children. The LEA's recommendations for teaching English and reading appear to be written for adults teaching other adults. There is little evidence of any insight into *how* children think and learn, *what* they can learn, and in what order. Lists of skills and goals predominantly apply to advanced readers, but there is no guidance on how to train children to *become* an advanced reader.

More problematic is the fact that curriculum advisers never actually produce a *curriculum*. Instead, they offer 'suggestions' from which the teacher is encouraged to construct her own. She is supposed to do this from scratch, sequenced appropriately for the developmental level of young children, without any guidance other than it should be 'meaningful'. The good reading curricula reviewed in this book were based on years of research, hundreds of sessions with children in classrooms and poor readers receiving remedial help, plus intense analytic work, in order to put together programmes that truly work for everyone. How can teachers be expected to do this on their own and be in the classroom every day? No one should be surprised that nearly every teacher falls back on some reading scheme, hoping that education publishers know what they are doing. Unfortunately, they do not.

This problem is best summed up by the NFER report, *What Teachers in Training Are Taught About Reading*:

> ... the National Curriculum does not require that teachers should have a knowledge of the main features of the sound system (or phonology) of English. Neither does it require that teachers should have a knowledge of the complex ways in which those elements of the sound system that distinguish vowels and diphthongs, for example, relate to the orthography of English. This information is of particular relevance to the diagnosis of systematic errors that pupils may make in reading aloud, for example. Such knowledge is also necessary for an intelligent interpretation of different approaches to the teaching of phonics and the claims made with respect to these. It is clear, however, from the review of the reading assignments associated with the courses taken and from interviews with teaching staff that the systematic study of language is not a significant component of the majority of the courses taken by the graduates. (page 87)

There are solutions to the problems that the National Curriculum is attempting to solve, but the National Curriculum isn't one of them. First, adopt a method with solid scientific support, one with a comprehensive curriculum. Provide clear, operationally defined goals, and make sure that each sub-goal or sub-skill is developmentally appropriate, so that every child can learn to read, write and spell. Design objective, up-to-date standardized tests, normed on large populations over a wide age-range. Get outside testers to administer these tests to find out if goals were met. Publish the test results of every school at regular intervals.

Second, foster and support scientific research on education. The output of good educational research in Britain, meaning properly controlled studies with *real data*, is marginal. All but a few of the quality studies reported in this book come from somewhere else. Educators, especially at the university level, must keep up to date with current research, and people who are completely unaware of this research should never be placed in decision-making positions.

Third, politicians need to exert the highest level of caution when they try to 'fix' education. People appointed to ministerial positions in education, both in Britain and the US, typically know little or nothing about education. They then rely on advice from the very people who are responsible for the problems they are trying to solve. This is analogous to employing architects whose buildings always collapse. Politicians consistently underestimate the complexities of the educational process and then register dismay and surprise when their citizens can't read, spell, or do maths.

Finally, in Britain far too much energy and rhetoric is expended on blaming political parties or ideologues of the right or left for absolutely everything that's wrong with society. This is a dangerous and overly parochial outlook, because it obscures the real problems. Politicians are not responsible for the education establishment. They did not create it; they got saddled with it. The problem of declining educational standards is not unique to Britain, and the time-frame is considerably longer than the last few elections. The problem is a consequence of universal education itself.

The Legacy of Universal Education

Although universal education developed slowly during the nineteenth century, it became practically an overnight emergency when it was made compulsory in 1880. There were millions of children who needed to be taught, but not enough teachers to teach them, nor enough money to pay the teachers. As salaries shrank, the good teachers (largely male) retreated totally into the private sector or left teaching altogether. The teaching profession became female and synonymous with poor pay and low prestige. A profession with low wages and no status, yet with high value to society, attracts two kinds of people: idealists with a sense of vocation who care little for money and prestige, and those who don't qualify for more highly paid work. How long idealists stay in the system depends upon how well they are trained. People who want to 'make a difference' suffer incredibly when they see they are making no difference.

In tandem with the need for new teachers was an urgent need for people to train them, but there was no mechanism for this. Formerly, teachers had been well educated, often with a university degree in a solid academic discipline. Noah Webster, of dictionary fame, taught primary school on and off for years. He had a degree in classics from Yale University. Neither he nor Dr Johnson in England considered teaching beneath their talent and training.

In Britain, teacher training colleges were created with a mandate to train teachers to teach the basics to the children 'of the workers'. A solid, classical education was the province of the elite private schools as it always had been. As lecturers in teacher training colleges were in no way comparable to university lecturers, this meant that the less able academically were in charge.

It should be noted that this problem cannot be solved by the recent sleight-of-hand of pulling teacher training colleges under the umbrella of universities and renaming them 'university departments'. This makes matters worse by lending undeserved authority to pronouncements of education lecturers. A primary school teaching credential is not an academic degree. The only way that departments of primary education can justify their existence within a university setting is through scientific research, but education teachers traditionally ignore and misunderstand scientific research.

It doesn't take much imagination to see that a system where the less well educated teach a curriculum with little scientific or academic foundation is doomed to spiral down out of control. As time goes by, mediocre minds become the arbiters of a collective 'wisdom' (or 'dumbdom') in which rational thought is rare. They misunderstand what they read and ignore the research in their own discipline because they have no understanding of how to read scientific reports. They jump on bandwagons because they're afraid of being 'out of date' or 'out of step'. Knowing little, they can at least be 'in the know'. Lecturers in departments of education often say things like: 'Oh we don't do *that* any more! Everybody knows that that method/theory/practice is out!' They then smile the knowing smile of the insider talking to the uninformed outsider, in the same disdainful manner as if you hadn't noticed that hemlines had just gone up or down.

If the only thing you can know is what's 'in' or 'out', it doesn't matter whether the fad of the moment makes any sense, whether the rhetoric is completely illogical, or whether words keep changing their meaning. Myth substitutes for reality and lip-service for deeds. All of this contributes to the classroom teacher's lack of knowledge and skill, and ultimately lack of confidence, causing her to lose respect even for herself. If parents sometimes find their child's teacher defensive and self-righteous, this is the reason. People are rarely defensive when they truly know what they are doing. (I know first-hand that when teachers are able to teach all children how to read, their joy radiates to everyone.)

Anyone who thinks rigorously and logically can't survive in this kind of environment. Thus, university departments of education succumb to the evolutionary imperative of the loss of the 'fittest' to more suitable ecological niches – the only 'academic' discipline that weeds out the wise. Teacher training gets worse, the children learn less and less, and the whole system begins to implode. Furthermore, until grammar schools were nearly erased out of existence or driven into the private sector, at least 20 per cent of the population got a good education. Now only people who can pay for it do. We have come full circle, from private education for the rich to private education for the rich, and no consistently good education for anyone else.

Class in the Classroom

It is impossible to separate educational policy and legislation in Britain from the issue of social class. Nearly every Education Act has had an influence, intentional or otherwise, on enhancing rather than weakening class barriers. The 1870 Education Act specifically targeted the workers ('manual labourers') as being different from everyone else. Compulsory education from 1880 inadvertently led to an explosion of independent fee-paying schools as parents fled in panic lest their child be in the same classroom as children of 'the workers'.

One of the indirect consequences of the proliferation of independent schools was 'accent raising'. Children were goaded to speak only with received pronunciation, and were ridiculed by their peers if they did not succeed. RP became the route by which school-leavers could move into the most prestigious occupations. It was a badge of class and of being 'properly educated', which meant: 'not in the state schools'. RP gave you such an edge it could even substitute for being bright or knowing anything. Although 'accent levelling' is currently the vogue, and public-school pupils feel pressure from the media and peers to refrain from speaking in 'super-posh' or 'la-di-da' accents, nevertheless some accents are still widely regarded as much better than others. This has fostered the notion that if you couldn't (or wouldn't) change your accent and 'speak properly', then you were basically ignorant and ineducable.

Meanwhile, the struggle goes on, and the mindset of many educators towards the working classes is firmly lodged in nineteenth-century practice and belief. This has led to reverse snobbery among working-class populations to protect their sense of self-worth. They eschew reading books, taking GCSE and A-level exams, or going on to university. In large cities like London, these attitudes have been easier to document, but they are festering, insidious and hidden, in smaller towns scattered across Britain. In towns where the vast majority are 'those members of the population who support themselves by manual labour', the attitudes of heads, teachers, boards of governors, and even parents lead to lower expectations, infrequent and undemanding homework, and a weak curriculum – almost as an expression of contempt. This gives the children the message that they are basically too dim to learn.

An example is a middle-size market town in southern England which shall remain nameless. The year is 1995. In this town, all children are considered to be too ineducable to go on to higher education. Educators and members of boards of governors, when speaking about this issue, use phrases like: 'Everybody knows that no one from this town ever goes to university.' 'It is well known that there are no bright children in this town.' 'This town is famous for having a "skew" in student test scores. Most students score at the lower end.'

Intrigued by the phenomenon of universal stupidity in an entire town, a well-known psychologist began a project to find out if this was, in fact, true. What she discovered was astonishing. Nine hundred comprehensive school pupils between the ages of eleven and fourteen were given the Cognitive Abilities Test (CAT) developed by the NFER. This is similar to an IQ test and measures verbal ability (verbal reasoning, analogies, etc.) and non-verbal ability (spatial/mechanical reasoning, etc.). Verbal and non-verbal scores on the CAT are standardized so that the average is 100 and the standard deviation is 15. The test is constructed so that students have comparable scores on both measures.

On the non-verbal test, the pupils scored completely normally in line with the general population, and the distribution of scores was normal as well. However, on the verbal test, they scored considerably below normal, and the entire school population was shifted to the left in the direction of lower scores. This was not a 'skew' (a long leftward tail in a distribution of scores) as local educators claimed, but a total shift. The shift was so large that the average verbal score was nine standard score points below the national average (well beyond half standard deviation). This value is enormous, and compares to the IQ differences between urban whites versus inner-city blacks in the US. How could it be that 900 students had a completely normal distribution of scores for non-verbal IQ, but such abnormal scores for verbal IQ?

One way this could happen is through a self-fulfilling prophecy in which working-class children are expected to have poor verbal skills. No such expectations would occur for non-verbal skills because these have no obvious connection to what is taught in the school system. If this was happening across the entire town, what did the children look like lower down the system? When did this deviation begin?

Two primary schools feeding into this comprehensive school were only about half a mile apart. One school was considered to be of a higher academic level than the other for no particular reason, other than that one neighbourhood was a council estate and one was not. Slightly more of the council estate students were receiving state-supported school meals, indicating that parents had somewhat lower incomes. We'll call the 'higher academic' school, School A, and the other school, School B. Students were given the two CAT IQ tests, the Peabody Picture Vocabulary Test, several reading tests, and a test of phoneme-awareness, similar to the Pig Latin test described earlier. The reasoning was that if children had low verbal IQ scores, then this could be caused by reading problems, which in turn could be a consequence of weaker phoneme-awareness and vocabulary skills, possible evidence for a biological/hereditary effect.

In both schools, children scored normally on the non-verbal portion of the test, but School A scored 10.5 standard score points above School B on the verbal IQ test, well within the normal range. Furthermore, on every reading test (word recognition, reading irregularly-spelled sight words, reading decodable nonsense words, and comprehension of fiction and non-fiction texts), School A was far ahead of School B. Was this a consequence of a superior aptitude in vocabulary and phoneme-awareness skills? *Not at all.* Scores on these two tests did not differ significantly between the schools, and were virtually identical when test scores were adjusted (co-varied) for non-verbal IQ.

The inescapable conclusion from these results is that a large proportion of children from School B were very poor readers, and this had nothing to do with IQ, with vocabulary, or with a phoneme-processing deficit. The cause was a toxic school *environment*, not genes. Children scored badly on the CAT verbal test *because they had such poor reading skills.* These children were not taught to read properly, didn't learn to read at an age-appropriate level, didn't develop verbally because they couldn't read, and no one appeared to care enough to do anything about it.

As the children from School B went through the system and into secondary school, their deficient reading skill would make matters worse, and they would fall further behind. As for the children from School A who started out scoring in the normal range on everything, these students also fell behind in secondary school. The function of the majority of schools in this town is to *reduce* children's ability so that everyone turns out 'below average' – a reverse 'Lake Wobegon effect'. (Lake Wobegon is American humorist Garrison Keillor's mythical town where 'all the children are above average'.) The same finding was reported in Nation and Hulme's study on 'lower middle class' children in York, where, compared to national norms, reading scores declined systematically year by year from Year 1 on (see Chapter 7).

This is a shocking example of extraordinary prejudice on the part of school officials and teachers who actively conspire to marginalize their own pupils, and it is by no means an isolated case. Good education is supposed to *overcome* social and economic handicaps and not reinforce or create them. As noted by Richard Herrnstein and Charles Murray, intelligence test scores have been rising during the twentieth century mainly due to improvement in the *lower* end of the distribution. As they put it: 'Egalitarian, modern societies draw the lower tail of the distribution closer to the mean and thereby raise the average.' Far too many schools in Britain do the reverse.

The fact that attitudes of teachers and school officials can profoundly affect a child's success in the school system has been detailed in a ground-breaking book, *Diverging Pathways* by Alan Kerckhoff. Kerckhoff analysed the data from the National Child Development Study which began in 1958. This consisted of every child born in England, Scotland, and Wales in the first week of March that year, a total of 17,733 children. These children have been followed through school and into the workforce. Kerckhoff's analysis ends when these people are twenty-three years old.

The evidence is overwhelming that children begin their school experience on an equal footing at infant schools, which are typically unstreamed. But once streaming begins in junior school, and especially in secondary school, the fate of each child is sealed. It might be imagined that streaming was a function of school performance and ability as measured by objective tests, but this is only a small portion of the answer. At junior school, roughly 49 per cent of all children were streamed. Streaming at this level was mainly determined by teacher ratings in maths and reading rather than by actual test results. Kerckhoff looked for factors that correlated to teacher ratings. There were three main ones: test performance, father's education, and mother's education.

The deviation between actual ability and teacher expectation began to be pronounced at the age of eleven. The strongest predictors of a child's maths performance at eleven were teacher ratings in maths, mother's education, teacher ratings in reading, and father's education. Actual maths ability (independent test scores) was a distant fifth in this prediction. These predictors were identical for both boys and girls.

At the time these children began attending secondary school, the system was in transition from secondary modern and grammar schools to all-ability comprehensive schools. The proportion of children attending comprehensives was about 60 per cent, with 20 per cent still in secondary moderns, 10 per cent (boys) and 13 per cent (girls) in grammar schools, and the remainder in private schools.

Who was able to attend grammar schools? The strongest predictors were the junior school teacher's ratings in maths and reading. Actual ability as measured by objective tests came a distant third. Ability grouping made a profound difference for girls. Once again, the teacher's *opinion* of a child mattered more than actual ability. (I can't resist an aside here in recollecting that my son's final-year teacher in junior school strongly urged me on several occasions not to embarrass my son by putting him forward for the County exam for a grammar school place, as 'he isn't smart enough'. He was awarded a scholarship to Haberdashers' Aske's.)

In secondary school, nearly all children were streamed by ability. Once again, junior school teacher ratings were the strongest predictors, followed by parents' education. A new factor appeared, which was teacher rating on the child's 'adjustment'. Actual test performance was less important. In fact, when looking at comprehensive schools alone, academic tests at eleven years had virtually no impact on which ability group the child was put into. Furthermore, when Kerckhoff looked at the maths and reading test scores across the different types of schools, he found no connection whatsoever between true ability and whether a child was streamed into a 'high', 'middle', or 'low' ability group from one type of school to another. There were even 'low ability' classes in grammar schools, despite the fact that these were supposed to be the top 10–13 per cent of all schoolchildren.

When these children had reached school leaving age at sixteen, the strongest effect on maths achievement tests, and the number and quality of O-level exams, was the type of school attended and the child's secondary school ability group. By now the difference between the high ability grammar-school child and children in middle/low ability groups in either secondary modern or comprehensive schools, was well over one standard deviation in maths test scores. The same difference was found *within* comprehensives between high and low ability groups. What is more, long-ago school experiences still contributed to student success or failure. The next strongest predictors apart from school type, ability group, and actual test scores, was the junior school teacher ratings, father's occupation, and parents' education.

At sixteen, more than half the students dropped out of school. Due to the fact that the UK has a wide range of options for further education, many young men subsequently returned. The largest majority of those who stayed on after sixteen returned to get middle or good O-levels and CSE exams. The next largest group completed various levels of City and Guilds. About 9 per cent of students received a degree, and only 1 per cent a postgraduate degree.

What determined who would continue and who would succeed? The data show that teacher ratings of 'academic promise' were about as important as actual O-level exam results. This effect was extremely strong for women. Teachers' opinions were based on secondary school ability group, parents' education and father's occupation, and junior school teacher ratings. All of these factors were stronger than actual exam results. Success at the age of twenty-three could be predicted first by secondary school exams, next by which ability group you were in, by teacher ratings of 'academic promise', and lastly by attitude to school. A strong predictor of a young adult's quality and prestige of employment was father's education, and this was equally true for men and women.

It goes without saying that children streamed into low ability groups were most likely to leave at sixteen and drop out of education altogether. But the different outcomes for men and women is striking. By the age of twenty-three, 21 per cent of the men had failed to complete any further education. This figure was 42 per cent for women. These women are now forty years old. Bear in mind that a large proportion of them (70 per cent) had been stuck in low ability groups for most of their education, receiving inferior instruction. Although girls had better CSE and O-level passes than boys, they were twice as likely to drop out of school. No doubt they came away hating school, humiliated by their school experience. *Today, these women, and women just like them, are responsible for raising children in a very large proportion of British families.* It comes as no surprise then, that reading researchers in Britain consistently report that mother's education is the highest contributor to a child's reading skill (40 per cent of the variance), whereas other countries do not report this.

Kerckhoff draws inferences about what lies behind the opinions teachers form of their students. One obvious inference is that teachers identify children by their social class early on and make assumptions about their ability on the basis of social class. If this wasn't the case, then social class would not have such a strong connection to school ability group and final level of employment. Teachers also do something else. They believe that ability is fixed; that skill in an academic subject area is 'given by birth'. So instead of a 'low ability group' being remedial, with the purpose of bringing children up to their other classmates, it is just that: *a group of children with 'low ability'*. As teachers believe that low ability children 'can't learn', their beliefs about a child's ability then become a self-fulfilling prophecy which is translated up the system at every level, and reinforced by the next tier of teachers.

Mother's education has a powerful impact, as we have seen. It matters in two ways. The mother is the person whom the classroom teacher meets most often. Mother's dress, accent, manner, etc. will telegraph her status in the social hierarchy. More than that, educated mothers have a greater concern that their children succeed in the system. They are much more likely to protest when told their child is not academic material. They are more likely, as I was, to go against a teacher's perception of their child, especially if that perception is grossly in error. Mothers who have been defeated and humiliated by the system may be too lacking in confidence to fight for their children. Having been taught that they are 'too stupid to learn', they may believe their children are as well.

The facts are clear that teachers form biased and unfounded opinions about a child's ability, and this has a powerful impact on a child's success. This means it is a highly retrograde step to replace objective testing with classroom teacher assessments, as recommended by the National Curriculum guidelines. The key to breaking out of the pattern of condemning a large proportion of women and men to an inferior education is through independent, objective testing. Furthermore, each child's performance in comparison to national or local norms should be reported to parents. A major message of Kerckhoff's analysis is that *teachers cannot be trusted to evaluate their pupils*.

The second important message is that the test results should not be used for the purpose of putting students into ability groups. Kerckhoff concludes that the negative consequences of streaming by ability far outweigh any positive benefits for the talented few. This means that the purpose of objective test scores is to provide information on who needs *extra help* with reading, maths, or other academic subjects. The purpose should *not* be to strengthen a belief in fixed ability, or to condemn children of 'low ability' to educational ghettos.

These studies point to one major conclusion: teachers simply must be better trained. They must learn that there is no such thing as a constant or uniform 'fixed ability' that holds true for every academic subject. They must learn how to teach fundamental skills like reading and maths so that everyone succeeds. They must have more knowledge about how children learn, and the emotional consequences of being ridiculed or labelled 'too stupid to learn'. They need courses on social issues, and to be alerted to their own potential biases. They must have more ammunition for how to think critically, and how to value children. We have known for at least thirty years from studies in both the UK and the USA that teacher expectation profoundly affects student performance. It's time that this kind of information was brought into teacher training.

Meanwhile, what's a parent to do? First and foremost, protect your own self-interest. Teach your children to read or find someone else who can. Monitor what your children are learning in the classroom. Insist upon excellence, but be cooperative and not adversarial. Remember, the teacher is as much a victim of the system as you are. She isn't responsible for her inadequate training, and she is well aware of its shortcomings. If you happen to live in a working-class area, you will need to be especially vigilant. Do not accept that your child is 'below average' and can never go to university just because he or she lives in a particular neighbourhood, speaks with a particular accent, or because you or members of your family have particular types of employment. Do everything in your power to get your child out of a low ability group.

Another alternative is to become an activist, though most people don't relish this role. It requires commitment, passion, and a lot of time and know-how. If you decide to take it on, be aware of what you're up against. Speaking at PTA meetings or writing vitriolic letters to the newspaper won't help very much. Unless you have good organizational and leadership skills, your best alternative is to bombard your elected officials with information about what you, other parents, and teachers really think. California turned its back on 'real books' for three major reasons: overwhelming proof of skyrocketing illiteracy rates; lots of media attention; *and* parents' outrage voiced to legislators.

There is an insidious belief among many journalists and others that the majority of British parents are too uninformed or too badly educated to know what to protest about. This is utter nonsense.

Everybody knows that a primary function of a school system is to teach children how to read. Nothing is more obvious or indisputable.

As we approach the twenty-first century, we have solved the mystery of literacy. We have pinned down *exactly* what skills and knowledge a child needs to be able to read and spell. We have proved this in careful research. We have shown that *everyone* can learn to read unless they are mentally retarded. We have shown that it isn't even *hard* for children to learn to read if they are taught properly. This is exciting news, but there has to be a major groundswell, a grass-roots movement, before anything can change.

Until then, parents and teachers are left holding the baby while they and other taxpayers foot the bill for a system that hasn't worked for over a hundred years. I have done my best to give you a better idea of the scope and seriousness of the problem. I have also tried to give you something practical to do to rescue your children. I hope I have succeeded.

1 *The Reading Report Card*

Notes

1. An international survey (W. B. Warwick, *The IEA Study of Reading Literacy: Achievement and Instruction in Thirty-Two School Systems*, Pergamon Press, London, 1994), reports American fourth-graders (aged eight to nine) as scoring just behind top-ranked Finland (for narrative prose) and behind only Finland and Sweden (for expository prose) in a survey of thirty-two countries. This study lacks the rigorous controls of the NAEP (National Assessment of Educational Progress) study (it included unsupervised testing by the classroom teacher, multiple choice answers only, sampling problems, etc.). In the US sample, 7 per cent of the children were excluded as 'untestable' and there was an 82.5 per cent compliance rate for the remainder. Thus, only 75 per cent of the US sample was represented in these data. Most countries had 99–100 per cent compliance rates. The author states that compliance rates of less than 80 per cent are regarded as 'suspicious'. Despite this, the study is frequently cited as proof that there is nothing wrong with American education.

Secretary of Education, Robert Riley (*C-Span* on CNN, 17 June 1996) stated that the discrepancy in the IEA and NAEP reports was due entirely to the higher difficulty level of the NAEP tests. According to this interpretation, American children are reading just fine compared to the rest of the world, but Americans have higher standards for literacy. This conclusion is not supported by the results from an international adult literacy survey conducted by Statistics Canada in 1995. This study used similar methodology to the 1993 US Adult Literacy Survey, and also measured US and Swedish literacy rates. For the youngest group tested (16–25 years), Statistics Canada report that six times more Americans scored at Level 1 (functionally illiterate) than top-ranked Sweden (23.5 per cent versus 3.8 per cent), and there were more Americans

373

scoring at Level 1 than Canadians. Forty per cent of Swedes scored at the proficient and advanced levels (Levels 4 and 5), versus 21.5 per cent in the US. The literacy rates for Americans in the Statistics Canada study were nearly identical to the rates from the US Adult Literacy Survey across all age groups, indicating solid methodology. Unless we assume that American children read superbly in fourth grade (IEA study) but suddenly become illiterate in high school (US and Canadian data), the only possible conclusion is that the IEA study is methodologically flawed and grossly inflates US fourth-grade literacy levels.

2. Educational Testing Service (an independent body funded by the US government) personnel reported to me that the IEP exclusion rates are beyond their control under Federal law. The IEP team consists of parents and special education teachers who have full authority to declare a child 'untestable'. Preliminary research on this issue has shown that a proportion of children declared 'untestable' are, in fact, testable. The ETS team has available a number of options (unlimited time, oral reporting of answers, Braille versions of the test items) to accommodate IEP students. This is a problem they recognize and are attempting to solve.

References

Adult Literacy in America (Office of Educational Research and Improvement, US Department of Education, 1993).

G. Brooks, T. Gorman, L. Kendall, A. Tate, *What Teachers in Training are Taught About Reading* (National Foundation for Educational Research, 1992).

J.J. Cannell, 'Nationally normed elementary achievement testing in America's public schools: How all 50 states are above the national average', *Educational Measurement Issues and Practice 7* (1988).

J. Davies, I. Brember, P. Pumfrey, 'The first and second reading standard assessment tasks at Key Stage 1: A comparison based on a five-school study', *Journal of Research in Reading 18* (1995), 1-9.

'Key Stages 1 and 3: United Kingdom National Curriculum Assessment for 1992 and 1993', *Schools Update* (Department for Education, 1993).

R. L. Linn, *Test Misuse: Why is it so prevalent?* (Office of Technology Assessment, US Congress, 1991).

Literacy, Economy and Society: Results of the First International Literacy Survey (Organization for Economic Cooperation and Development and Statistics Canada, 1995).

Literacy Skills: Further Results from the Second International Literacy Survey (Organization for Economic Cooperation and Development and Statistics Canada, 1997).

NAEP [National Assessment of Educational Progress] 1992: Reading Report Card for the Nation and States (Office of Educational Research and Improvement, US Department of Education, 1993).

NAEP 1994: Reading Report Card for the Nation and States (Office of Educational Research and Improvement, US Department of Education, 1996).

National Foundation for Educational Research, *Language for Learning: A summary report on the 1988 APU surveys of language performance* (SEAC and Central Office of Information).

The Primary Language Record: Handbook for Teachers (Centre for Language in Primary Education, London, 1992).

Projections of Education Statistics to 2003 (US Department of Education, 1993).

R. E. Slavin, 'Students at risk of school failure: The problem and its dimensions' in R. E. Slavin, N. L. Karweit and N. A. Madden (eds), *Effective Programs for Students at Risk* (Allyn and Bacon, Boston, 1989).

C. J. Sykes, *Dumbing Down Our Kids* (St Martin's Press, New York, 1995).

The Teaching and Learning of Reading in Primary Schools (A Report by HMI, Department of Education and Science, 1991).

2 *How Do Readers Read?*

References

P. E. Bryant, M. MacClean, L. L. Bradley, J. Crossland, 'Rhyme, alliteration, phoneme detection and learning to read', *Developmental Psychology 26* (1990), 429–38.

V. Cato, C. Fernades, T. Gorman, A. Kispal, J. White, *The Teaching of Initial Literacy: How Do Teachers Do It?* (National Foundation for Educational Research, 1992).

R. Flesch, *Why Johnny Can't Read* (Harper and Row, New York, 1955 and 1985).

K. Goodman, 'Reading: A psycholinguistic guessing game', *Journal of the Reading Specialist* (May 1967), 126–35.

'Key Stages 1 and 3: United Kingdom National Curriculum Assessment for 1992 and 1993', *Schools Update* (Department for Education, 1993).

D. McGuinness, 'Decoding strategies as predictors of reading skill', *Annals of Dyslexia 47* (1997), 117–50.

K. Rayner & A. Pollatsek, *The Psychology of Reading* (Prentice Hall, New Jersey, 1989), Chapter 4: 'The work of the eyes'.

Dr Seuss, 'How the Grinch Stole Christmas' in *Six by Seuss* (Random House, New York, 1991).

The Teaching and Learning of Reading in Primary Schools (A Report by HMI, Department of Education and Science, 1991).

3 *Transcribing Talk*

Notes

1. G. Childe, *Man Makes Himself* (Watts, London, 1941), 187.
2. 'Schooldays' translated by S. N. Kramer in his book *The Sumerians* (Chicago University Press, 1963), 237–40.
3. C. Chomsky, 'Approaching reading through invented spelling' (paper presented at a conference on Theory and Practice of Beginning Reading Instruction, University of Pittsburgh, 1976; EDRS document ED 155 630), 3.
4. C. Weaver, *Reading Process and Practice* (Heinemann, New Hampshire, 1988), 178. Cited in P. Groff, 'Teachers' Opinions of the Whole Language Approach to Reading Instruction', *Annals of Dyslexia 41*, 83–95.
5. F. Smith, *Reading* (Cambridge University Press, New York, 1985), 146. (Cited ibid.)
6. F. Smith, *Psychology and Reading* (Holt, Rinehart and Winston, New York, 1973), 79. (Cited ibid.)
7. F. Smith, *Reading* (Cambridge University Press, New York, 1985), 53. (Cited ibid.)
8. C. Weaver, *Psycholinguistics and Reading* (Winthrop, Massachusetts, 1980), 86. (Cited ibid.)
9. Ibid.
10. K. Goodman, *What's Whole in Whole Language?* (Heinemann, New Hampshire, 1986), 37. (Cited ibid.)
11. F. Smith, *Understanding Reading* (Lawrence Erlbaum, New Jersey, 1986), 188. (Cited ibid.)

References

PAGES 33–35: WHOLE LANGUAGE THEORIES

K. Goodman, 'Behind the eye: What happens in reading' in H. Singer and R. Ruddell (eds), *Theoretical Models and Processes in Reading* (International Reading Association, New York, 2nd edition 1976).

K. Goodman, *Phonics Phacts* (Heinemann, New Hampshire, 1993).

PAGES 36–53: EARLY WRITING SYSTEMS

E. A. W. Bridge, *The Book of the Dead: The hieroglyphic transcript of the papyrus of Ani* (University Books Inc., New Jersey, 1977).

F. Coulmas, *The Writing Systems of the World* (Blackwell, 1993).

D. Crystal, *The Cambridge Encyclopedia of Language* (Cambridge University Press, 1987).

C. H. Gordon, *The Ancient Near East* (W. W. Norton, New York, 1965).

S. N. Kramer, *The Sumerians* (Chicago University Press, 1963).

S. N. Kramer, *History Begins at Sumer* (University of Pennsylvania Press, 1981).

M. Lichtheim, *Ancient Egyptian Literature Vol I: The Old and Middle Kingdoms* (University of California Press, 1975).

S. Lloyd, *The Archaeology of Mesopotamia* (Thames and Hudson, 1978).

I. M. Lui, C. J. Chiang, S. C. Wang, *Frequency Count of 40,000 Chinese Words* (in Chinese) (Luck Books, Taiwan, 1975).

T. McArthur (ed.), *The Oxford Companion to the English Language* (Oxford University Press, 1992).

J. Oates, *Babylon* (Thames and Hudson, 1979).

K. Rayner & A. Pollatsek, *The Psychology of Reading* (Prentice-Hall, New Jersey, 1989), Chapter 10: 'Stage of Reading Development'.

A. Robinson, *The Story of Writing* (Thames and Hudson, 1995).

L. Schele & D. Freidel, *The Forest of Kings: An Untold Story of the Ancient Maya* (William Morrow, New York, 1990).

I. Taylor & D. R. Olson (eds), *Scripts and Literacy* (Kluwer Academie Publishers, Netherlands, 1995), see chapters by Che Kan Leong, 162–83; Shin-ying Lee, D. H. Uttal, Chuansheng Chen, 247–63.

PAGES 54–59: WHOLE LANGUAGE ISSUES

P. Groff, 'Teachers' opinions of the whole language approach to reading instruction', *Annals of Dyslexia 41*, (1991), 83–95.

The Primary Language Record: Handbook for Teachers (Centre for Language in Primary Education, London, 1992).

H. W. Stevenson, J. W. Stigler, W. Lucker, Shin-ying Lee, 'Reading disabilities: The case of Chinese, Japanese and English', *Child Development 53* (1982), 1164–83.

I. Taylor & D. R. Olson, *Scripts and Literacy* (Kluwer Academie Publishers, Netherlands, 1995), see chapter by Takeshi Hatta & Takehito Hirase, 230–46.

4 *Alphabets: Splitting Sounds*

References

J. Chall, *Learning to Read: The Great Debate* (McGraw-Hill, New York, 1967, 1983, 1996).

F. Coulmas, *The Writing Systems of the World* (Blackwell, 1993).

D. Crystal, *The Cambridge Encyclopedia of Language* (Cambridge University Press, 1987).

P. B. Denes & E. N. Pinson, *The Speech Chain* (W. H. Freeman, New York, 1993).

R. Flesch, *Why Johnny Can't Read* (Harper and Row, New York, 1955, 1985).

J. F. Healey, *The Early Alphabet* (British Museum, 1990).

I. Gelb, *A Study of Writing* (Chicago University Press, 1963).

S. Kramer, *The Sumerians* (Chicago University Press, 1963).

A. Robinson, *The Story of Writing* (Thames and Hudson, 1995).

L. Schele & D. Freidel, *The Forest of Kings: An Untold Story of the Ancient Maya* (William Morrow, New York, 1990).

H. W. Stevenson, J. W. Stigler, W. Lucker, Shing-ying Lee, 'Reading disabilities: The case of Chinese, Japanese and English', *Child Development 53* (1982), 1164–83.

I. Taylor & D. R. Olson, *Scripts and Literacy* (Kluwer Academie Publishers, Netherlands, 1995).

5 *The English Alphabet Code*

Notes

1. The opening lines of the *The Vision of Piers Plowman (C text)* by William Langland, written 1385–6. The translation is mine. (Bodleian MS 814, Bodleian Library, Oxford.)

2. E. Raleigh, letter to Sir Robert Cecil (HMS Cecil 5, p. 396, Hatfield House).

3. Preface to S. Johnson, *A Dictionary of the English Language* (Strahan, London, 4th edition 1773), 21.

4. Preface to N. Webster, *A Dictionary of the English Language* (English edition, Black, Young and Young, London, 1828) iv–v.

5. All quotes are from N. Webster, *Improved Spelling Book* (Abel Heywood, Manchester, 1870), 8–11.

6. N. Webster, *A Grammatical Institute of the English Language: Part 1* (1783) (facsimile published by The Scholar Press, England, 1968), 29.

7. The probability structure of American spelling as set out in these tables is based upon over 3,000 common English words. This probability structure is *not* based upon the work of P. R. Hanna, J. S. Hanna and R. E. Hodges, *Phoneme-grapheme Correspondences as Cues to Spelling Improvement* (OE-32008, US Department of Health, Education, and Welfare, 1966). This is a 1,716-page document which estimates the probability structure of spelling patterns in over 17,000 words by the position of each phoneme in the syllable. This was a valuable and important undertaking and it is a minor tragedy that there are so many errors in this work. For example, the

authors state that there are 52 (not 40–44) phonemes in English, and their classification duplicates many vowel and consonant sounds. (Silent /h/ is classified as a phoneme.) They misunderstand the consonant spellings which use e̲ as a diacritic: c̲e̲, s̲e̲, z̲e̲, v̲e̲, g̲e̲, d̲g̲e̲, l̲e̲, t̲h̲e̲, and classify them instead as vowel spellings. Examples are: choose = o̲o̲–e̲; juice = u̲i̲–e̲; license = e̲–e̲, dodge = o̲–e̲. There are hundreds of phonological errors in the word lists themselves (too many to count), possibly the fault of data-entry personnel. For example, words containing the vowel phoneme /o̅o̅/ (soon) are classified with words that contain the phoneme /ue/ (cue) (but cue is not 'coo', nor cute 'coot'). These problems make it impossible to rely on Hanna *et al.*'s probability estimates of American English spelling patterns.

A further problem is that the frequency estimates are based upon the entire corpus of 17,000 words. However, spelling patterns and hence their probabilities for common English words (including those of French origin) differ from the probabilities for Latin-origin words, and should be analysed separately. This is especially important for designers of early reading and spelling curricula.

Richard Venezky in *The Structure of English Orthography* (Mouton, The Hague, 1970) worked out all possible spelling patterns (letters) for a corpus of 20,000 words. These were set out from letter(s) *to* sounds (code overlaps only). This effort is of academic interest, but this is not how the alphabet code was written, nor how it works. No attempt to assess the probability structure of these overlaps was provided. Spelling patterns are illustrated with only a few examples, and rare spellings are given equal prominence to common spellings. Again, this type of analysis is of little use to people who design reading or spelling curricula.

References

PAGES 82–87: OLD ENGLISH WRITING

King Alfred, Preface to Pope Gregory's 'Pastoral Care', AD 890–95 (MS Hatton 20, Bodleian Library, Oxford).

Ælfric, 'A Grammar', AD 987–8 (MS 154, St John's College Library, Oxford).

Asser, *Life of King Alfred*, AD 893–4, translated by L. C. Jane (Cooper Square Publishing, New York, 1966).

Bede, *Ecclesiastical History of the English People*, AD 731, translated by L. Sherley Price, revised R.E. Latham (Penguin Books, 1990).

P. B. Ellis, *Celt and Saxon* (Constable, 1995).

M. Grant, *Dawn of the Middle Ages* (Weidenfeld & Nicolson, 1981).

C. Jones, *A History of English Phonology* (Longman, 1989).

A. H. Marckwardt & J. L. Rosier, *Old English* (Norton, New York, 1972).

T. W. Moody & F. X. Martin (eds), *The Course of Irish History* (The Mercier Press, Cork, 1978).

A. P. Smyth, *King Alfred the Great* (Oxford University Press, 1995).

C. Sprockel, *The Language of the Parker Chronicle Vol. 1: Phonology and Accidence* (Martinus Nijhoff, The Hague, 1965).

M. Wood, *In Search of the Dark Ages* (BBC Books, 1981).

PAGES 87–90: MIDDLE AGES TO THE EIGHTEENTH CENTURY

G. K. Anderson, *The Literature of the Anglo-Saxon* (Russell and Russell, New York, 1962).

J. A. Burrow & T. Turville, *A Book of Middle English* (Blackwell, 1992).

M. T. Clanchy, *From Memory to Written Record: England 1066–1307* (Blackwell, 1994).

R. S. Gottfried, *The Black Death* (Free Press, New York, 1983).

R. Jordon, *Handbook of Middle English Grammar: Phonology* (Mouton, The Hague, 1974).

C. Platt, *Medieval England* (Routledge, 1994).

D. G. Scragg, *A History of English Spelling* (Manchester University Press, 1974).

PAGES 90–94: SAMUEL JOHNSON

S. Johnson, *A Dictionary of the English Language* (Strahan, London, 4th edition 1773).

Mr William Shakespeare's Comedies, Histories and Tragedies, published by J. Heminge & H. Condell in 1623 (facsimile published as *The First Folio of Shakespeare,* W. W. Norton, New York, 1968).

J. Wain, *Samuel Johnson* (Papermac, 1994).

PAGES 94–98: NOAH WEBSTER

R. M. Rollins, *The Autobiographies of Noah Webster* (University of South Carolina Press, 1989).

N. Webster, *A Grammatical Institute of the English Language: Part I* (1783) (facsimile published by The Scholar Press, 1968).

N. Webster, *A Dictionary of the English Language* (English edition, Black, Young and Young, London, 1828).

N. Webster, *The Illustrated Webster Spelling Book* (Ward and Lock, London, 1856).

N. Webster, *British and American Spelling and Reading Book* (Dean and Son, London, 1858).

N. Webster, *Improved Elementary Spelling Book* (Abel Heywood, Manchester, 1870).

PAGES 99–103: THE LOGIC OF THE CODE

M. J. Adams, *Beginning to Read* (M.I.T. Press, Massachusetts, 1990).

K. H. Pribram, *Languages of the Brain* (Prentice-Hall, New York, 1971).

M. L. Stanbach, 'Syllable and rime patterns for teaching reading: Analysis of frequency-based vocabulary of 17,602 words', *Annals of Dyslexia 42* (1992), 196–221.

6 *Not So Universal Education*

References

M. J. Adamson, *A Short History of Education* (Cambridge University Press, 1930).

G. L. Bond & R. Dykstra, 'The co-operative research programme in first-grade reading instruction', *Reading Research Quarterly 2* (1967), 5–142.

G. Brooks, T. Gorman, L. Kendall, A. Tate, *What Teachers in Training are Taught About Reading* (National Foundation for Educational Research, 1992).

J. Chall, *Learning to Read: The Great Debate* (McGraw-Hill, New York, 1967, 1983, 1996).

N. Dale, *The Walter Crane Readers* (J. M. Dent, London, 1898).

N. Dale, *On the Teaching of English Reading* (J. M. Dent, London, 1898).

N. Dale, *The Dale Readers: Book I* (G. Philip and Son, London, 1902).

N. Dale, *Further Notes on the Teaching of English Reading* (G. Philip and Son, London, 1902).

N. Dale, *The Dale Readers: Book II* (F. H. Gilson, New York, 1907).

J. C. Daniels & H. Diack, *Progress in Reading* (Nottingham School of Education, 1956).

J. C. Daniels & H. Diack, *Progress in Reading in the Infant School* (Nottingham School of Edcuation, 1960).

J. L. Dobson, 'English studies and popular literacy in England (1870–1970)' in G. Brooks, A. K. Pugh, N. Hall (eds), *Further Studies in the History of Reading* (United Kingdom Reading Association, 1993).

R. Flesch, *Why Johnny Can't Read* (Harper and Row, New York, 1955, 1985).

E. Foner & Garraty (eds), *The Reader's Companion to American History* (Houghton Mifflin, Boston, 1991) 'Education', 313–27.

E. B. Huey, *The Psychology and Pedagogy of Reading* (Macmillan, New York, 1908).

M. Montessori, *The Montessori Method*, translated by A. E. George (Frederick A. Stokes, New York, 1912).

J. M. Morris, 'Phonics: From an unsophisticated past to a linguistics-informed future' in G. Brooks & A. K. Pugh (eds), *Studies in the History of Reading* (University of Reading Press, 1984).

M. Phillips, *All Must Have Prizes* (Little, Brown, 1996).

D. G. Scragg, *A History of English Spelling* (Manchester University Press, 1974).

L. C. Stedman & C. F. Kaestle, 'Literacy and reading performance in the United States from 1880 to the present', *Reading Research Quarterly 22* (1987), 8–46.

M. Thatcher, *The Downing Street Years* (HarperCollins, 1993).

The Welfare State: Education (BBC television documentary broadcast in June 1995).

7 Science to the Rescue

Notes

1. K. Goodman, *Phonics Phacts* (Heinemann, New York, 1993), 57–8.
2. M. Rutter & W. Yule, 'The concept of specific reading retardation', *Journal of Child Psychology and Psychiatry 16* (1975), 181–97 (quote on p. 194).
3. J. M. Fletcher, S. E. Shaywitz, D. P. Shankweiler, L. Katz, I. Y. Liberman, K. K. Stuebing, D. J. Francis, A. E. Fowler, B. A. Shaywitz, 'Cognitive profiles of reading disability: Comparisons of discrepancy and low achievement definitions', *Journal of Educational Psychology 86* (1994), 6–23 (quote on p. 20).
4. K. E. Stanovich & L. S. Siegel, 'Phenotypic performance profile of children with reading disabilities: A regression-based test of the phonological-core variable-difference model', *Journal of Educational Psychology 86* (1994), 24–53 (quote on p. 48).
5. B. Pennington, *Diagnosing Learning Disorders* (The Guilford Press, New York, 1991), 53, 54.
6. Ibid 55.
7. Rosner and Simon were not the first to publish this type of test. A phoneme deletion test was published by D. J. Bruce in Britain – 'The analysis of word sounds by young children', *The British Journal of Educational Psychology 34* (1964), 158–70. However, children younger than seven could not perform this test. Further, Bruce never correlated performance on his test to reading and reported that it *did not* correlate to oral spelling. I do not know whether Rosner and Simon were aware of Bruce's work. They do not cite it in their paper.
8. H. Aasved, 'Eye Examinations' in H-J. Gjessing & B. Karlsen (eds), *A Longitudinal Study of Dyslexia* (Springer-Verlag, New York, 1989) 192–209 (quote on p. 209).

References

PAGES 129–33: WHAT SCIENCE IS AND ISN'T

K. Goodman, *Phonics Phacts* (Heinemann, New Hampshire, 1993).

PAGES 134–40: IS DYSLEXIA A SPECIAL READING DISORDER?

J. M. Fletcher, D. J. Francis, B. P. Rourke, S. E. Shaywitz, B. A. Shaywitz, 'The validity of discrepancy based definitions of reading disabilities', *Journal of Learning Disabilities 25* (1992), 555–61.

J. M. Fletcher, S. E. Shaywitz, D. P. Shankweiler, L. Katz, I. Y. Liberman, K. K. Stuebing, D. J. Francis, A. E. Fowler, B. A. Shaywitz, 'Cognitive profiles of reading disability: Comparisons of discrepancy and low achievement definitions', *Journal of Educational Psychology 86* (1994), 6–23.

A. M. Galaburda, 'Ordinary and extraordinary brain development: Anatomical variation in developmental dyslexia', *Annals of Dyslexia 39* (1989), 67–93.

G. W. Hynd, M. Semrud-Clikeman, A. R. Lorys, E. S. Novey, D. Eliopulas, 'Brain morphology in developmental dyslexia and attention deficit disorder/hyperactivity', *Archives of Neurology 47* (1990), 919–26.

J. P. Larsen, T. Hoien, I. Lundberg, H. Odegaard, 'MRI evaluation of the size and symmetry of the planum temporal in adolescents with developmental dyslexia', *Brain and Language 39* (1990), 289–301.

C. M. Leonard, L. J. Lombardino, L. R. Mercado, S. R. Browd, J. I. Breier, O. F. Agee, 'Cerebral asymmetry and cognitive development', *Psychological Science 7* (1996), 89–95.

C. M. Leonard, K. K. Voeller, L. J. Lombardino, M. K. Morris, A. W. Alexander, H. G. Andersen, M. A. Garofalakis, G. W. Hynd, J. C. Honeyman, J. Mao, O. F. Agee, E. V. Staab, 'Anomalous cerebral structure in dyslexia revealed with magnetic resonance imaging', *Archives of Neurology 50* (1993), 461–9.

B. F. Pennington, *Diagnosing Learning Disorders* (The Guilford Press, New York, 1991).

B. F. Pennington, J. Gilger, R. K. Olson, J. C. DeFries, 'The external validity of age- versus IQ-discrepancy definitions of reading disability: Lessons from a twin study', *Journal of Learning Disabilities 25* (1992), 562–73.

S. O. Richardson, 'Specific developmental dyslexia: Retrospective and prospective views', *Annals of Dyslexia 39* (1989), 3–23.

M. Rutter & W. Yule, 'The concept of specific reading retardation', *Journal of Child Psychology and Psychiatry 16* (1975), 181–97.

D. L. Share, R. McGee, W. S. McKenzie, P. A. Silva, 'Further evidence relating to the distinction between specific reading retardation and general reading backwardness', *British Journal of Developmental Psychology 5* (1987), 35–44.

S. E. Shaywitz, M. D. Escobar, B. A. Shaywitz, J. M. Fletcher, R. Makuch, 'Evidence that dyslexia may represent the lower tail of a normal distribution of reading ability', *The New England Journal of Medicine 326* (1992), 145–50.

K. E. Stanovich & L. S. Siegel, 'Phenotypic performance profile of children with reading disabilities: A regression-based test of the phonological-core variable-difference model', *Journal of Educational Psychology 86* (1994), 24–53.

PAGES 140–42: A GENE FOR BAD READING?

R. Olson, H. Forsberg, B. Wise, J. Rack, 'Measurement of word recognition, orthographic, and phonological skills' in G.R. Lyon (ed.), *Frames of Reference for the Assessment of Learning Disabilities* (Paul Brookes, Baltimore, 1994), 243–77.

R. K. Olson, B. Wise, F. Conners, J. Rack, D. Fulker, 'Specific deficits in component reading and language skills: Genetic and environmental influences', *Journal of Learning Disabilities 22* (1989), 339–48.

B. F. Pennington, *Diagnosing Learning Disorders* (The Guilford Press, New York, 1991).

PAGES 142–56: PHONOLOGICAL AWARENESS AND READING

M. J. Adams, *Beginning to Read* (M.I.T. Press, Massachusetts, 1990).

I. Ben-Dror, R. Frost, S. Bentin, 'Orthographic representation and phonemic segmentation in skilled readers: A cross-language comparison', *Psychological Science 6* (1995), 176–81.

L. Bradley & P. E. Bryant, 'Difficulties in auditory organization as a possible cause of reading backwardness', *Nature 271* (1978), 746–7.

L. Bradley & P. E. Bryant, 'Categorizing sounds and learning to read – a causal connection', *Nature 301* (1983), 419–21.

L. Bradley & P. E. Bryant, *Rhyme and Reason in Reading and Spelling* (University of Michigan Press, 1985).

S. A. Brady & D. P. Shankweiler, *Phonological Process in Literacy: A Tribute to Isabelle Y. Liberman* (Lawrence Erlbaum Associates, New Jersey, 1991).

R. C. Calfee, P. E. Lindamood, C. H. Lindamood, 'Acoustic-phonetic skills and reading – kindergarten through 12th grade', *Journal of Educational Psychology 64* (1973), 293–8.

M. B. Denckla, 'Color-naming deficits in dyslexic boys', *Cortex 8* (1972), 164–76.

M. B. Denckla & R. G. Rudel, 'Rapid automatized naming (RAN): Dyslexia differentiated from other disorders', *Neuropsychologia 14* (1976), 471–9.

A. M. Liberman, F. Cooper, D. Shankweiler, M. Studdert-Kennedy, 'Perception of the speech code', *Psychological Review 74* (1967), 431–61.

I. Y. Liberman, 'Segmentation of the spoken word and reading acquisition', *Bulletin of the Orton Dyslexia Society 23* (1973), 65–77.

I. Y. Liberman, D. Shankweiler, F. W. Fischer, B. Carter, 'Reading and the awareness of linguistic segments', *Journal of Experimental Child Psychology 18* (1974), 201–12.

C. H. Lindamood & P. C. Lindamood, *Lindamood Auditory Conceptualization Test* (Pro-Ed, Texas, 1971).

I. Lundberg, A. Olofsson, S. Wall, 'Reading and spelling skills in the first school years predicted from phoneme-awareness skills in kindergarten', *Scandinavian Journal of Psychology 21* (1980), 159–73.

V. A. Mann & I. Y. Liberman, 'Phonological awareness and verbal short-term memory', *Journal of Learning Disabilities 17* (1984), 592–8.

D. McGuinness, *When Children Don't Learn* (Basic Books, New York, 1985).

D. McGuinness, C. McGuinness, J. Donohue, 'Phonological training and the alphabet principle: Evidence for reciprocal causality', *Reading Research Quarterly 30* (1995), 830–52.

D. McGuinness, 'Decoding strategies as predictors of reading skill', *Annals of Dyslexia 47* (1997), 117–50.

J. Morais, L. Cary, J. Alegria, P. Bertelson, 'Does awareness of speech as a sequence of phones arise spontaneously?', *Cognition 7* (1979), 323–31.

J. Morais, P. Bertelson, L. Cary, J. Alegria, 'Literacy training and speech segmentation', *Cognition 24* (1986), 45–64.

K. Nation and C. Hulme, 'Phoneme segmentation, not onset-rime segmentation, predicts early reading and spelling skills', *Reading Research Quarterly 32* (1997), 154–67.

C. Read, Z. Yun-Fei, N. Hong-Yin, D. Bao-Qing, 'The ability to manipulate speech sounds depends on knowing alphabetic writing', *Cognition 24* (1986), 31–44.

J. Rosner & D. P. Simon, 'The auditory analysis test: An initial report', *Journal of Learning Disabilities 4* (1971), 384–92.

D. P. Shankweiler, I. Y. Liberman, L. S. Mark, C. A. Fowler, F. W. Fischer, 'The speech code and learning to read', *Journal of Experimental Psychology: Human Learning and Memory 5* (1979), 531–45.

D. L. Share, A. F. Jorm, R. Maclean, R. Matthews, 'Sources of individual differences in reading acquisition', *Journal of Educational Psychology 76* (1984), 1309–24.

M. C. Vandervelden & L. S. Siegel, 'Phonological recoding and phoneme-awareness in early literacy: A developmental approach', *Reading Research Quarterly 30* (1995), 854–75.

R. K. Wagner & J. K. Torgesen, 'The nature of phonological processing and its causal role in the acquisition of reading skills', *Psychological Bulletin 101* (1987), 192–212.

R. K. Wagner, J. K. Torgesen, C. A. Rashotte, 'The development of reading-related phonological processing abilities: New evidence of bi-directional causality from a latent variable longitudinal study', *Developmental Psychology 30* (1994), 73–87.

M. Wolf, 'The word retrieval deficit hypothesis and developmental dyslexia', *Journal of Learning and Individual Differences 3* (1991), 205–23.

H. K. Yopp, 'The validity and reliability of phonemic awareness tests', *Reading Research Quarterly 23* (1988), 159–78.

PAGES 156–62: SPEECH AND LANGUAGE AND READING

D. V. M. Bishop & C. Adams, 'A prospective study of the relationship between specific language disorders and reading retardation', *Journal of Child Psychology and Psychiatry 31* (1990), 1027–50.

F. M. Hull, P. W. Mielke, R. J. Timmons, J. A. Willeford, 'The national speech and hearing survey: Preliminary results, *ASHA 3* (1971), 501–9.

D. McGuinness, 'A developmental study of nonsense word repetition' (unpublished data).

M. M. Merzenich, W. M. Jenkins, S. L. Miller, C. Screiner, P. Tallal, 'Temporal processing deficits of language-learning impaired children ameliorated by training', *Science 271* (1996), 77–81.

L. C. Moats, 'Honing the concept of listening and speaking' in G. R. Lyon (ed.), *Frames of Reference for the Assessment of Learning Disabilities* (Paul Brookes, Baltimore, 1994), 229–41.

Y. V. Post, B. R. Foorman and M. Hiscock, 'Speech perception and speech production as indicators of reading difficulty', *Annals of Dyslexia 47* (1997), 3–27.

D. Shankweiler, S. Crain, L. Katz, A. E. Fowler, A. M. Liberman, S. A. Brady, R. Thornton, E. Lundquist, L. Dreyer, J. M. Fletcher, K. K. Stuebing, S. E. Shaywitz, B. A. Shaywitz, 'Cognitive profiles of reading-disabled children: Comparison of language skills in phonology, morphology, and syntax', *Psychological Science 6* (1995), 149–56.

L. S. Snyder & D. M. Downey, 'Serial rapid naming skills in children with reading disabilities', *Annals of Dyslexia 45* (1995), 31–49.

P. Tallal, 'Auditory temporal perception, phonics, and reading disabilities in children', *Brain and Language 9* (1980), 182–98.

P. Tallal, 'Developmental language disorders' in J. F. Kavanagh & T. J. Truss (eds), *Learning Disabilities: Proceedings of the National Conference*, (York Press, Maryland, 1988), 181–272.

P. Tallal, S. I. Miller, G. Bedi, G. Byma, X. Wang, S. Nagarajan, C. Schreiner, W. M. Jenkins, M. M. Merzenich, 'Fast-element enhanced speech improves language comprehension in language-learning impaired children', *Science 271* (1996), 81–4.

P. Tallal & M. Piercy, 'Developmental aphasia: rate of auditory processing and selective impairment of consonant perception', *Neuropsychologia 12* (1974), 83–93.

P. Tallal & R. E. Stark, 'Speech acoustic-cue discrimination abilities of normally developing and language-impaired children', *Journal of the Acoustic Society of America 69* (1981), 568–74.

P. Tallal, R. E. Stark, D. Mellits, 'The relationship between auditory temporal analysis and receptive language development: Evidence from studies of developmental language disorder', *Neuropsychologia 23* (1985), 527–34.

W. E. Tunmer, A. R. Nesdale, A. D. Wright, 'Syntactic awareness and reading acquisition', *British Journal of Developmental Psychology 5* (1987), 25–34.

J. F. Werker & R. C. Tees, 'Speech perception in severely disabled and average reading children', *Canadian Journal of Psychology 41* (1987), 48–61.

PAGES 162–64: INTELLIGENCE AND READING

L. Bradley & P. E. Bryant, *Rhyme and Reason in Reading and Spelling* (University of Michigan Press, 1985).

P. E. Bryant, M. Maclean, L. L. Bradley, J. Crossland, 'Rhyme, alliteration, phoneme detection and learning to read', *Developmental Psychology 26* (1990), 429–38.

H-J. Gjessing & B. Karlsen, *A Longitudinal Study of Dyslexia* (Springer-Verlag, New York, 1989).

D. McGuinness, C. McGuinness, J. Donohue, 'Phonological training and the alphabet principle: Evidence for reciprocal causality', *Reading Research Quarterly 30* (1995), 830–53.

K. E. Stanovich, A. E. Cunningham, D. J. Feeman, 'Intelligence, cognitive skills, and early reading progress', *Reading Research Quarterly 19* (1984), 278–303.

R. K. Wagner, J. K. Torgesen, C. A. Rashotte, 'The development of reading-related phonological processing abilities: New evidence for bi-directional causality from a latent variable longitudinal study', *Developmental Psychology 30* (1994), 73–87.

PAGES 164–67: VISION AND READING

H. Aasved, 'Eye examinations' in H-J. Gjessing and B. Karlsen (eds), *A Longitudinal Study of Dyslexia* (Springer-Verlag, New York, 1989), 192–209.

R. C. Calfee, L. W. Fisk, D. Piontowski, 'On-off tests of cognitive skill in reading acquisition' in M. P. Douglas (ed.), *Claremont Reading Conference: 39th Yearbook* (Claremont Graduate School, California, 1975).

H-J. Gjessing, 'Function analysis of literacy behaviour' in H-J. Gjessing and B. Karlsen (eds), *A Longitudinal Study of Dyslexia* (Springer-Verlag, New York, 1989), 106–59.

K. Rayner, 'Do faulty eye movements cause dyslexia?', *Developmental Neuropsychology 1* (1985), 3–15.

K. Rayner & A. Pollatsek, *The Psychology of Reading* (Prentice Hall, New Jersey, 1989).

J. F. Stein & M. S. Fowler, 'Unstable binocular control in dyslexic children', *Journal of Research in Reading 16* (1993), 30–45.

8 *The Child's Mind and Reading*

Notes

1. Ælfric 'A Grammar', AD 987–8 (MS 154, St John's College Library, Oxford), quote is from the Introduction starting at the first lines in English (the preceding text is in Latin).

2. J. Piaget, 'Development and learning' in M. Gauvain & M. Cole (eds), *Readings on the Development of Children* (Scientific American Books/W. H. Freeman, New York, 1964, 1993), 25–33 (quote is on p. 32).

References

PAGES 171–76: MAKING SENSE OF THE WORLD

J. H. Flavell, *The Developmental Psychology of Jean Piaget* (Van Nostrand, New Jersey, 1963).

B. Landau & L. R. Gleitman, *Language and Experience: Evidence from the Blind Child* (Harvard University Press, 1985).

D. McGuinness, K. H. Pribram, M. Pirnazar, 'Upstaging the stage model' in C. N. Alexander & E. J. Langer (eds), *Higher Stages of Human Development* (Oxford University Press, New York, 1990), 97–113.

M. Montessori, *The Discovery of the Child* (Ballantine Books, New York, 1972).

J. Piaget, *The Construction of Reality in the Child* (Basic Books, New York, 1954).

J. Piaget, 'Development and learning' in M. Gauvain & M. Cole (eds), *Readings on the Development of Children* (Scientific American Books/W. H. Freeman, New York, 1964, 1993), 25–33.

J. Piaget, 'The theory of stages in cognitive development' in D. R. Green, M. P. Ford and G. B. Flamer (eds), *Measurement and Piaget* (McGraw-Hill, New York, 1971).

PAGES 177–82: LOGICS FOR THE ADVANCED CODE LEVEL

S. J. Ceci & A. Roazzi, 'The effects of context on cognition' in R. J. Sternberg & R. K. Wagner (eds), *Interactionist Perspectives on Human Intelligence* (Cambridge University Press, New York, 1994).

J. Piaget, *The Development of Thought: Equilibration of Cognitive Structures* (Viking Press, New York, 1977).

S. Pinker, *The Language Instinct* (William Morrow, New York, 1994).

F. A. Richards & M. L. Commons, 'Postformal cognitive-developmental theory and research: A review of its current status' in C. N. Alexander and E. Langer (eds), *Higher Stages of Human Development* (Oxford University Press, New York, 1990).

E. Rosch, 'Principles of categorization' in E. Rosch & B. Lloyd (eds), *Cognition and Categorization* (Lawrence Erlbaum, New Jersey, 1978).

PAGES 182–85: THE DEVELOPMENT OF LANGUAGE AND LEARNING TO READ

L. R. Gleitman, 'Maturational determinants of language growth', *Cognition 10* (1981), 103–14.

L. R. Gleitman & E. L. Newport, 'The invention of language by children: Environmental and biological influences on the acquisition of language' in L. R. Gleitman & M. Liberman (eds), *Language: Vol. 1* (MIT Press, Massachusetts, 1995).

A. M. Liberman, F. S. Cooper, D. P. Shankweiler, M. Studdert-Kennedy, 'Perception of the speech code', *Psychological Review 74* (1967), 431–61.

D. McGuinness, *When Children Don't Learn* (Basic Books, New York, 1985).

R. C. Tees & J. F. Werker, 'Perceptual flexibility: Maintenance or recovery of the ability to discriminate non-native speech sounds', *Canadian Journal of Psychology 38* (1984), 579–90.

J. F. Werker & R. C. Tees, 'Cross-language speech perception: Evidence for perceptual reorganization during the first year of life', *Infant Behavior and Development 7* (1984), 49–63.

J. F. Werker & R. C. Tees, 'The organization and reorganization of human speech perception', *Annual Review of Neuroscience 15* (1992), 377–402.

J. F. Werker, 'Exploring developmental changes in cross-language speech perception' in L. R. Gleitman & M. Liberman, *Language: Vol. 1* (MIT Press, Massachusetts, 1995), 87–106.

PAGES 185–89: CONTROL OF ATTENTION

E. L. Deci & R. M. Ryan, *The Initiation and Regulation of Intrinsically Motivated Learning and Achievement* (Cambridge University Press, New York, 1992).

R. J. Haier, B. V. Siegel, A. MacLachlan, E. Sonderling, 'Regional glucose metabolic changes after learning a complex visuspatial motor task: A positron emission tomographic study', *Brain Research 570* (1992), 134–43.

R. J. Haier, B. V. Siegel, K. H. Neuchterlein, E. Hazlett, 'Cortical glucose metabolism rate correlates of abstract reasoning and attention, studies with positron emission tomography', *Intelligence 12* (1988), 199–217.

R. J. Haier, B. Siegel, C. Tang, L. Abel, 'Intelligence and changes in regional cerebral glucose metabolic rate following learning', *Intelligence 16* (1992), 415–26.

L. Katz, 'Early education: What should young children be doing?' in S. L.

Kagan & E. F. Zigler (eds), *Early Schooling* (Yale University Press, 1987).

D. McGuinness, *When Children Don't Learn* (Basic Books, New York, 1985), Chapters 9 and 10.

D. McGuinness, 'Attention deficit disorder, The Emperor's Clothes, Animal Pharm and other fiction' in S. Fisher & R. Greenberg (eds), *The Limits of Biological Treatments for Psychological Distress* (Lawrence Erlbaum, New York, 1989).

D. McGuinness, 'Behavioral tempo in preschool boys and girls', *Journal of Learning and Individual Differences 2* (1990), 315–26.

D. McGuinness & K. H. Pribram, 'The neuropsychology of attention: Emotional and motivational controls' in M. C. Wittrock (ed.), *The Brain and Educational Psychology* (Academic Press, New York, 1980).

K. H. Pribram & D. McGuinness, 'Arousal, activation and effort in the control of attention', *Psychological Review 82* (1975), 116–49.

M. E. Raichle, J. A. Fiez, T. O. Videen, A-M. K. McLeod, 'Practice-related changes in human brain functional anatomy during nonmotor learning', *Cerebral Cortex 4* (1994), 8–26.

P. Williamson, *Good Kids: Bad Behavior* (Simon and Schuster, New York, 1989).

9 *The Proof of the Pudding*

References

PAGES 194–99: TRAINING STUDIES ON PRE-SCHOOL CHILDREN

E. W. Ball & B. A. Blachman, 'Phoneme segmentation training: Effect on reading readiness', *Annals of Dyslexia 38* (1988), 208–25.

E. W. Ball & B. A. Blachman, 'Does phoneme-awareness training in kindergarten make a difference in early word recognition and developmental spelling?', *Reading Research Quarterly 26* (1991), 49–66.

B. A. Blachman, E. W. Ball, R. S. Black, D. M. Tangel, 'Kindergarten teachers develop phoneme-awareness in low-income, inner-city classrooms', *Reading and Writing 6* (1994), 1–18.

B. Byrne & R. Fielding-Barnsley, 'Phonemic awareness and letter knowledge in the child's acquisition of the alphabetic principle', *Journal of Educational Psychology 81* (1989), 313–21.

B. Byrne & R. Fielding-Barnsley, 'Evaluation of a program to teach phonemic awareness to young children: A 1-year follow-up', *Journal of Educational Psychology 85* (1993), 104–11.

D. B. Elkonin, 'The psychology of mastering the elements of reading' in B. Simon & J. Simon (eds), *Educational Psychology in the USSR* (Routledge and Kegan Paul, 1963).

B. R. Foorman, D. J. Francis, T. Beeler, D. Winikates, J. M. Fletcher, 'Early interventions for children with reading problems: study designs and preliminary findings', *Learning Disabilities: A Multi-Disciplinary Journal 8* (1997), 63–72.

R, S. Johnston and J. Watson, 'Developing Reading, Spelling and Phonemic Awareness Skills in Primary School Children', *Reading* (July 1997), 37–40.

I. Lundberg, J. Frost, O-P. Petersen, 'Effects of an extensive program for stimulating phonological awareness in pre-school children', *Reading Research Quarterly 23* (1988), 263–84.

D. M. Tangel & B. A. Blachman, 'Effect of phoneme-awareness instruction on kindergarten children's invented spelling', *Journal of Reading Behavior 24* (1992), 233–61.

D. M. Tangel & B. A. Blachman, 'Effect of phoneme-awareness instruction on the invented spelling of first-grade children: A one-year follow-up', *Journal of Reading Behavior 27* (1995), 153–84.

PAGES 199–208: PREVENTIVE PROGRAMMES FOR AT-RISK CHILDREN

B. A. Blachman, 'An alternative classroom reading program for learning disabled and other low-achieving children' (proceedings of The Orton Dyslexia Society symposium on 'Dyslexia and Evolving Educational Patterns', Airlie, Virginia, 19–21 June 1987).

B. A. Blachman, 'Early literacy acquisition: The role of phonological awareness' in G. P. Wallach & K. G. Butler (eds), *Language Learning Disabilities in School-Age Children* (Merrill, New York, 1994).

B. A. Blachman, (ed.), *Foundations of Reading Acquisition and Dyslexia: Implications for Early Intervention* (Lawrence Erlbaum Associates, New Jersey, 1997).

L. Bradley, 'Categorizing sound, early intervention and learning to read: A follow-up study' (paper presented at the British Psychological Society Conference, London, December 1987).

L. Bradley & P. Bryant, *Rhyme and Reason in Reading and Spelling* (University of Michigan Press, 1985).

L. Bradley & P. E. Bryant, 'Phonological skills before and after learning to read' in S. A. Brady & D. P. Shankweiler (eds), *Phonological Processes in Literacy* (Lawrence Erlbaum Associates, New Jersey, 1991).

R. E. Slavin, N. L. Karweit, N. A. Madden, *Effective Programs for Students at Risk* (Allyn and Bacon, Boston, 1989).

R. E. Slavin, N. A. Madden, L. J. Dolan, B. A. Wasik, *Every Child, Every School. Success for All* (Corwin Press, California, 1996).

M. A. Wallach & L. Wallach, *Teaching All Children To Read* (Chicago University Press, 1976).

PAGES 208–10: SCHOOL-BASED STUDIES USING AVERAGE CHILDREN

M. Howard, 'Ultilizing oral-motor feedback in auditory conceptualization', *Journal of Educational Neuropsychology 2* (1982), 24–35.

M. Howard, 'Effects of pre-reading training in auditory conceptualization on subsequent reading achievement' (doctoral dissertation, Brigham Young University, 1986).

P. C. Lindamood, N. Bell, P. Lindamood, 'Issues in Phonological Awareness Assessment', *Annals of Dyslexia 42* (1992), 242–59.

D. McGuinness, *When Children Don't Learn* (Basic Books, New York, 1985). Chapter 11 reports on the Santa Maria study.

D. McGuinness, C. McGuinness, J. Donohue, 'Phonological training and the alphabet principle: Evidence for reciprocal causality', *Reading Research Quarterly 30* (1995), 830–52.

PAGES 211–23: REMEDIAL PROGRAMMES

A. Alexander, H. Andersen, P. Heilman, K. K. Voeller, J. Torgesen, 'Phonological awareness training and remediation of analytic decoding deficits in a group of severe dyslexics', *Annals of Dyslexia 41* (1991), 193–206.

Y. Center, K. Wheldall, L. Freeman, L. Outhred, McNaught, 'An experimental evaluation of Reading Recovery', *Reading Research Quarterly 30* (1995), 240–63.

D. B. Clark, revised edition with J. K. Uhry, *Dyslexia: Theory and Practice of Remedial Instruction* (York Press, Maryland, 1988, 1995).

J. M. Fletcher & P. Satz, 'Lag-deficit characterization of the disabled reader: Some alternative interpretations' (paper presented at the 80th annual meeting of the International Neuropsychological Society, San Francisco, February, 1980).

C. Juel, 'Learning to read and write: A longitudinal study of 54 children from first through fourth grades', *Journal of Educational Psychology 80* (1988), 437–47.

C. Juel, P. Griffith, P. Gough, 'Acquisition of literacy: A longitudinal study of children in first and second grade', *Journal of Educational Psychology 78* (1986), 243–55.

C. McGuinness, D. McGuinness, G. D. J. McGuinness, 'Phono-Graphix™: A new method for remediating reading difficulties', *Annals of Dyslexia 46* (1996), 73–96.

G. S. Pinnell, C. A. Lyons, D. E. De Ford, A. Bryk, M. Seltzer, 'Comparing instructional models for the literacy education of high-risk first graders', *Reading Research Quarterly 29* (1994), 8–39.

T. Shanahan & R. Barr, 'Reading Recovery: An independent evaluation of the effects of an early instructional intervention for at-risk learners', *Reading Research Quarterly 30* (1995), 958–96.

B. A. Shaywitz, T. R. Holford, J. M. Hoahan, J. M. Fletcher, K. K. Stuebing, D. J. Francis, S. E. Shaywitz, 'A Matthew effect for IQ but not for reading: Results from a longitudinal study', *Reading Research Quarterly 30* (1995), 894–907.

S. Truch, 'Stimulating basic reading processes using Auditory Discrimination in Depth', *Annals of Dyslexia 44* (1994), 60–80.

J. P. Williams, 'The ABDs of reading: A program for the learning disabled' in L. B. Resnick & P. A. Weaver (eds), *Theory and Practice of Early Reading: Vol. 3* (Lawrence Erlbaum, New Jersey, 1979), 179–95.

J. P. Williams, 'Teaching decoding with an emphasis on phoneme analysis and phoneme blending', *Journal of Educational Psychology 72* (1980), 1–15.

11 *Mastering the Advanced Code*

References

B. Byrne, P. Freebody, A. Gates, 'Longitudinal data on relations between word-reading strategy, comprehension, and reading time', *Reading Research Quarterly 27* (1992), 141–51.

B. R. Foorman, D. J. Francis, S. E. Shaywitz, B. A. Shaywitz, J. M. Fletcher, 'The case for early reading intervention', in B. Blachman (ed.), *Cognitive and Linguistic Foundations of Reading Acquisition: Implications for Intervention* (Lawrence Erlbaum, New Jersey, in press).

C. Juel, P. L. Griffith, P. B. Gough, 'Acquisition of literacy: A longitudinal study of children in first and second grade', *Journal of Educational Psychology 78* (1986), 243–55.

12 *Helping Those Who Didn't Make It*

References

C. H. Lindamood & P. C. Lindamood, *Lindamood Auditory Conceptualization Test* (Teaching Resources Corporation, Boston, 1971).

C. McGuinness, D. McGuinness, G. D. J. McGuinness, 'Phono-Graphix™: A new method for remediating reading difficulties', *Annals of Dyslexia 46* (1996), 73–96.

J. Rosner & D. P. Simon, 'The auditory analysis test: An initial report', *Journal of Learning Disabilities 4* (1971), 384–92.

J. Rosner & D. P. Simon, 'The auditory analysis test: An initial report', *Journal of Learning Disabilities 4* (1971), 384–92.

R. E. Slavin, N. L. Karweit, N. A. Madden, *Effective Programs for Students at Risk* (Allyn and Bacon, Boston, 1989).

S. Truch, *The Missing Parts of Whole Language* (Foothills Educational Materials, Calgary, 1991).

13 *What Parents Can Do*

References

D. J. Bruce, 'The analysis of word sounds by young children', *British Journal of Educational Psychology 34* (1964), 158–70.

J. Corcoran, *The Teacher Who Couldn't Read* (Focus on the Family, Colorado, 1994).

B. Hart & T. R. Risley, *Meaningful Differences* (Paul Brookes, Baltimore, 1995).

14 *Is Anyone in the Schools Listening?*

References

G. Brooks, T. Gorman, L. Kendall, A. Tate, *What Teachers in Training are Taught About Reading* (National Foundation for Educational Research, 1992).

J. Chattin-McNichols, *The Montessori Controversy* (Delmar, New York, 1992).

R. J. Herrnstein & C. Murray, *The Bell Curve* (Free Press, New York, 1994).

A. C. Kerckhoff, *Diverging Pathways* (Cambridge University Press, 1993).

'Key Stages 1 and 2: United Kingdom National Curriculum Assessment 1992 and 1993' in *Schools Update* (Department for Education, March, 1993).

R. McCrum, W. Cran, R. McNeil, *The Story of English* (Penguin Books, 1993).

M. Phillips, *All Must Have Prizes* (Little, Brown, 1996).

C. J. Sykes, *Dumbing Down Our Kids* (St Martin's Press, New York, 1995).

M. Thatcher, *The Downing Street Years* (HarperCollins, 1993).

AAT	Rosner & Simon's Auditory Analysis Test (see Chapter 7).
ADD	Auditory Discrimination in Depth – a remedial reading programme developed by Pat Lindamood.
alphabet	a writing system based on the phoneme.
categorical perception	the inability to hear acoustic transitions between two speech sounds, and the tendency to hear only one *or* the other.
character	in Chinese writing, a symbol standing for a word or syllable.
classes	in categorizing, where objects sharing similar features are grouped together.
class inclusion	one class nested within another class (red balls versus balls).
code overlap	all possible phonemes that a letter or letter-pattern can represent.
consonant	a phoneme which involves movement and/or contact of one or more of the speech articulators. A *voiced consonant* engages the vocal folds. An *unvoiced consonant* does not engage the vocal folds.
consonantal alphabet	a writing system based on the consonant in which vowels are inferred from context.
consonant cluster	Two or three consonants in sequence in a word, for example 'str' in street.

decoding	translating from symbols into words or into speech sounds.
DES	Department of Education and Science.
determinative	in Sumerian and Ancient Egyptian a written symbol that represents a category.
diacritic	a special mark written above, below, or beside a letter to indicate pronunciation.
digraph	two letters standing for one phoneme, for example *ch* in 'church'.
diphone system	a writing system where a symbol represents a consonant-vowel (CV) pair.
diphthong	a vowel sound which combines two vowels in rapid succession, for example /e/ + /ee/ = /ae/ in 'late'.
e-control principle	the letter *e* used as a diacritic to signal a vowel sound, in combination with the letters a, e, i, o, u only. Extends backwards across one consonant, but not two (for example, hat, hate, hated, hatted).
encoding	translating words or sounds in speech into symbols.
etymology	the study of the origin of words.
hieroglyphic	a writing system used on religious or public monuments for sacred or political purposes.
homophones	words that sound exactly alike but have different meanings.
invented spelling	a spelling method in which the child creates their own spelling system based upon knowledge of letter names and/ or sounds.
LAC test	Lindamood Test of Auditory Conceptualization (see Chapter 7).
logograph	an abstract symbol standing for a word.
mapping	a process by which units of one type are assigned to units of another type (for example, units of sound can be mapped by written letters).

NFER	National Foundation for Educational Research in England and Wales.
onset-rime	initial consonant plus rhyming ending.
orthography	consistent spelling patterns within a system of spelling.
phoneme	the smallest unit of sound in a word that people can hear.
phoneme-awareness	the ability to hear and remember the order of phonemes in words.
phonics	a generic term for any reading method that teaches the sounds of letters.
phonogram	three or more letters standing for one phoneme, for example 'ough' in plough.
phonological processing	a generic term for the ability to hear and remember various units of sound within a word: syllable, rhyme, syllable fragment, phoneme.
phonology	the study of sounds in a language.
pictograph	a pictorial symbol standing for a word.
prefix	a syllable added to the beginning of a word to change meaning, for example, 'un' in unfit.
propositional logic	the ability to simultaneously think of an entity in two or more classes at the same time.
'real books'	an approach to learning to read in which the child relies on natural language ability to discover how the writing system works.
relations	in categorizing, where objects share some features but not others.
schema	a mental structure which integrates dimensions or features of perceptual experience.
sight word	a word memorized by sight rather than sounded out phonetically.
silent letter	a letter in a word that isn't sounded – 'de*b*t'.

spelling alternatives   all possible spellings of one phoneme.

standardized test   a test for which norms have been established, allowing an individual's performance to be measured against a wider population. The results will fall along a normal distribution curve.

standard deviation   used to determine standard units of a population (the square root of the sum of the squared difference of each score to the mean for all scores in a population).

statistical significance   a probability estimate in which the outcome of a measurement is less than 5% (5 in 100) likely to have occurred purely by chance.

suffix   a final syllable added to a word to change meaning.

syllabary   a writing system based on the syllable.

syllable   a unit within a word containing only one vowel plus any consonants.

whole language   another term for the 'real books' approach.

word-family   vowel+consonant endings to words, also known as rimes. Identical rimes rhyme.

PENGUIN ONLINE

READ MORE IN PENGUIN

In every corner of the world, on every subject under the sun, Penguin represents quality and variety – the very best in publishing today.

For complete information about books available from Penguin – including Puffins, Penguin Classics and Arkana – and how to order them, write to us at the appropriate address below. Please note that for copyright reasons the selection of books varies from country to country.

In the United Kingdom: Please write to *Dept. EP, Penguin Books Ltd, Bath Road, Harmondsworth, West Drayton, Middlesex UB7 0DA*

In the United States: Please write to *Consumer Sales, Penguin Putnam Inc., P.O. Box 12289 Dept. B, Newark, New Jersey 07101-5289*. VISA and MasterCard holders call 1-800-788-6262 to order Penguin titles

In Canada: Please write to *Penguin Books Canada Ltd, 10 Alcorn Avenue, Suite 300, Toronto, Ontario M4V 3B2*

In Australia: Please write to *Penguin Books Australia Ltd, P.O. Box 257, Ringwood, Victoria 3134*

In New Zealand: Please write to *Penguin Books (NZ) Ltd, Private Bag 102902, North Shore Mail Centre, Auckland 10*

In India: Please write to *Penguin Books India Pvt Ltd, 11 Community Centre, Panchsheel Park, New Delhi 110017*

In the Netherlands: Please write to *Penguin Books Netherlands bv, Postbus 3507, NL-1001 AH Amsterdam*

In Germany: Please write to *Penguin Books Deutschland GmbH, Metzlerstrasse 26, 60594 Frankfurt am Main*

In Spain: Please write to *Penguin Books S. A., Bravo Murillo 19, 1° B, 28015 Madrid*

In Italy: Please write to *Penguin Italia s.r.l., Via Benedetto Croce 2, 20094 Corsico, Milano*

In France: Please write to *Penguin France, Le Carré Wilson, 62 rue Benjamin Baillaud, 31500 Toulouse*

In Japan: Please write to *Penguin Books Japan Ltd, Kaneko Building, 2-3-25 Koraku, Bunkyo-Ku, Tokyo 112*

In South Africa: Please write to *Penguin Books South Africa (Pty) Ltd, Private Bag X14, Parkview, 2122 Johannesburg*

READ MORE IN PENGUIN

POLITICS AND SOCIAL SCIENCES

The Unconscious Civilization   John Ralston Saul

In this powerfully argued critique, John Ralston Saul shows how corporatism has become the dominant ideology of our time, cutting across all sectors as well as the political spectrum. The result is an increasingly conformist society in which citizens are reduced to passive bystanders.

A Class Act   Andrew Adonis and Stephen Pollard

'Will Britain escape from ancient and modern injustice? A necessary first step is to read and take seriously this ... description of the condition of our country. Andrew Adonis and Stephen Pollard here destroy the myth that Britain is a classless society' *The Times Higher Education Supplement*

Accountable to None   Simon Jenkins

'An important book, because it brings together, with an insider's authority and anecdotage, both a narrative of domestic Thatcherism and a polemic against its pretensions ... an indispensable guide to the corruptions of power and language which have sustained the illusion that Thatcherism was an attack on "government"' *Guardian*

Structural Anthropology Volumes 1–2   Claude Lévi-Strauss

'That the complex ensemble of Lévi-Strauss's achievement ... is one of the most original and intellectually exciting of the present age seems undeniable. No one seriously interested in language or literature, in sociology or psychology, can afford to ignore it' George Steiner

Invitation to Sociology   Peter L. Berger

Without belittling its scientific procedures Professor Berger stresses the humanistic affinity of sociology with history and philosophy. It is a discipline which encourages a fuller awareness of the human world ... with the purpose of bettering it.

READ MORE IN PENGUIN

POLITICS AND SOCIAL SCIENCES

Anatomy of a Miracle Patti Waldmeir

The peaceful birth of black majority rule in South Africa has been seen by many as a miracle – or at least political magic. 'This book is a brilliant, vivid account of this extraordinary transformation' *Financial Times*

A Sin Against the Future Vivien Stern

Do prisons contribute to a better, safer world? Or are they a threat to democracy, as increasingly punitive measures are brought in to deal with rising crime? This timely account examines different styles of incarceration around the world and presents a powerful case for radical change.

The United States of Anger Gavin Esler

'First-rate . . . an even-handed and astute account of the United States today, sure in its judgements and sensitive in its approach' *Scotland on Sunday*. 'In sharply written, often amusing portraits of this disconnected America far from the capital, Esler probes this state of anger' *The Times*

Killing Rage: Ending Racism bell hooks

Addressing race and racism in American society from a black and a feminist standpoint, bell hooks covers a broad spectrum of issues. In the title essay she writes about the 'killing rage' – the intense anger caused by everyday instances of racism – finding in that rage a positive inner strength to create productive change.

'Just like a Girl' Sue Sharpe

Sue Sharpe's unprecedented research and analysis of the attitudes and hopes of teenage girls from four London schools has become a classic of its kind. This new edition focuses on girls in the nineties and represents their views on education, work, marriage, gender roles, feminism and women's rights.

READ MORE IN PENGUIN

PHILOSOPHY

Brainchildren Daniel C. Dennett

Philosophy of mind has been profoundly affected by this century's scientific advances, and thinking about thinking – how and why the mind works, its very existence – can seem baffling. Here eminent philosopher and cognitive scientist Daniel C. Dennett has provided an eloquent guide through some of the mental and moral mazes.

Language, Truth and Logic A. J. Ayer

The classic text which founded logical positivism and modern British philosophy, *Language, Truth and Logic* swept away the cobwebs and revitalized British philosophy.

The Penguin Dictionary of Philosophy Edited by Thomas Mautner

This dictionary encompasses all aspects of Western philosophy from 600 BC to the present day. With contributions from over a hundred leading philosophers, this dictionary will prove the ideal reference for any student or teacher of philosophy as well as for all those with a general interest in the subject.

Labyrinths of Reason William Poundstone

'The world and what is in it, even what people say to you, will not seem the same after plunging into *Labyrinths of Reason* ... holds up the deepest philosophical questions for scrutiny in a way that irresistibly sweeps readers on' *New Scientist*

Metaphysics as a Guide to Morals Iris Murdoch

'This is philosophy dragged from the cloister, dusted down and made freshly relevant to suffering and egoism, death and religious ecstasy ... and how we feel compassion for others' *Guardian*

Philosophy Football Mark Perryman

The amazing tale of a make-believe team, *Philosophy Football* is the story of what might have happened to the world's greatest thinkers if their brains had been in their boots instead of their heads ...

READ MORE IN PENGUIN

LITERARY CRITICISM

The Practice of Writing David Lodge

This lively collection examines the work of authors ranging from the two Amises to Nabokov and Pinter; the links between private lives and published works; and the different techniques required in novels, stage plays and screenplays. 'These essays, so easy in manner, so well-built and informative, offer a fine blend of creative writing and criticism' *Sunday Times*

A Lover's Discourse Roland Barthes

'May be the most detailed, painstaking anatomy of desire we are ever likely to see or need again ... The book is an ecstatic celebration of love and language ... readers interested in either or both ... will enjoy savouring its rich and dark delights' *Washington Post*

The New Pelican Guide to English Literature Edited by Boris Ford

The indispensable critical guide to English and American literature in nine volumes, erudite yet accessible. From the ages of Chaucer and Shakespeare, via Georgian satirists and Victorian social critics, to the leading writers of the twentieth century, all literary life is here.

The Structure of Complex Words William Empson

'Twentieth-century England's greatest critic after T. S. Eliot, but whereas Eliot was the high priest, Empson was the *enfant terrible* ... *The Structure of Complex Words* is one of the linguistic masterpieces of the epoch, finding in the feel and tone of our speech whole sedimented social histories' *Guardian*

Vamps and Tramps Camille Paglia

'Paglia is a genuinely unconventional thinker ... Taken as a whole, the book gives an exceptionally interesting perspective on the last thirty years of intellectual life in America, and is, in its wacky way, a celebration of passion and the pursuit of truth' *Sunday Telegraph*

READ MORE IN PENGUIN

LANGUAGE/LINGUISTICS

Language Play David Crystal

We all use language to communicate information, but it is language play which is truly central to our lives. Full of puns, groan-worthy gags and witty repartee, this book restores the fun to the study of language. It also demonstrates why all these things are essential elements of what makes us human.

Swearing Geoffrey Hughes

'A deliciously filthy trawl among taboo words across the ages and the globe' *Observer*. 'Erudite and entertaining' Penelope Lively, *Daily Telegraph*

The Language Instinct Stephen Pinker

'Dazzling . . . Pinker's big idea is that language is an instinct, as innate to us as flying is to geese . . . Words can hardly do justice to the superlative range and liveliness of Pinker's investigations' *Independent*. 'He does for language what David Attenborough does for animals, explaining difficult scientific concepts so easily that they are indeed absorbed as a transparent stream of words' John Gribbin

Mother Tongue Bill Bryson

'A delightful, amusing and provoking survey, a joyful celebration of our wonderful language, which is packed with curiosities and enlightenment on every page' *Sunday Express*. 'A gold mine of language-anecdote. A surprise on every page . . . enthralling' *Observer*

Longman Guide to English Usage
Sidney Greenbaum and Janet Whitcut

Containing 5000 entries compiled by leading authorities on modern English, this invaluable reference work clarifies every kind of usage problem, giving expert advice on points of grammar, meaning, style, spelling, pronunciation and punctuation.

READ MORE IN PENGUIN

PSYCHOLOGY

How the Mind Works Steven Pinker

This brilliant and controversial book explains what the mind is, how it evolved, and how it allows us to see, think, feel, interact, enjoy the arts and ponder the mysteries of life. 'To have read [the book] is to have consulted a first draft of the structural plan of the human psyche . . . a glittering *tour de force*' *Spectator*

The Uses of Enchantment Bruno Bettelheim

'Bruno Bettelheim's tour of fairy stories, with all their psychoanalytic connotations brought out into the open, is a feast of understanding' *New Statesman & Society*. 'Everything that Bettelheim writes about children, particularly about children's involvement in fiction, seems profound and illuminating' *Sunday Times*

Evolution in Mind Henry Plotkin
An Introduction to Evolutionary Psychology

Evolutionary theory holds a vital key to understanding ourselves. In proposing a more revolutionary approach to psychology, Professor Plotkin vividly demonstrates how an evolutionary perspective brings us closer to understanding what it is to be human.

The Man Who Loved a Polar Bear Robert U. Akeret

'Six fascinating case histories related with wit and humanity by the veteran psychotherapist Robert Akeret . . . a remarkable tour to the wilder shores of the human mind' *Daily Mail*

Private Myths: Dreams and Dreaming Anthony Stevens

'Its case for dreaming as something more universally significant than a tour across our personal playgrounds of guilt and misery is eloquently persuasive . . . [a] hugely absorbing study – its surface criss-crossed with innumerable avenues into science, anthropology and religion' *Spectator*